ASD
the complete
autism
spectrum
disorder
health
& diet guide

R. Garth Smith, MBBS, FRCPC,
Susan Hannah, BA, BScH, and
Elke Sengmueller, BASc, RD

Robert
ROSE

For complete cataloguing information, see page 385.

Disclaimer
This book is a general guide only and should never be a substitute for the skill, knowledge and experience
of a qualified medical professional dealing with the facts, circumstances and symptoms of a particular case.

The nutritional, medical and health information presented in this book is based on the research,
training and professional experience of the authors, and is true and complete to the best of their
knowledge. However, this book is intended only as an informative guide for those wishing to know more
about health, nutrition and medicine; it is not intended to replace or countermand the advice given by the
reader's personal physician. Because each person and situation is unique, the authors and the publisher
urge the reader to check with a qualified health-care professional before using any procedure where there
is a question as to its appropriateness. A physician should be consulted before beginning any exercise
program. The authors and the publisher are not responsible for any adverse effects or consequences
resulting from the use of the information in this book. It is the responsibility of the reader to consult a
physician or other qualified health-care professional regarding his or her personal care.

This book contains references to products that may not be available everywhere. The intent of
the information provided is to be helpful; however, there is no guarantee of results associated with the
information provided. Use of brand names is for educational purposes only and does not imply endorsement.

The recipes in this book have been carefully tested by our kitchen and our tasters. To the best of our
knowledge, they are safe and nutritious for ordinary use and users. For those people with food or other
allergies, or who have special food requirements or health issues, please read the suggested contents of
each recipe carefully and determine whether or not they may create a problem for you. All recipes are used
at the risk of the consumer. We cannot be responsible for any hazards, loss or damage that may occur as
a result of any recipe use. For those with special needs, allergies, requirements or health problems, in the
event of any doubt, please contact your medical adviser prior to the use of any recipe.

Design and Production: Daniella Zanchetta/PageWave Graphics Inc.
Editor: Bob Hilderley, Senior Editor, Health
Copyeditor: Sheila Wawanash
Proofreader: Kelly Jones
Indexer: Gillian Watts
Illustrations: Kveta (Three in a Box)
Cover image: Puzzle pieces © iStockphoto.com/Rinelle

The publisher gratefully acknowledges the financial support of our publishing program by the Government
of Canada through the Canada Book Fund.

Published by Robert Rose Inc.
120 Eglinton Avenue East, Suite 800, Toronto, Ontario, Canada M4P 1E2
Tel: (416) 322-6552 Fax: (416) 322-6936
www.robertrose.ca

Printed and bound in Canada

1 2 3 4 5 6 7 8 9 MI 22 21 20 19 18 17 16 15 14

Contents

Letter to Parents
from Heidi Penning, MPA, PhD (candidate) 6
Preface by R. Garth Smith, MBBS, FRCPC 7
Introduction by Susan Hannah, BA, BScH 9

Part 1: Understanding Autism

1. What Is Autism? 15
Autism Basics 15
Developmental Milestones 21
Checklist of Signs and Symptoms 33

2. How Is Autism Diagnosed? 37
Diagnostic Steps 37
Screening Tools 41
Associated Conditions 49

3. What Causes Autism? 55
Contributing Factors 55
Genetic Mutations 57
Environmental Neurotoxins 63
Oxidative Stress 69
Hormone Imbalance 71
Brain Dysfunctions 73
Gastrointestinal Theories 83
Nutritional Deficiencies 85
Food Sensitivities, Intolerances, and Allergies 86

Part 2: Managing Autism Spectrum Disorders

4. Standard Treatments 91

Standards and Guidelines for Care 92
Therapies and Interventions 100
Behavioral Therapies 101
Medications and Supplements 108
Sensory Therapies 110
Communication Therapies 112
Complementary and Alternative Medicines 114
Dietary Interventions 116

5. Feeding Therapy 121

Mealtime Challenges 121
Common Eating Problems 122
Developmental Food Issues 124
Sensory Food Issues 131
Environmental Food Issues 139
Practical Food Preparation Tips 141

Part 3: Dietary Therapy

6. The Gluten-Free, Casein-Free Diet Program . . . 147

Exclusionary Diets 147
GFCF Diet Principles 148
Immunity, Inflammation, and Antibodies 149
Food Sensitivity 150
Gluten-Free 150
Casein-Free 152
GFCF Diet Risks and Benefits 156

7. Eight Steps for Implementing the GFCF Diet Program. 161

The Challenge of Changing Diets 161
Step 1: Develop an Attitude for Success. 162
Step 2: Set a Physical and Behavioral Baseline. 162
Step 3: Gather Groceries. 163
Step 4: Manage Your Child's Weight. 164
Step 5: Avoid Foods Containing Gluten and Casein 165
Step 6: Rotate Your Child's Diet 166
Step 7: Seek Support. 166
Step 8: Work with a Meal Plan 167

Part 4: The Gluten-Free, Casein-Free Cookbook

Gluten-Free, Casein-Free Meal Plans 170
Introduction to the Recipes 183
Baby Food and Kids' Fare 185
Breakfast. 201
Breads and Muffins. 217
Appetizers, Dips and Sauces. 243
Soups and Salads 261
Meatless Mains. 285
Seafood and Meaty Mains. 305
Side Dishes 325
Desserts 347
Snacks and Beverages 369

Contributing Authors. 384
Acknowledgments. 386
Resources 386
References 389
Index 399

Letter to Parents
from Heidi Penning

Dear Friends,

Welcome to a community of parents, caregivers, doctors, teachers, dietitians, and friends who love and care for individuals on the autism spectrum. Our family has been part of this wonderfully unique community since May 30, 1997, the day that my beautiful son, Hayden, was diagnosed with what was then known as autistic disorder. By picking up this book, you are probably reaching the same conclusion I did so many years ago: autism involves so much more than social and communication deficits and repetitive behaviors.

I could not get my child to eat!

Let me qualify that. He would eat certain things, under certain circumstances, in certain combinations. I truly felt at times that I also needed to align the stars and stand on my head to get him to eat! It felt like every mealtime was a battle of wills. Looking back, I now recognize that we had a disordered relationship with food. Sadly, at the time, there were no resources available, such as the one you are holding in your hand right now.

Now the autism community — and that includes the authors of this brilliant book — know so much more about what gives rise to food selectivity in our "picky eaters." This book is chock-full of incredibly useful information that I only wish I'd had access to in those early years. In today's sea of resources about autism spectrum disorder, this one is a must-have.

Best of luck in your family's journey. Know that you are not alone, and take good care.

Sincerely,
Heidi

P.S. I am glad to say that Hayden now enjoys a wide range of healthy food choices, though he does persistently lobby for more chocolate chip cookies. That is autism for you!

Heidi Penning, MPA, PhD (candidate), Member, Autism Ontario

Preface

▬ ▬ ▬ ▬ ▬ ▬ ▬ ▬ ▬ ▬ ▬ ▬ ▬ ▬ ▬ ▬ ▬

Autism is a spectrum, and for those of us who have worked with these children and adolescents for more than 20 years, we can attest to the accuracy of this description. I have seen children and adolescents with autism spectrum disorder (ASD) who were aloof and pedantic, self-assured and indifferent to the opinion of others, and others who were withdrawn and timid and appeared to be "in their own world." I have also seen a young patient who, when given my birth date, in seconds told me the day of the week I was born. One such patient always arrived in my office with a novel challenge for me. "Dr. Smith," he asked me, "please tell me all of the countries of the world in alphabetical order, with their capitals." He already knew that I could not answer and took great pleasure in expounding his phenomenal rote memory while I listened in awe! He taught me many things, including all the different types of jellyfish and what they dined on, and the different types of sharks and whales. He also taught me about the ecosystem and how I could help preserve it.

> **"Dr. Smith,"** he asked me, **"please tell me all of the countries of the world in alphabetical order, with their capitals."**

Not all autistic children have such a wealth of esoteric knowledge. Some are creatures of habit, ritualistic in their routines, and, like a blind person, dislike change in meal schedules and bedroom organization. Others have been collectors and hoarders of rocks, seashells, receipts, and bubblegum wrappers. An explosive "meltdown" would ensue if their parents ever attempted to purge their room of any of these collections.

Many patients eat the same breakfast religiously for weeks on end and demonstrate extreme inflexibility to change. Then, just as their parents were starting to adjust to this ritual, they would change abruptly from eating pancakes every day, for example, to eating only Cheerios. One patient ate a particular brand of canned spaghetti and tomato sauce and french fries for breakfast, lunch, and supper for a year, and refused to take vitamins or supplements. This resulted in him developing a severe anemia and his serum ferritin (iron storage) and vitamin B_{12} were both close to zero. His hemoglobin was 4 grams per deciliter (4 g/dL, or 40 g/L)! He required admission to hospital, where further investigations were conducted to rule out bowel-related disorders, such as celiac disorder and inflammatory bowel disease. His blood zinc level was also critically low, and we recognized that this could further contribute to selective intake through poor taste sensation, or hypogeusia.

Many children with autism suffer with sleep-related disorders, anxiety, ADHD (attention deficit hyperactivity disorder), and sensory dysfunction. Many are also diagnosed with "intellectual disability" although we recognize that children with ASD are often not as interested in pleasing others or performing optimally "on demand," which affects the interpretation of the cognitive assessment.

Despite our efforts to understand the causes of ASD, the incidence of this condition is apparently increasing. Is this due to increased awareness among parents and in society? Is it the result of broadening the definition over the years? Is it because of overdiagnosis and the clouding of the margins of so-called "normality"? Where does eccentricity end and ASD begin? How is "impairment" defined objectively? Is there an "environmental" contribution — a Hurricane Katrina and ice storm phenomenon? Does increased maternal stress in our modern society play a role? Autistic kids seem to have a significant affinity for technological devices, even those kids with apparent intellectual disability. Our society is becoming more technological. Are kids with ASD evidence of an epigenetically directed evolutionary mechanism to meet the needs of our future societies? The current epigenetic research certainly gives us food for thought.

So why this book? There is clearly a paucity of practical, easy-to-read, yet evidenced-based books that cover the nutritional and gastrointestinal issues in ASD and how to manage them. Many of my patients are picky eaters and react adversely to food textures, food tastes, and even food appearances. We also hear and read about the high rate of gastrointestinal issues that these children experience. In my office, I am frequently bombarded with questions about gluten-free, casein-free diets, fish oil supplements, and probiotics.

In response to these questions and concerns, we decided to write this book, bringing together the experience and expertise of an ASD research assistant, a childhood dietitian, and a developmental pediatrician. We believe we have gathered the best evidence available to date and put it together in an accessible and practical format that parents, nutritionists, dietitians, pediatricians, counselors, and others caring for kids with ASD should find useful. I believe we have achieved this goal, for the ultimate good of children with this challenging disorder.

Dr. Garth Smith

> **There is clearly a paucity of practical, easy-to-read, yet evidenced-based books that cover the nutritional and gastrointestinal issues in ASD and how to manage them.**

Introduction

Autism is a challenging medical condition that leaves many parents feeling inadequate to the task of caring for their child and robbed of the intimacy they long to have with this child. Consider these behaviors, common among children with autism.

How would you feel and what would you do:

- If your infant doesn't smile or look you in the eye?
- If your baby doesn't want cuddles and hugs?
- If your baby doesn't laugh much or play peekaboo?
- If your child doesn't take an interest in looking at the baby in the mirror?
- If your child seems to live in his own little world?
- If your toddler doesn't talk, other than repeating whatever is said or repeating the same word over and over?
- If your toddler seems to constantly have temper tantrums or meltdowns?
- If your child rocks incessantly while sitting in a chair and flaps her hands uncontrollably?
- If your toddler insists on following the same routine in every aspect of life?
- If your school-age child is sad because he feels different from his classmates and doesn't have friends?
- If your growing child is extraordinarily picky about the foods she will eat?
- If your teenage son has difficult behaviors at mealtime?
- If your child seems to be hitting all the developmental milestones for behavior as a baby and toddler until, sometime after the age of 1, she reaches a plateau or even regresses to earlier behaviors?

> Currently, approximately one out of every 88 children — or more — is diagnosed with autism spectrum disorder.

If you recognize these behaviors in your child, you are not alone. Currently, approximately one out of every 88 children — or more — is diagnosed with autism spectrum disorder, the technical name given to autism in the *Diagnostic and Statistical Manual of Mental Disorders* 5, used by medical professionals.

Worldwide, families are in need of support and guidance for this condition. With a more accurate set of diagnosis criteria, health-care providers will be able to design more effective treatment interventions that focus on the specific needs of each child. The development of new treatments indicates a higher reliance on behavioral and dietary therapies than on medications to address specific symptoms.

To detect whether your child has autism, health-care providers screen, or test, children during regular visits, looking for basic skills or developmental milestones that are typically met over a range of months; for example, rolling over, sitting up, and first words for babies. These well-child visits to your doctor or pediatrician typically occur at 9, 18, 24, and 30 months. Some children are at higher risk of developing autism — premature babies, low-birth-weight children, or sometimes children born to a family with a brother or sister with autism. These kids should be screened more often for autism. In some regions, a multidisciplinary team (neurologist, psychologist, speech therapist, and more) will complete an in-depth cognitive test, language test, and neurological assessment for children who are suspected of having autism. Hearing and vision tests are also done to rule out deafness and visual impairments as a cause for behaviors that can be mistaken for autism.

The parents' observations are also very important in recognizing developmental delays. Early recognition of symptoms of autism leads to the best outcome. Typically, parents who have recognized difficult behaviors in their children will look to health-care providers, concerned that their child is not meeting developmental milestones or that their child may be deaf because she rarely responds when she's spoken to. One out of three children whose parents do raise concerns about development are later given a confirmed medical diagnosis for some form of developmental delay. In fact, parents' concerns about their child's development have been recognized as a factor in successful screening mechanisms for autism and, when an autism diagnosis follows, may lead to early intervention — the best predictor for improved outcomes.

Responding to these behaviors at the onset of symptoms may open doors to treatments, such as behavior therapies, medications, and dietary interventions, that might help your child reach his full potential, along with providing some financial aid for his care, depending on where you live. Just as important, this might provide emotional support for you. For some parents, a diagnosis of autism may help them accept that their child has some limitations but may also help them remain optimistic for a better outcome. And that is the aim of this book — to inform parents and caregivers about the symptoms, causes, treatments, and resources available for improving your child's quality of life, if not cure the disease.

> Early recognition of symptoms of autism leads to the best outcome.

> What is known for sure is that parenting behavior is not a cause of autism!

Many parents feel stigmatized, however, by having a child with autism and do not report the symptoms. Like most stigmas, this one arises from a lack of understanding. Sometimes, not understanding exactly what autism is, how symptoms may appear, possible outcomes, or even how therapies may reduce symptoms, parents may delay the decision to have a child assessed for autism. Socioeconomic status and language have also been seen as factors that may delay diagnosis and the beginning of treatments.

Although this view is not common today, "bad" parenting was at one time seen as the cause of autism. The exact cause of autism is unknown, but research suggests that this disorder is a combination of genetic, biologic, and environmental factors. What is known for sure is that parenting behavior is not a cause of autism!

In some ways, parenting a child diagnosed with autism is no different from parenting any other child — identifying behaviors that need support and finding solutions as a family with the help of a health-care team. In other ways, parenting a child with autism is more challenging. It can be a 24-hour, 7-days-a-week job, with little respite, under highly stressful conditions, and with little feedback from your child in the way of smiles and cuddles. Autism ranges from mild to severe, with some children showing high-level language skills but with social behavior issues at the mild end, to children who are nonverbal and lower-functioning and will need care of some sort throughout their lifetime. Other children develop normally but may regress (often between the ages of 1 to 3 years) and begin to show behaviors identified with autism.

Most of the time, families of children with autism are passionate about knowing everything they can about this disease. They become involved with a multidisciplinary health-care team to learn how to work with physicians to develop reasonable treatment goals and expectations based on their child's symptoms; to understand the positive and negative impacts of specific therapy interventions; and, importantly, to recognize, acknowledge, affirm, and celebrate incremental developmental gains as they occur. We encourage parents to exercise caution in adopting any therapy, to consult with a qualified health-care professional, and not to adopt therapies found on the Internet that are purely anecdotal.

ASD: The Complete Autism Spectrum Disorder Health & Diet Guide is based on the best and most current medical research available and on conversations with families that include children with autism, to learn what type of information these families are looking for. Interviews with parents help us all to understand the scary, strong, and mixed feelings parents

> We encourage parents to exercise caution in adopting any therapy, to consult with a qualified health-care professional, and not to adopt therapies found on the Internet that are purely anecdotal.

> This book is based on the best and most current medical research available and on conversations with parents of children with autism.

experience when their child is diagnosed with autism. They describe being tense as they waited for the health-care provider to identify how their child is "different." Some parents experience shock and grief at the loss of what they might consider to be a normal life for their child, but learn that life is still good, just different. For many parents who were resistant to having their child assessed for autism, participating in research was not something they were interested in or comfortable with. But most parents whose child has been diagnosed are keen to do something to help other families as well as their own.

> Picky eating, combined with difficult behaviors around eating, can make mealtimes stressful and restaurant meals impossible.

Mealtimes for families with an autistic child are sometimes described as "mealtime madness." Picky eating, combined with difficult behaviors around eating, can make mealtimes stressful and restaurant meals impossible. Descriptions of cognitive behavioral therapies to address mealtime madness are included in this book, as well as healthy meal plans for children who have preferences for soft or crunchy foods but exclude other types. Recent research shows that a gluten-free, casein-free (GFCF) diet can be effective in reducing symptoms for some children with ASDs who have gastrointestinal symptoms (upset stomach, constipation, or diarrhea), food allergies, and suspected food sensitivities. One of the issues associated with the use of a GFCF diet plan has been a concern about a loss of nutrients in this diet. The meal plans and recipes in *ASD: The Complete Autism Spectrum Disorder Health & Diet Guide* meet the criteria for Canada's Food Guide and the USDA MyPlate nutritional goals. For extremely picky eaters, supplements may be a necessary part of their treatment plan.

Part 1 of *ASD: The Complete Autism Spectrum Disorder Health & Diet Guide* follows the standard pattern of clinical reasoning, from the presentation of signs and symptoms to diagnosis and prognosis, followed by therapies and practical applications.

Part 2 presents a management plan for ASD, including

- Behavioral therapies and interventions
- Prescription medications
- Complementary and alternative therapies
- Nutritional supplements

Part 3 is devoted to specific nutritional issues and feeding behaviors associated with children with ASD. Here, the theory behind the evidence-based gluten-free, casein-free diet is explained, its principles and practices outlined, and sample meal plans for regular, soft, and crunchy diets provided, followed by a cookbook that includes 175 healthy recipes.

The authors of *ASD: The Complete Autism Spectrum Disorder Health & Diet Guide* bring together their diverse set of skills to provide guidance and support to families who have a child diagnosed with or suspected to have autism spectrum disorder.

Dr. R. Garth Smith, MBBS, FRCPC, is the medical adviser for *ASD: The Complete Autism Spectrum Disorder Health & Diet Guide*. He is a developmental pediatrician and the medical director of the Child Development Centre at Hotel Dieu Hospital in Kingston, Ontario, as well as a research board member of the Autism Spectrum Disorders, Canadian–American Research Consortium (ASD-CARC), a multidisciplinary research team of more than 70 researchers and clinicians working with more than 3,000 families in Canada and internationally, collecting anonymous physical and genetic data from families by mail and statistical data via their website (www.asdcarc.ca), using surveys, questionnaires, and emails. Dr. Smith brings to the book his many years of experience in diagnosing and providing care to children and families with children with autism spectrum disorders.

Susan Hannah, BA, BScH, is a former research assistant at ASD-CARC at Ongwanada Hospital and research associate in the Department of Family Medicine, Queen's University in Kingston, Ontario. She is a co-author of *The Complete Migraine Health, Diet Guide & Cookbook* and the *The pH Balance Health & Diet Guide for GERD, IBS and IBD*.

Elke Sengmueller, BASc, RD, is a registered dietitian with more than 16 years of experience providing pediatric nutritional care for a wide array of health conditions in acute care, community, and home-based settings. She is passionate about helping kids and adolescents meet their nutritional needs to optimize their growth and development. She runs a private practice, Family Nutrition Counselling. She has reviewed the dietary information in this book and prepared the gluten-free, casein-free meal plans.

The authors recognize that the stress that accompanies an ASD diagnosis affects all aspects of family life. We encourage you to discuss all aspects of your child's behaviors and possible therapies with health-care professionals before beginning any therapies or special diets. Remember to identify behaviors that interfere with your child's quality of life, and celebrate each and every success that may lead to improvement in the whole family's quality of life.

> **Discuss all aspects of your child's behaviors and possible therapies with health-care professionals before beginning any therapies or special diets.**

Part 1:

Understanding Autism

"Children are people to be unfolded, not things to be molded."

– Jesse Lair

Chapter 1
What Is Autism?

CASE STUDY
Regression

When Stephen was 2 years old, his parents took him to see his doctor because they were worried about his development. By that point, Stephen had some recognized autism symptoms. Although his language skills had been strong between 15 and 18 months, using words appropriately and responding to questions as well as asking them, he had regressed. Now Stephen barely spoke, repeating only a few words from a television commercial. He also yelled a lot when he was disturbed, which was whenever his schedule, space, or toys were disturbed. His appetite, too, had suffered; Stephen would eat only a few foods, typically bland and pale in color (bread, milk, pudding, cereal, pasta, and cookies), and would go hungry rather than eat other foods offered. Stephen was not interested in cuddling anymore, something that made his father especially sad because they used to read together before bedtime, all cuddled up on the couch with his younger sister. Stephen would not look anyone in the eye, and he ran in circles or flapped his hands if anyone tried to touch him. Stephen would watch his favorite DVD, *The Lion King*, over and over but, otherwise, he would not pretend play or play with other children. Stephen had many strep throat infections and was often constipated. He wasn't sleeping well either, often keeping everyone in the house awake with his shouts. The final blow was a seizure... *(continued on page 37)*

Autism Basics

"Autism" is short for autism spectrum disorder (ASD), which is a complex neurobiological and developmental disorder that can affect your child's brain development, immune system, gastrointestinal tract, and other organ systems. Autism may affect your child's ability to communicate and interact socially with other people. The term "neurobiological" means that autism is associated with brain anatomy (the physical structures) and brain physiology (how these structures function). Autism may also cause problems with the way the nervous system works.

Spectrum

The name of the condition includes the word "spectrum" because different people have different kinds and degrees of symptoms — there is no one face of autism.

- Roughly 50% of children with ASD have some intellectual disability, whereas the other 50% do not.

- Some children with autism symptoms have an abnormally large brain, whereas others do not.

- One in three children with autism has more than two epileptic seizures by the time they are a young adult, whereas the other two in three don't.

- About half of all children diagnosed with ASD are described as having severely impaired speech, whereas the other half don't.

- Approximately one in three children diagnosed with autism has disabilities that are lifelong and require a significant amount of social and educational support, whereas the other two in three don't.

- Autism occurs in children of every race and in every ethnic and socioeconomic group.

- Although typical onset is during the toddler years, autism symptoms can appear at any time from early infancy to young adulthood.

The degree of symptoms ranges in a spectrum from mild to severe and everything in between, so children may show some symptoms from both ends of the spectrum.

> ## Did You Know?
>
> **No Reliable Tests**
>
> To date, there is no reliable medical test or definite biomarker to identify autism, making this condition more difficult to diagnose and then to develop an effective treatment plan.

Incidence of Autism

Since 2009, the incidence of autism diagnoses has increased a great deal, from one out of every 110 children being diagnosed with ASD to the current rate of one out of 88 children. Boys are diagnosed three or four times more often than girls (one out of 54 boys). In the United States, around 36,500 out of the four million children born every year have autism.

Increased Awareness

It is difficult to tell whether there has been a real increase in the numbers of children diagnosed with autism or an increase in awareness of autism symptoms during the past 20 years. Families with an autistic child have been generous in providing research scientists with information and donations as they look for answers and appropriate treatments. There has been a rapid growth in research conducted and evidence collected about autism, but no cure. The increased number of ASD diagnoses could also be the result of a better understanding of the items or criteria that lead to an autism diagnosis and improved screening throughout the developmental years.

The true reason for the increase is hard to say. Although exact numbers of children with autism worldwide are not known, the rates of diagnosis are consistent across many countries where assessments are done. Unfortunately, many children are never diagnosed or treated.

Signs and Symptoms

Parents are often the first to identify the symptoms of autism in their child, long before a diagnosis by a health-care professional, even though most children are screened for autism at regular visits with their doctors. Showing some signs of autism does not always indicate a diagnosis however! Because autism can affect social, communication, and cognitive functions, each child will show a different, or heterogeneous, set of symptoms. Some children who are identified as having ASD at an early age make great strides in social and language skills because of early interventions.

Baby Behavior

Your baby's behavior can alert you to possible signs of autism. Do you find that your baby doesn't respond with smiles and coos when you play peekaboo? Does your 1-year-old not wave bye-bye or hold eye contact with you or other relatives when she is being fed? When your baby wakes after a nap, does he smile and put out his arms to be picked up? Are you able to have shared experiences with your baby? Does looking at and

Profile: Olivia

Olivia is 4 years old and has ASD. She has a twin sister, Alicia, who does most of the talking wherever they go. Olivia loves being read to more than anything, and her favorite book is *Olivia* (the pig). She likes stickers, especially horse stickers, and likes to play with her My Little Pony collection.

Most Common Symptoms of Autism

The most common symptoms of ASD include a range of mental and emotional impairments, including cognitive and intellectual problems, difficulties with regulating emotions, challenging behaviors, abnormal sleep patterns, seizures, and gastrointestinal disturbances that can be classified as mild, moderate, or severe. For a diagnosis of ASD, symptoms can begin at birth but are usually recognized as being different before the age of 3. Even though symptoms and the severity of ASD may vary, abilities to communicate and interact with others will be affected to some degree in every child who has autism.

pointing out your baby in the mirror lead to her looking at herself in the mirror, then back to you? Language development usually begins with cooing, moving on to babbling and copying sounds you may make. Does your baby cover his ears when you talk to him? If your baby isn't interested in working hard to "talk" to you with lots of expressions, you may have an early indicator of autism.

Social Symptoms

At the age when children typically enjoy playtime with other children, some children with autism are withdrawn, do not make friends, do not play interactive games, and may prefer to spend time alone rather than with other children or adults. They may show little imaginative or pretend play, may not copy the actions of other children or adults, and some children seem to prefer rituals as a form of play.

Sensory Symptoms

Often, children with autism have sensory issues, in that they perceive the world around them differently than do typically developing children. They may not startle at loud noises but may find a normal level of noise to be painful and are often seen holding their hands over their ears. You may see children with autism occupying themselves with odd sensory behaviors, such as rubbing surfaces, licking or mouthing objects, or chewing articles of clothing. Children with mild autism may be overly sensitive to colors, lights, smells, sounds, or textures or less sensitive to heat, cold, or discomfort. They may be either numb or overly sensitive to pain. Responses to sensory issues might include rocking, hand flapping, twirling, or repetitive sounds.

Behaviors Common to Children with Autism

- Short attention span
- Very strong requirement for sameness
- Repetitive physical movements
- Extremely narrow interests
- Aggressive behaviors to self or other children
- "Meltdowns," being overwhelmed, or extreme temper tantrums

Mild Autism

Children with a diagnosis of mild autism are more likely to appear to be a typically developing child with good language skills. They are socially aware but may have speech and language delays and difficulties with receptive language. Children with a mild form of autism may have developed vocabularies but may speak in awkward, monotone, or high-pitched tones or voices. The mild form of autism may also cause behavioral issues such as anxiety over simple transitions between activities and a strong compulsion to stick with very regimented routines. This group of children may not handle change well.

Although it is fairly well-known that children with autism are picky eaters, often choosing bland-colored and bland-tasting foods, they may be picky about clothing choices as well, finding many fabric textures uncomfortable. At school, children with mild autism may be allowed to type rather than write. Teachers use a gentle but firm approach, with a structured day, and provide brief, direct instructions, understanding that many children with autism may be visual thinkers.

Severe Autism

Children with more severe autism experience impairment in developmental areas, may be mentally handicapped, may have low awareness of their environment, and will be socially impaired. These children are more likely to self-injure, to have severe memory impairment, and to show severe disabilities, poor expressive or receptive language, and obviously odd behaviors, gestures, or rituals.

Q. **What do you mean by "expressive and receptive language" skills?**

A. Expressive language is the communication of your thoughts, ideas, information, and feelings using a collection or system of signals (gestures, voice sounds, sign language, or written symbols) and doing more than repeating what another person is saying. Receptive language is the ability to comprehend body language, gestures, what you hear other people say, or what you read. Broadly stated, expressive language means speaking, whereas receptive language means hearing and understanding.

Language Development

From the moment of her first cry at birth, your child begins to develop her language skills, listening and paying attention to what you say to her and making sounds of her own. For most children, the acquisition of language comes naturally; for some children with ASD, however, support is needed to develop these skills. If you have concerns about your child's ability to speak or understand language, consult your family physician or pediatrician as soon as possible. Your child may be referred to a pediatric speech pathologist.

Expressive Language Problems

Problems with expressive language skills are typically categorized as a delay or disorder. These categories can overlap. Expressive language *delay* describes a child who shows a typical speech development pattern but at a date relatively later than most other children. An expressive language *disorder* describes a language development pattern that is different in some way other than delay. In addition, language development may be affected by physiological and motor problems. It is difficult to speak if the mouth and tongue are somehow impaired.

Assessing Expressive Language Skills

Speech pathologists use three terms to assess expressive language problems — form, content, and use.

Form
Some children struggle with the form, structure, or grammar of language:
- Using logical sentence structure
- Following word order or word endings
- Using plural words, possessives, prepositions, and verb tenses

Content
Some children have issues with understanding the meaning or semantics of words:
- Finding the right word for the situation
- Putting words into categories
- Explaining things they understand
- Speaking about abstract concepts — something that doesn't have a physical presence you can point to

Use
Some children have problems with the use or pragmatics of language:
- Using the right word for the occasion
- Asking meaningful questions that lead to action

Receptive Language Skills

The ability to understand language involves the orchestration of several specific skills, including the ability to:

- Hear well
- Govern the speed or rate of taking in or processing language
- Pay attention and maintain attention
- Tell the difference between specific speaking sounds
- Understand language in different settings
- Remember how speech sounds come together in strings (similar to an automatic phone answering system being able to identify and understand what you are saying)
- Follow a narrative sentence structure if there is an action and if a time element is included: "Mommy is coming right back; you are going to wait here with your sister"
- Comprehend the meaning of commonly used words

If any one of these skills is impaired, communication may be impeded.

Receptive Language Problems

Assessing receptive language skills can be difficult because children may be able to understand what is being said based on the setting, facial expressions, gestures, or body language (not on speaking or reading). Behavior-related issues (including disinterest) may also interfere with understanding what is being said. Be concerned if your child's ability to understand language develops later than expected for his age.

Developmental Milestones

According to the Centers for Disease Control and Prevention (CDC), children should be checked to be sure they are meeting typical developmental milestones in every area — moving, behaving, learning, speaking, and playing — from ages 2 to 5. The following chart shows samples of typical development and is not intended to replace regular appointments with your child's health-care professional.

CDC Developmental Milestones

Age	Area of Development	Behavior
2 months	Social/emotional	Smiles at people sometimes Can sometimes self-soothe for a short period (hands to mouth, sucking on hand or fingers) Takes great interest in looking at parents
	Communication/language	Makes deliberate gurgling sounds and coos Able to turn toward sounds
	Learning/thinking/problem solving (cognitive)	Pays close attention to faces, staring and looking from one feature to another Starting to follow moving things with eyes Able to recognize familiar people from far away Starts to cry or fuss (act bored) when activity stays the same for long periods
	Physical development and movement	Able to hold up head and is starting to push up on arms when lying on belly Movements with arms and legs are smoother
◆ **Warning signals at 2 months to discuss with your child's doctor**		If he makes no response to loud sounds If she doesn't watch moving things If he doesn't bring hands to mouth If she isn't able to hold up her head when on tummy and pushing up
4 months	Social/emotional	Spontaneous smiles, especially at familiar faces Likes playtime with familiar people, may fuss or cry when it ends Parrots some facial expressions or movements (smiling, frowning)
	Communication/language	Babbling starts Copies heard sounds, expressive babbling Communicates emotional states through different cries: hunger, pain, tiredness, fear, anger
	Learning/thinking/problem solving (cognitive)	Responds to affection Shares feelings of happiness or sadness through smiles or crying Able to use eyes and hands together (seeing a toy and reaching for it) Able to reach for toys with just one hand Watches faces closely for cues Follows moving things from one side to the other Recognizes familiar people and things from a distance

Age	Area of Development	Behavior
4 months	Physical development and movement	May be able to roll from tummy to back Brings hands to mouth When on tummy, pushes up onto elbows Holds head up on neck, steady when unsupported When feet are on a hard surface, will push down on legs Can swing at dangling toys, can hold a toy and shake it
◆ Warning signals at 4 months to discuss with your child's doctor		If he doesn't watch things when they move If she can't hold her head up unsupported and steady If he doesn't coo or make any sounds If she doesn't smile at familiar people If he has some trouble moving one eye or both eyes from side to side and up and down If she doesn't push down with her legs when her feet are on a hard surface
6 months	Social/emotional	Knows familiar faces and begins to understand what a stranger is Likes playtime, especially with parents Often seems happy and responds to familiar people's emotions Likes to look at himself in a mirror
	Communication/language	Responds to her name Makes sounds to express joy or displeasure Responds to sounds heard by making sounds Strings vowel sounds together during babbling and likes to mimic parents by making sounds (*ah, eh, oh,* etc.) Starts to make consonant sounds by babbling *mmmm* or *bbbbb,* etc.
	Learning/thinking/problem solving (cognitive)	Brings things to mouth Shows curiosity about things and tries to reach or get things out of reach Starts to pass things from one hand to the other Looks at things nearby
	Physical development and movement	Starts to sit without any support Rocks to and fro while on hands and knees; for some, crawling backward before going forward Rolls in both directions (from tummy to back, from back to tummy) Supports weight on legs when standing, might bounce

What Is Autism? **23**

Age	Area of Development	Behavior
◆ Warning signals at 6 months to discuss with your child's doctor		If she shows no affection for caregivers If he doesn't try to get things even if they are within reach If she doesn't respond to sounds around her or directed at her If he has some difficulty getting things to his mouth If she doesn't laugh or make squealing sounds If he seems stiff, with tight muscles If she seems floppy, something like a rag doll
9 months	Social/emotional	Might be afraid of unfamiliar people or strangers Might be clingy with familiar people Has toys that are favorites
	Communication/language	Makes many different sounds (*mamamamam* and *bababab* and *dadadadad*) Copies gestures and sounds other people make Uses fingers to point to things Understands what "no" means
	Learning/thinking/problem solving (cognitive)	Looks for things he sees you hide Plays peekaboo Watches the path of something when it falls Puts things in her mouth Moves things from one hand to the other hand smoothly Picks up things, such as cereal, between thumb and index finger
	Physical development and movement	Can get into sitting position Pulls on something to stand up Crawls Stands, holding on to something Sits without support
◆ Warning signals at 9 months to discuss with your child's doctor		If he doesn't bear weight on legs with support If she doesn't sit with help If he doesn't babble If she doesn't play back and forth games with other people (passing a ball, etc.) If he doesn't look in the direction you point If she doesn't respond to her name If he doesn't appear to recognize familiar people If she doesn't move toys from one hand to the other

Age	Area of Development	Behavior
1 year	Social/emotional	Has favorite people and things Is fearful in some situations Cries when left by Mom or Dad Is nervous or shy with unfamiliar people Repeats actions or sounds for attention Puts out hands, feet, legs, and arms to help with dressing Brings a book to you when it's story time Plays peekaboo, pat-a-cake, and other stories
	Communication/language	Is using simple gestures (shaking head, no, bye-bye) Says "Mama," "Dada," and "uh-oh" appropriately Tries to repeat words you say Starting to make sounds and include tone changes (sounding more like language)
	Learning/thinking/problem solving (cognitive)	Investigates objects with shaking, throwing, and banging Easily finds anything you hide Looks at the right thing when you name an object or picture Will copy gestures you make Uses objects correctly, such as drinking from a cup or brushing hair Holds things in both hands and bangs them together Puts objects in containers, then takes them back out Lets go of things without your help Will poke things, or you, with a pointer or index finger Is able to follow directions if they are simple ("Pick up the truck")
	Physical development and movement	Able to change to a sitting position by himself Pulls herself up on furniture to stand, and walks along furniture or anything that offers security (called cruising) Might be able to take a couple of steps without any support Might be able to stand by himself
◆ Warning signals at 1 year to discuss with your child's doctor		If he is not crawling If she isn't able to stand, even if supported If he isn't interested in searching for objects that you hide in front of him If she isn't saying single words ("Mama," "Dada")

continued...

Age	Area of Development	Behavior
◆ Warning signals at 1 year to discuss with your child's doctor		If he isn't learning any gestures (waving, shaking head no) If she isn't pointing at things If he loses abilities he had mastered or regresses
18 months	Social/emotional	Might be afraid of unfamiliar people Might have temper tantrums Shows affection to people she knows Likes the game of handing objects to people Pretend plays (feeding dolls, driving trucks) Might be clingy with parents or caregivers in new situations Uses pointing to share something she finds interesting Is able to explore by himself, as long as a parent is nearby
	Communication/language	Has a vocabulary of several single words Says no and shakes head Consistently uses pointing for something she wants
	Learning/thinking/problem solving (cognitive)	Understands what everyday objects (brush, spoon, phone) are used for Uses pointing to get attention Pretends to feed dolls or stuffed animals Uses pointing to bring attention to one body part Able to scribble by himself Able to complete actions correctly when given single-step verbal commands ("Sit down")
	Physical development and movement	Able to walk by herself Might be able to run or walk up stairs Able to walk and pull toys at the same time Helps to undress himself Able to eat by herself with a spoon Able to drink from a cup by himself
◆ Warning signals at 18 months to discuss with your child's doctor		If he isn't able to point to share interest If she isn't able to walk If he doesn't understand what everyday objects are used for If she doesn't copy other people If he isn't adding new words to his vocabulary If she doesn't know at least six words If he doesn't mind or even notice if a caregiver leaves or when she comes back If she loses abilities she had mastered or regresses

Age	Area of Development	Behavior
2 years	Social/emotional	Is excited when she is with children Copies older children and adults Is becoming more independent Starting to be defiant (looks at a parent while doing what he has just been told not to do) Plays some games with other children, such as chase games, but mostly plays beside other children
	Communication/language	Able to point to pictures or objects you name Recognizes names of body parts and familiar people Able to say two- to four-word sentences Able to follow simple directions Is repeating words that she hears in conversations between other people Is pointing to objects in books
	Learning/thinking/problem solving (cognitive)	Able to find objects you hide, under several layers of covers, for instance Starting to sort colors and shapes Able to complete whole sentences, as well as rhymes from familiar books Plays simple pretend games Able to build towers using at least four blocks May be using one hand more than the other Able to follow directions with two steps ("Pick up your boots and put them in your room") Able to say the names of objects seen in picture books ("bird," "cat," "dog")
	Physical development and movement	Able to stand on tippy-toes Able to kick a ball Starting to run Able to climb up onto and down from the furniture by himself Able to walk up and down the stairs if holding on to the railing Able to throw a ball overhand Able to copy or make straight lines and circles
◆ Warning signals at 2 years to discuss with your child's doctor		If he doesn't understand how to use everyday objects (fork, spoon, brush, phone) Doesn't use two-word phrases (for example, "drink milk") If she isn't able to follow simple directions If he isn't steady when he walks If she doesn't copy your words and actions If he has lost skills he had mastered or regressed

continued...

Age	Area of Development	Behavior
3 years	Social/emotional	Copies actions and words of friends and adults Shows affection for friends without being prompted Is good at taking turns when playing games Is concerned for friends if they are crying Able to understand the concept of his, hers, and mine Shows emotions ranging from anger to joy Is easily able to be apart from Mom and Dad Might be upset when major routine changes happen Able to undress and dress by herself
	Communication/language	Able to follow directions that include two to three steps Able to name most things that are familiar Able to understand more difficult concepts (in, on, and under) Able to say age, gender, and first name Able to say a friend's name Has a more complex vocabulary, with "I," "me," "we" and "you," and some plural words ("cats," "dogs," "cars") Strangers can understand most words/sentences said Conversations extend to two or three sentences
	Learning/thinking/problem solving (cognitive)	Able to make toys work that have moving parts, levers, and buttons Engages in pretend play with animals, people, and dolls Able to complete simple puzzles that have three to four pieces Comprehends concept of two Able to copy a circle using pencils or crayons Able to turn pages of a book one page at a time Able to build towers six or more blocks high Able to turn door handles and screw jar lids on or off
	Physical development and movement	Able to run easily Able to climb easily Able to pedal a three-wheel bicycle Able to walk up and down the stairs with one foot per step

Age	Area of Development	Behavior
◆ Warning signals at 3 years to discuss with your child's doctor		If he falls down a lot or struggles with getting up or down stairs
		If she drools or has very garbled speech
		If he isn't able to make simple toys work (turning handles, doing simple puzzles, and using things like Peg-Boards)
		If she isn't able to speak in full sentences
		If he isn't able to understand simple directions
		If she isn't able to pretend play
		If he isn't interested in playing with toys or other children
		If she doesn't make eye contact with others
		If he loses abilities he had mastered or regresses
4 years	Social/emotional	Takes pleasure in new activities
		Pretends to be Mom or Dad
		Pretend play has become more and more creative
		Is happier playing with other children than playing by herself
		Is cooperative when playing with other children
		Can't always tell the difference between what is make-believe and what is real
		Talks about what he is interested in and what he really likes
	Communication/language	Understands some basic grammar rules (correctly uses "he" and "she")
		Able to sing a short song or recite a poem that she has memorized ("Itsy Bitsy Spider" or "Wheels on the Bus")
		Makes up or tells stories he has heard
		Able to say first and last name
	Learning/thinking/problem solving (cognitive)	Able to name some numbers and colors
		Able to understand the concept of counting numbers
		Beginning to understand how time works
		Able to remember part of a story
		Able to understand the concept of things being either the same or different
		Able to draw a person with two to four body parts
		Able to use scissors
		Beginning to copy a few capital letters
		Able to play some card or board games
		Able to tell you what she thinks might happen next in a story

continued...

Age	Area of Development	Behavior
4 years	Physical development and movement	Able to hop and stand on one foot for up to two seconds Mostly able to catch a bouncing ball Able to pour fluids, to cut food with some supervision, and to mash her own food
◆ **Warning signals at 4 years to discuss with your child's doctor**		If he isn't able to jump in the same spot If she has some trouble with scribbling If he doesn't show any interest in make-believe or interactive games If she doesn't respond at all to people who aren't part of her family or ignores other children If he is resistant to dressing himself, sleeping, or using the toilet properly If she isn't able to tell a favorite story she has heard many times If he isn't able to follow three-part directions If she isn't able to understand how objects might be either the same or different If he isn't able to use "me" or "you" appropriately If she is not speaking clearly If he loses abilities he had mastered or regresses
5 years	Social/emotional	Pleasing friends matters Wants to be like friends More willing to go along with rules Singing, dancing, and acting are sources of happiness Displays concern and sympathy for people Understands what gender means Understands the difference between real and make-believe Shows more independence (might visit next-door neighbors by herself, with adult supervision) Can be demanding or very cooperative
	Communication/language	Able to speak clearly Able to use full sentences to tell a simple story Able to understand future tense ("Grandma will be here") Able to say full name and where he lives

Age	Area of Development	Behavior
5 years	Learning/thinking/problem solving (cognitive)	Able to count more than 10 objects Able to make a drawing of a person who has six or more body parts Able to print some numbers or letters Able to copy geometric shapes, such as a triangle Understands everyday objects (for example, food, money)
	Physical development and movement	Able to stand on one foot (for at least 10 seconds or more) Able to hop and might be able to skip Able to do a somersault Able to use a fork and spoon properly and sometimes to use a table knife Able to go to the toilet by himself Able to climb and swing
◆ Warning signals at 5 years to discuss with your child's doctor		If he doesn't display the full range of emotions If she displays extreme behavior (unusually fearful, aggressive, shy, or sad) If he is extremely inactive and withdrawn If she is easily distracted and has trouble focusing on an activity for more than 5 minutes If he responds to people in a superficial way or not at all If she is not able to tell the difference between what is real or make-believe If he isn't interested in a variety of games and activities If she isn't able to say full name If he isn't able to use plural words or the past tense appropriately If she isn't able to talk about experiences or daily activities If he isn't able to draw pictures If she isn't able to brush teeth, get undressed by herself, or wash and dry hands If he loses abilities he had mastered or regresses

Q. What should we do if our child is rocking, twirling, or flapping her hands while playing with other kids? We don't want her to look "different" in the school playground.

A. Even though repetitive or stereotyped behaviors are recognized as signs of ASD, and hand flapping, twirling, and rocking are considered possible ASD symptoms for children older than 3, it is typically when these behaviors are taken to an extreme that they are a possible indicator of autism. Although all children will repeat behaviors or line toys up in a row, children with autism will be more difficult to distract from these games and will become very upset if their arranged toys or household items are disturbed. In some regions, babies are not diagnosed for ASD until they are older than 2 years old, because a wide range of developmental stages are common in infants and young children. If you are concerned, you should always check with your family physician or pediatrician in case some interventions are available even without a formal diagnosis.

Since we are all "different," it may be helpful to explain to your child's schoolmates that your child shows she is stressed by flapping her hands, and give them possible ways to help her to calm down.

DocTalk:
Responding to Language Regression

Q. My 3-year-old child doesn't talk at all; he used to say all the normal things until he was around 2; now he doesn't even look up when we say his name. What should we do?

A. This is not uncommon among children with ASD. One-third of children with autism have what is called regressive autism. They appear to develop language normally and then lose this ability. It has been suggested recently that regression may be an almost universal finding in ASD. To confirm this diagnosis, these children should have a hearing assessment and be referred for a speech-language evaluation. Your family doctor may refer you to a developmental pediatrician or psychologist to rule out ASD. A delay in diagnosis may result in a delay in treatment or intervention, which does affect outcomes.

Checklist of Signs and Symptoms

Tracking signs and symptoms of ASD shown by your child will help your physician or pediatrician in making a diagnosis and developing a treatment plan. Children may show one or several signs or symptoms of autism from as early as 3 months to 24 months of age. If you are worried that your child has autism, check off the relevant boxes on this list. This is a tool for you to review your child's behavior. Mark the severity or extremity of the symptom on a scale of 1 to 3, with 3 being the most severe or extreme. Indicate how often your child exhibits that behavior (monthly, weekly, daily, hourly).

Category	Sign or Symptom	Mild: 1	Moderate: 2	Severe: 3	Frequency
Behavioral	No or little eye contact				
	Failure to bond to parents				
	No imitation of facial expressions or movements				
	No interest in cuddling				
	Not easily soothed				
	No joint attention (following pointing finger)				
	Impaired empathy for others				
	Mind blindness (inability to imagine the thoughts and emotions of other people)				
	Insistence on sameness				
	Repetitive behavior, also known as stereotyped behavior (spinning, hand flapping, head banging, making the same noise or saying the same word over and over again)				
Psychiatric	Obsessions				
	Superior detection of change				
	Precocious understanding of machines				
	May not respond to sounds or rarely responds				

continued...

Category	Sign or Symptom	Mild: 1	Moderate: 2	Severe: 3	Frequency
Physiological	Chronic gastrointestinal problems (diarrhea or constipation; rumination)				
	Normal development followed by a return to behavior seen at an earlier age (called regression), often occurring between 2 and 3 years old				
	Impaired language, nonverbal, typical language development that is later lost, or high level of language but lack of knowledge of when to use specific language in social situations				
Behavioral/ Physiological	No pointing or not following pointing by others				
	Little interest in play with other children (known as impaired reciprocal social interaction or social affect)				
	Extremely picky eater				
Psychological/ Psychiatric	Sensory-perceptual issues				
	Sleep issues (not sleeping, different sleeping patterns)				
	Gait and motor coordination problems				
Language For frequency, rate as: Rarely = **R** Sometimes = **S** Frequently = **F**		Slow/ Quiet	Modulated/ Typical	High/ Loud	Frequency (R/S/F)
	Phrasing				
	Rate				
	Stress				
	Pitch				
	Loudness				
	Resonance				

Category	Sign or Symptom	Poor	Average	High	Frequency (R/S/F)
Motor movements For frequency, rate as: Rarely = **R** Sometimes = **S** Frequently = **F**	Posture				
	Balance				
	Motor dexterity				
	Coordination of movement				
Emotional, social, and cognitive processing For level, rate as: Mild = **1** Moderate = **2** Extreme = **3**		**Rare**	**Sometimes**	**Often**	**Level**
	Cognitive impairment				
	Deficits of executive function (reasoning, problem solving, planning)				
	Expressive language impairment (understanding and using language)				
	Affective blunting, or disinhibition (lack of emotional expressiveness)				
	Implicit timing impairments (remembering past social events to understand current situations and respond appropriately: affecting social cues)				
Social deficits linked to immune dysfunction	Deficits in social interactions and communications				
	Aberrant behaviors				
	Lack of sense of mind (consciousness)				
Gastro-intestinal	Abdominal pain				
	Constipation				
	Diarrhea				
	Gas				
	Bloating				
	Vomiting				
	Headaches				

If your child exhibits these behavioral, psychiatric, language, or physiological problems, see your physician or pediatrician for a possible diagnosis for ASD.

Research Spotlight

Symptoms of Regression

Approximately 30% of children with autism follow a typical development pattern and then regress to an earlier development pattern. This regression is typically diagnosed as ASD. Most often, regression happens between 18 and 24 months of age. Approximately one of three children with ASD have a regressive onset.

Recent research has identified four specific forms of regression that affect children diagnosed with ASD:

1. *Regression in language and social skills:* children who have been putting words together, responding to questions appropriately, and are socially active (saying hello, giving hugs and cuddles, playing with toys and other children or adults) suddenly regress to no language or do not respond to social cues.

2. *Regression in motor skills:* a child who has started walking and has some control over toilet training regresses to crawling and diapers.

3. *Regression in adaptive functioning skills,* which is the ability to cope with the everyday demands in life (and is usually compared to others of a similar age and background). For young children, the ability to wait for a short period to have their needs met while their caregiver tends to someone else is an example. Some children may actually do some things as well as or better than others, but still have coping issues in some areas.

4. *Regression unspecified.*

Chapter 2
How Is Autism Diagnosed?

CASE STUDY (continued from page 15)
Diagnostic Shock

After Dr. Parker reviewed the results of his physical examination of Stephen and the outcome of his Autism Diagnostic Interview — Revised (ADI-R) screening test, he called the family and asked them to meet at his office. Stephen's mother covered her eyes when their physician told her: "I'm sorry to have to tell you that Stephen meets all the criteria for a diagnosis of autism spectrum disorder." He went on to explain that children who were diagnosed early and received behavioral therapy often showed improvement in some symptoms, but all Stephen's mother could think was, "What did I do wrong?" She also asked if the diagnosis could be mistaken. She asked their doctor if he could explain in greater detail how autism spectrum disorder is diagnosed — and what they could do to help Stephen improve his quality of life... *(continued on page 55)*

Diagnostic Steps

There is no laboratory test or medical marker that identifies autism, so health-care professionals must revert to using patient histories and observations of behavior to identify the signs and symptoms. Diagnosis is further complicated by the wide range of screening tests available. In addition to identifying and recording developmental delays and anomalies specified in the Centers for Disease Control growth charts, an official diagnosis of autism must meet criteria established by the American Psychiatric Association. The APA offers reliable and sensitive guidelines for making a diagnosis, starting with a simple developmental history.

There are three basic steps in diagnosing autism, though descriptions of these steps may differ from one public health-care jurisdiction to another:

1. Surveillance by parents or caregivers
2. Screening by primary health-care professionals
3. Assessment by an interdisciplinary group of mental health-care professionals

Surveillance

During baby visits with your pediatrician, you will be asked if you have seen any problems with your child's development. Long-term research has shown that parents' concerns about their 6-month-old child did not correctly predict developmental outcome, but parents' concerns about their 12-month-old child were correct more often than chance. These families each had an older child who had been diagnosed with autism.

Parents tend to recognize excessive behavior — prolonged crying, feeding problems (shorter periods between feedings, longer feedings, food refusals, excessive vomiting), sleep problems, and failure to thrive in general — when they see and hear it. More persistent problems have been found to relate to later behavior problems, parent stress, and even maternal depression, but most infant crying, fussing, and sleep issues during the first 2 years are temporary.

Be sure to bring to the attention of your health-care provider any concerns you have about feeding, sleeping, or extreme crying to rule out autism.

Screening

APA guidelines recommend that when parents have concerns about their child's development, especially at or before the 18-month assessment, a screening or assessment tool for autism should be used (M-CHAT or equivalent). Each screening tool uses a specific set of questions or items using a rating scale directed at a particular age. Routine screening, however, is controversial, since some of the factors that warrant population screening are not present here: effective treatment or preventative measures for ASD, appropriate and effective screening tests, or a population-wide need for these tests.

Did You Know?

Early Diagnosis

Although ASD can be identified in some children at the age of 12 to 18 months, a diagnosis by an experienced professional at 24 months is considered more reliable. Early diagnosis of autism is one of the predictors of a better outcome, along with higher IQ, imitation behavior, and receptive language skills. Identifying autism at an early age permits earlier interventions that may reduce the severity of symptoms and even negate the diagnosis altogether. Some parents wait for a late diagnosis, however, because they fear being stigmatized by the "autism" label; others simply do not recognize the signs and symptoms of this condition.

A positive result from a screening test will lead to a referral to a specialist for more in-depth testing using the ADOS or ADI-R assessment. See page 44 for descriptions of screening and assessment tools.

Assessment

Current best practice for diagnosing autism involves a multidisciplinary clinical team, with the smallest group including a physician (developmental pediatrician, child neurologist, or psychiatrist), psychologist, and speech-language pathologist. Other health-care professionals who may be involved include occupational therapists, physical therapists, and audiologists. Any clinician involved in diagnosing autism requires clinical experience, specialized training, and direct experience with children with autism.

Assessment Stages

1. Developmental and family history
2. Physical examination
3. Identification of autism risk factors
4. Consideration of possible associated medical conditions
5. Differential testing to confirm or rule out any conditions suspected as a result of history or physical examination
6. Genetic screening with DNA and microarray analysis for fragile X syndrome
7. Metabolic screening, or EEG if indicated

In some cases, tests for allergies, immunologic abnormalities, or vitamin, mineral, and heavy metal levels may be used as required. The assessment process may vary, depending on your region.

Did You Know?

Diagnostic Systems

Diagnostic systems provide models of problems, signs, symptoms, restrictions in function, and physical or biological markers or test results for recognized disorders and disease states in psychiatric medicine. For mental health professionals, that diagnostic system is the *Diagnostic and Statistical Manual of Mental Disorders* (American Psychiatric Association, 1980, 1987, 1994, 2000, 2010, and the 2013 version, *DSM-5*), and for clinicians, the World Health Organization's Family of International Classifications on diseases and disorders is the standard tool for diagnosis, epidemiology, health management, and clinical purposes.

DSM-5 Assessment Standards

The *Diagnostic and Statistical Manual of Mental Disorders* 5 (*DSM-5*) is the diagnostic tool most often used in mental health-care and clinical practice around the world. The *DSM* provides models of mental health disorders, and if an individual shows the signs and symptoms that meet the criteria describing that disorder, and if the diagnostic process has shown that other medical conditions are not responsible, the person is thought to have that disorder unless new information proves otherwise.

Diagnostic Domains

Autism interrupts normal infant development in two areas, or domains, and they are described in the *DSM-5* and reproduced here:

1. Social-communication deficits
2. Restricted and repetitive interests/behaviors (RRB), including unusual sensory responses

Your health-care professional will check off the behaviors your child is exhibiting in each domain:

1. Persistent deficits in social communication and social interaction across multiple contexts
   - Deficits in social-emotional reciprocity
   - Deficits in nonverbal communicative behaviors used for social interaction
   - Deficits in developing, maintaining, and understanding relationships
2. Restricted, repetitive patterns of behavior, interests, or activities
   - Stereotyped or repetitive motor movements, use of objects, or speech
   - Insistence on sameness, inflexible adherence to routines, or ritualized patterns of verbal or nonverbal behavior
   - Highly restricted, fixated interests that are abnormal in intensity or focus
   - Hyper- or hyporeactivity to sensory input or unusual interest in sensory aspects of the environment

Severity

Symptoms are classified according to their severity into mild, moderate, or severe. These classifications are affected by intellectual disability, impaired language, and other medical or behavioral diagnoses.

Screening Tools

Screening tools are intended to identify developmental delays or specific behaviors in the age group for which the tool was designed. Some are used in pediatric care, and others are useful in the school setting. Screening tools are developed by research teams and tested vigorously again and again to be sure the behaviors they are intended to test are "validated." Screens are "reliable" when the scores are found to be accurate time after time, and "sensitive" when they score intended behaviors at a consistently high level. Used alone, however, scores from a screening tool will not indicate a diagnosis of autism.

Did You Know?

Older Screening Tools

Most screening tools for ASD have been developed under earlier versions of the APA *Diagnostic and Statistical Manual*. Research comparing results of diagnostic tools based on *DSM-IV* and *DSM-5* criteria show that, using combined ADOS (Autism Diagnostic Observation Schedule) and ADI-R (Autism Diagnostic Interview — Revised) ratings, high percentages of patients met criteria for both *DSM* versions.

Q. **Who conducts screening tests?**

A. Many health-care specialists are involved in administering and evaluating tests for ASD. Trained clinicians typically administer and monitor the tests, and a group of health-care professionals are involved in diagnosing autism spectrum disorder. Some screening tests are designed for parents or caregivers to complete at home (on paper or online). Screenings identify children or adults who might benefit from a thorough assessment with a clinical team. Behavioral screens are completed by psychologists, family physicians, or pediatricians. Some require a psychologist or someone at the masters' level with specific training (school counseling, occupational therapy, speech-language pathology, social work, special education). Medical testing, including referrals for hearing, lead screening, and screening for nutritional deficiencies, is done by a primary care physician. Audiologic evaluations to determine whether a physiological issue may be affecting language development or hearing are done by an audiologist. More specific genetic and metabolic testing is done by geneticists or developmental pediatricians.

$Q.$ Can I use screening tools at home?

$A.$ If you are thinking of trying a screening tool at home, start by answering these questions:

- *How do I know which questions are appropriate for my child?* If you have been tracking your child's behavior and health concerns, you will be able to decide which questions your child needs to answer.

- *Will a screening test identify specific delays or conditions?* Screening tests help identify children at risk for a specific diagnosis, but further in-depth testing by clinical health-care professionals is required to confirm a diagnosis.

- *How can I be sure that the screening test is the right one for my child?* Different screening tools are designed for specific ages and risk factors.

- *How can I tell if the screening tool is okay to complete at home?* Different tools are intended to be given in a health-care provider's office, in a community setting, such as a daycare, or in the home. However, parents should not attempt to interpret screening tests on their own.

- *Are there at-home screening tools available for children younger than 2?* Some screening tests have been designed to identify high-risk infants and will help monitor development as time goes by. Steady surveillance is key for early diagnosis.

Did You Know?

Ages and Stages Questionnaires (ASQ)

Various Ages and Stages Questionnaires in English, Spanish, or French are used to monitor developmental and social-emotional stages in children from 1 month to over 5 years old. The questionnaire takes about 10 to 15 minutes to complete and, if completed online, provides a score in 2 to 3 minutes, with a cutoff where scores below the cutoff point suggest further assessment, scores around the cutoff might recommend discussion and monitoring, and scores above the cutoff suggest that the child is developmentally on track. The website for the questionnaires — www.agesandstages.com — also provides an opportunity for managing your child's questionnaire data and referrals.

Did You Know?

Gold Standard for Diagnosing Autism

The Autism Diagnostic Interview — Revised (ADI-R) and the Autism Diagnostic Observation Schedule — Generic (ADOS-2) are recognized as the gold standard for autism screening tests.

- The ADI-R involves a standardized interview with the caregiver for children over 18 months of age. Although interview questions are intended to distinguish between deviance from typical development and developmental delay, cutoff scores are supplied for autism only, with recommended diagnoses for communication, social interaction, and restricted or repetitive behavior.

- The ADOS-2 is valid from 12 months to adulthood. This tool has different modules to be used for specific language and developmental levels. It uses structured play. Diagnostic decisions from a clinical team are made based on cutoff scores that recognize impaired communication or reciprocal social interaction, or a combined communication and social interaction score.

Q. Where can I find copies of these screening tools and questionnaires?

A. If you are interested in trying screening tools at home, some of the autism associations provide links to screening tools:

- Autism Canada
- Autism Research Institute
- Autism Spectrum Disorder Canadian-American Research Consortium (ASD-CARC)

We have provided a list of resource websites at the back of this book for your convenience.

Also consider becoming involved in a research study that gives you access to some screening tools. Other options for information, depending on your child's age, include calling a health line (typically run by nurses), contacting your family physician's or pediatrician's office, calling your local school or school board, or calling your public health office.

Guide to ASD Screening Tools

All screening tools are considered part of a diagnostic assessment; no one questionnaire or interview will give a diagnosis of autism. A diagnosis of autism syndrome disorder can only be given by a team or a qualified clinician who has the education and experience to interpret all information collected through questionnaires and medical history (called quantitative data) and through interviews (called qualitative data) with parents and caregivers, and teachers, if appropriate.

Questionnaires and Interviews for Screening Development and Diagnosing Autism

1. Screening tools for development

Screening tool (by age)	Age	Description	Notes
Sense and Self-Regulation Checklist (SSC)	Birth to 6 years	Measures and monitors sensory and self-regulatory symptoms (pain, clothing preferences, communication issues, vision, hearing, taste, smell, digestion, irritability, aggression, and self-injury).	
Brigance Inventory of Early Development-II (IED-II)	Birth to 7 years	Identifies range of learning and developmental issues. Creates appropriate instructional goals and monitors progress.	
Parent's Evaluation of Development Status (PEDS)	Birth to 8 years	Screens development and behavior status.	Ongoing monitoring tool.
Communication and Symbolic Behavior Scales (CSBS)	Infancy to preschool	Standardized (consistent and objective) assessment and evaluation tool for functional levels in communication, social-affective, and symbolic ability.	Identifies children at risk for developing communications impairment.
Ages and Stages Questionnaires (ASQ)	1 month to 5 years	Monitors developmental and social-emotional stage.	English, Spanish, and French versions. ASQ website offers data management (questionnaire data, referrals, etc.).
Autism Observation Scale for Infants (AOSI)	6-, 12-, 18-month infants	Detects and monitors high-risk infants when a sibling has ASD. Identifies autism characteristics.	Research tool only. High reliability overall for identifying ASD in 6-, 12-, and 18-month-olds, but less reliable item by item for 6-month-olds.

Screening tool (by age)	Age	Description	Notes
Screening Tool for Autism in Toddlers and Young Children (STAT)	12 to 24 months	12 questions to assess social and communication-based behaviors (imitation, directing attention, communication, and play).	This screening tool is not intended for diagnosing autism.
Pervasive Developmental Disorders Screening Test-II Primary Care Screener (PDDST-II PCS)	12 to 24 months	22 questions to identify challenges in typically developing children.	Provides a reliable parent/caregiver report. Positive responses score 1 point.
Child Behavior Checklist (CBCL) CBCL/1.5–5 CBCL/6–18	1 to 18 years	CBCL/1.5–5 has 99 questions, and CBCL/6–18 has 118 questions. Both screens assess problem behaviors with *DSM*-related categories.	
Early Screening of Autistic Traits (ESAT)	14 months	14-question screen completed by health-care providers during well-baby visits, following a parent/caregiver interview.	Failure on three or more items in the ESAT suggests the need for a more intensive assessment for autism.
Child Development Inventory (CDI)	15 months to 5 years	Assesses symptoms, behavior problems, development (social, self-help, motor, language, and communication).	Parent report completed at home. Development, strengths, and possible issue profile.
Modified Checklist for Autism in Toddlers (M-CHAT)	16 to 30 months	23 questions that assess autism symptoms for parents/caregivers to complete (written at grade 6 literacy level).	Validated in English, Spanish, Turkish, Chinese, and Japanese. Also available in other languages. Warning: may miss subtle signs of autism.
Baby and Infant Screen for Children with Autism Traits (BISCUIT – Parts 1, 2, and 3)	17 to 37 months	Part 1: 62 questions about ASD. Part 2: 65 questions about co-morbid mental health conditions. Part 3: 17 questions about challenging behaviors.	Identifies ASD; provides information for treatment plans and ongoing monitoring.

continued...

Screening tool (by age)	Age	Description	Notes
Quantitative Checklist for Autism in Toddlers (Q-CHAT)	18 to 24 months	25 questions that assess possible autism behaviors in toddlers.	
Autism Treatment Evaluation Checklist (ATEC) Scale	2 years or more	Single-page form for parents/caregivers or teachers to assess four categories: speech/language/communication (14 questions); sociability (20 questions); sensory/cognitive awareness (18 questions); health/physical behavior (25 questions).	Total score from four categories may indicate level of autism.
Social Responsiveness Scale (SRS)	2 to 5 years	Measures social awareness, ability for back-and-forth social communication, social information processing, social avoidance/anxiety, autism-related preoccupation or traits.	Uses natural settings; designed for parents' and teachers' assessment.
Short Sensory Profile (SSP)	3 to 10 years	38-question assessment for tactile sensitivity, taste/smell sensitivity, movement sensitivity, under-responsive/seeks sensation, auditory filtering, low energy/weak and visual/auditory sensitivity.	Overall score indicates level of sensory dysfunction.
Gilliam Autism Rating Scale – Second Edition (GARS-2)	3 to 22 years	42 questions to assess severity of stereotyped behavior, communication, and social interaction. Includes structured interview about early childhood.	Includes treatment recommendations, educational objectives, and goals for discussion.
Autism Quotient (AQ-Child)	4 to 11 years	Assesses social skills, attention switching, attention to detail, communication, and imagination.	Scores higher than 32 indicate some level of autism.
Childhood Asperger's Syndrome Test (CAST)	4 to 11 years	37 yes or no questions completed by parents/caregivers in a research setting. Assesses social behaviors, communication skills, and other possible medical conditions.	

Screening tool (by age)	Age	Description	Notes
Autism Screening Questionnaire/ Social Communication Questionnaire (SCQ)	4 to 40 years	40-question screening tool for use with ADI-R. Evaluates communication skills and social function. Lifetime form evaluates developmental history. Current form focuses on recent history for education support and is a monitoring tool.	Scores of 15 or more may indicate an autism diagnosis.
Behavior Rating Inventory of Executive Functioning (BRIEF)	5 to 18 years	Assesses executive functioning. 80 questions evaluate learning disabilities, low birth weight, attention deficit hyperactivity disorder, Tourette's syndrome, traumatic brain injury, and pervasive developmental disorders or autism.	
Aberrant Behavior Checklist (ABC)	School-aged	58 questions (5 categories) to rate severity of specific behaviors, using a four-point scale (0: not a problem; 3: a severe problem) for irritability (15 questions), lethargy (16 questions), stereotypy (7 questions), hyperactivity (16 questions), and excessive speech (four questions).	Measures mental abilities and processes (called psychometrics). Developed for school use.
Australian Scale for Asperger's Syndrome	6 to 12 years	25 questions to identify Asperger's syndrome, to assess social, emotional, communication, and cognitive skills, specific interests, movement skills, and more.	
Autism Spectrum Screening Questionnaire (ASSQ) for school-age children	6 to 17 years	27 questions to assess ASD symptoms: social interaction, communication skills, repetitive or restricted behaviors, motor skills, and other possible symptoms (such as vocal tics).	Important question: Does the child stand out in some way from his peer group?
Yale-Brown Obsessive-Compulsive Scale – II (Y-BOCS–II)	6 to 69 years	10 questions to rate types of obsessive and compulsive behaviors (OCD) and severity of symptoms.	
Autism Quotient – Adolescent (AQ-Adol)	10 to 19 years	50 questions for parents/caregivers to complete that assess social skills, attention switching, attention to detail, communication, and imagination.	

continued…

2. Assessment and screening tools and interviews for diagnosing autism

Assessment tool (by age)	Age	Description	Notes
The Autism Diagnostic Observation Schedule – 2 (ADOS-2) Replaces the ADOS-T and ADOS-G	12 months to adulthood	A standardized behavior observation and coding tool for autism, with ranges of concerns for toddlers. Modules 1 to 4 provide cutoff scores for ASD. Modules 1 and 2 provide a score that measures and compares levels of ASD symptoms with similar children diagnosed with ASD.	Requires a masters' degree in psychology, school counseling, occupational therapy, speech-language pathology, social work, education, special education, or related field.
Childhood Autism Rating Scale, Second Edition (CARS2) Separate rating booklets for standard, CARS2-ST, and high-functioning autism, CARS2-HF	2 to 6 years (CARS2-ST) or estimated IQs below average; 6 years or older (CARS2-HF) IQ scores above 80	15 items to test frequency, intensity, duration, and quirkiness. CARS2 identifies ASD and assesses severity (mid to moderate and severe autism).	Identifies develop-mentally handicapped children who do not have autism. A questionnaire for parents or caregivers (CARS2-QPC) collects data to help make ratings for the CARS2-ST and CARS2-HF.
Social Responsiveness Scale, Second Edition (SRS-2) Four forms: preschool, school-age, adult, and adult self-report	2.5 to 4.5 years (preschool), 4 to 18 years (school-age), 19 years and up (adult and adult self-report)	65 questions to identify ASD and severity. Measures social awareness, social cognition, social motivation, social communication, restricted interests, and repetitive behavior.	Provides means to compare some areas with *DSM-5* ASD criteria (social communication and interaction, restricted interests, and repetitive behavior responses).
Autism Diagnostic Interview — Revised (ADI-R)	Over 18 months	Standardized interview for diagnosing autism with parents/caregivers. Identifies developmental deviance or delay. Cutoff scores give diagnoses for communication, social interaction, and restricted or repetitive behavior, with separate cutoff scores for verbal and nonverbal children.	5 questions assess for developmental abnormality before 3 years.
Diagnostic Interview for Social and Communication Disorders (DISCO)	Children and adults	362-question semi-structured interview to evaluate social interaction, social communication, social imagination, and repetitive behaviors.	

Associated Conditions

In many cases, autism can be difficult to diagnose because of associated health conditions. For example, epilepsy and intellectual disabilities are associated with autism, especially in cases of severe autism. Some associated conditions are often seen with children who are diagnosed with autism but are not included in the *DSM-5* criteria. Be especially alert for language and motor development problems.

Unusual language development and abilities

- Age < 6 years: frequently uses language in an unusual way, and may be delayed in comprehension; two-thirds have difficulty with using correct words, pronunciation, and grammar structure for the situation.
- Age ≥ 6 years: a difference in or lack of understanding of the meaning of some commonly used words or sentence structures, or of how to use language in social situations, but still able to speak reasonably well (that is, some early difficulties are resolved).

Motor abnormalities

The different areas of the brain work together to produce fluid movements that usually progress as infants develop, from being able to lift their heads, roll over, grasp their hands, and so on. Developmental milestones help us to determine if our child is within the typical range of development for moving as well as for language and social development skills. Identifying areas of motor development that are different when your child is very young allows for early interventions that address specific symptoms. Some motor abnormalities affect daily function, such as speaking, eating, and moving.

Did You Know?

Attention to Detail

You might wonder how attention to detail relates to motor skills. One of the types of memory or recall is called procedural memory, where actions are remembered. Procedural memory guides the actions we perform on a regular basis and is involved in learning new activities (riding a bicycle, for example). Conscious control or attention is only involved as procedural learning for the new activity takes place, repeating the activity over and over until it becomes "automatic," when all mental systems related to that activity work together automatically to produce it. Some conditions related to problems with procedural memory include language deficits, alcoholism, schizophrenia, and epilepsy.

Kinds of Associated Motor Delays

Hypotonia

Your child with ASD may have decreased muscle tone (called hypotonia), which is sometimes described as being floppy or ragdoll-like. Typically, muscles have some "spring" even when relaxed. Hypotonia can coexist with muscle weakness, but not always. Because it can indicate some damage to the brain, nerves, or muscles, it is important to report any concerns if you think your child is "floppy." Some issues related to hypotonia are joint issues, poor reflexes, breathing difficulties, mobility, posture, and speech problems. Some conditions that may be associated with hypotonia include Down syndrome, muscular dystrophy, cerebral palsy, Prader-Willi syndrome, myotonic dystrophy, and Tay-Sachs disease, among others. Once the condition causing the hypotonia is identified and treated, physical, occupational, and speech therapy can help. Sensory stimulation therapy may also be beneficial.

Dyspraxia

Praxis is the name for our ability to make decisions, act, move, and react in our world. Our memory of movement activities is stored, develops over time, and increases in skill from infancy. Deficits in coordination, movement preparation, and planning can impact your child's praxis by causing clumsiness, disorganized behavior, and speech difficulties. Your child may be easily distracted or frustrated and exhibit low self-esteem. He may be a daydreamer and slow to dress.

Therapy for dyspraxia, after a careful assessment to identify specific needs, would include individualized motor training and speech therapy from a trained therapist through occupational activities in different settings as appropriate.

Gait and Balance

The process of walking is called gait. Balance is involved in gait, which is a separate but overlapping process. Both rely on different areas of the body, including the brain, muscles, eyes, and ears. Problems in either area can cause falls, dizziness, walking issues, or injury. Gait or balance issues can be caused by muscle weakness, loss of balance, poor posture, pain, muscle tightness, spasticity, numbness, fatigue, or limited range of motion. A careful assessment for possible causes of gait or balance problems will lead to appropriate treatment and support.

Comorbidity

Sometimes, when you read about typical ASD symptoms, you are confused because it doesn't describe your child's symptoms, even though he has been diagnosed with autism. The range of symptoms for autism spectrum disorder can overlap with other medical conditions that are commonly linked to ASD. One of the reasons for commonly linked conditions is that the genes that are thought to be associated with ASD are also linked with other conditions. Any child diagnosed with autism should be assessed for fragile X or Rett syndrome.

Fragile X Syndrome

Fragile X syndrome is the most common genetic disorder. An inherited intellectual disability, fragile X causes symptoms similar to autism but is caused by a mutation of the X chromosome, which appears pinched and fragile when viewed through a microscope. One out of every three children diagnosed with fragile X syndrome also meets diagnostic criteria for autism, and 1 in 25 children who are diagnosed with autism also has the mutation for fragile X syndrome. Because of this relationship between the two conditions, children with autism should also be tested for fragile X. Any other children born to the parents may also have this syndrome.

Rett Syndrome

Rett syndrome (RTT) mostly affects girls, who develop normally for 6 to 18 months, then begin to regress and show autism-type symptoms. RTT is a neurodevelopmental condition, with symptoms that include difficulties with coordination and gait, distinctive repetitive hand movements, and loss of speech. Rett syndrome is caused by a specific genetic mutation that can be identified. In the previous edition of the *DSM* (IV), Rett syndrome was included as an autism spectrum disorder, but since Rett syndrome has a short period of social withdrawal and is not a behavior-related condition — unlike autism, which is a lifelong condition — it is not included in *DSM-5*.

Sample Screening and Diagnosing

(Understanding that every child has a unique story)

Parent, caregiver, or teacher raises concerns about developmental, medical, behavioral, and/or dietary issues with family physician, pediatrician, or health-care provider.

Screening

Screening takes place (at home, online, or in a caregiver's office). The screening tool used would depend on the child's age, whether they are in school and the specific concerns being addressed. The child is given a screen for developmental issues either at home (paper or online) or in a clinic setting. Screening in the school setting may also be needed, in order to establish special educational services. A parent interview is often part of the screening process for a social and developmental history and to determine the current level of development. Family health, social, and developmental history might also be obtained. Observation of the child in multiple settings is typically part of many assessments.

If the screen is negative   **If the screen is positive**

Health-care provider discusses results and concerns with family/caregivers.

Health-care provider gives support and information for monitoring further development. No immediate action is required. Rescreen at next well-baby visit.

A more thorough assessment is conducted, or a referral to a specialist for assessment. Support and information are provided.

Further concerns

- Refer to appropriate early intervention services if child is < 3 years old, or special education services if child is > 3 years old.
- Book appointments for a full set of assessments and possible medical tests.
- Under guidelines in the region where you live, a group of clinical professionals would be involved in the diagnostic process.
- A differential diagnosis would also take place to rule out other possible or co-occuring medical conditions.

If diagnosis is negative for Autism Spectrum Disorder:

- Further tests would be done to determine proper diagnosis.
- Optimal therapy would be identified to address symptoms and behaviors.

If diagnosis is positive for Autism Spectrum Disorder:

- Child would be assessed for optimal treatment plan.
- Child would be monitored by health-care provider on a regular basis for symptoms and possible need for revision of therapy for best outcome.

Adapted from CDC (2013)

Conditions that Co-exist with Autism

Health conditions that are most commonly diagnosed along with autism fall under these categories:

1. *Developmental:* intellectual disability, language disorders, attention deficit hyperactivity disorder, tic disorders, motor abnormalities.
2. *General medical conditions:* epilepsy, gastrointestinal problems, immune function problems, genetic-based disorders (fragile X, Rett syndrome, Down's syndrome, tuberous sclerosis, to name a few), sleep disorders.
3. *Psychiatric:* anxiety, depression, obsessive-compulsive disorder, psychotic disorders, substance use disorders, oppositional defiant disorder, eating disorders, personality disorders.
4. *Behavioral:* aggressive behaviors, self-injurious behaviors, pica (eating nonfood items such as soil and paper), suicidal ideas or attempts.

Research Spotlight

Social Behavior

Why do children with autism have trouble with social behaviors? Soon after birth, children will usually show preferences for social experiences, preferring human voices to silence, and the sound of their mother's voice over that of someone they don't know. They are also able to tell if a person's face is directed toward or away from them. Face recognition develops quickly for typically developing children, with looking at the eyes more than other facial features, and at the face more than the body preferred. As well, 3-month-old babies will mimic facial expressions made by a person but not by machines, even when the movements are similar.

This is not the case for some children with autism, who have reduced social engagement and reduced interaction with other people. Typically developing children tend to make contact directly with other people's eyes, whereas children with ASD look more at people's mouths and body. It is believed that these preferences lead to increased social interactions through understanding social cues and social adaptations, and increased understanding of other people's emotions. It is thought that children with autism may be fixating on the mouth as an alternative mechanism for learning language, but this results in reduced ability to understand the emotional content of speech (speech that may have a double meaning; for example, sarcasm).

DocTalk:
Sensory Overload

Q. My 4-year-old child screams a lot when we are out in public. If I pick her up, she gets really stiff. Sometimes I worry that people think I'm abusing her. What should I do?

A. You are not alone. These behaviors are very common in children with ASD. Consider this to be "sensory overload" or an anxiety disorder, or both. Busy, noisy, unpredictable environments often overwhelm these children. If noise is the main issue, try using earmuffs or earphones. If this occurs mainly in busy, noisy environments, keep your child in a stroller, which can be at least partially covered up. If the problem persists, ask for a referral to an occupational therapist and seek the help of a behavioral therapist.

Chapter 3
What Causes Autism?

CASE STUDY (continued from page 37)
Sibling Risk

Following Stephen's diagnosis, his parents became concerned that his younger sister might also be at risk of developing autism. Adela was born 4 years after Stephen, but unlike her boisterous brother, she was calm, apparently happy to be in her crib, and spent her time looking at the sun on the wall across the room. She did seem like she was daydreaming even then. She rarely cried, even when you would think she was hungry.

By the time Adela was 7 months old, there were signs that something wasn't quite right. She didn't talk much — Stephen liked to talk for her, and talked nonstop. As time passed, Adela would often ignore her family when they said her name but did talk to herself and the toys she lined up in the hallway. She screamed if anyone tried to move them. Her parents didn't think she had autism so much, since she was affectionate and would look directly at her parents and Stephen. During well-baby visits to their family doctor, Adela was at the lower end of the growth charts, still small for her age. She was monitored closely, first because her older brother had been diagnosed with autism, which increased her genetic risk, but also because of her size and some developmental concerns.

Adela was finally diagnosed with autism at the age of 3 and began to bite other people, a behavior that kept her out of school and socially separated from her peers. Solving this problem proved to be next to impossible…

(continued on page 91)

Contributing Factors

What causes autism? What is known for sure is that no one factor is at the root of the disorder. Although genetics is likely one of the factors behind ASD, even this factor is complex, because different people with autism have different combinations of genetic mutations. Making it even more complex, some people who have the same configuration of mutations do *not* have autism.

It is thought, however, that some genetic configurations may make a child more susceptible to autism after exposure to toxic elements in the environment, either before or after birth.

Theories of Autism

Genetic (DNA) mutations
- Single nucleotide polymorphisms (SNPs)
- Chromosomal abnormalities (also known as submicroscopic cytogenetic anomalies)
- Copy number variations

Environmental neurotoxins

Oxidative stress

Hormone imbalance
- Extreme male theory

Brain dysfunctions
- Imprinted brain theory
- Clustering
- Mirror neuron hypothesis
- Prenatal and birth trauma

Gastrointestinal theories
- Gut-brain axis model
- Leaky gut theory
- Opioid excess theory

Nutrient deficiencies
- Folic acid deficiency
- Enzyme deficiencies
- Vitamin B_5 deficiency

Food sensitivities, intolerances, and allergies
- Intolerances, allergies, and intoxication
- Gluten and casein sensitivities

Gene-Environment Co-relations

For years, genetic and environmental factors were seen as exclusionary. Now it is understood that a number of relationships between our genes and our environment affect our behavior:

1. Gene-environment correlations: Genetic factors affect how exposure to specific environments may increase the risk of ASD, based on parent or child genes. Through twin and adoption studies, research examines potential behavioral mechanisms by which genes may influence environmental exposure, with genes, parenting, and the school environment all factors that influence development.

2. Gene-environment interactions: Children play an active role when they shape their environment by selecting activities, peers, and interests. The responses they draw from others also play a role. In addition, they affect the environment around them through behaviors, interests, and decision making.

3. Heritability-environment interactions: Genes and environment continue to match over time.

4. "Epigenetics" refers to external modifications to DNA that turn genes "on" or "off."

Genetic Mutations

Autism seems to be a collection, or family, of diseases that, even though they look alike (called having common phenotypes), are linked to a series of genetic errors (called anomalies). Each of these genetic errors can account for 2% to 3% of all the cases of autism that can be attributed to genetics (30% to 40% of all cases). Specific genes at several points in our DNA (chromosomes 7q, 15a, and 16p) have been identified as increasing the risk for autism syndrome disorder. New mutations in DNA have been identified as causing random cases of autism, and recent research has identified several hundred copy number variants linked to autism.

Profile: Yan

Yan is 7 years old. Although she doesn't talk much, she always has a big smile for her Teetay. She loves to read, and her favorite book is *The Story About Ping* because her Teetay has ducks and a creek on her farm, just like in the story.

Q. If I have a child with autism, will other children born to our family have autism too?

A. Research reports show that brothers or sisters of children who have a diagnosis of ASD have an increased risk — between 13% and 18% — of also having autism. Research to test for a higher risk is conducted by following families who already have a child who has been diagnosed with ASD. Doing genetic testing and observations on twins where at least one of the two children has a diagnosis of ASD also provides good information about an increased genetic risk in families. Family members provide a genetic sample from either saliva or blood tests, and chromosomes are assessed to see if there is any association between genes or sets of genes (called suites) for specific ASD symptoms or behaviors within families or between children who show similar symptoms.

How Genes Work

So what are genes and how do they work? That's not an easy question to answer. Let's start with the function of DNA and work forward to traits and alleles.

DNA: Every cell of your body has a part called the nucleus, which carries a blueprint of how to build an individual human being. Deoxyribonucleic acid (DNA) carries this blueprint information as a code broken into a ladder-like double helix strand that is joined by four molecules, or nucleotide building blocks. A (adenine) always connects to T (thymine), and C (cytosine) always connects with G (guanine) to form genes. Each strand of DNA is about nine feet (3 m) long and fits into each cell because it is packaged into chromosomes.

Genes: One strand of DNA contains many genes. We have 25,000 genes in our bodies that maintain growth and development.

Mutation: If the information provided by the genes has an error in it — for example, if an A is connected to a C instead of a T — that gene may not provide the correct instructions and a mutation may occur.

Chromosomes: To pack DNA into the compact storage units called chromosomes, the double helix is wrapped around proteins, which are then tightly curled together to form a chromosome. Each human cell carries 46 chromosomes, two paired sets of 23 chromosomes, with one set of our genetic material coming from each parent. The two sex chromosomes, the only ones that are not paired, determine the sex of an individual: males have one X and one Y chromosome, and females have two X chromosomes.

Proteins: Proteins work together like a machine to complete tasks that together form organs or body systems that help our bodies function. The cells of our bodies contain thousands of different proteins, each of which is shaped differently, depending on its function. When the brain sends a message to a cell that a particular protein is needed, specialized equipment in the cell nucleus reads the DNA gene code and produces a molecule, called RNA (ribonucleic acid). RNA acts as a messenger that moves out of the nucleus to a cell part called the ribosome, which then produces a protein based on the RNA code instructions. The new protein travels to the area of the cell where it is required and begins its task.

Traits: The instructions encoded in the two sets of chromosomes passed randomly from each parent (what we inherit from them) define our traits: definable features (physical traits), qualities, behaviors, or predisposition for a medical condition — for example, whether we have blue eyes like our father, instead of brown like our mother and grandmother, or curly hair like our grandfather's. We each have a distinct collection of traits. The random selection process means that each child born is an individual. Sometimes, however, that first single cell splits into two cells and becomes identical twins, who will have exactly the same sets of chromosomes.

Alleles: Each of the traits received from one of your parents is called an allele. Traits are connected to alleles. If you have one allele for a characteristic, such as predisposition for a medical condition, you may not have the condition, but if you have two alleles, one from each parent, you may be diagnosed with the condition at some point. If you have one of each allele, the alleles may interact and one allele trait may be masked by the other, with the visible allele being the dominant one and the masked or recessive allele being invisible.

Complex traits: The term used for having two different alleles is heterozygous, and when the alleles are the same, it is called homozygous. Incomplete dominance occurs when the trait from a heterozygous set of alleles is different from either of the parent alleles. Traits that are influenced by one gene are rare — a person's sex is an example of a single-gene trait. In general, traits are influenced by several to many genes, which is called complex traits.

Genetic Theories

For many years, researchers have worked hard to identify an autism-specific genetic factor, but current genetic theories are now suggesting that the risk of autism is more likely dependent on collected gene point mutations that happen through each of our lifetimes and may be passed on to our children as well.

Types of DNA Mutations Likely Implicated in ASD

1. Single nucleotide polymorphisms (SNPs)

> **The risk of autism is more likely dependent on collected gene point mutations that happen through each of our lifetimes and may be passed on to our children.**

The most common type of genetic variation that has been identified in individuals with ASD is called a single nucleotide polymorphism, or SNP. An SNP is a difference in a single DNA building block, such as replacing the nucleotide thymine (T) with a cytosine (C) at a particular point in DNA. SNPs are common in our DNA, occurring once in every 300 building blocks, which can add up to approximately 10 million SNPs in the entire human DNA makeup, or genome. Most of the time, though, SNPs happen in the DNA that is in between genes (the packing). If an SNP is within a gene or a region of the DNA that regulates a gene, it could affect that gene's function and increase the risk of autism or susceptibility to environmental factors.

Recent research has identified SNPs in two genes — exportin 1 (XPO1) and orthodenticle homolog 1 (OTX1) — as being associated with the severity of deficits in social interaction, verbal communication, and repetitive behaviors. These two genes may be related to physically expressed traits (called phenotypic) seen in some children with autism, intellectual disabilities (IDs), and congenital craniofacial/central nervous system malformations (called dysmophology) in deletion and non-deletion cases of ASD mapping that occur in this particular chromosomal region.

2. Chromosomal abnormalities (also known as submicroscopic cytogenetic anomalies)

These are irregular chromosomes, with missing or extra chromosomes or a structural abnormality that make up cytogenetic anomalies not visible through a microscope. Whenever chromosome number or structure is disrupted, the process causes an abnormality. When chromosomal abnormalities are the result of conception, the error is present in every cell of the body. "Mosaicism" is the term used to describe chromosome abnormalities that happen after the egg and sperm have joined (conception) — in this case, some cells have the abnormality, but not all.

A numerical abnormality happens when a person is missing a chromosome from a chromosome pair (called monosomy). Turner syndrome occurs when a female is born with only one X sex chromosome; typically, two X chromosomes are present for a female. When a chromosome pair has more than two chromosomes (called trisomy), Down syndrome occurs (a person has three copies rather than two of chromosome 21). Chromosome abnormalities can be passed from parent to child (translocations are an example) or be a new error. Deletions associated with a chromosome (16p11.2) and thought to cause autism were found in 2008, but that specific deletion is also involved in intellectual disability without autism present, and deletions in that same region are associated with obesity.

> Whenever chromosome number or structure is disrupted, the process causes an abnormality.

Abnormalities

Structural abnormalities arise when chromosome structure is altered by:

Duplication: Part of the chromosome appears twice.

Deletion: Part of the chromosome is missing.

Inversion: Part of the chromosome is attached upside down.

Translocation: Part of one chromosome is missing but has been attached to another chromosome. Translocation can be reciprocal, where portions of two chromosomes are exchanged. One particular case is a Robertsonian translocation, when one chromosome is attached to another chromosome close to the middle and may have an impact on the next generation.

Rings: Part of a chromosome has broken away and has joined to itself to form a circle.

3. Copy number variations (CNVs)

Genetic variation in human genomes is caused by small changes in nucleotide building block pairs, small insertions, or even large rearrangements of chromosomes. Crossover errors between the egg and sperm during conception are likely the cause of copy number variations, or CNVs, which indicate that an intermediate-scale change has occurred to the genome, usually DNA segments that are more than 1,000 base pairs but less than five megabases (one megabase is one million nucleotides). Due to their size, a CNV can change the genome structure and may account for much of the variability seen across the human species. CNVs of less than 10 kilobases are called copy number polymorphisms (CNPs) and occur at a rate of more than 1% in the genome. These CNPs are known to code for proteins that detoxify drugs and raise immunity. The second category of CNVs are longer (from hundreds of thousands to more than one million base pairs) and are called microdeletions and microduplications. These CNVs are rare and genetically recent, having been passed down over a few generations, and have been reported to be associated with developmental delay, mental delay, autism, and schizophrenia. CNVs may explain why many children with autism also have other conditions, such as developmental delay or epilepsy.

Profile: Nahia

Nahia is 8 years old and has sparkly brown eyes. Her autism does not stop her from dancing. She knows everything there is to know about insects, and loves reading books. Her favorites are *Puff the Magic Dragon*, *Madeline*, *The Girl Who Loved Wild Horses*, and *Jumanji*. Her favorite game is jump rope, which she often plays at lunchtime and during recess at school.

Environmental Neurotoxins

Environmental factors are also implicated as possible causes of autism, with toxic chemicals possibly causing damage or injury to the developing infant brain through direct exposure to toxins. Genetic expression can also be changed by toxic chemicals.

Environmental and Genetic Interactions

According to the National Research Council, approximately 25% of neurobehavioral disorders are caused by interactions between environmental factors and inherited genetic susceptibilities. The greatest danger is that symptoms that are not recognized by family or health-care professionals or identified by current available tests (called subclinical dysfunction) can go undiagnosed for many years.

Sensitivities

Allergies and sensitivities caused by hyperactive mast cells in many organs and genes can trigger ASD. For this possible subgroup of children, exposure to environmental and stress triggers could cause or worsen ASD symptoms.

Did You Know?

Dangers of Synthetics
In the past 50 years, more than 80,000 chemical synthetics have been invented, but only about 20% of widely used chemicals have been tested for possible toxicity before being fully developed.

Did You Know?

Maternal Infection During Pregnancy
Maternal viral infection during the first trimester of pregnancy may increase the risk of autism for children who are genetically susceptible. Research assessing children born between 1980 and 2005 for any associations between viral infection, admission to hospital, and ASD found that admission to hospital during the first trimester for viral infection (such as rubella or cytomegalovirus) and maternal bacterial infection during the second trimester increased the risk of an ASD diagnosis.

Biologic Risks for Autism

In addition to genetic and environmental risks, there are also biologic risks for developing autism:

Birth weight: Low birth weight may indicate possible fetal growth and development problems that can trigger ASD.

Age: While most genes express both copies of chromosomes, in some cases one of the two chromosomes may be silenced — known as imprinted genes. Due to imprinted genes, the father's age can indicate accumulated mutations in the sperm. The mother's age may increase risk of chromosomal abnormalities in the eggs.

Birth order: In families with two children, a child with autism tends to be the firstborn, possibly because parents choose not to have more children after one has developed autism, and in families with more than two children, a child with autism tends to be later-born.

Low fetal oxygen: Excessive bleeding, complications around the cord, hypertension, extremely long labor, fetal stress, or cesarean delivery may indicate risk for autism. The Apgar score, performed twice by a physician, a midwife, or a nurse, gives some indication of any stress from the birthing experience (1 minute after birth), and the second (at 5 minutes) assesses the baby's breathing, heart rate, muscle tone, reflexes, and skin color now that he is breathing on his own. Scores lower than 7 indicate that baby needs help.

Gestational diabetes: A biological reason for gestational diabetes is not known, but hormonal and metabolic abnormalities, along with oxidative stress, are possible causes that may also instigate the onset of autism.

Multiple births: Possible higher risk of autism is associated with multiple births.

Use of medications: Psychiatric medication, synthetic hormones, and psychoactive drugs can trigger ASD, but no significant association with autism has been seen for antiepileptics, antihypertensives, cardiovascular drugs, toxolytics, or steroids.

Season or month of birth: Interestingly, onset of autism seems to be dependent on birth month. March and August have both been suggested to have a higher risk of autism. Summer births have also shown a higher risk, possibly due to variation in viral or other infections or nutritional factors.

Did You Know?

Toxic Regression

Regression may be the result of exposure to environmental toxins. For those children who hit all the developmental markers but then regress, typically around the age of 18 months, possible causes for regression include infection and allergies.

Prenatal Exposure to Neurotoxic Chemicals

Chemical exposures may be an environmental factor in the development of autism. Pregnant women may be exposed to many of these chemicals on a daily basis.

Neurotoxic Chemicals Suspected of Causing Developmental Neurotoxicity

Chemical	Where it is found	How to reduce impact	Research studies
Lead	Gasoline, paint, pigment, mining materials, ceramic glazes, lead solder and pipes, herbal traditional medicines, folk remedies, cosmetics, toys, industrial sites, electronic or e-waste, burning waste that contains lead, eating food that has been grown in contaminated soil (or the soil itself). Children with pica are at a higher risk of ingesting lead from contaminated soil or dust.	Neurobehavioral impact from early exposure to lead appears to be permanent and cannot be undone. Removing lead from gasoline was an important first step in reducing worldwide blood lead concentration. Lead in paint and pigment remains a danger in homes built before 1978 and on new and used toys. Lead from recycled car batteries also poses a danger. Chelation does not reduce blood lead levels. Prevention is the answer to reducing blood lead levels. Meals high in fats and oils increase our body's ability to absorb lead, and eating foods high in vitamin C and calcium reduces the amount of lead absorbed.	Jusko et al., 2008. Landrigan et al., 2012. Minnesota Department of Health, 2013. WHO, 2010.
Methylmercury	Contaminated fish and shellfish, and rice grown in contaminated soil. Beauty creams, hair treatments and cosmetic products. Fossil fuels (coal, in particular), pesticides, gold and mercury mining, power stations for electricity, cement manufacturing, chlorine, caustic soda, mirrors, equipment for medicine, leaks from industries, dental practice, burning waste, and corpse disposal.	Exposure to and use of mercury must be reduced and eliminated, and alternatives promoted. The impact from methylmercury has been reduced by taking an essential fatty acid (EFA), omega-3 EPA, found in cold-water fish. EPA is a polyunsaturated fat that regulates cell activity and promotes healthy cardiovascular function. Selenium, a potent antioxidant, protects against heavy metals.	Landrigan et al., 2012. Li et al., 2010. Oken et al., 2008. WHO, 2007.

continued...

Chemical	Where it is found	How to reduce impact	Research studies
Polychlorinated biphenyls (PCBs)	Manufacturing process for heat exchangers and electrical equipment for hydraulic systems and other specialized situations until the later 1970s. Contaminated soil, and repair and maintenance of PCB transformers.	PCBs have been phased out since 1977. Handling, storage, transport, and destruction of PCBs is regulated by state and provincial regulations. Spills and fires are the main sources of PCB exposure. PCBs can leave the body through feces but may be held in organs and tissue for many years. There is no known treatment to reduce PCB body levels.	Environment Canada, 2013. Landrigan et al., 2012. Mount Sinai Children's Environmental Health Center, 2008. Winneke, 2011.
Organo-phosphate pesticides (for example, DDT)	Used in some countries to control pests. Used in the U.S. for vector (insect) diseases and body lice.	UN banned persistent organic pollutants (POPs) in 1996. DDT is permitted for indoor use in South America, Africa, and Asia to combat malaria. DDT is stored in fatty tissues of the body. During periods of starvation, breakdown products of DDT may be released into the bloodstream with toxic effect.	Eskenazi et al., 2007. Landrigan et al., 2012. London et al., 2012. U.S. Environmental Protection Agency, 2012.
Endocrine disruptors (pharma-ceuticals, dioxin, dioxin-like compounds, poly-chlorinated biphenyls, DDT and other pesticides, bisphenol A)	Natural and manufactured. Household and industrial products, pesticides, cosmetics, plastic bottles, flame retardants, food, metal food cans, detergents, and toys.	More comprehensive testing is needed to find all the endocrine disruptors, along with their sources and exposure routes. More research is also needed on mixtures of endocrine disruptors, as well as improved reporting of endocrine disruptors from chemicals in products, materials, and goods. Scientists in and between countries will need to share data. Living a simpler lifestyle, as seen in Old Order Mennonite (OOM) communities, with fresh food and limited use of processed products and gas-fueled transportation, appears to reduce exposure to endocrine disruptors.	Landrigan et al., 2012. Martina et al., 2012. Miodovnik et al., 2011. National Institute of Environmental Health Sciences, Health and Education, 2013. WHO, 2013.

Chemical	Where it is found	How to reduce impact	Research studies
Automotive exhaust, isocyanic acid (HNCO), isocyanate (CNO-)	Automobile engine parts (catalytic converters, automobile catalytic reduction catalyst systems, byproduct from urea-based selective catalytic reduction catalyst systems used on heavy-duty diesel vehicles and light-duty trucks to satisfy stricter nitrous oxide emission requirements.)	Efforts to reduce and capture HNCO and CNO- will help reduce exposure.	Green Car Congress, 2013. Landrigan et al., 2012. Volk et al., 2011.
Polycyclic aromatic hydrocarbons (PAHs)	Natural and manufactured sources. Forest fires and volcanoes produce PAHs. PAHs are made when coal, gas, oil, other organic material, and garbage don't burn completely. In crude oil and coal tar, creosote, roofing tar, some medicines, dyes, plastics, and even pesticides. In cigarette and cigar ingestion and smoke. Long-term sun exposure. Residential wood-burning and aluminum smelters. Foods cooked on open fires and barbecues. Small amounts are found in other foods, such as roasted coffee beans or peanuts, grains, refined vegetable oil, vegetables, and fruits. Shampoos and cosmetics made with coal tar; cleaning supplies and mothballs. Products treated with creosote. Petroleum product spills, metallurgical and coking plants, and deposition of atmospheric PAHs.	If soil contains PAHs, neither your children nor your pets should be allowed near bare earth. No gardening should be permitted in areas with PAHs, and contaminated soil should not be allowed indoors. To protect children from soil with PAHs, always wash their hands before eating and after playing outside. Outdoor toys should be washed frequently to reduce risk.	Environment Canada, 2013. Government of South Australia, 2009. Illinois Department of Public Health, 2009. Landrigan et al., 2012. Perea et al., 2009.

continued...

Chemical	Where it is found	How to reduce impact	Research studies
Brominated flame retardants (BFRs): tetrabromo-bisphenol A, polybromo-diphenyl ethers, polybromo-biphenyls, hexabromo-cyclo-dodecanes	BFRs are applied to combustible materials (wood, plastics, electronics, textiles, and paper) to meet fire regulations. Contaminated foods, water; ingestion and inhalation of dust. Combustion of waste containing BFRs, accidental fire of products that contain BFRs, BFR-containing product emission, blending of BFRs with polymers, BFR-containing plastic product recycling, textile finishing with BFRs.	Measure trace levels and identify all sources of BFRs in water, sediment, and waste. Define processes that transport BFRs. Identify ecologic impact of BFR exposure. BFR-free alternatives include wool and Kevlar. Safe disposal of electronics can reduce dispersal of BFRs.	Herbstman et al., 2010. Kefeni et al., 2011. Landrigan et al., 2012.
Perfluorinated compounds (PFCs)	Consumer and industrial products. Repellents (stain/water/grease) for carpets and clothing. Nonstick coatings for cooking. Contaminated foodstuffs or water. Indoor or outdoor air.	Phase out use of PFCs. Reduce use of microwave popcorn, grease-proof paper and packaging (for example, pizza boxes). Reduce use of packaging in general. Read labels on items like shampoo and dental floss to be sure they are PFC-free.	Landrigan et al., 2012. National Institute of Environmental Health Sciences, 2012. Stahl et al., 2011. Stein and Savitz, 2011.

Profile: Emil

Emil learned to collect stamps from his grandfather and asks everyone to save their stamps for him. He is 11 years old. He laughs a lot and goes everywhere with his older sister, Clara. He loves to watch wrestling on TV, but has learned that he can't try these moves on other children (or adults)! This year, Emil is taking judo, which is helping him learn self-discipline.

Oxidative Stress

Increased oxidative stress is also considered a possible cause of ASD symptoms. Oxygen is necessary to live, but like everything else in life, balance is key to good health. The most familiar and visual example of oxidative stress is rust. Oxidation in a cell is the process of removing an electron from an atom or molecule in our body, so changing the molecule's ability to function normally (creating a free radical). Too much oxygen can be toxic to cells in our bodies. Factors that lead to an increase in oxidative stress include:

- Natural or artificial radiation (too much sun exposure, airplane travel, working with hazardous chemicals or wastes, X-ray exposure)
- Food, water, or airborne toxins (tobacco smoke, vehicle-polluted air, food grown in contaminated soil)
- Stress (physical stress, such as overexercise, or emotional stress)

> A healthy diet rich in antioxidant foods, daily exercise, and reducing stress are important for neutralizing free radicals.

Free Radicals

Throughout the day, every cell in our bodies is at risk of damage from molecules called free radicals. Free radicals are byproducts of the metabolic processes that are a normal part of maintaining life. Some are built to fight invading viruses, and some may be caused by environmental factors. To regain balance, these unstable molecules strip electrons — the source of the electrical energy in our bodies — from cells they contact, thereby creating a wave of unstable molecules.

Antioxidants

As the name suggests, antioxidants (such as vitamins C and E) reduce the possible harm from free radicals by donating electrons. Certain diseases and even aging can have an impact on how well our bodies fight against free radicals. A healthy diet rich in antioxidant foods, daily exercise, and reducing stress are important for neutralizing free radicals.

Free Radicals and Antioxidants

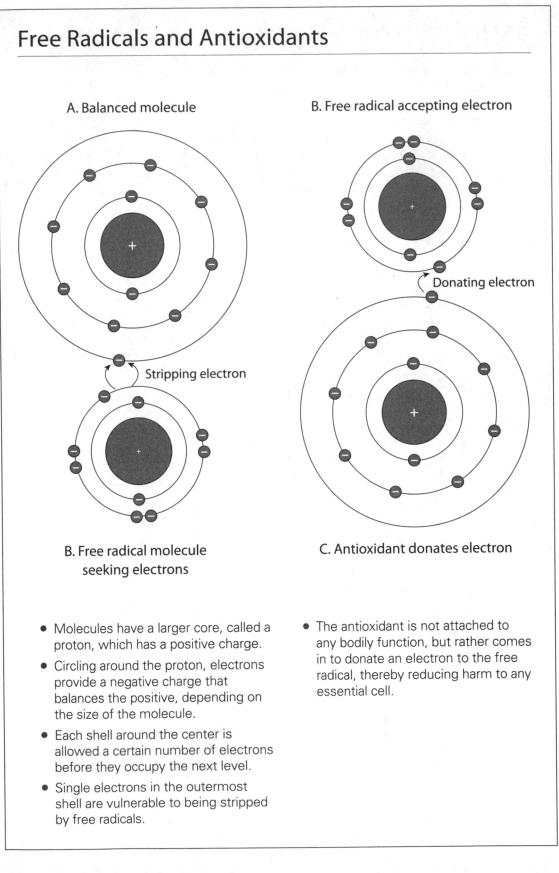

A. Balanced molecule

B. Free radical accepting electron

Stripping electron

Donating electron

B. Free radical molecule
seeking electrons

C. Antioxidant donates electron

- Molecules have a larger core, called a proton, which has a positive charge.
- Circling around the proton, electrons provide a negative charge that balances the positive, depending on the size of the molecule.
- Each shell around the center is allowed a certain number of electrons before they occupy the next level.
- Single electrons in the outermost shell are vulnerable to being stripped by free radicals.

- The antioxidant is not attached to any bodily function, but rather comes in to donate an electron to the free radical, thereby reducing harm to any essential cell.

Hormone Imbalance

The role of hormones in the onset and further development of autism has been studied in some detail, but more evidence is needed before these theories gain credibility.

Extreme Male Theory

Women and men have been identified (in general) as having strengths that are usually but not always related to their gender. Women are seen as having a higher level of empathy — the ability to identify with and understand another person's situation, feelings, and motives and to then respond appropriately. Men are seen as being better able to systemize — to analyze and predict how something works from just looking at the rules that govern a system. Children with autism show an impaired or reduced ability to empathize and an increased ability to systemize, often referred to as an extreme male brain.

Gender Gap

Concern has been voiced that girls who have autism are not being diagnosed at the same rate as boys, not that ASD is a condition that affects boys more than girls. Research done since 2006 has suggested that autism symptoms are different for most girls than for boys, that many girls with autism have a non-male

Extreme Male

Differences between the sexes have been assessed at the population level but not individually.

Females were strong in

- recognition of emotions
- social sensitivity
- verbal fluency
- early language development

Males were strong in

- spatial recognition
- ability to perform mental rotation of objects
- increased play with mechanical toys
- engineering and physics problems, where they had higher scores

typical presentation of symptoms and therefore may go undetected. Areas of difference include cognition, hormones, genetics, and early brain overgrowth. Examination of structural neuroimaging studies have shown that the brain areas of girls with autism show differences from typically developing female brains in different areas from those of boys. If you are concerned about your daughter due to physical, social, emotional, or intellectual issues, contact your family physician.

Sex Hormones

The extreme male brain theory has been confirmed as appropriate to describe girls with autism with more typically male-like behavior and physiological profile, but not in young boys.

Behaviors such as rate of language development, eye contact, empathy, systemizing, and attention to detail are all controlled by

Research Study: Thomas the Tank Engine

In a U.K. National Autistic Society survey of children who watched *Thomas the Tank Engine* on television and played with the replica toy, one in four parents described how their child's fascination with Thomas the Tank Engine helped them learn about colors, numbers, and language in a way that related to them — especially language, which is so often late to develop for children with autism, sometimes with just a few words but sometimes with no language at all.

Parents describe their child's fascination with Thomas as a "gateway" to learning: Thomas motivated their child to take an interest in new skills — for example, computer skills that helped them play Thomas the Tank Engine games.

- "He always watched Thomas on TV with so much concentration. It encouraged him to speak; he would look you in the eye and tell you about what Thomas was doing." (Low-functioning 13-year-old boy)
- "He learned numbers and colors from playing (constantly) with Thomas and grew more confident when he was right." (High-functioning 6-year-old boy)
- "Even though he has little speech, he is able to say their names (Thomas and Gordon) when he is watching or wants to watch TV." (Very-low-functioning 3-year-old boy)
- "He could say 'Thomas' and 'Gordon' well before he ever said 'Mommy' or 'Daddy.'" (Higher-functioning 5-year-old boy)

Children with ASD often associate with Thomas first, sooner than with any other children's cartoon characters, such as Elmo and Dora. They also keep their relationship with Thomas longer, usually 2 years longer than typically developing children. One out of three parents thinks their child with autism has an obsession with Thomas.

The study concluded that Thomas can be a valuable tool for learning and communication for children with autism. For some children with autism, Thomas helps them understand emotions, imagination, and symbolic play.

an area of the brain called the anterior cingulate cortex. Early development is a time when we all have high levels of sex steroid receptors, so we may have an increased sensitivity to androgen in our prenatal state. Even though a girl who has been diagnosed with autism may engage in less of the typical patterns and behaviors of play for girls, her period may begin at a later age than her friends and, later in life, she might show higher rates of androgen-related medical and developmental conditions (polycystic ovary syndrome being one), as well as elevated testosterone (serum) and masculinized physical features. This possibility of increased sensitivity to hormone activity during early development is part of the imprinted brain theory for autism (see the section on brain dysfunctions).

Brain Dysfunctions

There are several theories of autism based on brain dysfunctions, ranging from neural defects to brain trauma. Autism can also affect specific functions of the brain.

Brain-Related Factors in Autism

- Imprinted brain
- Clustering
- Mirror neuron hypothesis
- Perinatal and neonatal trauma
- Cerebrovascular lesions
- Severe encephalopathy (viral infection or toxins in the blood)
- Infections of the brain (such as cytomegalovirus or herpes simplex)

Anatomy of the Brain

With the folds straightened out, the outside (or cortex) of the brain is about the size of a newspaper.

The brain maintains constant communication with all body organs through two means:

- The nerves of the central and peripheral nervous system
- Messages passed across the membrane of the cell or through chemical messages that originate from the brain and travel through the bloodstream (hormones are an example of this type of communication)

Structure of the Brain

An average adult human brain weighs around 3 pounds (1400 g) and is deeply wrinkled, or folded. It looks a bit like a walnut, but is a pink-gray color. The folds increase the surface area, for the size of our heads, and make our brains more efficient. With the folds straightened out, the outside (or cortex) of the brain is about the size of a newspaper, about 324 square inches (2100 sq cm).

The lobes, or distinct areas shown in the diagram (at right), are separated by fissures (called sulci) and raised sections, or bumps (called gyri). Our brains are just as individual as we are, with unique patterns of sulci and gyri organizing the different areas of our brains.

Q. How does autism affect the brain?

A. "Clattering, hissing, whistling, blowing off gauge-cocks, ringing his bell, thundering over bridges with a row and a racket like everything going to pieces, whooping through tunnels, running over cows… for three dreadful hours he kept it up" — Mark Twain's description of a blind youth on a train who could not talk but rocked wildly in his seat, imitating the noises of the express.

A neurodevelopmental condition such as autism can affect the development of our brain from an early age, perhaps even during prenatal development. Understanding the structures of our brains and how they work together may aid in a better understanding of how autism affects development and behavior.

Parts of the Brain

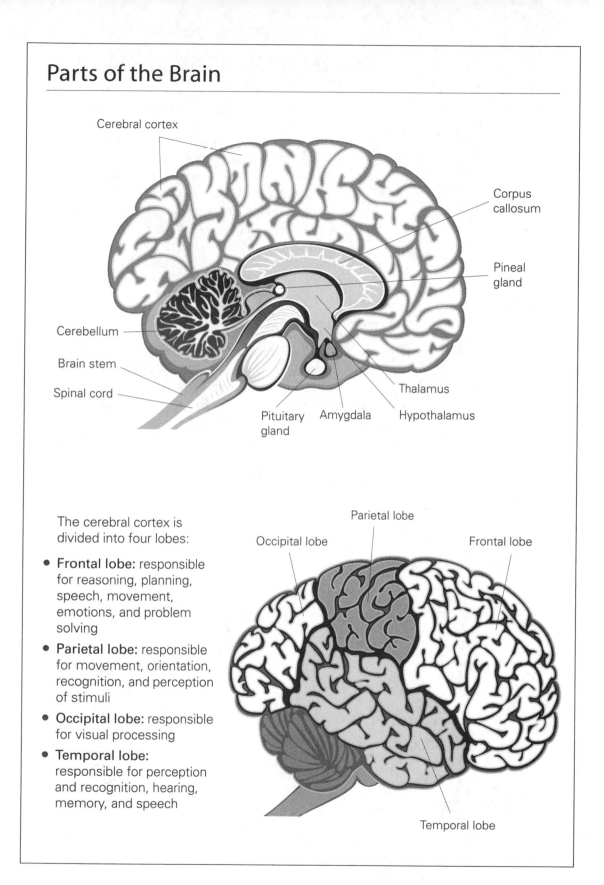

Cerebral cortex

Corpus callosum

Pineal gland

Cerebellum

Brain stem

Spinal cord

Pituitary gland

Amygdala

Thalamus

Hypothalamus

The cerebral cortex is divided into four lobes:

- **Frontal lobe:** responsible for reasoning, planning, speech, movement, emotions, and problem solving
- **Parietal lobe:** responsible for movement, orientation, recognition, and perception of stimuli
- **Occipital lobe:** responsible for visual processing
- **Temporal lobe:** responsible for perception and recognition, hearing, memory, and speech

Occipital lobe

Parietal lobe

Frontal lobe

Temporal lobe

The Nervous System

Your central nervous system is the combination of your brain and your spinal cord. Your skull protects your brain and your spine protects your spinal cord. Attached directly to your brain, or by nerves that extend to every part of your body, your peripheral nervous system transmits signals between different body parts and coordinates both voluntary (moving your hand to turn the pages of this book) and involuntary actions (your heartbeat, breathing, and digestion are all involuntary actions).

Nerves are the long fibers that connect the central nervous system to the peripheral nervous system and are collections of neurons, also known as nerve cells. Glial cells (also called neuroglia or just glia) are also part of the nervous system.

Neurons

The structure of a neuron allows signals to be transmitted swiftly and precisely from one neuron to another. When an electrical reaction and a chemical diffusion happen at the same time in a neuron, it is called an electrochemical wave. Electrochemical waves travel along thin extensions, or fibers, called axons. The waves cause the release of chemicals (called neurotransmitters) to occur at axon junctions, called synapses. The connections where neurons come together form neural circuits that are responsible for how we perceive the environment and also determine behavior.

Neuron Anatomy

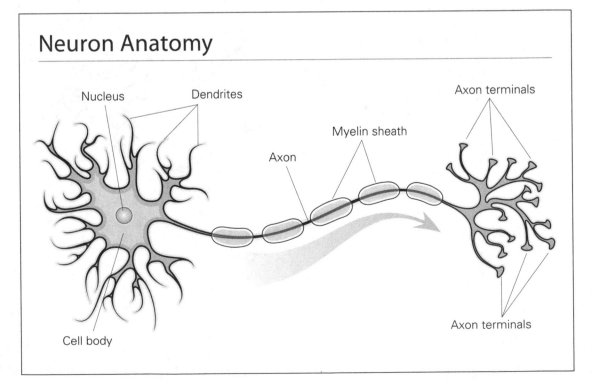

Nucleus

Dendrites

Axon terminals

Myelin sheath

Axon

Cell body

Axon terminals

Glial Cells

The glia provide structural and metabolic support by holding the neural structure in place, by insulating the neuron to protect the integrity of the electrochemical wave action, by providing nutrients and oxygen to the neurons, by protecting neurons from pathogens, and by removing any neurons that are not functioning or dead. Glial cells also assist neurons to build new synaptic connections and are involved in respiration. Astrocytes, a form of glial cell, sense increased blood acidity from high carbon dioxide levels and trigger a deeper respiratory response (deeper breathing), bringing higher levels of oxygen into the body.

Myelin Sheath

Another form of glia is myelin cells, called the oligodendrocytes in the central nervous system and Schwann cells in the peripheral nervous system. In both cases, the cells form the myelin sheath, a protective case, or envelope, around the axons. The myelin cells insulate the axons (the myelin sheath is 70% lipids, or fat), but gaps between myelin sheath cells, called the nodes of Ranvier, help increase the speed of the electrochemical wave action moving along the axon as the electrical impulse jumps from one node to the next (called saltatory conduction).

Axons

The axon is the long, thin part of the neuron that sends information from the senses to the brain via the neurons and delivers information to different parts of the brain or to muscles and glands. Axons can connect to one other neuron but usually connect to many others. Axon terminals (also called terminal buttons, or boutons) are the endpoints of the axon branch and affect the dendrites of other neurons.

Did You Know?

Consciousness (Sense of Self)
One of the mind-related symptoms of autism is a lack of a sense of consciousness — being able to look in the mirror and identify the "me" that you see there. Children will usually show a sense of "self" around the age of 2. If you put a mark on their face (lipstick, for example) and hold them up to a mirror, typically developing children will touch the mark on their face, but a child with autism does not recognize himself and doesn't touch the lipstick on his face.

Mind

Beyond the physical control that our brain has over our body, it is also the structure that houses our mind. The mind includes:

- Cognition (knowing)
- Attention (understanding)
- Memory
- Language (production and understanding)
- Learning
- Problem solving and decision making

Dendrites

Dendrites are short, branching protrusions that increase the surface area of the neuron cell body. They receive incoming information from other neuron cell axons and then transmit electrical stimulation to the cell body (called the soma). Neurons may have as few as one dendrite, but typically have many. According to recent research, the dendrite may also sort and interpret information to determine the appropriate brain area to which the information should be sent.

Gray Matter and White Matter

These are the terms used to describe the thin, folded layer of neural tissue that covers the outside of the brain. Gray matter is made up of neural cell bodies, dendrites, and axon terminals of neurons. It gathers information from sensory organs and other gray matter cells and redirects it as needed. Gray matter is also located inside the two hemispheres of the brain and in the front end of the brain stem. White matter is made of nerve fibers and is white because of the myelin sheath that covers and protects the fibers as information is moved along them. Its function is to connect different areas of gray matter.

Function of Brain Hemispheres

LEFT Hemisphere

- Right side of body control
- Number skills
- Math/scientific skills
- Analytical thought
- Objectivity
- Written language
- Spoken language
- Logic
- Reasoning

RIGHT Hemisphere

- Left side of body control
- Visual-spatial skills (3-D object, distance and depth perception)
- Music/art awareness
- Imagination
- Subjectivity
- Intuition
- Creativity
- Emotion
- Face recognition

Hemispheres of the Brain

When you look at the brain from the top, you can see the two halves, called hemispheres, the left and the right. Each hemisphere functions slightly differently and is connected to the other hemisphere through a nerve bundle called the corpus callosum.

Imprinted Brain Theory

The conception, development, and birth of a new person requires one complete copy of the human genome (a complete set of DNA) from the mother and the father, and not two sets of either the mother's or father's genome.

Genetic experiments using mice have demonstrated that duplication of specific regions of mouse chromosomes in the egg and sperm resulted in different appearances depending on which parent the chromosomes were from. With more sophisticated laboratory techniques, the specific genes that activate the change in the genes (called imprinted genes) were pinpointed by the addition or removal of a chemical molecule to the DNA. The result is the expression of genes from one parent only, rather than a mix of both parents (through recombination).

It is now common knowledge that genetic imprinting is a key point in physiology, especially in the brain. The mother's and father's genomes activate changes in neurodevelopment in specific regions of the human brain, in particular behavior and neurodevelopmental disorders, and affect from 5% to 10%

Functional Magnetic Resonance Imaging (fMRI)

Images of internal body structures are produced by exposure to a very strong magnetic field that uses radio frequency pulses. Functional magnetic resonance imaging, or fMRI, measures the level of brain activity through any changes in blood flow in the brain while an action, either mental or physical, occurs. Comparing fMRI images of children with autism to typically developing children helps us understand the areas of the brain that are different for children with autism and may lead to more successful therapies.

The ability to look at a developing brain through the magic of fMRI is a fairly recent addition to the collection of tools, such as EEGs (electroencepholographs), used by our health-care professionals to understand how our brains and bodies work. Understanding the impact of autism on our child's developing brain through observed behaviors has been accomplished with the use of questionnaires completed by parents, caregivers, and health professionals over time. Developing databases of the collected information helps establish grades for the severity of symptoms, provide developmental benchmarks for assessments of infants and young children, and alert health-care professionals and families to early signs of autism. Questionnaires are divided into domains, which identify language, communication, and social impairment, behavioral issues, intellectual delays, motor problems, gastrointestinal challenges, and sensory issues.

Health-care professionals are trained specifically to deliver and analyze each assessment tool and to use their education and experience to establish a diagnosis of autism.

of the brain overall. In the development of the child from the fertilized egg, the imprinting process effectively silences the gene that has the added chemical group — and that change in the gene lives on in future generations. It is bizarre to think that imprinting genes is a form of conflict between the mother and father, but this appears to be the case.

Another theory is that imprinting is how the next generation "evolves," providing the means for faster changes over a few generations.

Clustering

Our brains are like constellations of stars where each star is a "node" and nearby stars are closely connected by clusters of neural axon networks. The clusters form hubs of organization within the brain, allowing local function, such as happens in the area of the brain devoted to language development, but also allowing global functions, such as listening to others (or reading this text), making decisions based on the information received, and discussing those thoughts with others.

Human Neural Network

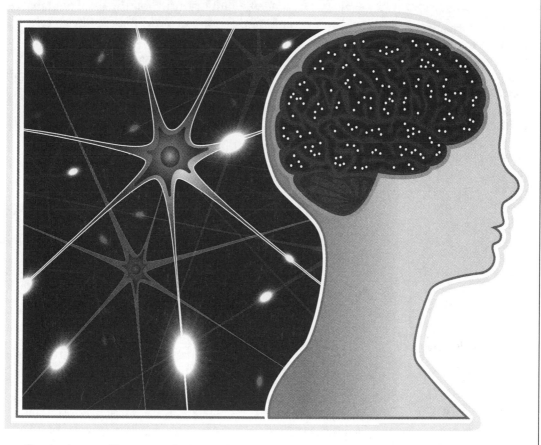

Our brains are like constellations of stars where each star is a "node" and nearby stars are closely connected by clusters of neural axon networks.

This clustering network is controlled by genes and reaches its optimum in early development, around the age of 2. Typically developing children have many more connections and axons in their brains than adult brains, but strong development of clustering indicates better cognitive abilities in adulthood.

Pruning

Pruning of unused short-range neural connections, along with the growth of myelin on the axons that travel longer distances, happen as a normal part of development. The outcome of the pruning is less strength in the local connections and more strength in the (longer) global axons. The usual electrical activity seen in the brain is described as spontaneous slow and fluctuating activity in the cortex, rather than high-frequency waves, suggesting more communication in global function between brain areas than within local areas. If these development processes are disturbed on the local or global level, the resulting communication networks may not be as effective or may not work at all — as can be seen in children with autism.

Research has shown that in children with autism, the organization of their brain has reduced levels of the clustering that is so essential, and less efficient local and global communication clusters. Electronencephalography (EEG) tests show a disrupted ability to work together or in sequence (called synchronization) in the networks, likely reducing the effectiveness of communications between brain regions.

Mirror Neuron Hypothesis

This popular theory is based on the belief that "mirror" neurons are active in learning, copying, and understanding actions, imitation, behavior, and language acquisition. This hypothesis suggests that people with autism do not have working mirror neurons and are not sensitive to the intentions and emotions of other people. Until recently, this theory failed to explain how the mirror system is defective or how the defects may happen. Recent research has used fMRI imaging to identify patterns of mirror neuron activity in regions rather than single cells, as well as in regions other than those initially identified. The parietal lobe may be the basic hub for human mirror neural systems (HMNS). If there is a connection between children with autism and a lack of mirror neurons, this would further support the theory that the networks are lacking in long-range communications, as would be required for a working HMNS hypothesis.

Perinatal and Neonatal Trauma

Some of the perinatal and neonatal risk factors for autism that affect the brain include asphyxia, neonatal anemia (not enough oxygen-carrying red blood cells), and meconium aspiration (when the unborn infant who is under stress and not getting enough oxygen inhales excreted waste while inside the uterus). Maternal hemorrhage has been shown to double the risk of autism, and incompatible blood type with the mother increased the risk four-fold. Umbilical cord complications, fetal distress, breech, and other abnormal birth positions have all been cited as increasing the risk for autism.

Gastrointestinal Theories

According to a recent seminar on autism published in *The Lancet* (2013), gastrointestinal problems are present in 9% to 70% of children who are diagnosed with autism. The most common symptoms experienced are chronic constipation or diarrhea, abdominal pain, and gastroesophageal reflux, with frequent bloating, belching, vomiting, and flatulence. Other related disorders include gastritis, inflammatory bowel disease, esophagitis, celiac disease, Crohn's disease, and colitis. Children with autism also tend to have higher incidences of food selectivity. Problems with communicating GI symptoms to caregivers may often be the cause of sleep disturbance, hyperactivity, aggressive behavior, and feeding issues.

> **Problems with communicating GI symptoms to caregivers may often be the cause of sleep disturbance, hyperactivity, aggressive behavior, and feeding issues.**

Gut-Brain Axis Model

Soon after birth, our intestines are populated with trillions of microorganisms (bacteria) that are essential in the normal development of our immune system and in breaking down dietary food particles, and thus to our overall health. Pathways of communication are established between the autonomic nervous system (ANS), the endocrine system, the enteric nervous system (ENS), and the immune system. This collection of bacteria is known as the micobiome, or gut flora, and the variability of the bacteria in individuals' intestines is based on geography, genetics, metabolism, age, diet, stress, and antibiotic therapy.

Did You Know?

Probiotics

The connection between the gut and the brain is called the brain-gut axis, which may be affected by poor intestinal bacterial populations. Antibiotics given to combat infection may kill off beneficial gut bacteria. Probiotics are colonies of the beneficial bacteria that are taken as supplements or are available in some foods. Beneficial gut bacteria may reduce some of the symptoms experienced in GI issues (constipation, diarrhea, gas, or bloating). Anecdotally, many children with ASD have a history of exposure to multiple antibiotics in the first few years of life, and that, coupled with known immunological issues in this population, suggests that gut flora may be somewhat compromised in this subset of children. Though controversial and lacking in evidence-based research, it may be worth considering a trial of probiotics in this subgroup, especially if they have a history of gut-related symptoms, such as loose stools, diminished appetite, and irritability.

Understanding the microbiome of an individual may lead to a better understanding of the risk of illness, the progress of disease, and the effectiveness of treatment. The gut (called the enteric nervous system) is made up of cells along the lining of the esophagus, through the stomach, the small intestine, and the colon. If communications within the brain are not working properly, communications to and from the gut may also be altered, resulting in GI problems.

Leaky Gut Theory

The microvilli (fingers) that stick out into the interior of the intestine regulate digestion and absorb micronutrients in a healthy environment, but in other-than-optimal conditions, macromolecules (protein fragments) may move beyond the gastric-intestinal barrier and become the target of an immune system response. Dysfunction of the typically tight junctions across cell wall barriers can occur in systemic inflammatory disease, food allergies, inflammatory bowel disease, and celiac disease — all possible factors in autism.

Ingesting biological contaminants and a possible overgrowth of candida are two of the factors that may unbalance beneficial gut bacteria populations, resulting in clinical signs and symptoms. In a 2010 study, 37% of children with autism were found to have abnormal intestinal permeability, compared with 21% of first-degree relatives and 0% of the control group children. Other studies have not found signs of leaky gut, however, which suggests that leaky gut may occur in a subgroup of children with autism and their first-degree families. This theory is still controversial; more research is required.

Opioid Excess Theory

Compared to typically developing people, children with autism feel little to no pain. Increased numbers of peptides (protein fragments from digestion) that are opioid-like have been found in the urine of some children with autism. The enzyme that is known to break down such peptides was found to be low or absent altogether in the urine of some children with autism, compared to typically developing children, which may explain the elevated numbers.

The opioid excess theory claims that the excessive level of unmetabolized peptide fragments from dietary proteins that contain gluten and casein are able to pass through both the intestinal and blood-brain barriers (digestive and brain cell walls have tight cell-to-cell junctions to control which substances are able to cross and when), where they have a morphine-like impact on behavior (reduced social contact, insistence on routine, developmental milestone delay, and decreased pain response). More recent studies have not found opioid peptides in autistic children's urine. Due to the variability of autism symptom presentation, it is possible that the subpopulation who experienced the opioid symptoms earlier were not part of the later study.

Nutritional Deficiencies

Selective eaters are at the highest risk of vitamin and nutrient deficiencies. Children with autism are excessively selective eaters, more likely to resist new food, and less likely to eat a variety of foods. Vegetables are high on the list of being refused. Children with autism were seen to have poorer self-feeding skills and higher food avoidance. A 2010 systematic review showed that children with autism received calcium, vitamin D, and vitamin A supplements more often than typically developing children. An abnormally high level of vitamin B_6 compared to typically developing children suggests an impaired enzyme system, because pyridoxal kinase, which is necessary for metabolizing vitamin B_6, may be present.

Enzyme Deficiencies

Children with autism have been studied for their ability to break down, or metabolize, phenols (found in food additives, dyes, and some medications), amines (dietary protein fragments), and sulfur. Enzymes are necessary for this digestive process, and a reduced level or deficiency of enzymes leads to an inability to digest nutrients. This deficiency could lead to a buildup of dopamine, serotonin, or noradrenaline, and alternative metabolism pathways may result in substances similar to toxins produced by plants (called phytotoxins). To break down possible phytotoxins, children with ASD may be using up their bodily supply of sulfate. Abnormal sulfation may contribute to leaky gut syndrome as well.

Transsulfuration

Vitamin B_5 is critical to many metabolic pathways in our bodies. In the transsulfuration pathway, homocysteine is converted to cystathionine and then cysteine. This conversion matters because cysteine is a conditionally essential amino acid

> ### Did You Know?
> **Folic Acid Deficiency**
> Folic acid is known to reduce neural tube defects that occur during early development, but studies conducted in 2013 illustrate that taking this supplement before conception and during pregnancy significantly reduces the numbers of children born with autism (0.1% of children of mothers who took folic acid compared to 0.2% of children of mothers who did not).

totally dependent on the status of methionine. The pathway happens mostly in the liver, where a decrease in the availability of cysteine due to genetic or nutritional deficiencies would negatively affect antioxidant abilities in tissues such as the brain, intestine, and thymus. This deficiency has been seen to increase the vulnerability of these tissues to environmental stressors and may have an impact on neurologic, gastrointestinal, and immune system dysfunction for people with autism.

Food Sensitivities, Intolerances, and Allergies

Keeping a health and diet diary for your child will help if he ever experiences symptoms of food sensitivities, allergies, intolerances, or intoxication. Being able to inform health-care professionals about the food that has been ingested over the 48 hours previous to symptoms — and being able to accurately describe the onset of symptoms — will help them give your child relief. This is especially true if your child is nonverbal or has an intellectual disability.

Food sensitivities, intolerances, and allergies are considered illnesses that may affect some individuals any time they eat certain foods or food ingredients that the general population is able to tolerate without any problems. Food sensitivities only affect certain individuals in the population, not everyone. Food sensitivities differ from food-borne infections, or food poisoning, that come from infectious bacteria, viruses, or parasites. Anyone is likely to be affected by food-borne infections if they eat foods that are tainted, even though some individuals will be affected differently than others.

Food Sensitivities

With food sensitivities, individuals who are affected experience adverse reactions from eating even a small amount of a food or food category that most other people are able to eat with no reaction at all. For anyone who is sensitive to a food, avoidance is the best therapy. Even so, it is still critical that your health-care professional follow through with a differential diagnosis to be sure that another medical condition is not responsible for your symptoms.

Food Allergies

Food allergies are bodily immunological responses to a food or food component. Immediate hypersensitivity reactions or delayed hypersensitivity are the two types of abnormal immunological responses that typically occur. Immediate hypersensitivity reactions are mediated by immunoglobulin E (IgE), with symptoms apparent almost immediately after eating the food. People who suffer from food allergies often carry automatic injector pens (for example, EpiPens) that contain epinephrene as an immediate response to an allergic reaction to foods that may cause anaphylaxis, a fatal reaction when the throat swells up to the point that it is impossible to breathe.

Food Intolerances

Food intolerances include metabolic food disorders and idiosyncratic reactions. In lactose intolerance, the digestive enzyme — lactase — to digest lactose is missing. People with this intolerance either avoid the food or take an enzyme supplement to overcome the response from consuming dairy products containing lactose.

Gluten and Casein Sensitivity

For some children with ASD who also have gluten and casein sensitivities, some of their symptoms may be improved with the gluten-free, casein-free (GFCF) diet. This diet is described in Part 4 of this book, which includes 175 GFCF recipes.

One percent of the people in the world have gluten sensitivity that manifests as celiac disease. There is no better way to confirm gluten sensitivity than an exclusion diet, which confirms the diagnosis if the symptoms go away when gluten-containing foods are reduced or eliminated from the diet. Once the symptoms have gone, a food challenge with gluten will confirm gluten sensitivity if symptoms reappear.

Did You Know?

Lactose or Casein
Lactose intolerance and casein sensitivity are often confused. Lactose is a sugar molecule found in milk products. Lactose intolerance is due to a deficiency of the enzyme lactase. It is not an immune system response. Casein is a protein found in mammalian milk, milk products, and other foods.

Current Models of Autism Symptoms

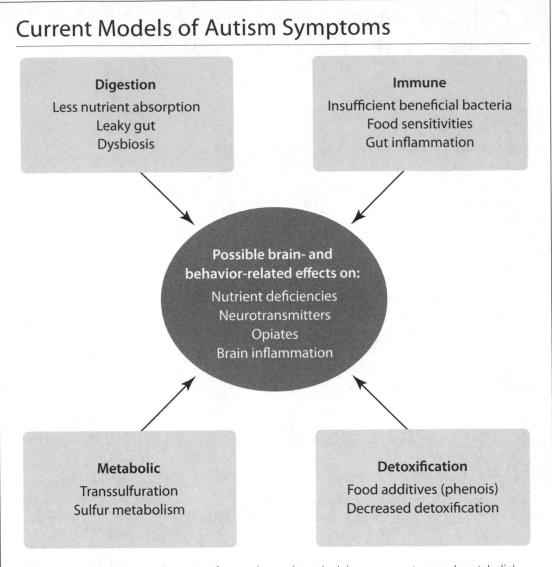

Digestion
Less nutrient absorption
Leaky gut
Dysbiosis

Immune
Insufficient beneficial bacteria
Food sensitivities
Gut inflammation

Possible brain- and behavior-related effects on:
Nutrient deficiencies
Neurotransmitters
Opiates
Brain inflammation

Metabolic
Transsulfuration
Sulfur metabolism

Detoxification
Food additives (phenois)
Decreased detoxification

These models suggest that many factors (gastrointestinal, immune system and metabolic) may contribute to autism symptoms.

Research Spotlight

Brain Balance

One of the many therapies available for children with autism is based on the functional disconnection syndrome. In this model, the higher-order functions of the brain (language, planning, and sensory information) that usually connect to the frontal lobes may become disconnected. This model is based on a small body of evidence, but it is worth following the research as it develops. Like many other models, this may be true for a subset of children with autism.

DocTalk:
Refrigerator Mothers

Dr. Leo Kanner, the first researcher to identify autism as a childhood health condition, laid the blame for the condition at the feet of mothers, claiming that emotionally cold "refrigerator mothers" were responsible for socially distant children with ASD. Kanner's theory has been discredited, but we do know that parents can affect autism-related behavior through problematic interactions with their children. Keep these parenting principles in mind.

Attention: As a parent, your attention, or lack of it, can directly affect your child's behavior. Giving your child your undivided attention for a short period and letting her know when you will be focusing on her once again will help her learn to self-manage for slightly longer periods of time. This is achieved in a gradual, baby-step process.

Follow-through: Consistent parenting is a critical tool in your toolbox when you have a child with autism. For those children who are inflexible, your continued stable direction and guidance help them learn how to cope within their world.

Appropriate response: Celebrating and congratulating your child for achieving a new behavioral goal is appropriate, but celebration is not appropriate for previously achieved goals unless there has been regression. Being consistent increases the value of goal setting and satisfaction in achieving each small goal.

Distractions: In this world of smartphones, tablets, computers, and televisions, it is hard for children to compete for your attention. Learn to ignore the beep of a new text or a ringtone if you're busy with your child. A distracted parent can increase the risk of a meltdown. If you find that you're trying to do too many things at once, try to set up some free time for yourself with the support of family and friends or through a support agency.

Part 2:

Managing Autism Spectrum Disorders

Chapter 4
Standard Treatments

- - - - - - - - - - - - - - - - - - - -

CASE STUDY (continued from page 55)
Making Plans

When Stephen's parents caught their breath, they asked their doctor what was next. Dr. Parker advised them to learn as much as possible about available therapies for autism because they would be making the decisions about Stephen's care, even though he would be advising them about best practices and medical evidence. He talked at length about the lifestyle and biomedical approach — specific diets for children who showed gastrointestinal symptoms, like Stephen, along with nutritional supplements where needed and medication to help Stephen get past some of the symptoms that interfered with his social life and learning (for example, his aggressive behavior, hyperactivity, and irritability). If more seizures were to occur, Stephen might be prescribed antiseizure medication to protect his brain.

Dr. Parker gave Stephen's parents a referral to a registered dietitian to talk about how to broaden Stephen's diet. He set up appointments for testing Stephen for gluten and milk sensitivity, in view of his GI symptoms. He also set up a blood test to assess Stephen's levels of vitamins and minerals before recommending supplements to support his diet (possibly zinc and iron). The doctor's final comments were to be mindful that any therapies they chose for Stephen should do no harm. "Look for evidence that the therapy is helpful for the symptoms you're targeting," he advised.

Stephen's parents left the doctor's office feeling a little overwhelmed, with pamphlets about autism spectrum disorder, behavioral therapies called ABA and IBI, nutritional information, an appointment card reminder for meeting with the dietitian, a prescription with clear warnings about possible side effects and how to cope with them, and a journal to keep track of Stephen's symptoms and diet. Despite information overload and some trepidation, they were feeling excited and hopeful, ready to move ahead with building a program focused on Stephen to help him reach his full potential — and to do it as a team, with a family-centered approach.

Standards and Guidelines for Care

Experienced family physicians know that parents are the experts when it comes to their children. This is doubly true when the child has autism, because each child is unique in the presentation of signs and symptoms of autism spectrum disorder. For parents with a child diagnosed with ASD — after the initial shock — the journey can be a long one, without a map or navigator. Depending on your location, social, medical, and financial support may or may not be available. Navigating through the decision-making process while continuing on with all other aspects of family life can be overwhelming.

To assist families in managing autism, standards of care and clinical guidelines have been established by health-care professionals. In effect, these standards and guidelines constitute a bill of rights for people undergoing treatment for autism.

Q. What should I do if I think my child has autism?

A. Proceed systematically in consultation with your family doctor.

1. **See your doctor.** Dismiss old wives' tales about autism and speak to the experts. Your doctor will likely conduct a physical examination, take a medical history of your family, and examine your child's patterns of growth. If symptoms seem to indicate ASD, your doctor will likely refer your child to a developmental pediatrician or behavioral specialist.

2. **Screen for autism.** Your child's specialist will likely run a screen to rule out associated conditions and to help make a diagnosis. There are many specialized screening tools available for this purpose. Discuss the possibilities with your doctor. If your child has special problems — with speech and hearing, for example — he may be referred to the appropriate specialist, such as a speech pathologist or audiologist.

3. **Keep a health journal.** This will help your health-care team monitor your child's social, language, and motor development as she proceeds through any prescribed treatments. Keep copies of any screening tests and comprehensive evaluation results. Prepare to be patient and persistent. Caring for a child with ASD is challenging. Nothing can quite prepare you for a diagnosis of autism, but once your child is diagnosed, there are many treatment interventions available, as well as support groups and individuals to help with any accommodation and financial demands. You and your child are not alone.

Q. What are standards and guidelines?

A. Standards and guidelines in the medical professions are based on the best available evidence, which is prepared by a group of expert clinicians, whose opinions and experience add to the validity of the document. Guidelines highlight important recommendations for clinical practice, in particular when uncertainty or some controversy has been encountered. For the care of children with ASD, the following standards have been established:

- Regardless of intellectual disabilities or other medical conditions that coexist with autism, children and young adults will have full access to health, social, and mental health services.
- Community- and specialist-based multidisciplinary teams in the fields of mental health, learning disabilities, and social care services will be responsible for assessing, managing, and coordinating care for children and young people with autism.
- These teams will receive training to increase all aspects of autism awareness, as well as to increase required skills for managing and preparing an individualized treatment plan and managing care for children and young people with autism.
- Health-care professionals will be aware of the individual's special needs and challenges in order to support and provide care by adapting to the social and physical environment and by being flexible around care processes.
- Interventions will address the core features of autism as well as any other identified challenges the individual faces, at the appropriate developmental level, while also supporting the individual and family, teachers and caregivers.
- Interventions will be delivered by trained professionals, with mediation by parents, caregivers, teachers, and siblings.
- Antipsychotics, antidepressants, anticonvulsants, and exclusion diets will be considered for managing core features of autism on a risk-to-benefit ratio.
- Physical, social, and environmental factors will be considered in developing targeted interventions that reduce the risk of challenging behavior for the individual and also address possible issues.
- Parents, siblings, extended family members, and caregivers will be provided with an assessment to develop support that meets their personal, social, and emotional needs and gives practical support for their caring role, including a future plan of care for their child or young person that covers the transition to adult care.
- All aspects of care planning, including transition to adult care services, will involve the autistic young adult (especially after they are 16 years of age) whenever possible for informed decision-making.

Planning Interventions

Before an individualized treatment plan can be devised and implemented, your child will likely undergo a series of exploratory evaluations:

Psychological and cognitive evaluation: This evaluation is designed to help determine the developmental and cognitive level your child has achieved and to assess social, emotional, and communication skills. Conducted by a behavioral therapist.

Speech-language communication: This evaluation assesses your child's basic language level and use of language in verbal and nonverbal children. Conducted by a speech pathologist.

Audiologic assessment: This evaluation aims to rule out hearing problems. Conducted by a pediatric audiologist.

Vision assessment: This goal of this assessment is to rule out visual impairment that can mimic and coexist with ASD.

Adaptive functioning assessment: This evaluation is designed to test how well your child copes with everyday demands. Challenging behaviors are addressed during this assessment.

Fine motor skills assessment: This evaluation is recommended for children who have sensory concerns and difficulties with fine motor skills. Conducted by an occupational therapist.

Academic functioning assessment: If your child is over 3 years old, general academic functioning should be assessed. Poor organization skills, attention issues, transition problems, and auditory processing problems can be barriers to succeeding in school. Your child's progress should be monitored, with ongoing access to clinicians to address any concerns, as well as medical and behavioral needs.

Intervention Plans

During the evaluation process, your health-care provider should continue to provide health promotion and disease prevention care for your child with autism, and may also monitor and treat some of the conditions associated with autism for some children (sleep issues, gastrointestinal problems, and seizures).

1. **Plans:** As evaluations are completed, intervention plans can be put together by experienced therapists, who should provide objectives and regular goals that fit with your child's developmental, medical, social, or dietary concerns.

2. **Goals:** Regular goals should be established, with monitoring done for progress and response to treatment, and results shared with family and health-care providers.

3. **Timing:** Intensive and early intervention is required (at least 25 hours per week throughout the year).

Safety Tips at Home

Childproof your home to prevent accidents and injuries. Many of these tips apply to all young children.

- Install locks, gates, and barriers to prevent escapes.
- Check with your local fire department for safety regulations before installing locks on windows.
- Tie back any cords on window blinds or tie them above your child's reach.
- Place child locks on all cabinets.
- Pad all sharp surfaces in your child's room and elsewhere if self-injury is a concern.
- Attach bookcases, dressers, and other heavy furniture to walls to prevent tipping.
- Use visual labels to reduce frustration. Green means go and red means stop signs may help your child to understand safety and danger.
- Mark off places where it is safe to play and places that are off-limits.
- Reduce mealtime injuries by tying utensils with short strings and attaching (unbreakable) dinnerware to surfaces with Velcro or suction cups.
- Be aware of any objects that may be thrown inside a vehicle, such as hard shoes.
- Ensure that car seats and seatbelts are installed properly.
- Protect the driver from being kicked from behind or having items pulled (hair, necklaces, ties, and scarves, for example).
- Check with your local fire and rescue force to be sure that you are observing fire and safety regulations in your region. Practice regular fire drills with your family.
- Discuss safety tips with other parents.

4. **Family:** All family members should be involved in the intervention process. All family members should be assessed to develop appropriate support for the entire family.

5. **Aggression:** In cases where aggression is a symptom, emergency response information needs to be discussed with the health-care and therapy team. Establish local emergency mental health and hospital emergency solutions and respite (relief for parents and caregivers) before the need occurs. All family members need to practice what to do in case someone is injured. If possible, your child with autism also needs to know how to respond, who to contact, and how.

Identification

Some children with ASD wander from home. Escape from caregivers may present a danger to the child. Having resources to protect your loved one will help your peace of mind.

- Inform local police and rescue departments that your child tends to wander so they can help immediately if your child goes missing.

- If your child cannot provide her name and a phone number or address, be sure that she carries some form of identification, such as an identification bracelet or a sewn-on or iron-on tag on her clothing.

- Introduce yourself and your child to organizations in your neighborhood, such as churches and athletic clubs, and explain how to react should your child appear at their door by themselves.

- Consider purchasing a GPS tracking device for your child to wear.

Family Stress

These can be stressful times for the whole family as the child with ASD is diagnosed and a treatment plan is developed.

Parental Stress

Parents with young children who have ASD are known to have higher stress levels than other parents, perhaps due to the need for close monitoring of their child, along with lack of sleep and concern about the challenges related to the core autism symptoms. Some therapies include or coach the parents and may be effective in lowering the parents' stress levels as well.

Sibling Stress

Workshops may help siblings cope with their family situation and make new friends who share their issues. Support for siblings is as important as support for parents.

Siblings may struggle with the amount of attention given to the child with autism — "They get away with everything; I would never be allowed to do that!" Other worries may include a fear that their sibling with autism may be dying and a feeling of being different from their friends. A real concern may be that they will be expected to take over as guardian for their sibling with ASD.

When you treat any child, you treat the whole family. Families should talk about sibling issues and help siblings by reaching out to chat groups, websites, or books written from the perspective of the sibling. Workshops may help siblings cope with their family situation and make new friends who share their issues. Support for siblings is as important as support for parents.

In more serious situations, autism-related behaviors or aggressions between siblings are best dealt with by a behavioral professional or social worker. Personal property belonging to the sibling should be protected and he should have a quiet space away from noise, tantrums, or intrusive behaviors. House rules about restricting time for TV or limiting time on the Internet should apply to all children. Quality time with parents is especially important for uninterrupted discussions about life, friends, school, the future, and the sibling's concerns.

DSM-5 Standards for Diagnosis and Treatment Care

The *Diagnostic and Statistical Manual of Mental Disorders 5* (*DSM-5*), published by the American Psychiatric Association in 2013, guides health-care professionals not only in diagnosing autism but also in designing improved treatment interventions that focus on the child's individual needs. A higher reliance on behavioral therapies and interventions to treat specific symptoms — rather than on medication — is central to the philosophy behind the *DSM-5* standards for ASD.

A.L.A.R.M. Guidelines

The Centers for Disease Control and Prevention (CDC), in cooperation with the American Academy of Pediatrics, the American Academy of Neurology, and the Child Neurology Society have established first-signs A.L.A.R.M. guidelines to standardize practices among health-care professionals, to simplify the screening process, and to ensure that all children receive appropriate screenings and therapeutic interventions:

A: Autism is happening more frequently. Numbers of children with developmental/behavioral issues are increasing, and early signs are easily missed.

L: Listen to parents. Autism symptoms are present for many infants younger than 18 months; parents' concerns are usually accurate; ask for their thoughts.

A: Act early. Participate fully in early screening for developmental delays; learn about milestones; and look for early intervention if problems are found.

R: Refer for an early intervention program or a special education program, depending on age; refer to clinical professionals for a definitive diagnosis (if autism); refer to an audiologist to rule out hearing issues; and provide information about community and family support.

M: Monitor. Follow up to continue to monitor and address concerns thoroughly; check for other co-occurring medical conditions associated with autism; continue to educate and advise parents to keep them current; be a family support advocate with intervention programs, respite care, special education, and insurance agencies.

Did You Know?

Going to School

Introducing your child with autism to teachers, administrators, support staff, and other children at the beginning of the school year may help raise awareness of the talents that make your child special. Planning playtime and establishing a play buddy for recess and lunchtime may help to reduce bullying or teasing, and may help your child to build friendships and a social network. Ask about policies to make the school environment safe for your child and others, and how students are educated to reduce bullying in the school setting.

Clinical Practice Recommendations

Developmental screening tools should be used at each well-child visit (infant to school-age) and any time parents and caregivers are concerned about development, social interactions, behavior, or learning.

1. Recommended screening tools include the Brigance screens, Ages and Stages Questionnaires, Parents' Evaluations of Developmental Status, and Child Development Inventories.

2. The Denver Developmental Screening Test II (DDST-II) and the Revised Denver Pre-Screening Developmental Questionnaire (R-DPDQ) are *not* appropriate for developmental screening in the primary care setting.

3. Further developmental screening is required when a child does not meet typical milestones: babbling by 12 months; pointing or waving bye-bye by 12 months; single words by 16 months; two-word phrases that are not parroting others by 24 months; or loss of language or social skills at any age.

4. Screening and monitoring should be done for any siblings of children with autism, focusing on acquisition of communication and social skills, play, or maladaptive behaviors. Screen for autism-related symptoms, language delay, social issues, learning problems, and depression or anxiety.

5. If any child does not meet the cutoff for regular developmental screening processes, autism assessment with a validated tool should be administered.

6. Any child who has been diagnosed with developmental delay and/or autism spectrum disorder should have audiologic assessment, as well as laboratory investigations and screening for lead exposure. Any child who has developmental delay and pica should have lead testing, with additional screening conducted periodically if the pica continues.

American Academy of Neurology and the Child Neurology Society Guidelines

In addition, the American Academy of Neurology and the Child Neurology Society recommend these clinic-based practices:

1. Genetic (microarray) testing for any child who is diagnosed with ASD — high-resolution chromosome testing and DNA analysis (fragile X testing).

2. Selective metabolic test to be initiated if the following presents: sluggishness, seizures early in life, cyclic vomiting, dysmorphic/coarse features, and intellectual disability (ID), or when newborn screening is not available or is inadequate.

3. Electroencephalogram study is recommended for children with autism who are sleep-deprived, if they suffer from clinical seizures, if there are some suspicions of the child having unidentified seizures, or if the child has experienced regression showing a medically significant communication and social function loss (the focus is on toddlers and preschoolers, but this recommendation applies to children at any age).

4. Event-related potentials (evaluates brain function) and magnetoencephalography (maps brain activity) are *not* recommended as a routine clinical test.

5. Clinical neuroimaging is not recommended for diagnostic evaluation of autism, even when megalencephaly (large head) is present.

6. Inadequate evidence exists for the following tests to be routinely done for autism diagnosis: hair analysis, allergy testing (candida or other molds, casein, or gluten), celiac antibodies, neurochemical or immunologic abnormalities, intestinal permeability studies, levels of vitamins, mitochondrial disorders (lactate and pyruvate levels), urinary peptides, tests for thyroid function, stool analysis, or erythrocyte glutathione peroxidase.

Q. What do you mean by the term "evidence-based"?

A. Evidence-based interventions are supported by validated research (research that obtains the same results when it is repeated by another research group with a similar population), and where the research question is based on experience and observation (will this therapy help a child of a certain age with certain symptoms reach a certain level over a certain time?). An evidence-based practice model is one that includes evidence-based interventions, with professional clinical judgment (often from a collaborative health-care team) that is patient- or client-focused — that takes into consideration specific values, preferences, and goals as discussed with individuals and their families.

Q. How do I know which research studies I can trust for the best information?

A. Finding reliable information can be a challenge for the parent who wants to know more about ASD and how to care for their child. How a study is designed is one way to test the credibility of the research.

- Gold standard research studies are randomized, double-blind, and placebo-controlled. Half of the participants in the study are randomly placed in the experimental group and half in the control group, where everything is handled in exactly the same way except that a placebo is used rather than the experimental treatment.

- Silver standard studies are open-label, which means everyone receives the treatment. Because there is nothing to compare the results against, it is more difficult to say whether any change is actually based on the experimental treatment.

- Bronze standard studies comprise survey data that may be affected by some bias on the part of the participants or the reviewers but may provide useful information that would be difficult and expensive to obtain otherwise.

Many early ASD therapies and interventions were based on weak study design, and the results may not stand up to close scrutiny. More recent research has stronger methodology but often finds fewer positive outcomes for the effectiveness of the therapy being assessed.

! CAUTION !

As you read through this chapter, be on the lookout for CAUTION boxes that look like this one. They highlight therapies that might not be appropriate because of concerns for safety, cost, and/or family time.

Therapies and Interventions

There are so many therapeutic approaches — where do you start? Autism therapies can be grouped into five categories according to the core and peripheral symptoms targeted for treatment:

- Behavioral therapies
- Biomedical (including pharmacological and nutritional) therapies
- Sensory therapies
- Communication therapies
- Educational interventions

The most common types of treatments used for ASD are behavioral interventions, speech and music therapies, and social stories.

However, treatments with little to no evidence of efficacy for treating ASD are also used by many families, including physiological treatments (auditory and sensory integration training, vitamin and mineral supplementation, alternative diets, and detoxification, for example), and some of the treatments reported as being effective are less commonly used.

Behavioral Therapies

Behavioral training programs are typically based on applied behavior analysis (ABA), which is proven to be effective for reducing core ASD symptoms. Be aware that behavioral training programs often do not entirely remove symptoms. They can also be expensive and demanding to administer. As your child ages, the interventions used will continue to shift to age-appropriate target goals for your child's level of development, social situation, and education. ABA therapy is not appropriate or effective for every child who has ASD.

Behavioral therapy is used for many conditions:

- Mental health conditions and social disorders
- Substance abuse
- Eating disorders
- Coping with chronic disease states, chronic pain, or emotional grief
- Autism

Individually designed treatment plans and exercises include:

- Relaxation methods and breathing exercises
- Social skills training
- Coping tools or mechanisms
- Exercises to increase focus

- Role playing in situations that cause anger, pain, or fear
- Writing (keeping a journal or diary)

Specific benefits from behavioral therapy include:

- Increased self-awareness in terms of emotional and physical needs
- Improved pain management
- Fewer emotional meltdowns
- Improved ability to cope with difficult, stressful, and unusual situations
- Social skills improvement
- More appropriate emotional behaviors

Therapeutic techniques derived from applied behavior analysis include:

- Pivotal response training (PRT)
- Discrete trial training (DTT)
- Aggression replacement training (ART)
- Picture exchange communication system (PECS)
- Intensive behavioral intervention (IBI)
- Verbal behavior analysis (VBA)

Applied Behavior Analysis (ABA)

ABA targets behaviors that are socially problematic for an individual and helps him make changes that can be measured and tracked. Optimistic attitudes and positive reinforcements are used, rather than avoiding or deterring behaviors (using a carrot instead of a stick). The ABA process has been researched

---

Did You Know?

Parent Dropout

Parents give many reasons for choosing, beginning, and ending specific therapies for treating their child with autism. Some factors proposed as influences include:

- The severity level of their child's ASD
- The impact of early intervention that may significantly and quickly alter behavior or symptoms
- Possible misunderstanding of their child's diagnosis
- Possible incorrect evaluation of an evidence-based intervention that can lead to a poorly informed decision
- Conflicting information from health-care professionals that can leave parents overwhelmed and vulnerable

Teams of health-care professionals can work with your family to arrive at the best therapy to meet your child's and your family's needs.

---

and validated for many years. ABA principles are used to build techniques that provide solutions to shape particular undesirable social behaviors. Treatment decisions are based on the information collected about behavior in particular situations.

Intensive Behavior Intervention (IBI)

Based on applied behavior analysis, intensive behavior intervention (IBI) is provided in a highly structured format with learning-to-learn behaviors described as imitation, cooperation, and attention, with a focus on preparing children with ASD for school learning.

Children are taught a wide range of skills and behaviors (communication, self-help, socializing, play, and learning skills). IBI goals are established to:

- Decrease ASD symptoms
- Increase rate of learning for each individual
- Prepare for an age-appropriate school setting

Average cognitive functioning is the best IBI therapy outcome, but IBI responses vary widely — some children meet the therapy goals, and some children get even worse.

Program guidelines recommend that progress be assessed every 6 months for ongoing measurement of IBI improvements and to assess the child's ongoing therapy needs. To continue in IBI, the child needs to demonstrate learning in language, general cognitive ability, and adaptive behavior. Parent education workshops are also included in the IBI program, to deepen parent understanding of IBI principles and techniques and show how to cope with possible challenging behaviors.

Early Intensive Behavior Intervention (EIBI) Programs

Because early treatment of autism is critical to the best outcome, programs that focus on very young children are important. EIBI targets play, self-helping, social, emotional, communication, and cognitive skills — a functional and adaptive skill set. Intervention goals are developed based on your child's age and the typical development milestone achievement pattern (what is missing) through one-on-one play and across a variety of settings, with constant monitoring through a child-specific logbook. Along with being updated at the end of each session, the logbook is updated during supervision meetings to discuss successes and newly identified targets.

> **Because early treatment of autism is critical to the best outcome, programs that focus on very young children are important.**

Two factors that have been associated with the most successful outcomes are intensive therapy and the use of trained professionals. One of the valuable outcomes for many children in the United States from EIBI therapy is that they were able to attend the mainstream school system. EIBI therapy responses increased inversely with the age that intervention began, more so than with the severity of ASD symptoms.

Reinforcers

Immediately after a targeted learning goal is met, a reward, or preferred reinforcer, is given. Some children like praise; most, but not all, children with autism prefer toys or behaviors that are child- and age-specific — tickles, raisins, crackers, music, computer games — for a brief, predetermined period. A token economy is another reward scenario where the child earns a token for each goal met, with the ultimate reward being given when a predetermined number of tokens have been earned. Reinforcers change with learning, and some of the learned behaviors may become preferred reinforcers themselves. For some children, receiving reinforcers may increase their preference for praise as a reward in itself.

Prompts

Prompts are used in the early stages of an intervention. When asking a question, the teacher may move the child's hand to make the correct response. For example, after the teacher says, "Touch the train," the child's finger would be moved to do so. In subsequent trials, more lag time would be given before the prompt, with the hope that the child would respond without help. Tasks are broken down into small, more manageable bits to provide more successful learning opportunities. Prompts and breaking down tasks are both examples of discrete trial teaching (DTT).

Learning trials happen quickly, with little time between (2 to 5 minutes). Natural environment teaching, a less structured teaching format than DTT, maximizes opportunities for learning throughout the child's day, during choosing clothes and dressing, meal preparation, bathing, social interactions, and play. Fewer reinforcers are used here.

Each child's therapy is designed to include teaching key behaviors (called behavioral cusps) that are usually divided between three levels of curriculum: beginning curriculum for basic skills; intermediate curriculum for more social skills and more advanced language and grammar — whether sign language, the picture exchange communication system (PECS), or verbal; and the advanced curriculum, which includes theory of mind, learning by watching, conversation, pretending, reading and writing, cooperating during play, and appropriate

Did You Know?

Pathways

Behaviorists theorize that autism may be caused by a specific deficit in social motivation, either from a disinterest in any aspect of social interaction or excessive interest in environmental or external stimuli. This model fits well with the theory that networks in the brain have become disordered, and that the pathways may be realigned with intense intervention.

attention skills in the classroom. The advanced curriculum prepares children for public school (mainstreaming), with the ability to work independently. As the child continues to show improvement in learning and in social interactions with school-age peers, EIBI and ABA sessions are slowly reduced. For children who continue to require more support, ABA sessions that target identified goals are given.

Pivotal Response Training (PRT)

Similar to the behavior cusps discussed in EIBI, pivotal response training builds on learning for further development, with a focus on target behaviors that initiate changes in behavior through four aspects of functioning:

- Motivation
- Self-initiation
- Responses to many cues
- Self-management skills

PRT appears to result in an increase in self-initiations, improvements in play skills, communication and language, and improved adaptation for many children, and PRT can be provided by family members and caregivers.

Managing Aggressive Behavior in Autism

Along with cognitive behavioral therapy, medications can be effective for some children and young people with autism when it comes to irritable, aggressive behavior, such as tantrums, destruction of property, arguing, and other behaviors that affect individuals and their families in a negative way. Aggressive behavior may lead to restrictions in access to the community, fewer social interactions, and a more isolated and restricted environment. Concerns for other, more vulnerable family members may even lead to removal from the household for safety concerns. Higher-functioning individuals are more likely to show aggressive behaviors, and sleep, mood, or GI disturbances may contribute to the problem. A multidisciplinary team can use functional behavioral assessment (FBA) to determine possible causes and provide appropriate treatment for such individuals. Behavioral interventions for aggressive behavior have been successful whether children with autism are medicated or not. Providing training for parents, caregivers, and teachers in how to reduce or calm aggression has also been successful.

> **Along with cognitive behavioral therapy, medications can be effective for some children and young people with autism when it comes to irritable, aggressive behavior.**

Parent-Child Interactive Therapy (PCIT)

An evidence-based therapy for young children (2 to 7 years old) and their parents or caregivers, parent-child interactive therapy is designed to improve the parent-child relationship and shift or change how interactions between the two happen during certain situations. PCIT is founded on research to help parents learn authoritative parenting skills, which is associated with fewer behavioral problems in the child. Parents are taught a collection of skills to use during time with their child:

- Praise (their child's positive actions)
- Reflect (on what their child says)
- Imitate (the play of their child)
- Describe (the child's actions)
- Enjoy (the special times)

Speech and Language Therapy

This treatment focuses on improving communication skills. For the speech and language therapist, the purpose of therapy is to improve the child's signs, sounds, and words, using a variety of techniques. An assessment of the child's existing use of receptive and expressive language establishes a starting point for a treatment plan. Depending on the child's preferences, different forms of play involving computers, games, and interactions with other people are used to build shared meanings.

Visual Schedules

One of the symptoms of children with autism is an inability to be sufficiently organized to complete tasks on their own. This can be frustrating for them in the school setting. Visual activity schedules are picture sets that show a sequence of events and are often used in classrooms to support children with disabilities by reminding them of the single steps in a more complex activity. As an aid for children with autism, visual supports help strengthen their communication skills because children with ASD tend to use visual imagery rather than listening as their primary learning mode. Visual supports are especially valuable for the transition moments — moving from one activity to another during the day, which is difficult for many children and young people with ASD. In one research study, visual schedules reduced the need for verbal and physical prompts, and allowed children to transition between learning centers independently. Importantly, the students appeared to enjoy using visual schedules.

Education Programs

Treatment and Education of Autistic and Related Communication Handicapped Children (TEACCH) is based on a social cognitive theory that accommodates visual schedules and work systems for the individual rather than having the individual adjust to the environment in order to increase engagement and learning. This model tends to result in children with ASD being segregated from typically learning peer groups.

Learning Experiences and Alternate Program for Preschoolers and their Parents (LEAP) is a learning therapy based on applied behavior analysis combined with early childhood education (ECE) theory. It aims to reduce autism symptoms that interfere with learning opportunities. The LEAP model of education teaches children with autism in the same classroom with typically developing peers. One outcome of this model is that the typically developing children provide social instruction and intervene on behalf of the children with autism.

Comparing these two educational models showed that the TEACCH group had significant improvements over time in all areas — autism characteristics and severity (ACS), communication, reciprocal social interaction (teacher- and parent-rated), and fine motor skills — but not for sensory and repetitive behaviors, and the students in the LEAP group showed significant improvements in sensory and repetitive behaviors and reciprocal social interactions. This comparison of these two programs did not show a significant difference in successful outcomes, although there was a range of different methods and theories.

> The LEAP model of education teaches children with autism in the same classroom with typically developing peers. One outcome of this model is that the typically developing children provide social instruction and intervene on behalf of the children with autism.

Did You Know?

Transition to School

Intensive behavioral intervention (IBI) therapy can be given in many settings — for example, at home, daycare, school, or treatment centers. IBI therapists require a safe, reasonably quiet, smoke-free, and work-friendly environment. For children transitioning from IBI to school, a transition classroom may be used to help the child adapt to learning in small groups, focusing on play and social skills. The child's IBI care team is made up of a supervising psychologist, a senior therapist, a school support consultant, and instructor therapists. Parents continue to be involved throughout the transition process, observing classroom therapy sessions regularly and engaging in update meetings on their child's progress.

To summarize, consider your child's symptoms and preferences, and research the educational programs available in your region before choosing the most appropriate school setting.

Social Workers

Services provided by social workers help families address issues and take a more active role in their child's ongoing care. Social workers provide counseling and support during periods of adjustment in sibling situations, related issues for couples, crisis, trauma, or grief. Social workers also coordinate with other service providers to meet the family's needs.

Medications and Supplements

Pharmacological interventions (drugs) are often prescribed for children who have autism. Medications are primarily recommended to support behavioral therapies when those therapies alone are not effective. There is no medication that will reduce all autism symptoms for every child. Research on effective medications for ASD has been focused on medications for reducing challenging behaviors.

Pharmacologic therapies are prescribed for some of the psychiatric symptoms that may coexist with ASD, such as hyperactivity, lack of attention, aggression, irritability, self-injury, rigidity, and impulsivity. In these cases, medications are used to facilitate other treatments (applied behavioral analysis or cognitive behavioral therapy). Unfortunately, side effects of most medications may sometimes outweigh the therapeutic benefits. Individual and flexible program development for each child is necessary.

Nutritional Deficiencies

The diet of many children with autism is deficient in vitamins and minerals. This is caused by limited food choices, picky eating habits, and, for some, a refusal to eat altogether. If you are concerned that your child has a nutritional deficiency, meet with your physician or dietitian to design a supplement program for your child.

! CAUTION !

While nutrient supplements are effective and safe for solving deficiency issues, they have not been proven to be a safe or effective therapy when taken in large doses or "megadoses." It is important to discuss the addition of any supplements to your child's diet with your health-care team before making any changes.

Q. How can I determine which complementary and alternative treatments are effective and safe for my child with autism?

A. A survey of parents of children with autism indicates how parents make treatment decisions. In order of choice, they rely on:

- Advice from other parents
- Information gathered from the Internet or from books
- Research published in peer-reviewed scientific journal articles
- Advice from health-care professionals
- Guidance from relatives and friends

Research published in peer-reviewed scientific journal articles and advice from health-care professionals are recommended as highly reliable sources of information.

Caution must be stated here, though, because unsubstantiated and unmonitored use of multivitamins and minerals does carry substantial risk (for example, vitamins B_6 and A or magnesium). Autistic children are picky eaters and should be assessed by a registered dietitian (or a qualified nutritionist, depending on your region) and supplemented according to the plan established by this professional. Many children with autism also refuse to take pills or supplements because of taste, texture, or a sensitive gag reflex, which creates further challenges. There *are* some encouraging findings that supplementation with omega-3 fatty acids has produced improvements in language skills and aggressive behaviors, but currently the evidence of effectiveness is weak.

Q. What treatments are preferred by parents?

A. At one end of the scale, occupational therapy, social skills training, and speech therapy were chosen by more than half the parents who participated in a survey and then rated them as "somewhat" or "dramatically" effective (70%). At the other end of the scale, auditory integration, Floortime, and music therapy were seen as the least effective ASD treatments. Parents' perceptions of the effectiveness of a treatment are essential when it comes to choosing to continue with that intervention or not. It is still not understood why families try many therapies and then discontinue them.

! CAUTION !

Used to eliminate specific metals, such as mercury and lead, chelation has been suggested as a treatment to improve ASD systems. Because of the possible harm that this treatment may cause, chelation is not recommended as an intervention for any child with ASD.

Sensory Therapies

Among sensory therapies used by health-care professionals and parents to care for children with ASD are sensory integration and auditory integration.

Sensory Integration

A form of occupational therapy that helps children organize or process bodily sensations coming from the surrounding environment, sensory integration is an effective treatment. Enjoyable activities, such as climbing, walking, and swimming, help realign miswired brain networks. For children who are hypersensitive to being touched, a gentle massage with their choice of powder, cream, or something soothing and fun, such as gelatin, may help them become more comfortable with touch. Sensory stories may also be included to help the child understand and adopt more appropriate behavior to sensory situations. **This treatment is widely used, but is still considered controversial.**

Auditory Integration

This therapy is directed toward individuals who experience auditory symptoms, such as a more acute, or hypersensitive, perception of some frequencies than others (a distortion), that may lead to difficulties in comprehension and perhaps also behavior issues. Some of the outcomes of this therapy include an increase in attention, increased interest in communication, better eye contact, improvement in auditory comprehension, reduced sensitivity to sounds, and a reduction in the incidence of temper tantrums and aggressive behavior. **Results are only anecdotal, and research reviews were at best equivocal.**

Swimming Therapy

Research has shown that structured physical activities benefit both motor and social symptoms. The therapeutic use of swimming in children with ASD is thought to improve language development and self-concept, improve adaptive behavior, and provide an appropriate setting for an early educational intervention to reduce antisocial behavior. **Only a few small studies have been reported; while they noted some positive results, further studies are needed.**

Floortime Therapy

Dr. Stanley Greenspan, a child psychiatrist, developed Floortime therapy. Research studies have reported that Floortime significantly improves emotional development while reducing the core symptoms of ASD.

Parents follow the Floortime philosophy by helping their child with ASD expand their communication by meeting them at their developmental level. Parents get down on the floor with their child and play with them, using activities enjoyed by the child. Parents are taught how to direct their child to increase the complexity of interactive play by opening and closing communication connections and circles. Floortime's goals for emotional and intellectual growth include:

- Interest in the world
- Regulation of self
- Engagement in relationships (intimacy)
- Communication (two-way)
- Communication (complex)
- Emotional ideas
- Emotional thinking

Floortime can be an effective form of therapy in the home or in a professional setting, with sessions lasting from 2 to 5 hours a day. Providing parental and caregiver training at the same time as interacting with the child increases the success of the program, creating shared attention, increasing engagement, and developing enhanced problem-solving skills.

Communication Therapies

Picture Exchange Communication (PEC)

For children with autism who have weak communication skills, this therapy uses pictures to communicate needs or thoughts, which is useful in either the home or classroom. Although picture exchange communication begins with the use of simple icons for communication, sentence structure skills can quickly be developed. Tablet computer companies, such as Apple with the iPad, have been partners in developing apps to support PEC for children with autism.

Six Phases of PEC

Phase 1
Exchange single pictures for items or activities.

Phase 2
Single pictures are used in different places, with different people, and over distances to develop persistent communication skills.

Phase 3
Two or more images are selected as favorites.
Communication book is created for regular use.

Phase 4
Simple sentences are constructed using communication images.

Phase 5
PECs are used to answer questions.

Phase 6
Interactions with the environment become part of the PEC process when the child answers questions such as "What do you see?" "What do you hear?" and "What is it?"

Verbal Behavior (VB) Therapy

Verbal behavior therapy is an individualized, one-on-one ABA method of teaching language where the meaning of a word is found in its function. VB improves cognitive scores, receptive and expressive language, and problem behavior scores. One of the assessment tools used for this therapy is the Verbal Behavior Milestones Assessment and Placement Program (VB-MAPP).

Signed Speech

Also known as simultaneous communication or total communication, signed speech is the process of speaking aloud at the same time as using sign language. Research reports suggest that teaching sign language along with speech will likely increase language abilities. Behaviors associated with autism, such as depression, aggression, self-injury, anxiety, and tantrums, are thought to be associated with the lack of ability to communicate. It is possible that learning to sign may also increase attention to and understanding of social gestures.

Social Stories

Written from a child's point of view in the first person at the child's vocabulary level, social stories help a child understand typical social scenarios they will encounter, such as visiting a museum or ordering and purchasing a food item in a restaurant. The story is put into booklet, audio, or videotape form for the child to review and learn the preferred behavior.

Complementary and Alternative Medicines

There are many complementary and alternative medical practices from many different regions of the world that have been used to treat ASD. However, very few have shown benefit when subjected to research scrutiny.

Homeopathy

Some studies have shown potential for homeopathic treatment as an alternative therapy for specific autism symptoms. Discuss any alternative therapies with your health-care team before proceeding (do no harm).

Following the principle of "like treats like," or the law of similars, homeopathy works on the premise that illness can be removed by a short-lived exposure to a similar illness of natural or medicinal origin. Once the effects from the first and second exposure have worn off, the body returns to a state of balance, or homeostasis. **Results of studies to date are largely inconclusive.**

> **! CAUTION !**
>
> Some homeopathic remedies from India and China have been found to be contaminated with steroids and arsenic. Exercise caution by consulting an experienced practitioner for help choosing safe remedies.

Acupuncture

Acupuncture has been practiced throughout China for hundreds of years and is now being practiced on a wider scale in many Western countries. Traditional Chinese medicine teaches that almost 400 key points on the body are linked with our organs or viscera by 14 meridians. The philosophy supporting Chinese medicine is that when we are healthy, we live in a state of balance between the two states of yin and yang, mediated by qui.

Some children with ASD seem to have experienced some cognitive and linguistic benefits as a result of acupuncture, but **research studies on this treatment to date have yielded inconsistent results and have not offered conclusive**

evidence for acupuncture as therapy for ASD. Further studies need to be conducted.

Massage

Thai traditional massage (TTM) has been seen to reduce anxiety in children with autism. Studies have shown that after receiving TTM, hyperactivity, inattention passivity, and sleeping patterns were all significantly improved. TTM is a yoga-based therapy that includes mindfulness elements, easy rocking, extended stretching, and measured compression. Described as noninvasive, TTM sessions are thoughtful, slow, considerate, and appropriate for vulnerable children. However, in a review of six articles, **limited evidence of the usefulness of massage therapy in treating autistic symptoms was found.**

Yoga

Specific yoga poses, along with breathing techniques, can reduce stress, build strength, and calm a child or adult. Breathing techniques are effective at any time to relieve stress, agitation, anger, or boredom. Although little research is available for how effective yoga may be for helping children with autism cope with symptoms, yoga is well-known as beneficial to reduce stress, anxiety, and possibly undesirable behaviors in neurotypical children.

! CAUTION !

While acupuncture for ASD has been shown in several trials to be effective for improving some children's cognitive and linguistic abilities, the possible side effects are significant: bleeding, crying from pain, irritability, sleep disturbance, and hyperactivity. Exercise caution.

Q. Is it true that trained dogs can be used in treating children with ASD?

A. Yes. Research suggests that learning how to react appropriately to a dog's social cues may help children with ASD learn how to interpret the social behavior of people. Various reports have also shown the overall relationship with a service dog to be a synergistic way to increase socially based events and improve important social systems — which is more important for a child who has a more severe form of autism, who often faces social discrimination.

For children with autism who are seeking stronger sensory stimulation, dogs may satisfy this need, with their unforgettable smell and mixture of tactile sensory factors — being licked, the sensation of a dog's wet nose as it touches you, the feel of its tail thumping against your leg, and the harder scratch of its nails compared to the soft or wiry fur — along with the doggy collection of strong, clear, sharp sounds that are easily understood (by most) and the graphic and often humorous visual images. Although service dogs show promising results for managing ASD symptoms, individual programs are required so that hypersensitivity is not increased by interactions with the dog.

Scripting

We have all laughed at the young child who parrots private conversations or repeats swear words endlessly, to the horror of her parents. Repetition of words, phrases, or even passages from conversations, films, books, and other sources by children after infancy is known as scripting. Among infants, repeating sounds or whole words is known as echolalia. Both are important for developing language skills.

Scripting among children with ASD is typically seen as socially unacceptable behavior, but this language habit can be used as a tool for language development in children who find it difficult to hold conversations. Scripting may be their form of communication, helping them to start talking when they can't find the right word or calming them when a situation is overwhelming. Your child may not even be aware that she is being vocal. Rather than discourage your child from scripting, encourage her to share her thoughts and feelings in this way, and reward her for limiting scripting in socially inappropriate occasions. So, if your child is scripting, be patient and listen up, she may have an important message for you as she develops her language and social skills by scripting.

Dietary Interventions

Some children with ASD appear to be prone to being deficient in specific nutrients and sensitive to specific food components. Talk to your physician or dietitian about possible solutions to the deficiencies and food sensitivities.

Deficiencies: The diet of some children with ASD is lacking in specific minerals, such as iron (iron deficiency), and specific vitamins, such as vitamin B_{12} (vitamin B_{12} deficiency).

Sensitivities: Some children with ASD may be sensitive to specific foods that are thought to be possibly associated with certain behaviors. Gluten from grains and casein from milk products may possibly trigger gastrointestinal symptoms in some children with ASD.

Exclusions: Anecdotally, some children with ASD have shown improvement in core and peripheral symptoms after changing to a diet that excludes possible food sensitivities. For some children, a gluten-free, casein-free diet is effective for reducing some symptoms — and more often for children with gastrointestinal symptoms. The GFCF diet excludes gluten (from wheat, barley, and rye) and casein (from mammalian dairy foods). This diet has been shown in some studies to improve behavior and enable development for some children, most often those with gastrointestinal issues. For some children, improvements in many symptoms have been seen after 8 weeks, and symptoms of ASD became worse when casein-based foods were reintroduced into the diet (called a challenge). Improvements in seizure activity were seen in a case report of a child on a gluten-free, casein-free ketogenic diet, where carbohydrates are severely restricted and fat intake is increased, but more long-term research is needed for specific diets and their effects on ASD symptoms.

Kinds of Dietary Therapy

Several dietary therapies have been suggested as ASD interventions. For most diets, there is limited evidence for success because many families drop out of such research because they have problems sticking with the diet being tested. Some of the difficulties include problems finding time to plan the diet, finding specific foods, or affording special foods required. Because children who have autism are often picky eaters, limiting their diet and asking this group of children to accept new foods can be challenging.

Specific Carbohydrate Diet

The theory behind the specific carbohydrate diet (SCD) is that undigested or unabsorbed carbohydrates that stay in the intestines may increase the growth of bacteria and yeast, possibly injuring intestinal walls and leading to impaired digestion. The specific carbohydrate diet is intended to reduce the overgrowth of bacteria and yeast in the intestines and to heal any leaky gut symptoms. This diet has been used for children with autism to treat GI symptoms.

Foods included in the specific carbohydrate diet:

- Simple sugars (some vegetables and fruits, honey)
- Vegetables that are not starchy (cauliflower, spinach, peppers, cabbage, onions)
- Soaked beans and lentils
- Nuts and nut flours (walnuts, almonds, Brazil nuts)
- Eggs, homemade yogurt, natural cheese
- Proteins such as unprocessed chicken, turkey, pork, lamb

Grains are excluded from this diet. The cost-benefit ratio associated with the SCD is the increased time and higher cost of some of the foods.

Antioxidant Diet

The theory behind the antioxidant diet is to reduce oxidative stress and inflammation. This diet has been seen to be effective for an overactive or dysfunctioning immune system. Oxidative stress is a result of physiological stress on our bodies, which happens from the additive damage done by free radicals that have not been removed by antioxidants. Free radicals are unusually reactive atoms, either produced in our bodies from natural biological processes or introduced by environmental toxins. Antioxidants inhibit oxidation and protect our bodies from free radicals.

Foods included in the antioxidant diet:

- Fresh vegetables and fruits
- Whole grains
- Cooked legumes and starchy vegetables
- Moderate amounts of lean meats
- Superfoods, such as berries, Brussels sprouts, broccoli, and seaweeds

This is a healthy diet, but there is no evidence of improvement in ASD symptoms with its use.

Research Spotlight

Leaky Gut

Leaky gut syndrome is a theory that increased inflammation in the gut may allow undigested fragments, such as opioid peptides, to cross the intestinal barrier, as well as crossing the blood–brain barrier via the bloodstream and affecting the opiate system and the central nervous system. In some studies, it has been suggested that this hyperpermeability at the intestinal level, and possibly in other bodily membranes, combines with inadequate breakdown of dietary gluten and milk-based proteins to produce ASD symptoms. Leaky gut has been diagnosed in between 25% to 33% of all children with autism who have been tested for it. Some reports show reduced incidences of leaky gut for children with ASD who have been on the GFCF diet. **This is still considered a controversial concept, however. More research is required.**

GFCF Diet

One of the most frequently used interventions for ASD, the gluten-free, casein-free diet is based on the theory that incomplete digestion of some foods may lead to opioid peptides (protein fragments), which could explain some behaviors associated with autism (stereotypical or ritualistic behaviors, excessive activity, speech and language delays, for example). Studies for the GFCF diet have shown some nutritional losses (calcium and vitamin D) for some children on this diet, but recent research indicates that this diet shows more promise than ketogenic and antioxidant diets for some children with autism.

The downsides of the GFCF diet are the inconvenience and the limitations of food choices for the child. Using this diet for children with ASD also carries some risks due to the need for a long-term intervention.

Vitamin D deficiency: Issues with functional levels of important vitamins linked to calcium homeostasis, such as vitamin D, have been identified.

Inflexibility: The introduction of a GFCF diet may upset inflexible children with ASD unless great care is taken to gradually shift to alternative foods.

Support: Everyone involved with the child's dietary changes (family, school, medical support services) must monitor the diet to ensure effectiveness, safety, and compliance. However, preparing food together may increase your child's interest and appetite for something new.

> **! CAUTION !**
>
> Inadequate calcium intake may be a concern following the exclusion of dairy products, but dietary intake is not necessarily negatively affected by removing dairy, especially with the increased availability of other GFCF foods.

Alleged GFCF Diet Benefits for Some Children with Autism

- Improved communication and use of language
- Improved attention and concentration
- Improved social integration and interaction
- Reduced self-injurious behavior, altered pain perception
- Reduced repetitive or stereotyped patterns of behavior
- Improved motor coordination
- Reduced hyperactivity
- Fewer functional bowel problems (diarrhea, constipation, alternating stools); **this is still controversial, and many children on this diet do not have this response.**

Q. My 5-year-old child doesn't have any friends; he is happiest when he is in the corner with his building blocks and books. We are worried for when he is older. What should we do?

A. This is not unusual for children with ASD. Even higher-functioning children with ASD prefer to be alone. If they approach other children, they prefer a single child rather than a group. This appears to be related to the lack of predictability of larger groups of children or the greater ability to maintain control ("run the show") with just one child. The lack of predictability of young children is probably also why they prefer adults or older children. Playing alone is simpler, because they have "full" control of their own activities.

Autistic children like structure and consistency and dislike change and lack of predictability. In puberty, some recognize or feel the need to "hang around" their peers but often lack the pragmatic skills and often fail to pick up on nonverbal cues necessary to be accepted by peers. Social skills can be successfully taught to school-age children with high-functioning ASD ("Asperger syndrome"), but difficulties with empathy and mind-reading persist. Using a "peer-buddy" system in the school setting can provide a mentor as well as protect against bullying.

Chapter 5
Feeding Therapy

CASE STUDY
Mealtime Madness

Every parent has tales to tell about throwing and refusing food, about toy trucks being driven across plates, and dolls being fed what was meant for the family. For most children, this mealtime madness is temporary. For families of children with autism, mealtime struggles may continue, as these excerpts from several case histories indicate:

- "My daughter will only ever eat crunchy food. She gags and vomits if she is forced to eat soft food."
- "My son eats mostly whipped or soft foods, and wipes his hands repeatedly on his clothes and hair, even if nothing is on them. Introducing new foods has to be done very slowly, and you need to be prepared that he may reject something that you thought he had accepted."
- "My son ate few foods other than macaroni and cheese. When I taught him that macaroni were noodles, I was able to convince him to try other noodles by telling him they were like macaroni. Now he has expanded to eating gluten-free spaghetti dishes and some spicy noodle dishes. His interest in trying new food did not happen overnight. Don't give up!"
- "Food etiquette is important for children to be accepted in social situations. Feeding therapy gives children the tools to cope with unfamiliar mealtime situations when food they are unable to eat is served. At camp, putting prepared snacks in your pocket for 'later' or spitting food you cannot eat into a napkin is okay."

Mealtime Challenges

What children with autism eat is no less important to their health and well-being than it is for other growing children, but *how* they eat raises a whole raft of behavioral issues that can develop into serious nutritional problems and family disturbances. More children with autism have gastrointestinal problems than do children without autism, for example, so families of children

> **For all children with ASD, teaching them how to eat appropriately is an important life skill that will ultimately help them realize their own dreams.**

with autism may be faced with severe diet-related issues and associated behavioral problems. One approach to treating these problems is sometimes called feeding therapy, a set of tools used to help children accept new foods, use appropriate eating behavior at the table, and participate in social behavior during meals. For all children with ASD, teaching them how to eat appropriately is an important life skill that will ultimately help them realize their own dreams.

"Feeding therapy has been a huge help to my daughter for learning how to sit properly at the table and use appropriate manners," one parent commented. "She still doesn't eat much, if any, food, but will say please and thank you and will try little bits of new foods, which is all any parent can ask. When she started feeding therapy 3 years ago, she would gag until she threw up if you put food like cut-up meat or eggs in her mouth."

Common Eating Problems

Eating is one of our most sensory-related pleasures, involving sight, smell, sound, taste, and touch. For children with autism, eating can be overwhelming. All children have eating behaviors we would rather not see at home, and especially not in public. Sometimes, when you look at the specific behavior that is troublesome, you may realize that it is a behavior you don't like in yourself. Some of the mealtime behaviors that are most often seen in children with ASD can take a family meal from fun to a challenge in a blink of an eye.

Similarity

A balanced meal can be sidelined by your child's need for sameness in all things: the same color (light brown, beige, or white shades), the same food brand, and even the exact same presentation, with each food served in the same place (usually never touching) on the same plate at the same temperature and at the same time. Meltdowns may be the result if different-colored or -textured food is served on different plates or with different utensils than the ones accepted by your child.

Selectivity

Extreme food selectivity can become a serious concern when your child refuses to eat new foods, foods from one food group, or any food you have prepared at home.

Sensitivity

Children with autism typically have a supersensitive sense of smell, taste, and temperature. Your child is able to perceive any change from what has been accepted before. Even chewing makes changes, so a mouthful of food may be rejected after being chewed.

Possible Solutions

Some unconventional eating behaviors may be the result of an oral motor control problem or other physical condition. Before starting any program for managing your child's eating behavior, consult your physician and arrange for a thorough physical examination.

Support: Discuss any possible solutions to specific behaviors with all members of your child's support team: health-care providers, school and support staff, therapists, friends, and family. When any new therapy, diet-related or otherwise, is taken on, set goals and a trial period, monitor as you continue, evaluate on a regular basis, and, at the end of the trial, assess for success before continuing.

Persistence: Keep offering previously rejected foods. For any child, new foods must be offered a number of times (typically 10 to 12) before they are accepted into the diet, so more time and patience may be required. Serve the new food — during snack time might be easier, or even before dinner — on a small, clean plate when your child is hungriest.

Participation: Including your child in meal planning, grocery shopping, and putting foods away, as well as washing and preparing food for meals, may increase her receptivity. Have her smell fresh fruits and vegetables in the market or grocery store. Serving dishes to others, cleaning up, and scraping dishes clean are all possible ways to participate in the mealtime experience.

> When any new therapy, diet-related or otherwise, is taken on, set goals and a trial period, monitor as you continue, evaluate on a regular basis, and, at the end of the trial, assess for success before continuing.

Pretending to cook, smelling, licking, and tasting foods with appropriate funny faces may make new foods more appealing.

Play: Try turning new foods into playthings; for example, pretend to be a food delivery truck, with your child unloading the food for dinner. Stack cucumber or carrot slices to make buildings. Pretending to feed stuffed toys or farm animals could all make the sight, smell, and feel of foods familiar enough to be added to your child's list of preferred items.

Mix up the medium: Make the smells and texture of soft food (pudding, soft tofu, or yogurt) more familiar by using it as a paint. Potatoes can be used for stamp art, but other fruits and vegetables can be used as well. Consider the kinds of foods that can be glued or shaved to become part of a piece of art to be kept on the fridge and admired (with the rule that it be displayed for a short period only, since any possible destruction may cause a meltdown).

Defer: If you can't track down a cause for mealtime behavior problems right away, the tried-and-true parent response of deferring response to the behavior as long as possible may be the best route — at least for the moment.

Developmental Food Issues

Because of the variable onset of autism, you need to be ready to solve problems in feeding from infancy to adolescence. Some of these problems are unique to the developmental stage, and others carry on into adulthood for some children with ASD. For these children, parents report that there seemed to be more problems feeding their baby than they had expected or what they saw in their nieces and nephews. If you are concerned about how your baby feeds, contact a health-care professional with experience in caring for children with ASD.

Baby and Toddler Food Issues

Oh, the wonderful moments breastfeeding your baby, holding her hand as she feeds, feeling the strong tug as the milk flows from your breast; she gazes into your eyes or watches the fan turn as she's feeding, looking very peaceful and falling asleep after she's finished, little milk bubbles at the corner of her mouth as her lips purse, suckling in her sleep.

Feeding your baby can also be a frustrating experience. We are all concerned that we may not be feeding our babies enough, feeding them too much, forcing the breast too far into their mouth, holding the bottle at the wrong angle, not burping often enough — the list goes on forever.

First Foods

Options for feeding your baby for the first year of life are breast milk or infant formula. Discuss the pros and cons of the different milk alternatives for infant formula with your health-care professional. Choose baby foods without added salt, fat, sugar, or other sweeteners, such as honey, or artificial flavors, colors, or preservatives.

Solids

When adding solid foods to your baby's diet, increase the amounts, textures, and variety of foods and flavors gradually. Begin to add food when your baby can sit up straight with support, has good head control, and can swallow food without sticking out his tongue (extrusion reflex), around 4 months, and definitely by 6 months. Waiting longer than 6 months to introduce some solids may increase the chance that your baby will prefer liquids and decrease your child's acceptance and tolerability of textures. Juice or extra water is not usually necessary for babies less than a year old. Adding solids helps your baby maintain nutrient intake to match growth. Vitamin D, iron, and vitamin C are especially important for this age group. By the time your baby is 1 year old, more food from the table can be added.

Textures

Textures are an important factor when introducing new foods. Babies are individuals when it comes to diet, like the rest of us, but most prefer soft, smooth-textured foods to start and gradually accept foods with a thicker texture.

Food Groups

Food is typically categorized into four food groups. We should eat from all four groups to maintain a balanced diet that sustains life.

- Fruits and vegetables
- Grains and cereals
- Meat and alternatives
- Dairy and alternatives

Fruits and Vegetables Eating Guide for Infants

1. Begin to feed your baby puréed vegetables and fruits sometime between 6 and 7 months.
2. Serve all varieties of fruit.

Baby Food Problems

Problems experienced at 9 to 12 months in the progression from smooth puréed foods to mixed texture (food with soft lumps):

- Many children with ASD struggle to accept food with soft lumps.
- Bite-size finger foods are a problem for some.
- Some children are fussy about food color.
- Many children are fussy about food presentation.

Food refusal behaviors from 6 months on:

- Head turning
- Batting at the spoon
- Throwing food (this can be a normal temporary developmental stage)
- Spitting food out
- Holding food in the mouth
- Screaming
- Leaving the table, refusing to sit
- Gagging, vomiting
- Talking and ignoring food
- Politely refusing

Eating abnormalities at all ages:

- Mechanical eating style
- Shoveling or gulping food into the mouth
- Spitting out
- Vomiting
- Throwing food
- Holding food tucked into a cheek for long periods
- Avoiding specific foods
- Not using utensils

Grains and Cereals Eating Guide for Infants

1. Serve single-grain, iron-fortified baby cereal to start. Rice is often the first grain chosen because it is less likely to cause an allergic reaction.

2. When adding a new food to your baby's diet, wait about 3 days so you are able to identify the food responsible if a reaction occurs.

3. Once your baby has become accustomed to each of the single-grain cereals, mixed cereals can be added.

4. Although feeding single-grain cereal has been the typical way to start feeding, giving puréed meat or poultry first may be better options to provide iron and zinc.

Meat and Dairy Eating Guide for Infants

1. Between 7 and 9 months, begin to add a protein source (red meat, poultry, fish, egg yolks, beans, or tofu) to your baby's diet.

2. Purée the meat, but other protein foods, such as tofu or egg yolks, can be mashed.

Food Hazards

Beware of firm foods at an early age, especially round foods like grapes, which can pose a choking hazard:

- Peanuts
- Popcorn
- Whole grapes (cut them into quarters)
- Edamame
- Raisins
- Sticky foods that might get stuck in the back of the throat, such as peanut butter

Troublesome New Food

Many children with autism are exceptionally hesitant to try new foods. In response, you can try these feeding therapy strategies:

1. Let your baby set the pace of feeding. Feeding too quickly can cause choking or upset stomach; feeding too slowly may cause frustration or loss of interest in eating.
2. Give your child time to pay attention to every spoonful before feeding more.
3. Allow your baby to feel and handle the food and spoon. Exploration is a healthy way of getting accustomed to the texture before eating.
4. Let your baby take over the feeding with finger foods when ready.
5. Let your baby say when dinner is over. Turning away from the spoon or falling asleep are two signs that dinner is over.

- Raw, hard fruits or vegetables (apples, carrots, green beans)
- Hot dog pieces
- Stringy uncut meat
- Big pieces of cheese, meat, or other foods that are hard to chew

Finger Foods

By the time your baby is able to sit in a high chair, pick up food, bring it to his mouth, and chew, you can start giving him soft foods, such as small pieces of fruit. Stay on guard for choking. The transition to finger food, like all other stages of development, is a gradual one, and one that is determined by your baby. At this point, cereal can be given once daily. Finger food choices include:

- Mashed or diced vegetables
- Oat ring cereals, soft bread, or crackers that dissolve easily
- Cooked short pasta (gluten-free)
- Bite-size soft fruit pieces: banana slices, ripe cantaloupe, peaches, or pears
- Small bits of tender meat, fish, tofu, or cooked egg

Solutions to Six Common Infant Feeding Problems

1. **No interest in feeding, even after a long period:** Stroke the face; tickle the feet; wipe the face gently with a cool cloth; take clothing off the baby for skin-to-skin contact with a parent.

2. **No crying when hungry (for infants with failure to thrive or at risk of dehydration):** Set an alarm clock for the typical feeding time; massage baby's body and tummy before feeding.

Be Safe

Safety is rule number one when feeding your baby:

1. Never leave a baby unattended when he is eating in his high chair.
2. Don't let your child crawl or walk with food in her mouth.
3. Examine all meat for bones, especially fish.
4. Cut all foods into small pieces, watching carefully for choking.
5. Avoid foods that might be aspirated into the lungs, such as whole nuts or carrots.
6. Don't give your baby any food that makes you worry.

Q. How many meals should my baby eat?

A. Your baby is likely to let you know when he is hungry and when he is full, usually about every 3 hours. When adding cereal to the diet, begin the meal with the cereal when your baby is most hungry and finish the meal with the breast or bottle. Feedings will likely develop into a regular schedule of two meals, then move on to three, and for some children even four meals per day. As your baby continues to grow, add morning and afternoon snacks to their meal schedule. Establishing a routine for mealtimes will help set up good eating habits and bring your baby into the family routine.

3. **Taking barely enough milk to thrive is a struggle:** When babies don't gain weight, allowing them to take the lead about how much to feed is difficult. Possible solutions are to change the bottle partway through the feed; change the nipple; change the temperature of the fluid, if a bottle is used; change the position if breastfeeding; try taking the baby's sleeper or nightie or clothing off or putting more on; try various ways of increasing stimulation. Other environmental ideas include sitting in a sunny room, opening a window to allow a fresh breeze, playing some upbeat music or animal sounds, singing to your baby, tickling your baby, or going for a walk.

4. **Seeming unsettled or in some discomfort (up to 8% of children under the age of 3 have food intolerances):** If breastfeeding, consider the food that Mom is eating — cruciferous vegetables are a common source of discomfort for a nursing baby. If bottle-feeding, perhaps a change in formula is needed — visit your health-care provider for advice here.

5. **Vomiting or gagging:** Your baby may be taking too much to be able to swallow or may have a problem with his swallowing mechanism. If your baby is breastfed, your nipples may be long or your breast may be over-full. Expressing a little milk beforehand or holding the nipple back with two fingers may help. Discuss this issue with a certified breastfeeding advisor (often a nurse). If your baby is bottle-fed, changing the nipple to another shaped nipple or holding it at another angle may help. Discuss this issue with your nurse or health-care provider.

Toddler to Adolescent Food Issues

At this stage in her eating development, your child with ASD may begin to present unique problems. If your child refuses many types of food as a toddler and beyond, you are not alone. If your child struggles to accept new foods, has troublesome mealtime behavior, or refuses healthy food choices, try reviewing how we typically introduce foods to babies and toddlers. These principles may help you, as a caregiver, help the child increase her appetite and the range of her diet. Keeping track of your child's daily activities before, during, and after meals by writing in a journal or recording comments on a smartphone may help you identify and reduce the causes of the more difficult issues related to food.

Did You Know?

Neural Networking

Remember that your child's behavior is not deliberate but is the result of neural networking in the brain that operates in an unusual way. Address behaviors that affect your child's quality of life (such as not taking pleasure in eating) or that reduce his state of nutrition.

Food Selectivity

Food selectivity, or selective eating, is the most common eating issue reported by parents of children with ASD. Food selection problems range from mild (refuses a few foods, like most developing children) to extreme (eats only two or three foods). Some children with ASD choose one type of food only (french fries or a brand, for example) or focus on a food texture, such as puréed foods. In severe cases of food refusal, malnutrition is a risk and tube feeding may be necessary.

Less Food

An overall problem associated with children with autism is that they eat less food from each food group than do children without autism. These behaviors have various causes:

- Unusual or impaired sensory satisfaction (sensory seeking or sensory avoidance)
- Aversion to oral care and absence of mouth exploration phase in development
- Overly sensitive to sight, smell, taste, and texture of food
- Gastrointestinal disorders, including gastroesophageal reflux
- Restricted range of foods
- Food refusal behavior
- Specific utensil requirements
- Stringent mealtime requirements
- Abnormal eating behaviors (pica or unusual food cravings)

Associated Food Behaviors

Typically, a child with autism at this stage will develop and repeat specific behaviors associated with eating:

- Reflexive sucking: The kind of automatic sucking you see babies doing in their sleep or if you put anything in their mouths.
- Vocal play or echolalia: Playing with sounds and repeating the same sound over and over.
- Oral exploration: Putting new objects and food into the mouth, smelling, licking, and feeling with their mouth.
- Sensory modulation: Interpreting and understanding changes in different sensory experiences.
- Intact constitutional capabilities: Physical, emotional, social, and intellectual development along the typical time frames.

Sensory Food Issues

Your child's sensory systems (taste, smell, sight, sound, feel) react in a different way than a typically developing child and may overwhelm her with physical reactions so that she has little interest in eating.

Health-Related Issues

A few health-related issues have an impact on feeding for children with autism. Be sure to attend to these if they occur:

- Colic
- Gastroesophageal reflux
- Latching problems with breastfeeding
- Allergies to breast milk or cow's milk protein-based formula
- Excessive wind
- Gagging, coughing, or choking while eating
- Oxygen loss (turning blue or purple)
- Liquid or food that comes out of nose
- Repeated respiratory problems, along with pneumonia
- Pica (eating nonfood items)

Sensory-Related Food Aversion

Most children with ASD are averse to trying new foods because of a sensory reaction to the smell, taste, or temperature and refuse anything different from what they prefer. Most children will choose the same food items repeatedly rather than try something new. The pattern of food choice varies from child to child, with a small group that refuses food from all categories. Sensory food aversion behavior may begin with the introduction of a new or different kind of food. From that point on, your child may refuse all new foods. Sensory food aversion may lead to dietary deficiencies. Oral motor or speech delay may also be involved. The child may avoid participation in the social aspect of mealtimes. Typically, no swallowing issues are present — sensory food aversion is not in any way related to GI issues or known food allergies or sensitivities.

Among the reasons given by children for refusing food, the most common include:

- Wrong, not preferred brand
- Preferred brand placed in wrong box
- Different appearance from preferred
- Bread cut into squares when whole bread slices preferred
- Specific food items served in wrong-colored bowls
- Food items touching on the plate
- Wrong food temperature (hot, not warm, for example)

If your child with ASD becomes underweight because of food aversion, it is time to consider how to improve feeding behaviors. Before you consider special diets, or even tube feeding for extreme cases, start with a complete physical checkup with your health-care provider and dentist. Assessing any physical or physiological reason for feeding issues will prevent your child from being put on a special diet for no good reason.

Hypersensitive or Hyposensitive Sensorimotor Behaviors

Hypersensitive Behaviors

Oral tactile	Negative response to specific textures Dislikes feeding tools Dislikes messiness around mouth
Olfactory and gustatory	Prefers bland foods Odors elicit vomiting Extreme sensitivity Gagging Food refusal

Hyposensitive Behaviors

How food and objects feel in the mouth (called oral tactile) Internally produced stimuli (called proprioceptive)	Pocketing in cheeks or somewhere in the mouth Swallowing whole or large pieces of food Chewing for a very long time Choking and/or vomiting Unusual chewing patterns Chewed food does not form a small ball, or bolus
Olfactory and gustatory	Food holding Prefers crunchy and highly flavored foods Disinterested in eating without enhancement of smell

Sensory- and Motor-Related Feeding Behaviors

Gagging

Sensory: Sight, smell, taste of food	Motor: Chewing development is delayed; swallows before food is broken down to smaller pieces; unusual pattern of the chewed food bolus as it moves through the GI tract

Drooling and teeth grinding

Sensory: Reduced oral awareness, open mouth or low muscle tone, disinterest in eating	Motor: Does not chew food; needs increased sensory stimulation to the jaw

Immature feeding behavior

Sensory: Aversion to touch, avoidance of molar surfaces, food texture preferences (soft or smooth), intact ability to initiate the task	Motor: Has motor planning problems but intact ability or potential to consume foods or liquids

(Adapted from Twachtmean-Reilly J, Amaral SC, Zebrowski PP. Addressing feeding disorders in children on the autism spectrum in school-based settings: Physiological and behavioral issues. *Lang Speech Hear Serv*, 2008:39:261-272.)

Food Preferences

"I won't eat that!"

Children with autism are famous for their food preferences. At one extreme, some children have as few as 20 food items in their diet, preferring to eat the same foods several times daily (leading to poor nutrition). Just as some children are averse to specific foods, others have specific food preferences, and many of these preferences may be linked to sensory issues related to brain function. Networks in the brain may be under- or oversensitive.

Preferred food groups typically (but not always) include starchy vegetables, refined carbohydrates, processed meat products, and dairy products. Children with autism have food preferences like any other child for crackers, chicken fingers, or french fries — and each child prefers something different. Some children with autism will refuse all foods besides their preferred foods, ignore their hunger, and go without food altogether rather than eat something else when their preferred food is not available.

The most common food preferences for children with autism include:

- Crunchy or dry texture
- Smooth consistency
- Specific appearance and presentation
- Specific brands and packaging
- Same foods (sameness in everything)
- Specific odor

Most children with autism:

- Refuse to eat eggs
- Refuse most meat alternatives, such as tofu
- Refuse most beans and lentils
- Refuse most dairy products

Some children with autism:

- Refuse to eat unprocessed meat or fish, and a few refuse processed meat
- Refuse to drink less fluid than is optimal for health

Behavioral therapy to widen the variety in their diet teaches children and their parents how to interact to improve mealtime behavior and food choices.

Did You Know?

Smell

Most children smell food before eating it, but children with ASD tend to be more sensitive to smell in general, and in particular to the sounds and smells of cooking. These smells may be a source of joy or the cause of nausea and vomiting. Some children are undersensitive to smells and prefer strong flavors and odors (vinegar, garlic, ginger, lemon, onions).

New Foods

Talk to support group members, health-care professionals, therapists, family, friends, schoolteachers, therapists, and even people in grocery stores about ideas for getting your child to try new foods. Everyone has different ideas that might do the trick. Here are a few to start:

- Start with making a big deal about washing hands so it becomes a habit at an early age. Make up a short silly song about washing hands.

- Make meal planning a family affair. Work with a menu plan worksheet. Use pictures of foods from old cookbooks, magazines, newspapers, or grocery store advertisements to build your meal plan. Assemble a photo binder that has plastic-covered pages that can be moved around easily — or, for high-tech families, take photos of food in grocery stores with a digital camera or

Physiological Reasons for Feeding Issues

Some feeding problems are caused by your child's physiology. Ask your doctor and dentist to examine your child for these disorders. Using smaller utensils, cutting food into smaller bites, and putting less food on a fork are all possible solutions.

- Poor tongue lateralization: Your child is not able to move food around in his mouth with his tongue or is tongue-tied (when the tongue is too closely attached in the mouth, reducing range of movement).

- Delayed chewing skills: Your child is not able to break food down into components before swallowing. This could lead to GI issues, choking, or refusal to eat out of fear of choking.

- Mouth formation (small palate): If the formation of your child's mouth is unusual, such as being small for her age group, she may choke or gag easily and more often than other children.

- Hypersensitive or hyposensitive gag reflex: An indication that your child may have an oversensitive gag reflex is if he gags whenever he brushes his teeth. Smaller bites of food and less food on a fork may help. Rather than brushing his tongue, use a clean damp washcloth to wipe it off.

- Poor endurance or weak muscles: Being impulsive or having weak muscles in the jaw (hyposensitive) may lead to not chewing food enough to break it down properly, which can lead to GI issues for your child. Taking small bites and chewing longer may help. It may also help to give your child a handheld mirror to check for herself that her mouth is empty before taking another forkful.

- Difficulty biting and tearing food: Problems with tooth and jaw alignment might make it difficult for your child to chew.

Did You Know?

Oral Solutions

Children with ASD often have issues with chewing. If your child has sensory issues but can calm them by chewing on ballpoint pens, rather than trying to stop her from chewing, give her oral motor tools designed for use in therapy in early childhood or for children with autism. Choices include teething toys, pencil toppers, jewelry, chewy tubes, alphabets, and more. Some have various smells: grape, lemon, or chocolate. Save favorites for difficult situations to help calm your child or as a reward for trying a new food. A speech pathologist may be able to help.

smartphone and add to a tablet for easy access (for verbal and nonverbal children). Planning meals once a week will help you manage your busy schedule and save money by purchasing only what you will need based on your plan.

- Plan a garden with your whole family. Use pictures of the foods to draw a map of the garden so everyone understands what is growing where. Let each family member choose a food to grow, to plant, and to care for (as much as possible). Small indoor window herb and leafy green gardens are great too.

- Become food poets. Make up names for foods so they become more personal. Eat Right Ontario suggests naming food after body parts: tell your child their hair is noodles or their brains are walnuts, so you'd like some hair with brains sprinkled on top for lunch, please! Obviously, for older kids, this may not be advisable!

- Put your kids to work in the kitchen. Plunk your little one into a high chair or bring your child's wheelchair into the kitchen and get him involved in helping prepare meals (to his level of development). Older children are able to help with salads, add premeasured ingredients to bowls, mix sauces and batters, help wash dishes — whatever you're comfortable with. Working together in the kitchen is a great time to talk about food. If your child is nonverbal, pay close attention to expressions and body language. Having helpers may actually add time to meal preparation, however, so start early.

- Babies like to help after watching as you wipe down kitchen and dining areas and wash foods before serving. Give them fruits and vegetables to wash — they will likely put them in their mouths (stay safe: stay close by and attentive).

Common Sensory Likes or Dislikes at Mealtime

These likes and dislikes are related to mealtimes for children with autism. There is nothing wrong with many of these preferences, even though some may be inconvenient:

- Dirty or sticky hands and face (finger foods) — more likely in boys than in girls
- Giving or receiving hugs
- Being touched — more likely in boys than in girls
- Wearing wet or smelly clothes
- Feel of metal or plastic utensils

Proprioception

Proprioception is a big word that describes our built-in ability to sense the position, location, movements, and orientation in space of our bodies as we move. If your child has issues with proprioception, take baby steps to develop his sense of where he is in the world, and as you do so you will build new connections in the brain. Your child may also have issues with being touched.

1. Talk to your child about specific actions, and what it feels like during these activities.
2. For tactile proprioception, help your child become more comfortable with being touched if that is something he struggles with.
3. Tell your child exactly what you are going to do, be positive, and complete your activity as quickly as possible.
4. Use a firm touch when wiping your child's face and hands and during bathtime.
5. Let your child watch while you brush your teeth and tell her exactly what you are doing and why before taking care of hers or helping her do it herself.
6. Increase positive touch in songs, clapping games, and other activities.

- Pretend your home is the family's favorite restaurant and have your child take on different roles: chef, waiter, or patron. Depending on development level, she will learn to set the table, describe new dishes, serve, order, and use table manners through play.

- Playing with your food can be a good thing. Have your child help by putting food on plates in more creative ways. Draw on egg shells, use fancy cutting knives to make vegetable and fruit shapes, or use toothpicks to attach small bites of fruit and vegetables and vegan cheese to a pineapple, squash, or pumpkin for an edible centerpiece. Watch out for the toothpicks, though; make a big deal about collecting them. Treat them like they are money and be sure to keep toothpicks away from babies and some older children, depending on their developmental level.

New Utensils

Many children show a preference for specific mealtime utensils and cutlery:

- Some children will only drink or eat from a specific cup, spoon, or plate.
- Most children prefer a spouted cup, a straw, or a water bottle rather than a cup.

- Most children choose specific cutlery from the kitchen and check cleanliness or smell before using.
- Some children prefer not to use cutlery and eat with their hands.
- Some prefer plastic rather than metal utensils.

Food Preparation

Choosing, cleaning, preparing, and cooking food can provide a gradual introduction to new foods. Helping to prepare and cook foods — for example, pulling the outer leaves off the

---

Solutions to Four Common Sensory-Related Eating Problems

Most of us have some sensory-related issues, whether it be washing our hands often out of concern about germs or eating foods on our plate in a specific order. And we are all guilty of teasing our loved ones for such nitpickiness. Some of the quirks that are considered sensory issues are also what make each of us special. No sensory issue needs to be considered for therapy unless it in some way interferes with your child's quality of life or health.

Problem: Your child swallows whole pieces of food without chewing.
Solution: Change food texture to chopped, and after improvement has been seen over time, offer food cut in smaller pieces rather than chopped.

Problem: Your child pockets food or holds food in her mouth.
Solution: Change how the food feels in your child's mouth. Try a different temperature — cold might be preferred — or a different way of presentation. If food is puréed, try chopped.

Problem: Your child loses interest in the food held in her mouth.
Solution: Change your pace of feeding or change the size of bites (smaller bits) to suit your child's ability to chew and swallow. Recognize when her interest in feeding has faded and help her with visual and verbal cues to say when she has had enough of that food.

Problem: Your child refuses to accept diet or food changes.
Solution: Take baby steps in changing food and diet. Make gradual and subtle changes to food choices. For example, when switching from a dairy to a non-dairy product, add the new product to the dairy product in small increments for several days, reducing the dairy gradually until there is none. Offer very small bites of the new food, asking that it be smelled, touched to the lips (kissed), licked, held in the mouth on the spoon or fork, chewed, and swallowed. Each step might take days to be accepted. Be patient but persistent in continuing to offer the new food.

---

broccoli so you can see the "trees" better — may increase the interest in the final product. Finally, assisting in the kitchen may help your child learn to identify new smells as the lead-up to preferred flavors.

Environmental Food Issues

The setting, or environment, for eating is as important as the food itself when encouraging your child with autism to eat well. Everything from the curtains to the cutlery plays a role.

Hypersensitive

If your child is hypersensitive, provide calm surroundings to reduce the upset caused by his meal experience:

- Use cloth pull-down blinds rather than metal or wooden ones that make noise.
- Install curtains to reduce the amount of light coming into the room where he eats.
- Use wood or plastic racks for dishes and pots to reduce rattling and banging.
- If smells are an issue, open windows or doors to let fresh air into the areas where food is prepared and meals are eaten. If possible, eat in a room other than where food is prepared.
- For nonverbal children, if possible, use a picture system (a binder, computer, or tablet) to involve them in choosing foods. You might try posting magnets of favorites on the fridge, including the children in meal preparation, and getting them to express themselves in their own way about likes and dislikes.
- Tablets and smartphones have apps that help nonverbal children and verbal children with communication issues, make themselves understood, and assist in decision making through games.
- Help your child (of any age) learn to use acceptable self-stimulation for staying calm and reducing feelings of being overwhelmed.
- Help a child who easily gags and vomits by talking about what brings on the feelings, but be sure to have her checked for mechanical issues (swallowing issues, cleft palate or other issues).

Hyposensitive

If your child is hyposensitive, provide an eating environment that is bright, with more food-related stimulation to increase his sensory experience and interest in eating:

- Sing songs or play word games about food during meals to keep your child engaged in eating.
- Provide a weighted toy or a blanket for your child's lap while she is in the high chair during meals.
- Offer a favorite book about cooking and eating meals, with big pictures of colorful food.

Eating Problems Caused by Environmental Issues:

- Will eat only while sitting in a specific chair
- Will eat only when a specific person is present
- Will not sit in a chair during mealtimes
- Will eat only if a set routine is followed (fixed mealtimes)
- Acts disgusted or feels the need to vomit when hearing other people chew
- Prefers mealtime distractions: reading books, listening to music, or watching specific television programs

Solutions for Environmental Feeding Issues:

- Distraction: If your child is not so interested in eating or is hypersensitive to aspects of his surroundings, such as light, sound, and colors, try changing your eating environment.
- Keep serving items like plates and serving dishes out of your child's reach — but keep extras on hand.
- Turn off noisy fans. If necessary, use comfortable earplugs that fit your child to reduce sound, but not so much that she can't hear you praise her.
- Stay close by your child when you are working to expand his diet.
- Sit at the level of your child's head so you see what she sees.
- Remove any distracting visuals.
- Think about his chair. Is it covered in a fabric that irritates him? Plastic may stick to him, as it gets hot or cold; textured fabric may be irritating; metal may be cold to the touch and make noise if something hits it. Try different solutions until you find the best chair for your child.

Dining Areas

For most families, the kitchen table or dining room is where the action is, where everyone comes home to, where everyone gets a chance to talk about their day, and where some of life's greatest moments play out.

Choosing your furniture and decorating your dining area may increase or decrease your child's autism symptoms. If your child uses a wheelchair, arrange the room for easy access to the table and the kitchen. Pay close attention to how your child behaves in your dining area. Does she cover her ears? Does he hide under the table? Does she bring toys or a tablet or a device to listen to music with? Your child's behavior in the dining space during meals will tell you if he needs less or more stimulation in that space so everyone can enjoy meals as a family.

> **Your child's behavior in the dining space during meals will tell you if he needs less or more stimulation in that space so everyone can enjoy meals as a family.**

Mealtime Location

Some children with ASD are very specific about the location of mealtimes, preferring to eat alone or with one main caregiver present. They tend to dislike eating with other people or in a public place. Maybe you could have one date night with your child every week where it is just the two of you. One-on-one is a great opportunity to introduce new foods.

Practical Food Preparation Tips

Spend some time each weekend washing, cutting, and cooking food for the week ahead. This will give you cut-up veggies, prepared protein sources, and washed fruit that you can eat right from the refrigerator. This session can also include some home-baked goodies for lunchboxes and some complete meals that just need to be reheated at serving time.

1. Have healthy snacks ready to go for the moment your child either wakes up hungry from a nap or arrives at the door after school, ready to clean out the fridge.

2. Take advantage of this time for your picky eaters. They may be more willing to kiss, lick, and taste new foods, especially if they are presented with fun and games.

Have your kitchen helpers make up new names (especially silly ones) for snacks. Keep a list on the fridge so they can ask for new snacks by name or point to them, and maybe add stars or other stickers for favorites.

Food Fun

Mealtime behavior can be a challenge, but it can also be fun if you are prepared to use your imagination and plan ahead.

Smart Smoothie

This is a great way to combine vegetables and fruit into a tasty snack. Let your child choose ingredients or make a smoothie as a surprise. Add frozen fruits (grapes, bananas, mango, mixed berries, cranberries), raw or slightly steamed greens (depending on your child's ability to digest raw), tofu, pudding, a milk alternative, or water. If sweetness is needed, add a little applesauce, honey, or maple syrup. Use your imagination to come up with new smoothie combinations or have a brainstorming session with plastic fruit and vegetables, sign language, or a picture system if your child is nonverbal. Oatmeal or other whole grains can be added in small amounts, and nuts that are well ground can be added too. If you give your child probiotics, smoothies are a good way to deliver them.

Fresh-Cut and Steamed Vegetables

Use fancy knives to cut carrots, radishes, snow or sugar snap peas, celery, peppers, cucumbers, and cherry tomatoes (cut in half or quarters for younger children) to eat plain or with a dip, dressing, or sauce. Serve steamed vegetables with a sauce or just a bit of lemon juice, a teaspoon (5 mL) of peanuts, toasted pine nuts, or broken-up tortilla chips on top for crunch. Make celery sticks ahead with natural smooth or crunchy peanut butter, almond butter, or any other butter; add raisins or other dried fruits if your child likes them. Have your kitchen helpers make up new names (especially silly ones) for snacks. Keep a list on the fridge so they can ask for new snacks by name or point to them, and maybe add stars or other stickers for favorites.

Fruit Salad

Keep on hand fresh pears, apples, grapes, strawberries, oranges, or watermelon, as well as dried fruit: raisins, apricots, apple slices, papaya, or berries. Add a bit of juice to moisten your salad and let your imagination go jungle wild. For special treats, add a few mini marshmallows or chocolate chips or a handful of well-chopped nuts. Let your kitchen helpers make up a new fruit salad (keep the portions small in case it is rejected) by choosing four items. Help with the cutting or give them safe kitchen tools. Cut open some dried figs and dates and let your little people make them into wrappers for other foods.

Trail Mix

Add mixed nuts, dried fruit, dark chocolate chips, small sesame crackers, and dried peas or other vegetables. Keep an eye out for different ideas. Stay away from artificial flavors and colors; choose flavors and textures that are distinctive. Adding one new taste at a time to a known trail mix may increase food choices. Present the same mix many times, even if the new addition is rejected (provide a small bowl, just in case). For safety, keep an eye on your child while eating nuts. Sitting at a table with her is best. This snack also presents a great opportunity to talk about shapes and numbers.

Egg Faces

How do you like your eggs? Use eggs as an instant snack or quick meal, scrambled, boiled, poached, fried, baked, or as an omelet with favorite ingredients. Draw happy faces or secret messages on boiled eggshells.

Instant Salad

Wash your greens when you get home from getting groceries (or when you get a chance), dry them, and keep them in a bag with holes cut in it to let them breathe in your crisper. Either make your salad ahead or have your kitchen helpers build a quick salad from their choice of vegetables. Add gluten-free croutons for crunch, cut-up meat or some other form of protein, such as nuts, and a favorite dressing or dip. A choice of two dips may persuade picky eaters to try something new.

Dips, Hummus, and Guacamole

Change up your hummus recipe with different bean and vegetable combos for a variety of colors and textures. Serve in small bowls for "experiments." Set out with your child's favorite gluten-free crackers, tortilla chips, or mixed vegetable sticks or cucumber slices. Have a contest to see which dip tastes the best (or the worst). See who can make the wildest face while trying a new dip (sticking their tongue WAY out to "taste" new flavors). Offer favorite hummus, salsa, and guacamole recipes with very small amounts of new flavors added for picky eaters.

Did You Know?

Instant Pizza
Keep gluten-free corn tortilla shells on hand to load up with toppings and slip under a broiler. Use leftover chicken, cut-up dried sausage, and whatever else strikes your child's fancy.

Chunky Applesauce

Chop up an apple, or cook it whole in your microwave or oven. Use your imagination. Add dried fruit with a bit of maple syrup or vanilla extract for flavor, a teaspoon (5 mL) of peanut butter, or a tablespoon (15 mL) of oats with maple syrup for a quick apple crisp.

Popcorn

Air- or stovetop-popped is a healthier choice than microwaved. Add different flavors to experiment: sweet, dill, salty, or savory. Use coconut oil or olive oil instead of butter — try different options to find new (healthier) favorites.

Leftovers

Chili and spaghetti make great fast snacks after school. Gluten-free toast with spaghetti sauce and 1 meatball, heated up in the microwave or in the oven, is a change from the ordinary, but any preferred healthy leftovers make good snacks.

Pancakes and Waffles

Freeze leftover homemade pancakes or waffles for a quick snack or meal. Add cut-up fruit, honey, maple syrup, sauces, or steamed vegetables for a different taste.

Research Spotlight

Diet Research on Children with ASD

Smaller subject group sizes, families dropping out of studies, and difficulties keeping the children with autism on the GFCF diet have been issues in four published randomized controlled clinical trials of this diet. The nature of diet issues for some children with autism will also have a negative impact on a typical study. Each child exhibits her own set of autism-related symptoms, so finding a group that has similar symptoms will be difficult. For the children who are inflexible (an autism-related trait), changing to a new diet will take time and patience, so more time may be required for a study to be successful in illustrating any success. In addition, the parents of children enrolled in studies may find that adding one more responsibility to their already packed schedule might be more than they can handle.

As a result, it is recommended that you discuss any diet changes with your health-care team and with a registered dietitian before adopting any new regimen, and monitor your child's nutrient levels on a regular basis.

DocTalk:
Eating Challenges

Q. My 3-and-a-half-year-old child won't eat. No matter what we try, she clamps her mouth shut and refuses to eat. What should we do?

A. Eating problems are very common in children and in adolescents with ASD. Many are described as "picky" eaters, with "highly selective" diets. This has been attributed to "sensory" issues, ranging from food texture selectivity to fixations on plain-colored foods, such as pasta. Some like sweet or spicy foods, and others are bothered by certain food odors. About 50% have bowel-related issues (constipation, gastroesophageal reflux, and chronic diarrhea or bloating/gassiness), all of which can further impact eating habits.

Consider an assessment by a dietician who understands autistic children, a pediatrician, or gastroenterologist to look at bowel-related issues, and an occupational therapist to look at sensory issues. Be careful about following diets on your own without professional guidance because certain nutritional deficiencies can ensue. Also certain underlying gut-related conditions, such as celiac disorder, can be missed. An organized approach to treatment, offering small quantities of a variety of foods and looking for reaction and acceptance/refusal can be informative.

In addition to the advice given here, you may want to visit a registered dietitian or nutritionist for more information about feeding therapy for your child with ASD and for your family at the table. Dietitians and nutritionists can be valuable members of your child's health-care team and an important source of support for you. They are trained to discuss:

- Balanced diets
- Varied diets
- Exclusion diets for ASD
- General dietary assessment
- Constipation and other gut-related issues
- Refusal or difficulty accepting new foods
- Underweight
- Overweight
- Unacceptable behavior during mealtimes
- Iron deficiency anemia
- Dietary supplementation

Registered dietitians are health-care professionals trained to provide evidence-based advice about diet, food, and nutrition. An RD career may be in health care, industry, government, and/or education, where they influence policy development, direct nutrition programs, manage quality food services, and conduct nutrition research. RDs must be registered with the regulatory body in the province or state where they practice and abide by the established guidelines.

A nutritionist is a professional trained in the science of nutrition, whose principal role is to educate groups and individuals about the benefits and health effects of optimal nutrition. Nutritionists also work directly with clients to identify and support solutions for nutritional causes of disease, and design personalized diet and lifestyle programs that optimize health.

Part 3:

Dietary Therapy

Chapter 6

The Gluten-Free, Casein-Free Diet Program

- -

CASE STUDY (continued from page 91)

Biting Behavior

One of the biggest issues with Adela was that she bit other people, even her mother, without warning. One time she bit her mother on the wrist and wouldn't let go. Her mother explained, "Her eyes were glazed over and nothing I did could get her to stop. The pain was terrible. My mother finally reached over and just pinched Adela's nose — it worked and didn't hurt Adela. The skin was broken on my arm, and it was painful for about a week. I guess that was foreshadowing what was to come."

When Adela did start school, her aggressive behavior toward other children was a constant issue. Her parents tried several different kinds of therapy to curb her biting behavior with little luck until they got help in using behavioral shaping — a program that has proven effective for intractable behaviors — to reward her for not biting. *(continued on page 161)*

Exclusionary Diets

Special diets that avoid, limit or exclude specific foods have been studied for children with ASD with varying and inconsistent degrees of success. Of these diet types, the gluten-free, casein-free (GFCF) diet may hold the most promise for some children with ASD, especially those with GI symptoms.

Did You Know?

GI Relief

More than half of all children with ASD have gastrointestinal conditions, including enterocolitis, esophagitis, gastritis, and all forms of inflammatory bowel disease (IBD). Dietary therapies are sometimes used to treat these conditions. Always discuss any dietary therapy or supplements with your family physician and a registered dietitian. Health-care professionals may not recommend these therapies, but they will, in most cases, support parents who want to try dietary therapy.

Nutritional Deficiencies

Before starting your child on an exclusionary diet, such as the GFCF diet, discuss this therapy with your doctor and dietitian, especially if your child has another medical condition, such as epilepsy. At the same time, your dietitian will check for any nutrient deficiencies and recommend supplements when a child's diet is found deficient. Omega-3 essential fatty acids (EFAs) and a full range of multivitamins are sometimes added to the diet. For some children, the addition of vitamin supplements, minerals, and EFAs has shown improvement in core and other ASD symptoms.

In one study, children on a GFCF diet were seen to be deficient in more than one essential amino acid. These nutrient-level reports suggest that some children with autism should be assessed for all vitamins and nutrients as part of any diagnosis and follow-up, with the expectation that some children may need to supplement their diet, especially in the case of selective eaters. Cognitive behavioral therapy can help increase food variability and improve mealtime behaviors.

GFCF Diet Principles

Simply put, the GFCF diet excludes foods with gluten and casein. The theory behind the GFCF diet is that food-based peptide fragments cross the intestinal barrier and are carried to the brain, where these molecules are able to cross the cell wall barrier between the bloodstream and the brain. The presence of the proteins and peptides in the brain is thought to affect the nervous system and creates a chronic effect throughout the body instead of a single effect, such as a headache or upset stomach. Research support of this model shows immune system production of antibodies to peptides, such as those from casein and glutenin and gliadin (both of the latter are gluten-related).

The GFCF diet model is based on investigations of conditions that have been linked to autism, and Dr. Leo Kanner, the first medical scientist to define autism, included GI problems and diet-related issues as symptoms for some children. Dr. Hans Asperger, who defined Asperger's syndrome, suggested a relationship between celiac disorder and autism. No universal link was ever established, but some children with autism show symptoms of celiac disease. Since the theory behind the GFCF diet is still controversial, more research is required. The GFCF diet is not included in current guidelines for ASD management.

> Dr. Leo Kanner, the first medical scientist to define autism, included GI problems and diet-related issues as symptoms for some children.

Immunity, Inflammation, and Antibodies

Our immune system is a network of cells, tissues, and organs that protect our bodies from infections that can be caused by foreign invaders (called antigens). Leukocytes are white blood cells that monitor for antigens as they move through the lymph and blood systems. Produced in the thymus, bone marrow, and spleen, leukocytes are stored in lymph nodes throughout the body. Several forms of white blood cells seek out and destroy invading antigens, or remember and recognize antigens from earlier encounters. Antibodies are produced to lock onto specific antigens so our bodies are protected from future attacks.

Inflammation is a short-term, rapid response by our immune system to infection from an antigen or injury or to a toxin. Histamine released from mast cells, where it is stored, sends messages to nearby blood vessels, causing dilation and reducing blood pressure to allow increased blood flow to the site. Dilation also increases the permeability of the blood vessels, permitting plasma and immune cells into the tissue area at the site. Inflammation symptoms may include pain, swelling, redness, heat, and, rarely, loss of function for the site.

Inflammation sometimes becomes chronic if the immune system misidentifies body cells or tissues as foreign invaders.

Food Sensitivity

Three types of antibodies are typically linked to food sensitivity: IgE, IgA, and IgG. Ig is the abbreviation for immunoglobulin, a protein made in our bodies to protect against foreign invaders (pathogens). Each Ig protein is specific for the pathogen it identifies. For example, celiac disease is confirmed or ruled out by a test called the tissue transglutaminase IgA/IgG test, where the antibodies would be produced when the enzyme tissue transglutaminase (tTG) is present in the intestines, but only when the person being tested has gluten included in their diet. Measuring IgA in the bloodstream is a better test because IgA is produced in the intestine.

Food Sensitivity Tests

Because GI symptoms usually occur after eating, it is not surprising that food is often blamed. True food allergies are rare and are unlikely to cause GI symptoms. They could, however, be caused by a food intolerance. There are many tests available commercially that claim they can diagnose food intolerance — for example, an IgG blood test, kinesiology, electrodermal (Vega) testing, and hair analysis. At this time, there is no convincing evidence to support any of these tests. The most reliable way to identify problem foods is by eliminating foods for a couple of weeks and reintroducing particular foods as a challenge to see if a reaction occurs.

Gluten-Free

"Gluten intolerance" and "gluten sensitivity" are two terms used to describe a condition where people experience a variety of symptoms when they eat foods containing gluten and the symptoms go away when they follow a gluten-free diet. Gluten is a large protein found in the endosperm of wheat, rye, and barley. Foods with gluten are widely used in baking because gluten is an effective binding agent.

Gluten Sensitivity

Symptoms of gluten sensitivity may be similar to those of celiac disease, but are usually not as severe. Research suggests that gluten sensitivity is caused when the presence of gluten triggers the immune system, but not by the same pathways as for celiac disease (which is more complex). More research is needed to fully understand both conditions.

Possible Gluten Sensitivity Symptoms

- Weight loss
- Joint pain
- Bloating
- Frequent gas
- Abdominal pain
- Nausea
- Constipation
- Diarrhea
- Headache
- Fatigue
- Heartburn
- Rash
- Tingling of hands and feet

Testing for Gluten Sensitivity

Because gluten sensitivity does not involve the immune system in the same way as an allergy, IgE and tissue transglutaminase (TTG) antibody testing will not identify the condition. Gluten sensitivity is considered a systemic autoimmune disease, and it is often genetic. If a biopsy of the small intestine is done, as in celiac disease, no damage to the small intestine will be found.

If you suspect your child may be sensitive to gluten, keep a meal-by-meal journal of what your child with ASD has eaten. Use the food journal to record all food eaten for a week and any symptoms of ill health. This will help your child's physician make a diagnosis.

Food Elimination

If your child's doctor chooses to try food elimination, you will be asked to continue with your food journal. To test for gluten sensitivity, you will write down all foods eaten and track all possible symptoms. You will then exclude gluten from your child's diet for several weeks while continuing to monitor and record symptoms. This will be followed by a food challenge where gluten is included in the diet for 3 months once again to see if symptoms change. A reduction or complete loss of symptoms indicates gluten sensitivity, especially if symptoms return after the gluten challenge.

> ## Profile: Harry
>
> Harry is 19 and has ASD. His sister, Gemma, posted on Facebook recently about her non-verbal brother's success story: "Yesterday, when I got home from school, I said 'Hi' to Harry, and for the first time in my life, I heard 'Hi' back! In the almost 17 years of my life, I've never been more proud or happy to hear someone's voice. Love you, buddy!"

Blood Test or Biopsy

Tests to rule out celiac disease start with blood tests for raised levels of specific antibodies in the bloodstream that would suggest that the immune system is reacting to gluten. If there is a positive reading for antibodies, an endoscope and biopsy is typically carried out, where the doctor looks at the inside of the small intestine through a scope, and a very small piece of tissue from the small intestine is removed and assessed for damage to the intestinal wall. If any damage is found, your child will be diagnosed with celiac disease and put on a strict gluten-free diet to prevent further damage to the intestine. If the blood test is negative, or if no damage is found in the intestine, celiac disease is ruled out, but gluten sensitivity may still be a possibility.

Single Treatment

The treatment is the same for celiac disease and gluten sensitivity — exclusion of all foods containing gluten. The terms used to describe these two different conditions that have similar symptoms and treatments are "IgE-mediated" or "non-IgE-mediated" immune mechanisms, meaning that the condition is based on an allergic reaction (IgE-mediated) or not (non-IgE-mediated).

Did You Know?

Food Rotation

For successful food rotation, test particular foods for exclusion from the diet. Exclude the food — gluten, for example, for 1 month — and continue to track foods and autism-related symptoms. After 1 month has passed, allow your child to include foods with gluten once weekly for 2 weeks. Your journal notes should also show if your child has any reactions to red food dye or other possible or known food sensitivities on days after eating food that contains gluten, in case a reaction to the red food dye is mistaken as a reaction to a food containing gluten. Food rotation takes a lot of planning and should be discussed with a dietitian to be sure that your child's diet continues to meet his nutritional needs.

Casein-Free

Casein is the main protein (80%) in all mammalian milk, but it is also found in other foods that have dairy or lactose as ingredients. If your child is on a casein-free diet, be sure to read food labels carefully. The food may contain casein even if it is lactose- or dairy-free. Many soy and imitation dairy products include casein as an ingredient.

Testing for Casein Sensitivity

Similar to gluten testing, blood tests for levels of antibodies against casein may be IgE or IgG positive or not, even if there is inflammation in the small intestine. In simple terms, testing may or may not reveal a response to eating casein, even when symptoms are present in the small intestine. Common gene mutations that are either inherited or environmentally caused may be factors in the response to these two proteins.

Following a GFCF diet: What foods are safe to eat? What foods should we avoid?

Safe Foods to Include	Foods to Avoid
Beans, seeds, nuts (unprocessed) Fresh eggs Fresh meats, fish, and poultry Vegetables, fruits Most dairy products (not for casein-free diet) Some grains: amaranth, arrowroot, buckwheat, corn and cornmeal, flax, gluten-free flours (rice, soy, corn, potato, bean), hominy (corn), millet, quinoa, rice, sorghum, soy, tapioca, teff	Barley (malt, malt flavoring, malt vinegar) and any other barley products Rye and rye products Triticale (wheat/rye mix) Wheat (white, whole wheat, wheat germ, wheat bran, bromated, enriched, phosphate, plain, self-rising) and any other wheat products Bulgar Farina, durum flour, graham flour, Kamut, semolina, spelt Oats, if grown, harvested, or processed together with wheat (look for gluten-free)
Look for a gluten-free label: Beer, breads, cakes, pies, pastries, muffins, candies, cereals, cookies, crackers, croutons, flour tortillas, couscous, french fries, gravies, imitation meat/seafood, matzo, pastas, processed luncheon meats, salad dressings, sauces (including soy sauce), seasoned rice dishes, seasoned snack foods (potato/tortilla chips), self-basting poultry, soups and soup bases, prepared vegetables in sauces, oats, dates, cooking sprays, flavored coffee or teas, coffee substitutes, baking powder, specialty mustards or curry pastes, cake icing or frosting, food additives, modified food starch, medications, vitamins with binding agents that include gluten, play dough	

(Gluten-related food lists adapted from Eat Right Ontario, www.eatrightontario.ca; Canadian Celiac Association, www.celiac.ca; American Diabetes Association, www.diabetes.org)

Safe Foods to Substitute	Foods to Avoid
For children >1 year: Soy drink (> 120 mg calcium/100 mL) Rice drink (>120 mg calcium/100 mL) Soy yogurt, soy cheese, soy sour cream, soy ice cream, sorbet, milk-free gelato, milk-free margarine (please check all labels for milk products) Milk-free chocolate; rice, soy, or potato-based milk; pareve creams and creamers (Kosher pareve foods are casein-free); coconut butter or milk	Milk, cheese, yogurt, yogurt products and drinks, butter, buttermilk, casein and caseinates, casein hydrolysate, cheese powder, condensed milk, cottage cheese, cream, light cream (5%), half-and-half (10%), table cream (18%), whipping or heavy cream (35%), curds, custard, dairy solids, hydrolysates (casein, milk protein, whey), evaporated milk, ghee, butter oil, butter fat, goat's and sheep's milk, ice cream, ice milk, infant formula (cow's milk–based), lactose, lactolose, lactalbumin, lactalbumin phosphate, lactoglobulin, low-fat milk, malted milk, milk derivative, powdered milk, milk protein, milk solids, nonfat dairy solids, nonfat milk solids, nougat, puddings, creamed soups and vegetables, probiotic drinks, skim milk, skim milk solids, sour cream, sour cream solids, sour milk, sour milk solids, whey (sweet, delactosed, protein concentrate)
	Foods likely to contain casein: Non-dairy coffee whiteners and creams, Naturlose (a sugar replacement made from whey), Tagalose (a sugar replacement made from whey), infant rusks, biscuits, breads, cakes, pastry, instant breakfast beverages and bars, nutritional bars, breakfast cereals (chocolate rice cereals and muesli), canned spaghetti, caramel or butterscotch desserts, nougats, custard, puddings, rennet casein, chocolate, confectionery, marshmallows, boiled sweets, drinking chocolate, gravy, instant mashed potatoes, malted milk powder, artificial butter, margarine, milk ice blocks, pasta sauces, processed meat (hot dogs, pies, ham sausage, pâté), salad dressings, snack foods, soups, frozen desserts, toppings, tuna fish, dairy-free cheese, cosmetics, medicines/pharmaceuticals, magnesium caseinate, sodium lactylate (may or may not contain casein), lactic acid, artificial flavorings, caramel coloring, semisweet chocolate, sports drinks, infant foods, pasta, Bavarian cream flavoring, natural chocolate flavoring, coconut cream flavoring, brown sugar flavoring A note about lactic acid: When reading ingredients, check the food source for lactic acid; it is found in sour milk, but also produced from cornstarch, potatoes, molasses, and whey.

(Casein-related food lists adapted from The Children's Hospital, Westmead, Australia, www.chw.edu.au/; Casein Products, 2013; http://nzic.org.nz)

Q. How do I know if a GFCF diet is helping my child?

A. For families of children with autism who have tried a GFCF diet, many have reported that some autism-related behavior improves when their child follows the diet.

Your child's health, diet, and symptom journal is the best tool you might have in your parental toolbox when deciding whether or not to continue with a special diet like the GFCF diet or any other therapy aimed at improving autism-related symptoms that affect your child's quality of life and health.

You can test the general health of your child by pinching the skin on the back of her hand (not to hurt but to assess the elasticity of the skin) to tell if she is dehydrated or by checking her daily bowel movements and comparing them to the Bristol Stool Chart (see box, below) for changes while on the diet. If your child is nonverbal, look for particular signals of ill health. Lay your hand on his belly to feel or listen for gut sounds or disturbances that might indicate some GI issues. Recording any changes will help you and your health-care team make the best decisions for your child.

Remember, gluten is found in wheat, barley, and rye, among other sources, and casein is found in all dairy products, plus more.

Did You Know?

The Bristol Stool Chart

The Bristol Stool Chart groups stools into seven categories to assess the effect of dietary therapies by checking stool consistency before and after treatment. Ask your health-care provider for a copy of the chart.

GFCF Diet Risks and Benefits

The GFCF diet is not a cure-all and can pose some risks, which, fortunately, can be mitigated by nutrient supplementation.

Nutritional Deficiencies

Nutritional deficiencies are a worry for all families with children with ASD, but calcium levels for children on the GFCF diet are of special concern. Research is showing that with appropriate education and support, dietary intake is not affected by the GFCF diet. Children who are following a GFCF diet are more likely to be taking nutritional supplements, and this is even more likely for those children who have GI issues.

Interactions

Because supplements may interact with each other or with medications, it is very important that your child's health-care team be aware of every nutritional supplement your child takes. Keeping track of which supplements, how much and when they are taken, along with your record of autism-related symptoms, in your child's journal is extremely helpful for your health-care team to identify any interactions or concerns.

Accessibility

Improved accessibility of GFCF foods and personal preferences for taste and texture are satisfied by a greater range of food products.

Growth Patterns

Recent research is showing that patterns of growth are normal for children on the GFCF diet compared to typically developing children.

Bone Health

Bone health has been a point of concern for the GFCF diet, but it is not known whether excluding dairy, abnormal eating patterns, or absorption problems are the cause. Bowel problems confuse the ability to point to a specific reason.

Commitment and Compliance

Any reduction in autism-related symptoms is usually seen in the first year, with a need to continue after confirmation that the GFCF diet has had some impact. Shorter-term commitments to the diet are not seen as effective; at least a 3- to 6-month trial is necessary. Food, eating, and mealtimes are a great source of pleasure, comfort, and a sense of belonging, so a special diet such as the GFCF diet may cause some upset for children with ASD. All support members of your child's team, including family, school, and health care, must be involved for effective safety monitoring and diet compliance.

> **Any reduction in autism-related symptoms is usually seen in the first year, with a need to continue after confirmation that the GFCF diet has had some impact. Shorter-term commitments to the diet are not seen as effective.**

Q. How long should my child stay on this diet?

A. If discussions with your health-care team lead your family to try the GFCF diet, research is showing that a period of 6 months to a year is the minimum time for the diet to show full effect. Any decisions about extending the diet beyond that time would be based on the impact of the diet on your child's symptoms and quality of life. A food challenge at the end of that time — by presenting in a controlled fashion the foods that have been avoided and keeping track in your child's journal to see whether symptoms that had been reduced or totally disappeared returned with the addition of the food to the diet — will help you make your decision.

Q. Is the GFCF diet expensive?

A. Looking through the recipes provided in Part 4 of this book will show you that many of the foods included are from a typical supermarket shelf. For the items that are more expensive, consider sharing costs with other families following this or a similar diet. You could even share prepared dishes in batches that can be frozen. Buying food in bulk or coupon cutting may also defray costs. Health food stores may be a good resource for casein-free foods, and supermarkets do carry vegan food choices.

Q. Is it difficult to make the recipes?

A. Begin making changes to the GFCF diet gradually rather than in one big step (baby steps all the way). By learning to understand the different forms of GF flours before moving on to casein-free foods, you will become more confident and enjoy your new meal-making adventures. Talking to other families and sharing meals with them will also make the process more fun.

Q. Is the GFCF diet safe?

A. One of the concerns raised by research studies done on the GFCF diet and children with autism is that they may not meet all the nutritional requirements for maintenance and growth. Excluding foods that contain gluten and casein may lead to malnutrition if diet planning and supplementation are not carried out. Gluten and casein are excellent sources of protein, calcium, vitamin D, and zinc, among other nutrients, which may need to be supplemented. See your family physician or dietitian for guidance in preventing any nutritional deficiencies.

Research Spotlight

GFCF Review

A review of research conducted on the GFCF diet for children with autism shows improvements in autism-related symptoms — for some children. For any diet that restricts foods, potential quality of life is an important factor to consider. Other family-related issues included the cost of diet-specific foods and the inconvenience factor of preparing several sets of meals.

Improvements in Autism Core and Related Symptoms for Some Children on a GFCF Diet

Symptom	Research
Communication and language use	Knivsberg et al., 1990, 1995, 2002; Lucarelli et al., 1995; Whiteley et al., 1999, 2010a; Johnson et al., 2011
Attention and concentration	Knivsberg et al., 1990, 1995, 2002; Lucarelli et al., 1995; Whiteley et al., 1999, 2010a
Social integration and interaction	Knivsberg et al., 1990, 1995, 2002; Whiteley et al., 1999, 2010a
Self-injury and increased or decreased pain perception	Knivsberg et al., 1990, 1995; Lucarelli et al., 1995; Whiteley et al., 1999
Repetitive or stereotyped patterns of behavior	Knivsberg et al., 1990, 1995, 2002
Motor coordination	Knivsberg et al., 1990, 1995; Whiteley et al., 1999
Hyperactivity	Whiteley et al., 2010a; Johnson et al., 2011
Improvement of diarrhea, constipation, or alternating conditions	Afzal et al., 2003
Reduction in seizure activity during diet and increased activity at diet challenge (consult prescribing physician before making any changes to medications)	Knivsberg et al., 1990, 1995; Lucarelli et al., 1995; Whiteley et al., 1999

DocTalk:
Child-Focused Parenting, or Life Drawing

Parenting children with autism requires that you bring your sense of humor and a big chunk of patience, washed down with a lot more flexibility, to stay in the moment and stay cool. Remember that your child doesn't need to be "fixed," and share her strengths, first with her, then with family members and friends, acquaintances, health-care providers, teachers, and just anyone who will listen.

We all need to use some of the philosophy that is taught to artists when they first take a life drawing course. You learn to unfocus your sexual eye. What you are really learning to do is to step away from your "ego" to observe the lines, planes, and curves of the figure in front of you without doing so from a sexual perspective — unless, of course, that is the angle from which you are painting your picture.

With your children, your ego may also need to be set aside. When you are upset about an event or a rude comment that you have just heard, stop for a minute and ask yourself if you are concerned for your child's sake or is it about you, the parent.

Q. When he is really upset, my 6-year-old hits other children and my wife sometimes too. It is very worrisome. He is a strong boy and big for his age. What should we do?

A. Aggression in children with ASD is often due to many things, including inability to communicate needs or frustrations, sensory-related issues, anxiety, ADHD, and unanticipated transitions. Alone or in combination, these challenges can result in aggression or self injury.

Consistent use of an ABC (Antecedent-Behavior-Consequence) approach often leads to an identification of possible cause(s) and the creation of a therapy plan. Behavioral approaches with or without medication (if behavioral approaches fail initially) are often successful. Medications are used only to facilitate behavioral interventions, in most cases.

Chapter 7
Eight Steps for Implementing the GFCF Diet Program

The Challenge of Changing Diets

Making changes to your child's established eating habits and developing better mealtime behavior requires an acceptance of the need to change. Success depends on your ability to motivate your child and family members to participate.

Where Do We Start?

Before making any major changes to your child's diet, try to improve your child's eating habits in general, without excluding foods with gluten or casein. You may see some improvements in behavior before implementing the GFCF diet.

Step 1: Develop an Attitude for Success

The first step in implementing a new diet is reducing or eliminating any barriers your child with ASD and your family may impose. Research studies have shown that barriers related to behavior can be overcome with appropriate information and motivation.

- Try to instill a positive attitude in your child with ASD and your family. Counteract common barriers to change, including lack of desire, interest, or awareness. Rather than thinking about foods you can't eat, focus on nutritious and delicious new foods your family will be enjoying.

- Give yourself 12 months to convert to the new diet. Be patient with your child with autism, who might resist change. Changing too much too soon may lead to a refusal to follow the GFCF diet. Be prepared to shift strategies.

- Make a list of single-step goals to follow that are more likely to be accepted by your child.

- Encourage the whole family to join in. You may find that it is easier and saves money for the whole family to switch to the new diet, rather than one person, and since food sensitivities are sometimes genetic, more members of your family may find that they feel better after the switch. Special diets can take a lot of your time and money, as well as special concessions for restaurants, travel, family and friend celebrations, and events.

Step 2: Set a Physical and Behavioral Baseline

This will help you to know for sure that the GFCF diet or improved nutrition in general is responsible for any improvements that may be seen. Work with your doctor or dietitian to use the developmental charts to establish not only baseline values but also daily or weekly goals. This is important because it will enable your family to make the decision whether to continue the GFCF diet at the end of your trial.

Step 3: Gather Groceries

Before beginning any new diet for your child or family, have a discussion with your child's health-care and support teams to be sure everyone is up-to-date and ready to provide support and monitor for GFCF-containing foods. This makes it easier to build a meal plan and diet that meet your child's nutritional needs.

Ask your physician and dietitian about possible supplements to prevent nutritional deficiencies. Your pharmacist will be able to check all medications and supplements for any interactions.

Grocery Shopping

Grocery shopping with your child with autism requires planning. Make careful lists showing where to buy GFCF products or arrange with other families to share groceries and costs. It may help to have a second person with you to take your child for a walk or to the car if he is overwhelmed by the grocery store experience — with so many bright colors, loud sounds, and moving people, meltdowns are a possibility.

Preparing to Shop

- Keeping a health and diet journal will help you recognize conditions that may overwhelm your child. Try to avoid more difficult conditions for shopping if possible.
- If your child has a meltdown, a bear hug may help prevent her from hurting herself.
- Try putting a heavy or weighted toy or blanket in your child's lap to soothe him and prevent meltdowns.
- Have your child wear sunglasses against the glare of the bright lighting.
- Play calming music on a set of headphones while shopping with your child.
- Eat a snack before shopping.
- Carry a favorite sippy cup to stay hydrated.
- In case things go wrong, plan ahead so someone else can pick up some of the groceries you need, or have them delivered in worst-case scenarios.

Finding GFCF Groceries

- Check Asian markets for inexpensive rice or buckwheat (gluten-free) noodles with a variety of textures and tastes. Experiment until you find a few that are acceptable. Asian grocery stores also carry a good variety of rice snack products.
- Check all household toiletry items (moisturizers, sunscreen, makeup, soap, shampoo, and conditioner) for gluten and casein.
- Look for gluten-free cereals with natural-source colorings and unmalted brown rice syrup, or apple juice or pear juice, as sweeteners.
- Try Italian gelato as a great replacement for an occasional ice cream cone.
- Try unsweetened gluten-free cereal for breakfast and snacks.

- Talk to your extended family and friends or the group of people your family frequently eats with to alert them to this dietary change and to ask them for their support. Improving everyone's health can be a collective goal.
- To reduce costs, think about sharing bulk purchases with other families following this diet.

Step 4: Manage Your Child's Weight

When your child's weight is below normal, this puts her at risk for other health problems. Keeping a health, diet, and symptom journal is very important to know how much food is being eaten and when.

- If your child prefers fluids, offer less fluid before meals (a smaller cup or less in the cup); offer a smoothie or high-calorie drink after a meal. Be aware that drinking too much fluid before or during a meal will reduce the amount of solid foods eaten.
- Add nut butters, olive paste with GF crackers, or GFCF puddings with cut-up fruit as snacks.
- Add GFCF gravies or sauces with meals.
- Add healthy high-energy snacks (trail mix snacks with dried fruit, nuts, and coconut, for example).

When your child's weight is above normal, this also puts him at risk for other health problems.

- Increase physical activity (using nonfood rewards, like a favorite game or movie or book).

Q. Do I have to make any changes in my kitchen?

A. If your child will be the only person on a GFCF diet, you will need to set up separate cooking areas with separate tools and pots and pans to prevent cross-contamination. You may find it easier to try your whole family on the GFCF diet for a trial period; research has shown that immediate family members are often sensitive to gluten and casein as well.

- Mark all grains clearly as gluten-free or not. Using a red sticker on food items containing gluten may keep people from using them in an absentminded way.
- If you have ingredients in the fridge that contain casein, it would be helpful to put a big red dot on them to remind people not to use them.

- Use smaller plates.
- Serve food away from the table.
- Monitor second helpings (if seconds are important to your child, make the first helping small to allow for a second helping — also small).
- Offer low-calorie beverages (water down or add a little soda water to juices).
- Offer water more often. Try a little lemon, orange, apple, or grape juice to flavor it. Sometimes hunger is mistaken for thirst.
- Put down fork between bites (slows down eating).
- Provide healthy snacks (from a locked snack drawer), with a timer set for when it's snack time.
- Introduce alternatives to fast foods. Ask for nutritional information.
- Use small plastic bags for portion control for school snacks or trips.
- Increase fiber intake (serve whole fruits and vegetables rather than juices).
- Limit 100% juice intake to $\frac{1}{2}$ cup (125 mL) per day.
- Reduce soda intake (replace soda by adding soda water to 100% juice).
- Schedule mealtimes and snack times. Set up a plan for days when you know you are busy, so you still have something ready in the fridge or freezer.
- Establish an emergency fast food that meets your nutritional needs (such as sushi or a dinner salad in a restaurant — hold the croutons — or look for restaurants in your region that have GF foods). Call ahead to ask if salads and dressings are GFCF.

Step 5: Avoid Foods Containing Gluten and Casein

Keep track of your grocery lists and read food label ingredient lists to establish a list of foods you will need to change because they contain casein or gluten.

- Make a quick list of excluded food ingredients: cheese, milk, powdered milk, malt, casein, caseinate, gluten, wheat, rye, barley. Share this with your child's immediate family, schoolteachers, and other social contacts.
- Make another list of allowed foods as you find delicious new foods.

Step 6: Rotate Your Child's Diet

Plan to replace or reintroduce one food item at a time.

- Milk is a good place to start. Buy the smallest size of a fortified alternative milk (rice milk, almond milk, hemp milk, or soy milk, if no allergy) to start to test on your family. Soy milk has the closest protein content to dairy milk.

- Introduce the new food replacement gradually, adding a little of the milk alternative to a container of milk and increasing the amount until everyone is accustomed to the new flavor.

- Do not substitute juice for milk. This may cause diarrhea. Diluting juices with water will provide a healthier drink.

- Try visiting Mexican, Chinese, and Thai restaurants, which are likely to have GFCF food choices. Discuss GFCF choices with the waiter right away or even call ahead.

Step 7: Seek Support

Meet with your dietitian or physician for information and support. Bring along a list of questions about your child's diet and how to go about making changes to it.

- How many servings of fruit and vegetables should my child eat now?

- Discuss which fruits and vegetables are accepted. Which are not?

- How can I add to this list?

- How much white bread, pasta, and desserts should my child eat now?

- How should my child feel about not eating some of these foods?

- How many servings of beans and less common vegetables, such as bok choy, should my child eat?

- Should my child eat a lot of one food or from only one food group?

- How can I help my child to commit to making diet changes?

- What steps do I need to take to shop, store, and prepare food for the GFCF diet?

Join support groups for diet ideas, to share food costs, and to swap recipes. Ask your child to help bake on a weekly basis. Older children can be a big help to read food ingredient lists for gluten- or casein-containing items.

ASD Picnic

Before sending GFCF lunches to school, try a "school lunch test run" for a couple of weekends. This might help you establish new habits in familiar surroundings. For the first weekend, make the lunch you plan to send to school, package the food up as if you were sending it off with your child, and then have a picnic at home. Start by eating your picnic lunch at the table where you usually eat meals. Next time, try a picnic with the packed lunch somewhere else in the house. For the second weekend, head out to the schoolyard to eat your picnic lunch at one of the tables there. For the third weekend, you could try to get permission from the school principal to open the doors for an hour or so while you eat inside in your child's homeroom or in the cafeteria. You might make this a tradition, eating at your child's grandparents' home or at a friend's place. Picnic in the park. Make eating the new GFCF diet an adventure.

Step 8: Work with a Meal Plan

To help launch your GFCF diet, we have provided sample meal plans that provide a nutritionally complete day. Each menu has been designed to meet the energy requirements for a child in the particular age group listed (2–3, 4–8, 9–13, and 14–18). Energy requirements for 14- to 18-year-olds may be different depending on level of activity, muscle mass, and individual differences.

Because children with autism are known to prefer specific types of food with similar mouth feel, or textures, three separate sample meal plans have been prepared for each age group:

- Regular diet, with a variety of textured recipes
- Soft diet, with soft and smooth foods
- Crunchy diet, with foods that have a crunch and bite to them

The 175 nutritious and appealing recipes chosen for the meal plans help us remember that choosing the foods we eat and preparing them for ourselves and those we love might fuel our bodies, but it also feeds our souls. Shopping for and preparing food, as well as the sight and smells from cooking meals, can be an ongoing source of pleasure.

Be proud of your decision to set a priority for nourishing your family!

Q. I'm worried about what will happen when my child grows up and I'm no longer here to look after him. What can I do to protect him?

A. Prognosis is quite variable in children with autism, and depends on cognitive level, communication skills, and presence of coexistent medical disorders, such as seizures, or neuropsychiatric conditions, such as severe anxiety and ADHD. The more comorbidities, the worse the prognosis. Sleep and dietary issues also affect prognosis. Push for early intervention and evaluation of cognitive abilities. Ask your treatment team for advice concerning interventions that may help optimize your child's prognosis. Identifying coexisting issues and addressing them in a timely manner may help achieve a desired outcome. A multidisciplinary team approach to management also tends to facilitate this transition.

DocTalk:
Barbed Tongues

For some families who have a child with ASD, rude and inconsiderate remarks from strangers or even seemingly helpful remarks from acquaintances can be painful. In some cases, when autism is an invisible disability, it can be mistaken for disobedience or lack of intelligence. Your response might be less than kind to these people who do not know the challenges of living with a child who has ASD.

What can you do? Try having a positive response ready for these remarks, whether they are well intentioned or otherwise. "Did you know that my daughter has ASD? It's not always easy for her and for our family to manage this condition, but things work out most of the time." A positive attitude will buoy up your self-esteem as a parent, and speaking up helps your children know you support them, not only your child with autism but also any typically developing children. It's not hard to stand up for any of your children.

Part 4

The Gluten-Free, Casein-Free Cookbook

Gluten-Free, Casein-Free Meal Plans

About the Meal Plans

To help you, the parents of and caregivers for the pickiest eaters club, we've provided sample meal plans in four age groups: ages 2–3, 4–8, 9–13, and 14–18. Each menu is designed to meet the energy requirements for that age group. We've prepared three sample meal plans for each age group: one for a soft, low-texture diet, which includes only recipes that are soft and smooth; one for a crunchy, high-texture diet, which includes only recipes that have a crunch and bite to them; and one for a regular, varied-texture diet.

CASE STUDY
A New Diet

Elia is sitting quietly with his headphones on, listening to a Yo-Yo Ma live performance. His mom took him to see Yo-Yo Ma as a reward for finishing his feeding therapy courses, and now he loves to listen to that performance. Elia uses the music as a way to calm himself — as a "stim." When he was younger, he used to do circles and rock, and sometimes hit his head on the wall, but now he knows that isn't acceptable in public places, so he listens to music instead.

At 11, Elia looks like most children his age, although he is very thin. He has striking features, pale skin, and very large eyes, which seem focused on a distant thought most of the time. Having been diagnosed with autism at an early age, Elia is an expert on therapy of all sorts, and going to therapy has helped him with troublesome symptoms that kept him from being part of his community to the extent he enjoys now. He swims with a local competitive team and is in a chess master club — and often brings home champion ribbons. He still finds social situations difficult, but has learned how to ask a couple of questions to get another person talking.

Elia's biggest ongoing issue is food. He used to throw food — the dining room was a bit of a war zone — but the therapy has helped him stop. His new doctor ran some tests and discovered that Elia has problems with his gastrointestinal tract that might be helped by probiotics. Luckily, they could be sprinkled on cereal and added to smoothies or muffins, since he gags on pills, and especially capsules.

A recent visit with his doctor, a registered dietitian, his education support from school, and his parents was uncomfortable for Elia, with too many people focused on him and talking about him. Fortunately, he was allowed to wear his headphones, though he still needed to kick his chair constantly just to stay in one place. But they came out of that appointment with a new diet for him to try: a gluten-free, casein-free diet. Elia has been on a gluten-free diet for more than a year, but he is a little stressed about this further change because it means no more ice cream.

His parents will continue to write down everything he eats (or what they think he eats) and any symptoms, be they physical or behavioral, and he needs to go back to the doctor once a month for blood tests and a checkup to be sure he is doing okay.

A week into the diet, Elia is liking most of the food and is not having stomachaches. He feels a little more in control some days and is happy about that. What he doesn't know yet is that his parents and his sister, Steph, have planned a surprise — they found dairy-free coconut milk ice cream.

How Much Food Is in a Serving?

Food Group	Size	Food Product
1 serving of vegetables	1 cup (250 mL)	Salad or raw leafy vegetable
	½ cup (125 mL)	Vegetable (fresh, frozen, canned) or 100% juice
1 serving of fruit	½ cup (125 mL)	Fruit (fresh, frozen, canned) or 100% juice
	1 medium fruit	Apple, orange, banana, pear, etc.
1 serving of grain product	1¼ oz (35 g)	1 slice bread, ½ pita, or ½ tortilla
	1½ oz (45 g)	½ bagel
	½ cup (125 mL)	Pasta, rice, quinoa, amaranth, etc.
	1 oz (30 g)	Cold cereal
	¾ cup (175 mL)	Hot cereal (oatmeal, quinoa, amaranth, cream of rice)
1 serving of non-dairy milk alternative	1 cup (250 mL)	Non-dairy fortified milk alternative
	¾ cup (175 mL)	Vegan yogurt
	1½ oz (45 g)	Vegan cheese
1 serving of meat and alternatives	2½ oz (75 g) or ½ cup (125 mL)	Lean meat, poultry, cooked fish, or shellfish
	¾ cup (175 mL)	Cooked beans
	2	Eggs
	2 tbsp (30 mL)	Peanut or nut butter

Source: Adapted from Canada's Food Guide

Soft, Low-Texture Meal Plans

AGES 2–4

Breakfast	Morning snack	Lunch	Afternoon snack	Dinner
¾ cup (175 mL) Sweet Banana Porridge (page 205) ½ cup (125 mL) Easy Homemade Applesauce (page 360) ¼ cup (60 mL) Almond Crème Fraîche (page 368)	1 Gingerbread Muffin (page 240)	¾ cup (175 mL) Sautéed Mushrooms and Potatoes with Garlic, Parsley and Poached Egg (page 290) 1 cup (250 mL) Prune Smoothie (page 379)	¾ cup (175 mL) Pumpkin Pudding (page 364)	½ cup (125 mL) Puréed Vegetables (page 194) ¼ cup (60 mL) cooked white rice ¾ cup (175 mL) soy milk ¾ cup (175 mL) Chickpeas in Tomato Sauce (page 302)

Soft, Low-Texture Meal Plans

AGES 4–8

Breakfast	Morning snack	Lunch	Afternoon snack	Dinner
1 Pumpkin Almond Flour Muffin (page 242) 1 cup (250 mL) soy milk	½ cup (125 mL) cooked oatmeal 1 cup (250 mL) Prune Smoothie (page 379)	1 serving Basic Beans (page 343) with Basic Tomato Sauce (page 257) 1 cup (250 mL) Apple Ginger Pudding Cake (page 351)	½ cup (125 mL) Strawberry Salad (page 269) 3½ oz (100 g) soy yogurt	1 cup (250 mL) Egg and Mushroom Fried Rice (page 346) ¼ avocado ½ cup (125 mL) Cold Mango Soup (page 262)

Soft, Low-Texture Meal Plans

AGES 9–13

Breakfast	Morning snack	Lunch	Afternoon snack	Dinner	Evening snack
1 Individual Salsa Fresca Omelet (page 212) 1/4 cup (60 mL) shredded non-dairy cheese 3/4 cup (175 mL) Cooked Oat Bran (page 186) 1/2 cup (125 mL) Easy Homemade Applesauce (page 360)	1 cup (250 mL) soy milk	2 slices Brown Sandwich Bread (page 220) 2 tbsp (30 mL) Creamy Crab Salad Spread (page 252) 1/2 cup (125 mL) Sweet Pea Soup (page 263) 1 cup (250 mL) Prune Smoothie (page 379)	1 cup (250 mL) Apple Ginger Pudding Cake (page 351) 1/2 cup (125 mL) Strawberry Salad (page 269)	1 serving Turkey Apple Meatloaf (page 314) 1/2 cup (125 mL) Tomato and Zucchini Sauté (page 332) 1/2 cup (125 mL) Mashed Sweet Potatoes with Rosemary (page 340) 1 Peaches and Cream Frozen Pop (page 363)	1 Carrot Oatmeal Muffin (page 237) 3 1/2 oz (100 g) soy yogurt

Soft, Low-Texture Meal Plans

AGES 14–18

Breakfast	Lunch	Afternoon snack	Dinner	Evening snack
1 Simple Corn Tortilla (page 229) 1 Individual Salsa Fresca Omelet (page 212) 1/4 cup (60 mL) shredded non-dairy cheese 1 1/2 cups (375 mL) Vanilla Soy Milk Rice Pudding (page 200) 1/2 cup (125 mL) chopped ripe melon	2 slices Brown Sandwich Bread (page 220) 2 tbsp (30 mL) Hummus (page 255) 1/4 sliced avocado 1 cup (250 mL) Strawberry Salad (page 269) 1 cup (250 mL) soy milk	1 Pumpkin Date Bar (page 375) 3 1/2 oz (100 g) soy yogurt	1 serving Thai-Style Coconut Fish Curry (page 307) 2 servings Steamed Rice Noodle Cakes (page 345) 1 cup (250 mL) Glazed Carrots (page 327), minced and well cooked 1 1/2 cups (375 mL) Banana Frappé (page 378)	1 Black Bean Brownie (page 350)

Recipe Options for Soft, Low-Texture Meals

- Egg Foo Yong (page 189), without the bean sprouts
- Puréed Meat (page 191)
- Spiced Bananas (page 198)
- Mashed Banana and Avocado (page 199)
- Breakfast Rice (page 204), made with short-grain white rice
- Sweet Banana Porridge (page 205)
- Cranberry Quinoa Porridge (page 206), well cooked
- Banana Pecan Waffles (page 213), without the pecans
- White Bread (page 218)
- Brown Sandwich Bread (page 220)
- Egg-Free, Corn-Free, Dairy-Free, Soy-Free Brown Bread (page 222)
- Date Cashew Loaf (page 228), without the cashews (or grind them well in a clean coffee grinder)
- Carrot Oatmeal Muffins (page 237)
- Pear Buckwheat Muffins (page 238)
- Almond Flour Blackberry Muffins (page 239)
- Gingerbread Muffins (page 240)
- Pumpkin Almond Flour Muffins (page 242)
- Creamy Crab Salad Spread (page 252)
- Egg Salad Spread (page 253)
- Fiesta Guacamole (page 254)
- Hummus (page 255)
- Tomatillo and Chia Seed Salsa (page 256)
- Cold Mango Soup (page 262)
- Sweet Pea Soup (page 263)
- Fresh Tomato Dill Soup (page 264)
- Coconut-Spiked Pumpkin Soup with Cumin and Ginger (page 265)
- Hungarian Chicken Soup (page 268)
- Grilled Portobello on Greens (page 286)
- Vegetarian Chili (page 287)
- Cold Buckwheat Noodles with Broccoli and Sesame Dressing (page 292)
- Rice and Black Bean–Stuffed Peppers (page 298)
- Mushroom and Chickpea Stew with Roasted Red Pepper Coulis (page 300)
- Chickpeas in Tomato Sauce (page 302)
- Asian Barbecued Tofu Cubes (page 303)

- Tofu Patties (page 304)
- Baked Mediterranean Salmon Fillets (page 306)
- Thai-Style Coconut Fish Curry (page 307)
- Rice Stick Noodles with Crab in a Basil-Tomato Sauce (page 308)
- Sweet Potato Coconut Curry with Shrimp (page 309)
- Glazed Carrots (page 327), well cooked
- Sautéed Spinach with Pine Nuts (page 330), without the pine nuts
- Sweet Baked Tomatoes (page 331)
- Tomato and Zucchini Sauté (page 332)
- Hot-Bag Vegetables (page 333)
- Squash with Quinoa and Apricots (page 334), without the apricots (or slice them finely)
- Ratatouille (page 336)
- Batter-Dipped Vegetable Fritters (page 338), cooled and kept in an airtight container, causing the outer layer to soften
- Sweet Potato "Fries" (page 339), cooked soft with moist heat (i.e., covered with foil in the oven)
- Mashed Sweet Potatoes with Rosemary (page 340), with tarragon instead of rosemary if rosemary is too textured
- Yukon Gold Bay Leaf Mash (page 341)
- Florentine Potato Cakes (page 342), cooked soft and covered to retain moisture
- Basic Beans (page 343)
- Caramelized Peppers and Onions with Pasta (page 344)
- Steamed Rice Noodle Cakes (page 345)
- Egg and Mushroom Fried Rice (page 346)
- Apple Ginger Pudding Cake (page 351)
- Harvest Cupcakes (page 352)
- The Ultimate Baked Apples (page 353), with apples peeled and ground nuts used in filling
- Easy Homemade Applesauce (page 360)
- Fruit Salad with Ginger and Honey (page 361)
- Fruit Salad with Flax Seeds (page 362), with ground flax seeds (or omit the seeds altogether)
- Berry Pops (page 362)
- Peaches and Cream Frozen Pops (page 363)
- Pumpkin Pudding (page 364)
- Coconut Butter Vanilla Icing (page 365)
- Chocolate Hazelnut Spread (page 366)
- Almond Crème Fraîche (page 368)

Crunchy, High-Texture Meal Plans

AGES 2–4

Breakfast	Morning snack	Lunch	Afternoon snack	Dinner
½ cup (125 mL) Tofu Quinoa Scramble (page 209) 1 Crispy Bacon Strip (page 209) 1 cup (250 mL) Berry Frappé (page 379)	1 Crunchy Flaxseed Cookie (page 348) 3½ oz (100 g) soy yogurt	1 wedge Honey Dijon Toastie (page 226) 1 cup (250 mL) Waldorf Parma Salad (page 282)	1 Fresco de Fruit Taco Cupita (page 358) ¼ cup (60 mL) Almond Crème Fraîche (page 368)	3 pieces Coconut-Battered Shrimp (page 310) 1 serving Florentine Potato Cakes (page 342) ½ cup (125 mL) Orange Broccoli (page 326) ½ cup (125 mL) soy milk

Crunchy, High-Texture Meal Plans

AGES 4–8

Breakfast	Morning snack	Lunch	Afternoon snack	Dinner
2 Maple Breakfast Biscotti (page 215) ½ cup (125 mL) firm blueberries ½ cup (125 mL) soy milk	1 cup (250 mL) Green Quinoa Smoothie (page 380)	1 Lettuce Wrap (page 190) 1 cup (250 mL) Vanilla Soy Milk Rice Pudding (page 200)	½ cup (125 mL) Easy Homemade Granola (page 202) 1 apple, sliced 3½ oz (100 g) soy yogurt	1 serving Taco Salad (page 280) ¼ cup (60 mL) shredded non-dairy cheese

Crunchy, High-Texture Meal Plans

AGES 9–13

Breakfast	Morning snack	Lunch	Afternoon snack	Dinner	Evening snack
1 cup (250 mL) Easy Homemade Granola (page 202) 1 apple, sliced 1 cup (250 mL) soy milk	1 cup (250 mL) Vanilla Soy Milk Rice Pudding (page 200) ¼ cup (60 mL) raisins 1 tbsp (15 mL) shredded coconut	1 serving Taco Salad (page 280) ¼ cup (60 mL) shredded non-dairy cheese	4 pieces Sesame Crispbread (page 234) 1½ cups (375 mL) Banana Frappé (page 378)	3 pieces Crispy Pecan Chicken Fingers (page 312) with 1 tbsp (15 mL) Honey Mustard Dipping Sauce (page 259) 1 serving Oven-Roasted Potato Wedges (page 196) 1 cup (250 mL) Kale Quinoa Tabbouleh (page 295)	3½ oz (100 g) soy yogurt + 2 cups (500 mL) hot-air popcorn

Crunchy, High-Texture Meal Plans

AGES 14–18

Breakfast	Lunch	Afternoon snack	Dinner	Evening snack
2 slices Crunchy Multigrain Bâtarde (page 224) 1 apple, sliced 1½ oz (45 g) soy cheese 1½ cups (375 mL) Banana Frappé (page 378)	2 Rolled Veggie Tacos with Spicy Asian Sauce (page 296), made with Simple Corn Tortillas (page 229) 1 serving Asian Barbecued Tofu Cubes (page 303) 1 cup (250 mL) soy milk	½ cup (125 mL) Spicy, Crispy Roasted Chickpeas (page 373) ½ cup (125 mL) cucumber slices 3½ oz (100 g) soy yogurt	1 serving Crispy Calamari (page 251) 2 servings Batter-Dipped Vegetable Fritters (page 338) 2 Peaches and Cream Frozen Pops (page 363)	1 Toasted Sesame Quinoa Bar (page 376) 1 cup (250 mL) grapes

Recipe Options for Crunchy, High-Texture Meals

- Easy Homemade Granola (page 202)
- Gluten-Free Muesli (page 203)
- Quinoa Crunch (page 204)
- Cranberry Quinoa Porridge (page 206)
- Baked Apple Quinoa (page 207)
- Crispy Bacon Strips (page 209)
- Maple Breakfast Biscotti (page 215)
- Cocoa Quinoa Breakfast Squares (page 216)
- Crunchy Multigrain Bâtarde (page 224)
- Honey Dijon Toastie (page 226)
- Date Cashew Loaf (page 228)
- Simple Corn Tortillas (page 229)
- Bacon and Tomato Biscuits (page 231)
- Breadsticks (page 232)
- Sesame Crispbread (page 234)
- Oven-Baked Tofu "Fries" (page 246)
- Thai Yellow Curry Mango Salad (page 270), made with green mango
- Festive Mexican Slaw (page 271)
- Kasha and Beet Salad with Celery and Feta (page 272), with the veggies slightly undercooked and the feta cheese omitted if necessary
- Roasted Sweet Potato Salad (page 273), with a shortened cooking time for firmer sweet potatoes
- Shrimp Caesar Salad with Garlic Croutons (page 276)
- Kale Quinoa Tabbouleh (page 295)
- Pacific Rim Coconut Ribs (page 318)
- Orange Broccoli (page 326)
- Glazed Carrots (page 327)
- Corn with Tomatoes and Basil (page 328)
- Green Beans with Mustard Seeds (page 329)
- Sautéed Spinach with Pine Nuts (page 330)
- Tomato and Zucchini Sauté (page 332)
- Hot-Bag Vegetables (page 333)
- Ratatouille (page 336)
- Batter-Dipped Vegetable Fritters (page 338)
- Sweet Potato "Fries" (page 339)
- Florentine Potato Cakes (page 342)
- Steamed Rice Noodle Cakes (page 345)
- Crunchy Flaxseed Cookies (page 348)
- Chocolate Chip Cookies (page 349)
- Medley of Fruit Crisp (page 357)
- Fresco de Fruit Taco Cupitas (page 358)
- Fruit Salad with Flax Seeds (page 362), made with crunchy fruits, such as apple, pear, firm grapes, pomegranate seeds, firm blueberries, green mango, dragon fruit, and firm fuyu persimmon
- Sage Potato Crisps (page 370)
- Fresh Tortilla Chips (page 371)
- Baked Candied Pecans (page 372)
- Spicy, Crispy Roasted Chickpeas (page 373)
- Chocolate Date Protein Bars (page 374)
- Pumpkin Date Bars (page 375)
- Toasted Sesame Quinoa Bars (page 376)

Regular, Varied-Texture Meal Plans

AGES 2–3

Breakfast	Morning snack	Lunch	Afternoon snack	Dinner
½ cup (125 mL) Breakfast Rice (page 204) ½ cup (125 mL) Grape and Melon Fruit Cups (page 197) ¾ cup (175 mL) soy milk	1 Carrot Oatmeal Muffin (page 237)	½ cup (125 mL) Hungarian Chicken Soup (page 268) 1 Tasty Potato Pancake (page 214) 2 tbsp (30 mL) Tangy Fruit Sauce (page 197)	½ cup (125 mL) Pumpkin Pudding (page 364)	¾ cup (175 mL) Sticky Rice Salad with Asparagus and Mushrooms in Soy Vinaigrette (page 275) 3 Oven-Baked Tofu "Fries" (page 246) 1 to 2 tsp (5 to 10 mL) Mock Soy Sauce (page 259) ½ Ultimate Baked Apple (page 353) ¾ cup (175 mL) soy milk

Regular, Varied-Texture Meal Plans

AGES 4–8

Breakfast	Morning snack	Lunch	Afternoon snack	Dinner
1 Bacon and Tomato Biscuit (page 231) 1 cup (250 mL) soy milk	½ cup (125 mL) Fruit Salad with Flax Seeds (page 362)	1 cup (250 mL) Mediterranean Tuna Risotto Salad (page 278) ½ cup (125 mL) Green Quinoa Smoothie (page 380)	½ cup (125 mL) Vanilla Soy Milk Rice Pudding (page 200)	½ Rice and Black Bean–Stuffed Pepper (page 298) ½ cup (125 mL) Sweet Pea Soup (page 263) 3½ oz (100 g) soy yogurt

Regular, Varied-Texture Meal Plans

AGES 9–13

Breakfast	Morning snack	Lunch	Afternoon snack	Dinner	Evening snack
1 cup (250 mL) Tofu Quinoa Scramble (page 209) ¼ cup (60 mL) Tomatillo and Chia Seed Salsa (page 256)	1 Carrot Oatmeal Muffin (page 237) 3½ oz (100 g) soy yogurt	¾ cup (175 mL) steamed brown rice ¾ cup (175 mL) Sweet Potato Coconut Curry with Shrimp (page 309) 1½ cups (375 mL) Prune Smoothie (page 379)	½ cup (125 mL) Strawberry Salad (page 269) ½ cup (125 mL) frozen soy or almond milk yogurt	1½ cups (375 mL) Buckwheat Noodle Bowls with Beef and Snap Peas (page 322) 1 Ultimate Baked Apple page 353) 2 tbsp (30 mL) Almond Crème Fraîche (page 368)	2 to 3 Chocolate Chip Cookies (page 349) 1 cup (250 mL) soy milk

Regular, Varied-Texture Meal Plans

AGES 14–18

Breakfast	Lunch	Afternoon snack	Dinner	Evening snack
1 Bacon and Tomato Biscuit (page 231) 1 cup (250 mL) Banana Frappé (page 378)	1½ cups (375 mL) Mediterranean Tuna Risotto Salad (page 278) 1 cup (250 mL) mixed greens ½ cup (125 mL) grapes 3½ oz (100 g) soy yogurt	1 slice Medley of Fruit Crisp (page 357)	1 to 2 servings Coconut Chicken with Quinoa (page 313) 1 cup (250 mL) Sautéed Spinach with Pine Nuts (page 330) 1 cup (250 mL) Fruit Salad with Ginger and Honey (page 361) 1 cup (250 mL) soy milk	½ cup (125 mL) Easy Homemade Granola (page 202) 1 cup (250 mL) frozen soy yogurt

Tips for Teens with Low Calorie Needs or Big Appetites

Kids should never be placed on strict weight loss diets. They are still growing. The healthier approach, for both body and mind, is for kids to grow into their weight. Remember, healthy kids come in all shapes and sizes. If you are concerned that your child may be overweight, please consult a qualified pediatric health-care provider for guidance.

Grains

- Choose filling, high-fiber whole grains (e.g., brown rice, steel-cut oats) with at least 4 grams of fiber per serving.
- Encourage your teen to fill up on high-fiber grains at mealtimes.

Fruits and Vegetables

- Leave edible peels on for more filling fiber and choose berries more often.
- Use vegetable-based sauces for pasta, casseroles, pizzas, and dips.
- Provide exotic fruits and vegetables from a local market for your teen to sample.
- Prewash and cut vegetables and fruits and keep them handy in the refrigerator.
- Keep a fruit bowl on the counter — it's a great visual reminder when your teen is faced with a craving for sweets.
- Limit fruit juice to $\frac{1}{2}$ cup (125 mL) per day. Better yet, offer the fruit instead — it has more nutrition and is more filling!
- Aim to fill half your child's plate with vegetables.
- Encourage your child to practice eating the rainbow, enjoying fruits and vegetables in all the different colors every day!

Meats and Alternatives

- Choose lean meats and cold cuts (chicken, turkey, roast beef, ham) or light soy-based protein products (tofu).
- Serve baked, steamed, or grilled fish or seafood at least twice a week.
- Choose high-fiber lentils, chickpeas, and baked beans a few times a week.
- Limit nuts to $\frac{1}{4}$ cup (60 mL) per day.

Dairy Alternatives

- Choose light and less-sweetened soy milk products.
- Shred cheese alternative to make it go farther on pizzas, pasta, salads, snack foods, baked goods, etc.

Miscellaneous

- Limit added fats and oils to 2 tbsp (30 mL) per day.
- Serve meals on small plates.

Tips for Teens with High Calorie Needs or Small Appetites

Growth should be monitored regularly by your health-care provider. If you think your child may be underweight, picky eating may be the culprit. Have your child's health monitored to ensure that there are no nutrient deficiencies or medical reasons for lack of weight gain. A knowledgeable dietitian or behavioral therapist with a specialty in food issues can help expand the diets of fussy eaters.

Grains

- Add an extra serving or two daily if your teen is feeling low-energy or hungry.
- For snacks, provide grain-based energy bars or popcorn with a dash of oil.
- Boost your teen's grain intake by breading pan-fried or roasted vegetables and meats.

Fruits and Vegetables

- Add oil to sauces for pasta, casseroles, pizzas, and dips.
- Provide dips for fruits and veggies.
- Liberally dress salads with olive, peanut, sesame, canola, flax, or walnut oil (or with your teen's favorite if not mentioned here).
- Encourage your teen to drink a smoothie if whole fruits and veggies are too filling. Pack the smoothie with high-energy foods, such as ground nuts, nut butter, flax or chia seeds, oat flakes, and dairy alternatives.
- Keep dried fruits handy for concentrated energy. They store well in gym bags, lockers, and cars.

Meats and Alternatives

- Choose oil-packed fish, such as tuna, salmon, and sardines.
- Add pasteurized liquid eggs to smoothies.
- Add whole, chopped, sliced, or ground nuts to baked goods, sauces, mixed dishes, and salads.
- Use nut butter in smoothies, as a spread for bread or crackers, in baking, and as a dip for fruits.

Dairy Alternatives

- Use dairy alternatives instead of water when making soups, baked goods, salad dressings, etc.
- Try adding cheese alternative to up the nutrient content of pasta, casseroles, salads, snack foods, baked goods, etc.

Miscellaneous

- Use spreads generously. Try mayonnaise, dairy-free margarine, jam, nut butter, hummus, tahini, baba ghanoush, etc.
- Mix together all of your teen's favorite snack foods to create a trail mix for him to nibble on.
- Include 3 tbsp (45 mL) of added fats and oils daily in the foods you prepare for your teen.

Introduction to the Recipes

The sample meal plans (pages 172–180) are built from the nutritious and appealing recipes found in this section. Following a special diet is hard work, but we have made every effort to ease your workload by giving you the information you need to understand how, for some children, avoiding gluten and casein may improve autism-related symptoms.

Providing a regular meal and snack plan, with plenty of fluids, may suit your child's preference for sameness and improve his health and energy levels in general. And although your child may begin with a preference for the crunchy or the soft meal plan, we hope you will be able to add more from the regular meal plan and other recipes as time goes by. Throughout the recipes, you will find tips on personalizing this diet to suit your child.

Remember that patience wins out. You may have to offer a new food to babies 10 to 15 times (or even more) before they will accept it into their diet.

About the Nutrient Analyses

The nutrient analysis done on the recipes in this book was derived from the Food Processor SQL Nutrition Analysis Software, version 10.9, ESHA Research (2011). Where necessary, data were supplemented using the USDA National Nutrient Database for Standard Reference, Release #26 (2014), retrieved January 2014 from the USDA Agricultural Research Service website: www.nal.usda.gov/fnic/foodcomp/.

Recipes were evaluated as follows:

- The larger number of servings was used where there is a range.
- The smaller quantity of an ingredient was used where a range is provided.
- Where alternatives are given, the first ingredient and amount listed were used.

- Optional ingredients and ingredients that are not quantified were not included.
- Calculations were based on imperial measures and weights.
- Nutrient values were rounded to the nearest whole number.
- Defatted soy flour and brown rice flour were used, including where these ingredients are listed as soy flour and rice flour.
- Calculations involving meat and poultry used lean portions without skin.
- Canola oil was used where the type of fat was not specified.
- Recipes were analyzed prior to cooking.

It is important to note that the cooking method used to prepare the recipe may alter the nutrient content per serving, as may ingredient substitutions and differences among brand-name products.

Baby Food and Kids' Fare

Cooked Oat Bran 186

Special Muffins for Kids 187

Vegetable Broth and Puréed Veggies 188

Junior Hot-and-Sour Soup 189

Egg Foo Yong 189

Lettuce Wraps 190

Puréed Meat 191

Basic Beef Mixture 192

Fruity Chicken 193

Puréed Sweet Potatoes 194

Puréed Vegetables 194

Fresh Vegetable Purée 195

Rice Salad 196

Oven-Roasted Potato Wedges 196

Tangy Fruit Sauce 197

Grape and Melon Fruit Cups 197

Spiced Bananas 198

Mashed Banana and Avocado 199

Vanilla Soy Milk Rice Pudding 200

Cooked Oat Bran

Makes 1 serving

Introducing your infant
to different hot cooked
cereals is a big moment
in her life. It can lead
to a lifetime of enjoying
the pleasure and
comfort of a hot cereal
start to the day. These
single-serve amounts
can be easily increased
according to your child's
appetite. Remember to
give small spoonfuls,
and watch your child
carefully to know when
she's ready for more.

Tips

This recipe is suitable for
babies over 8 months.

A great snack at any time.

This recipe keeps its
nutrient value for about
3 days in the fridge. Serving
at different temperatures
(hot, warm, cool or cold)
gives you more solutions
for busy days.

Nutrients per serving	
Calories	43
Fat	2 g
Carbohydrate	6 g
Fiber	1 g
Protein	3 g
Calcium	50 mg
Vitamin D	19 IU

1 tbsp	GF oat bran	15 mL
3 tbsp	water or formula	45 mL

Microwave Method

1. In a small microwave-safe bowl, combine oat bran
   and water. Microwave, uncovered, on High for about
   1 minute; stir. Let stand until appropriate serving
   temperature is reached and mixture has thickened.
   Stir and serve.

Stovetop Method

1. In a small saucepan, combine oat bran and water.
   Cook over medium-low heat, stirring frequently, for
   2 to 4 minutes or until mixture has thickened.

Variations

For a treat, add a sprinkle of ground nutmeg or cinnamon.

For children older than 12 months, try adding raisins
and chopped dried fruit. Prunes, apricots or apples are
appropriate. Add a few to each serving during cooking.

Special Muffins for Kids

Makes 6 muffins

Who can resist the combination of peanut butter, banana and chocolate? Kids of all ages will wolf these down and ask for more!

Tips

You'll need about 2 very ripe medium bananas for ¾ cup (175 mL) mashed. Do not add extra.

You can substitute GF smooth peanut butter for the crunchy.

Read chocolate ingredient labels carefully for gluten-, milk- and casein-related food products. Choose GFCF or vegan chocolate.

Ask your child if he feels his tummy rumbling when it's time to eat! Having a meal or snack every 3 to 4 hours helps children appreciate what it means to feel hungry, to enjoy eating and then to feel full.

Nutrients per muffin	
Calories	333
Fat	16 g
Carbohydrate	45 g
Fiber	5 g
Protein	6 g
Calcium	90 mg
Vitamin D	16 IU

- **6-cup muffin pan, lightly greased**

½ cup	sorghum flour	125 mL
¼ cup	quinoa flour	60 mL
2 tbsp	tapioca starch	30 mL
¼ cup	packed brown sugar	60 mL
2 tsp	GF baking powder	10 mL
½ tsp	baking soda	2 mL
1 tsp	xanthan gum	5 mL
¼ tsp	salt	1 mL
1	large egg	1
¾ cup	mashed bananas	175 mL
¼ cup	GF crunchy peanut butter, at room temperature	60 mL
2 tbsp	vegetable oil	30 mL
1 tsp	cider vinegar	5 mL
½ cup	GFCF semisweet chocolate chips (see tip, at left)	125 mL

1. In a bowl or plastic bag, combine sorghum flour, quinoa flour, tapioca starch, brown sugar, baking powder, baking soda, xanthan gum and salt. Mix well and set aside.

2. In a separate bowl, using an electric mixer, beat egg, bananas, peanut butter, oil and vinegar until combined. Add dry ingredients and mix just until combined. Stir in chocolate chips.

3. Spoon batter into prepared muffin cups, dividing evenly. Let stand for 30 minutes. Meanwhile, preheat oven to 350°F (180°C).

4. Bake for 18 to 20 minutes or until firm to the touch. Remove from the pan immediately and let cool completely on a rack.

Variation

Substitute ¼ cup (60 mL) unsalted peanuts for half the chocolate chips.

Vegetable Broth and Puréed Veggies

Makes 2 cups (500 mL) broth and 2½ cups (625 mL) vegetable purée

Tips

This recipe is suitable for babies over 6 months.

You can use the puréed vegetables to make a cream soup too! Add about ½ cup (125 mL) plain non-dairy milk to ½ cup (125 mL) of the vegetables. Simply delicious!

This recipe is a great way to add fluid and fiber to any diet, and aids children who are suffering from constipation.

The purée is an excellent selection of vegetables for kids who refuse their veggies.

- **Food processor or blender (optional)**

1 cup	sliced celery	250 mL
1 cup	sliced broccoli	250 mL
1 cup	sliced parsnips (or 1 medium)	250 mL
1 cup	sliced onions (or 1 small)	250 mL
1 cup	sliced leeks	250 mL
1 cup	sliced carrots (or 4 medium)	250 mL
4 cups	water	1 L

1. In a large pot, combine celery, broccoli, parsnips, onions, leeks, carrots and water. Bring to a boil over high heat. Reduce heat and boil gently for about 30 minutes or until vegetables are soft.

2. Strain, reserving vegetables and broth separately. Use broth immediately or transfer to containers for storage.

3. In food processor, or in a bowl, purée or mash vegetables to desired consistency. Serve immediately or transfer to containers for storage.

Nutrients per ½ cup (125 mL) soup, including puréed vegetables

Calories	31
Fat	0 g
Carbohydrate	7 g
Fiber	2 g
Protein	1 g
Calcium	30 mg
Vitamin D	0 IU

Junior Hot-and-Sour Soup

So easy and fast to
make, yet delicious
and tasty — and a
good way to introduce
kids to spicier foods.
Adjust the amount of
hot pepper sauce to
individual tastes.

Tip

This recipe is suitable for
children over 18 months.

6 cups	ready-to-use chicken or vegetable broth	1.5 L
3 tbsp	GF soy sauce	45 mL
4 tsp	ground ginger	20 mL
1 tbsp	rice vinegar	15 mL
2 tsp	granulated sugar	10 mL
½ to 1 tsp	hot pepper sauce	2 to 5 mL
1 tsp	sesame oil	5 mL
4 oz	silken tofu, diced	125 g
2	green onions, sliced	2

1. In a large saucepan, combine broth with soy sauce,
   ginger, vinegar, sugar, hot pepper sauce and sesame oil.
   Bring to a boil. Add tofu and green onions. Cook for
   1 minute longer and serve.

Nutrients per ½ cup (125 mL)			
Calories	34	Protein	3 g
Fat	1 g	Calcium	8 mg
Carbohydrate	3 g	Vitamin D	0 IU
Fiber	0 g		

Egg Foo Yong

The bean sprouts add
crunch to the softer
texture of the eggs in this
tasty Asian-style dish.

Tip

This recipe can be adapted
to the soft menu plan by
omitting the bean sprouts.
Once the recipe grows on
your picky eater, try adding
a few sprouts back in.

4	large eggs, lightly beaten	4
1	green onion, finely chopped	1
1 cup	bean sprouts	250 mL
½ cup	diced cooked pork, chicken or beef	125 mL
2 tsp	reduced-sodium GF soy sauce	10 mL
1 tbsp	canola oil	15 mL

1. In a small bowl, combine eggs, green onion, bean
   sprouts, pork and soy sauce.

2. In a skillet, heat oil over medium heat. Pour in egg
   mixture and cook, stirring, for 5 minutes or until egg
   is set. Serve warm.

Nutrients per 1 of 3 servings			
Calories	234	Protein	20 g
Fat	15 g	Calcium	55 mg
Carbohydrate	5 g	Vitamin D	37 IU
Fiber	0 g		

Lettuce Wraps

A great lunch or after-school snack, easy and quick to make, nutritious and yummy to boot! These finger foods are a great way to get kids to start putting together their own meals.

Tips

Boston lettuce has a softer texture than other lettuces, which makes it easier to roll. You can serve the filling in lettuce cups rather than rolls, or use small GF flour or corn tortillas.

Try telling your kids that lettuce wraps are like little green sleeping bags for food.

Variation

For a vegetarian version, use tofu or beans instead of the chicken or shrimp.

4 tsp	vegetable oil	20 mL
1 tbsp	rice vinegar	15 mL
1 tsp	reduced-sodium GF soy sauce	5 mL
1 tsp	sesame oil (optional)	5 mL
$\frac{1}{2}$ tsp	minced gingerroot (or pinch ground ginger)	2 mL
$\frac{1}{2}$ tsp	liquid honey	2 mL
	Salt and freshly ground black pepper	
1 cup	chopped cooked chicken or whole small cooked shrimp	250 mL
1 cup	halved or quartered cherry tomatoes	250 mL
$\frac{1}{2}$ cup	chopped English cucumber	125 mL
1	carrot, grated	1
1	green onion, sliced	1
8	leaves Boston lettuce	8

1. In a large bowl, whisk together vegetable oil, vinegar, soy sauce, sesame oil (if using), ginger and honey. Season to taste with salt and pepper. Add chicken, tomatoes, cucumber, carrot and green onion; toss to coat.

2. Spoon chicken mixture into the center of each lettuce leaf, dividing evenly. Fold in sides of lettuce leaves and roll up from the bottom.

Nutrients per wrap	
Calories	72
Fat	4 g
Carbohydrate	3 g
Fiber	1 g
Protein	6 g
Calcium	11 mg
Vitamin D	1 IU

Puréed Meat

Once your baby needs proteins, this puréed meat recipe provides lots of options. Adding juice from the meat during processing will make for a smoother texture.

• Food processor or blender

| ½ cup | cooked meat (chicken, beef, etc.), cut into small pieces | 125 mL |
| ¼ cup | water or cooking liquid | 60 mL |

1. In food processor, combine meat and water. Process for 1 to 2 minutes or until smooth.

2. Serve immediately or freeze in an ice cube tray for future use. Once frozen, transfer individual cubes to freezer bags.

Tips

This recipe is suitable for babies over 8 months.

Puréed meat is a great choice for a child of any age who prefers soft foods.

For an even smoother purée, cook the meat in a slow cooker.

Homemade baby food can be frozen and used for up to 3 months. Thaw overnight in the refrigerator, or defrost in a container of warm water.

Nutrients per serving (for 4 oz/125 g chicken drumstick meat)

Calories	67
Fat	3 g
Carbohydrate	0 g
Fiber	0 g
Protein	9 g
Calcium	7 mg
Vitamin D	3 IU

Nutrients per serving (for beef)

Calories	134
Fat	7 g
Carbohydrate	0 g
Fiber	0 g
Protein	18 g
Calcium	11 mg
Vitamin D	1 IU

Nutrients per serving (for lamb)

Calories	133
Fat	8 g
Carbohydrate	0 g
Fiber	0 g
Protein	14 g
Calcium	11 mg
Vitamin D	0 IU

Basic Beef Mixture

2 lbs	lean or medium ground beef	1 kg
4	cloves garlic, minced	4
2	onions, finely chopped	2
2 cups	tomato sauce or pasta sauce	500 mL
2 tsp	dried basil	10 mL
2 tsp	dried oregano	10 mL
½ tsp	salt	2 mL
¼ tsp	freshly ground black pepper	1 mL

Makes 6 cups (1.5 L)

Ground beef forms the basis of many dishes that kids love — including sloppy joes, pizza, shepherd's pie, chili, or just as a topping for baked or mashed potatoes. Make a big batch of this recipe and freeze in smaller amounts. The recipe originated from the Canada Beef Information Centre.

Tip

When adding new foods to your child's diet, be positive, even if it's not on your preferred menu list.

1. In a large skillet over medium-high heat, cook beef, garlic and onion, using a spoon to break up the meat, for 10 minutes or until beef is no longer pink. Drain fat.

2. Add tomato sauce, basil, oregano, salt and pepper. Bring to a boil; reduce heat and simmer for 5 minutes. Divide beef mixture into 1-cup (250 mL) portions. Refrigerate for up to 2 days or freeze for up to 3 months.

Uses

Sloppy Joes: In a saucepan, combine 1 cup (250 mL) Basic Beef Mixture, 2 tbsp (30 mL) finely chopped green bell pepper and 2 tbsp (30 mL) finely chopped celery. Heat thoroughly and serve over cooked rice, toasted GF bun or bread. Makes 1¼ cups (300 mL).

Baked Potato Topping: Bake or microwave 1 potato. Cut a cross in top of potato; squeeze to open. Top with ¼ cup (60 mL) heated Basic Beef Mixture and serve. Makes 1 serving.

Shepherd's Pie: In a shallow ovenproof casserole dish, combine 1 cup (250 mL) Basic Beef Mixture, ½ cup (125 mL) frozen mixed vegetables and ½ cup (125 mL) sliced canned mushrooms. Top with 2 cups (500 mL) cooked mashed potatoes. Bake in 350°F (180°C) oven for 15 minutes. Makes 3 to 4 servings.

Last-Minute Chili: In a small saucepan, combine 1 cup (250 mL) Basic Beef Mixture, ½ cup (125 mL) tomato sauce, ½ cup (125 mL) drained kidney beans and 1 tsp (5 mL) chili powder. Heat thoroughly. Makes 2 cups (500 mL).

Nutrients per ½ cup (125 mL)	
Calories	106
Fat	3 g
Carbohydrate	4 g
Fiber	1 g
Protein	16 g
Calcium	8 mg
Vitamin D	0 IU

Fruity Chicken

Kids love the flavor and sweetness of dried fruit — and it's a good source of iron as well. This recipe also provides lots of protein.

Tip

The vitamin C in fruit, combined with the protein from the chicken, aids your child's digestive process by increasing iron absorption.

- **Preheat oven to 400°F (200°C)**
- **Roasting pan with lid**

1	whole chicken (about 5 lbs/2.5 kg)	1
1 tsp	paprika	5 mL
½ tsp	salt	2 mL
¼ tsp	freshly ground black pepper	1 mL
½	package (9 oz/275 g) pitted prunes	½
½	package (9 oz/275 g) dried apricots	½
½ cup	dried cranberries	125 mL
2 tbsp	liquid honey	30 mL
½ cup	orange juice	125 mL
½ cup	water	125 mL

1. Season chicken with paprika, salt and pepper.

2. In a bowl, toss together prunes, apricots and cranberries until well mixed. Stuff chicken cavity with fruit and place in roasting pan. (Place any extra fruit around chicken in pan.)

3. In a small bowl, whisk together honey, juice and water. Drizzle over chicken.

4. Bake uncovered for 1 hour, then remove from oven, cover and bake for another 30 minutes or until chicken is no longer pink and juices run clear when pierced with a fork.

Nutrients per 1 of 6 servings	
Calories	507
Fat	23 g
Carbohydrate	42 g
Fiber	3 g
Protein	30 g
Calcium	31 mg
Vitamin D	15 IU

Puréed Sweet Potatoes

Makes 3 cups
(750 mL)

A wholesome and naturally sweet dish that is bursting with beta-carotene, vitamin A and fiber.

Tips

This recipe is suitable for babies over 6 months.

Homemade baby food can be frozen and used for up to 3 months. Thaw overnight in the refrigerator, or defrost in a container of warm water.

• **Food processor or blender**

2	large sweet potatoes, peeled and cubed (about 5 cups/1.25 L)	2

1. In a saucepan of boiling water, boil sweet potatoes for about 20 minutes or until tender. Drain, reserving $2/3$ cup (150 mL) of the cooking liquid.

2. Transfer potatoes to food processor and purée for 30 to 60 seconds, adding reserved cooking liquid as needed until smooth.

3. Serve immediately or freeze in an ice cube tray for future use. Once frozen, transfer individual cubes to freezer bags.

Nutrients per $1/4$ cup (60 mL)			
Calories	74	Protein	1 g
Fat	0 g	Calcium	11 mg
Carbohydrate	18 g	Vitamin D	0 IU
Fiber	2 g		

Puréed Vegetables

Makes 3 to
4 servings

Add new vegetable tastes and textures to your baby's diet, one at a time, with this simple and fresh puréed dish.

Tips

This recipe is suitable for babies over 6 months and is an excellent option for a snack at any time.

Try making purées from different-colored vegetables.

• **Food processor or blender**

$3/4$ cup	cooked vegetables, cut into small pieces	175 mL
3 tbsp	water or cooking liquid	45 mL

1. In a small bowl, microwave vegetables on High for about 1 minute or until warmed through. Stir in water. Transfer to food processor; process for 1 to 2 minutes, until purée is smooth.

2. Serve immediately or freeze in an ice cube tray for future use. Once frozen, transfer individual cubes to freezer bags.

Nutrients per 1 of 4 servings			
Calories	17	Protein	1 g
Fat	0 g	Calcium	6 mg
Carbohydrate	3 g	Vitamin D	0 IU
Fiber	1 g		

Fresh Vegetable Purée

To gain the optimal flavor, you should use only vegetables in season. Check out your local farmers' market.

Tip
Thoroughly rinse all fruits and vegetables under running water to remove any potential contaminants. This includes scrubbing the peel for fruits such as avocados and melons.

- **Food processor**

1	onion, quartered	1
3	carrots, sliced into 3-inch (7.5 cm) lengths	3
1 tbsp	vegan butter substitute	15 mL
3 lbs	butternut squash, peeled, seeded and cut into $\frac{1}{2}$-inch (1 cm) pieces	1.5 kg
1 cup	unsweetened apple juice	250 mL
2 tbsp	pure maple syrup	30 mL
$\frac{1}{2}$ tsp	freshly grated nutmeg	2 mL
$\frac{1}{4}$ tsp	ground coriander	1 mL
	Salt and freshly ground white pepper	

1. In food processor, pulse onion until chopped, about 5 times. Transfer to a bowl. Replace the metal blade with the slicing blade and slice carrots.

2. In a saucepan, melt butter substitute over medium heat. Add onion and sauté just until tender, about 3 minutes. Add carrots and squash and sauté until softened, 6 to 8 minutes.

3. Pour apple juice over vegetables and cover. Simmer on low until vegetables are softened, about 25 minutes. Stir in maple syrup, nutmeg and coriander.

4. In food processor fitted with metal blade, working in batches, process mixture until smooth. Season with salt and pepper to taste. Transfer to a serving bowl.

Nutrients per serving	
Calories	163
Fat	1 g
Carbohydrate	40 g
Fiber	6 g
Protein	3 g
Calcium	142 mg
Vitamin D	0 IU

Rice Salad

This tasty, sweet rice salad is a great accompaniment to just about any meat or fish.

Tips

This recipe is suitable for children over 18 months.

For increased flavor and nutrients, use half brown rice and half white rice.

Variation

Replace half the diced celery with diced red or green bell pepper.

3 cups	cooked white rice	750 mL
½ cup	diced celery	125 mL
½ cup	chopped onion	125 mL
10 oz	peas (canned or frozen), drained	300 g
¼ cup	vegetable oil	60 mL
2 tbsp	granulated sugar	30 mL
2 tbsp	reduced-sodium GF soy sauce	30 mL
1½ tbsp	rice vinegar	22 mL

1. In a large bowl, combine rice, celery, onion and peas.

2. In a small bowl, whisk together oil, sugar, soy sauce and vinegar. Pour dressing over rice. Toss and let stand for at least 1 hour before serving.

Nutrients per ¼ cup (60 mL)			
Calories	99	Protein	2 g
Fat	5 g	Calcium	13 mg
Carbohydrate	12 g	Vitamin D	0 IU
Fiber	1 g		

Oven-Roasted Potato Wedges

Makes 3 servings

These roast potato wedges are as crisp as french fries. Try the same thing with carrots, zucchini or sweet potatoes.

Tips

This recipe is suitable for children over 12 months.

Packaged herb blends can be found in the seasonings section of most supermarkets. Or make your own.

- **Preheat oven to 400°F (200°C)**
- **Nonstick baking sheet**

1 lb	baking potatoes, scrubbed and cut into wedges	500 g
2 tbsp	vegetable oil	30 mL
1 tbsp	garlic and herb blend (see tip, at left)	15 mL

1. In a large bowl, toss potatoes with oil and garlic and herb blend. Spread in a single layer on baking sheet. Bake in preheated oven for 40 minutes, turning halfway through cooking time, until potatoes are crisp on the outside and tender on the inside.

Nutrients per serving			
Calories	199	Protein	4 g
Fat	8 g	Calcium	27 mg
Carbohydrate	30 g	Vitamin D	0 IU
Fiber	3 g		

Tangy Fruit Sauce

Makes 1¼ cups		
(300 mL)		

¼ cup	granulated sugar	60 mL
2 tbsp	cornstarch	30 mL
½ cup	orange juice	125 mL
½ cup	water	125 mL
1 cup	sliced strawberries, raspberries, blueberries or sour cherries	250 mL
1 tsp	grated lemon zest	5 mL
1 tbsp	freshly squeezed lemon juice	15 mL

Tip

Try this sauce as a dip for new GF bread or cracker additions to your child's diet.

1. In a saucepan over medium heat, combine sugar, cornstarch, orange juice and water; bring to a boil. Reduce heat and cook, stirring constantly, until sauce has thickened. Stir in fruit, zest and lemon juice. Serve warm or cover and refrigerate until needed.

Nutrients per ¼ cup (60 mL)			
Calories	75	Protein	0 g
Fat	0 g	Calcium	8 mg
Carbohydrate	19 g	Vitamin D	0 IU
Fiber	1 g		

Grape and Melon Fruit Cups

Makes 4 servings	

1 cup	seedless grapes (see tip, at left)	250 mL
½	cantaloupe, seeded, peeled and cut into bite-size pieces	½
⅔ cup	water	150 mL
1 to 2 tbsp	granulated sugar	15 to 30 mL
1 tsp	ground ginger	5 mL

Tips

To minimize the risk of choking for children under the age of 4, always cut whole grapes in half.

Try this dish with any combination, such as pears and mandarin oranges, to entice your child to try new fruits.

If you wish, omit the syrup in step 2.

1. Arrange fruit in 4 small serving cups.

2. In a small saucepan over high heat, combine water and sugar; cook, stirring, until sugar dissolves and light syrup forms. Stir in ginger. Remove syrup from heat and let cool before pouring over fruit.

Nutrients per serving			
Calories	65	Protein	1 g
Fat	0 g	Calcium	14 mg
Carbohydrate	16 g	Vitamin D	0 IU
Fiber	1 g		

Spiced Bananas

Here's a zesty variation on bananas that will start your child's day (and yours) with a bang. Serve alone, with a slice of GF toast on the side, or as an accompaniment to GF pancakes or toaster waffles.

Tips

To make this recipe casein-free, be sure to use non-dairy cream cheese.

Top warm oatmeal with spiced bananas for a change from milk products and maple syrup.

¼ cup	orange juice	60 mL
1 tsp	grated orange zest	5 mL
2 tbsp	cream cheese (see tip, at left)	30 mL
Pinch	ground cinnamon	Pinch
Pinch	ground ginger	Pinch
2 tbsp	liquid honey	30 mL
4	bananas, cut into slices	4

1. In a bowl, using an electric mixer, combine orange juice and zest, cream cheese, cinnamon and ginger; beat until smooth. Transfer mixture to a large nonstick skillet. Add honey and cook, stirring, over medium heat until mixture is warm and thoroughly blended.

2. Add bananas to skillet; cook, turning slices frequently, until bananas are softened and warm. Serve banana slices topped with some sauce.

Nutrients per serving	
Calories	167
Fat	3 g
Carbohydrate	37 g
Fiber	3 g
Protein	2 g
Calcium	18 mg
Vitamin D	0 IU

Mashed Banana and Avocado

1	banana, sliced	1
1	avocado, cubed	1

**Makes 1 cup
(250 mL)**

Bananas and avocados are both great first foods. Their soft texture makes them easy to mash or cube, with no cooking required.

Tips

This recipe is suitable for babies over 6 months.

Let your baby mash small pieces of banana or avocado in her hands to get used to the texture.

Never take your attention away from your baby when he is eating; if the phone is ringing, let it go.

To keep unused avocado from turning brown, try storing the unused portion facedown on a plate in the refrigerator, or store in a covered container with the pit.

1. In a small bowl, using a potato masher or fork, mash banana and avocado to desired consistency.

2. Serve immediately or freeze in an ice cube tray for future use. Once frozen, transfer individual cubes to freezer bags.

Variation

You can try other fruits in combination with the avocado, including soft ripe peeled peaches or a peeled and cooked apple.

Nutrients per ¼ cup (60 mL)	
Calories	107
Fat	8 g
Carbohydrate	11 g
Fiber	4 g
Protein	1 g
Calcium	8 mg
Vitamin D	0 IU

Vanilla Soy Milk Rice Pudding

Makes 5 cups		
(1.25 L)		

The pudding can also be made with chocolate soy milk if you prefer. The spices can be tied in a cheesecloth bag, but if you don't have cheesecloth, you can just add them directly to the pudding and remove them once it's cooked.

Tips

This recipe is suitable for most babies over 8 months.

If you do not have whole cinnamon, cloves and cardamom, they can be replaced with ground spices. Use about ¼ tsp (1 mL) of each.

The soy milk will provide some sweetness, so you may find you prefer to reduce the sugar in the recipe.

If your child is sensitive to soy milk, try one of the other non-dairy milk products: almond, rice, coconut or hemp, for example.

Nutrients per ½ cup (125 mL)	
Calories	98
Fat	1 g
Carbohydrate	20 g
Fiber	1 g
Protein	3 g
Calcium	62 mg
Vitamin D	24 IU

¾ cup	short-grain rice (such as Arborio)	175 mL
2	cardamom pods (see tip, at left)	2
2	whole cloves	2
1	3-inch (7.5 cm) cinnamon stick	1
2 cups	vanilla-flavored soy milk	500 mL
⅓ cup	granulated sugar	75 mL
1	large egg	1
1 tsp	GF vanilla extract	5 mL

1. In a large bowl, cover rice with cold water. Stir until water becomes cloudy; drain. Repeat until water is no longer cloudy.

2. Place rice in a saucepan and add 2 cups (500 mL) cold water; bring to a boil over medium-high heat. Cover, reduce heat to low and cook for 15 minutes or until liquid is absorbed. Remove from heat and stir in cardamom, cloves and cinnamon. Let stand, covered, for 10 minutes.

3. Stir soy milk and sugar into rice; bring to a boil over high heat. Reduce heat to low and cook, uncovered, for 15 minutes, stirring constantly. Discard spices.

4. In a bowl, beat a small amount of hot rice mixture into egg; stir into saucepan and cook, stirring constantly, for 3 minutes or until slightly thickened. Remove from heat and stir in vanilla. Serve warm.

Breakfast

Easy Homemade Granola. 202

Gluten-Free Muesli. 203

Quinoa Crunch 204

Breakfast Rice. 204

Sweet Banana Porridge 205

Cranberry Quinoa Porridge 206

Baked Apple Quinoa 207

Quinoa Coconut Fruit Sushi 208

Crispy Bacon Strips. 209

Tofu Quinoa Scramble 209

Akoori (South Asian Scrambled Eggs) 210

Aamlete (South Asian Omelet). 211

Individual Salsa Fresca Omelets. 212

Banana Pecan Waffles 213

Tasty Potato Pancakes 214

Maple Breakfast Biscotti. 215

Cocoa Quinoa Breakfast Squares. 216

Easy Homemade Granola

With few ingredients, this granola is economical and easy to prepare. A small sealable bag of granola is a great take-along snack or topping for your favorite vegan ice cream.

Tips

Flax seeds are available in grocery and natural food stores either raw or toasted. Raw flax seeds may be toasted in a heavy skillet over medium-high heat while stirring constantly to prevent burning until seeds turn a golden brown. Store in an airtight container in the refrigerator for up to 3 weeks.

Sprinkle a little granola on top of a cut-up apple and bake in the microwave as a great shortcut for apple crisp.

Nutrients per ½ cup (125 mL)	
Calories	520
Fat	26 g
Carbohydrate	56 g
Fiber	13 g
Protein	15 g
Calcium	98 mg
Vitamin D	0 IU

- **Preheat oven to 250°F (120°C)**
- **Rimmed baking sheet, lined with parchment paper**

2 cups	certified GF large-flake (old-fashioned) rolled oats	500 mL
¾ cup	slivered almonds	175 mL
½ cup	sunflower seeds	125 mL
¼ cup	green pumpkin seeds (pepitas)	60 mL
2 tbsp	toasted flax seeds (see tip, at left)	30 mL
1¼ cups	unsweetened orange juice	300 mL
1 tsp	GF vanilla extract	5 mL
½ tsp	ground cardamom	2 mL
2 tbsp	sunflower oil	30 mL
¾ cup	dried blueberries	175 mL

1. In a large bowl, combine oats, almonds and sunflower, pumpkin and flax seeds, mixing well to combine.

2. In another bowl, combine orange juice, vanilla and cardamom. Stir into oats, mixing well to blend. Stir in oil and mix well to coat.

3. Spread mixture evenly on prepared baking sheet. Bake in preheated oven, stirring occasionally to ensure even crisping, until granola is crisp, about 1½ hours. Remove from oven, stir in blueberries and let mixture cool. Store in an airtight container for up to 2 weeks at room temperature or freeze for up to 2 months.

Variation

Use any nuts, seeds or dried fruit you happen to have on hand. Cranberries, raisins, dried apricots, papaya, mango and figs are excellent choices.

Gluten-Free Muesli

Makes 3 servings

Tip

If using soy milk, note that barley malt contains gluten, so use gluten-free or malt-free soy milk.

- **Preheat oven to 400°F (200°C)**

¼ cup	almonds	60 mL
1 cup	puffed brown rice cereal	250 mL
1 cup	puffed amaranth cereal	250 mL
½ cup	rice bran	125 mL
¼ cup	raw green pumpkin seeds (pepitas)	60 mL
½ cup	whole flax seeds	125 mL
¼ cup	lecithin granules (GMO-free soy)	60 mL
	Chilled malt-free soy milk or Almond Milk (page 377)	
	Liquid honey (optional)	
1	banana, sliced	1

1. Spread almonds on a baking sheet and toast in preheated oven for 4 minutes (do not burn them). Remove from heat and let cool.

2. Mix puffed rice, puffed amaranth and rice bran with the almonds, pumpkin seeds, flax seeds and lecithin. Store in an airtight container.

3. Serve 1 cup (250 mL) per person and add soy milk, honey and banana.

Nutrients per serving	
Calories	501
Fat	30 g
Carbohydrate	50 g
Fiber	17 g
Protein	16 g
Calcium	172 mg
Vitamin D	0 IU

Quinoa Crunch

**Makes about 1 cup
(250 mL)**

Here, quinoa is
transformed into a
crispy-sweet topping
that's heavenly sprinkled
on cereal or muffins,
mixed into trail mix
or simply eaten out of
hand.

Tip

An equal amount of pure
maple syrup, brown rice
syrup or agave nectar may
be used in place of the
honey. Remember, children
under 1 year should avoid
honey due to the risk of
botulinum toxin.

- Preheat oven to 375°F (190°C)
- Rimmed baking sheet, lined with parchment paper

1 cup	quinoa, rinsed	250 mL
1 tbsp	vegetable oil	15 mL
1 tbsp	liquid honey	15 mL
$\frac{1}{8}$ tsp	fine sea salt	0.5 mL

1. In a small bowl, combine quinoa, oil, honey and salt. Spread in a single layer on prepared baking sheet.

2. Bake in preheated oven for 11 to 13 minutes, stirring occasionally, until quinoa is crisp. Transfer to a large plate and let cool completely.

3. Transfer quinoa crunch to an airtight container and store at room temperature for up to 1 month.

Nutrients per $\frac{1}{4}$ cup (60 mL)			
Calories	207	Protein	6 g
Fat	6 g	Calcium	20 mg
Carbohydrate	33 g	Vitamin D	0 IU
Fiber	2 g		

Breakfast Rice

**Makes about
3 cups (750 mL)**

Tip
The rice will be a bit
crunchy around the edges.
If you prefer a softer version
or will be cooking it longer
than 8 hours, add $\frac{1}{2}$ cup
(125 mL) of water or rice
milk to the recipe.

Variations

Add fresh apples or pears.

Use half rice and half
wheat, spelt or Kamut.

- $1\frac{1}{2}$- to $3\frac{1}{2}$-quart slow cooker
- Lightly greased slow cooker stoneware

1 cup	brown rice	250 mL
4 cups	vanilla-flavored enriched rice milk	1 L
$\frac{1}{2}$ cup	dried cherries or cranberries	125 mL

1. In prepared slow cooker stoneware, combine rice, rice milk and cherries. Stir well. Place a clean tea towel, folded in half (so you will have two layers), over top of stoneware to absorb moisture. Cover and cook on Low for up to 8 hours or overnight or on High for 4 hours. Stir well and serve.

Nutrients per $\frac{1}{2}$ cup (125 mL)			
Calories	236	Protein	3 g
Fat	2 g	Calcium	212 mg
Carbohydrate	51 g	Vitamin D	67 IU
Fiber	4 g		

Sweet Banana Porridge

Children love this hearty, warm breakfast.

Tip

For a slightly crunchier texture that may please those more selective palates, reheat leftover porridge in a pan and top with a few GFCF chocolate chips or another family favorite, such as Tangy Fruit Sauce (page 197).

2 cups	certified GF large-flake (old-fashioned) rolled oats	500 mL
4 cups	water	1 L
4 tsp	pure maple syrup	20 mL
1 tbsp	ground flax seeds (flaxseed meal)	15 mL
1 cup	calcium-fortified soy milk	250 mL
1	ripe banana, thinly sliced	1

1. If possible, soak the oats overnight in the water to germinate the grain, making it more digestible and the nutrients more available.

2. Place oats and their water in a small saucepan. Bring to a boil and simmer for 5 minutes, stirring regularly, until cooked. Serve with maple syrup, flax seeds, soy milk and banana.

Nutrients per serving	
Calories	267
Fat	5 g
Carbohydrate	47 g
Fiber	6 g
Protein	9 g
Calcium	106 mg
Vitamin D	26 IU

Cranberry Quinoa Porridge

If you're not organized enough to make hot cereal ahead of time, here's one you can enjoy in less than half an hour, start to finish.

Tips

Unless you have a stove with a true simmer, after reducing the heat to low, place a heat diffuser under the pot to prevent the mixture from boiling. This device also helps to ensure the grains will cook evenly and prevents hot spots, which might cause scorching, from forming. Heat diffusers are available at kitchen supply and hardware stores and are made to work on gas or electric stoves.

Serve the dried cranberries on the side and let your child decorate his porridge with style.

Try topping with Tangy Fruit Sauce (page 197) to tempt a picky eater.

Nutrients per serving	
Calories	137
Fat	2 g
Carbohydrate	27 g
Fiber	2 g
Protein	4 g
Calcium	13 mg
Vitamin D	0 IU

3 cups	water	750 mL
1 cup	quinoa, rinsed	250 mL
½ cup	dried cranberries	125 mL
	Pure maple syrup or liquid honey	
	Plain non-dairy milk (optional)	

1. In a saucepan over medium heat, bring water to a boil. Stir in quinoa and cranberries and return to a boil. Reduce heat to low. Cover and simmer until quinoa is cooked (look for a white line around the seeds), about 15 minutes. Remove from heat and let stand, covered, about 5 minutes. Serve with maple syrup and non-dairy milk (if using).

Variations

Substitute dried cherries, dried blueberries or raisins for the cranberries.

Use red quinoa for a change.

Baked Apple Quinoa

Apples times two — diced and applesauce — add moistness and natural sweetness to this delicious, healthful baked quinoa breakfast. A light sprinkling of turbinado sugar adds a beautiful and tasty touch.

Tips

For the apples, try Gala, Braeburn or Cortland.

This is a great snack anytime for anyone, as well as an after-school crowd pleaser.

The combination of warm apples and cinnamon is always good if your child is a super-sniffer!

- **Preheat oven to 400°F (200°C)**
- **8-inch (20 cm) square glass baking dish, sprayed with nonstick cooking spray**

1 cup	quinoa, rinsed	250 mL
1½ tsp	ground cinnamon	7 mL
½ tsp	fine sea salt	2 mL
2 cups	plain non-dairy milk (such as soy, almond, rice or hemp)	500 mL
2	large eggs	2
½ cup	unsweetened applesauce	125 mL
¼ cup	pure maple syrup or liquid honey	60 mL
1 tsp	GF vanilla extract	5 mL
2 cups	diced peeled tart-sweet apples (see tip, at left)	500 mL
½ cup	dried cranberries, cherries or raisins (optional)	125 mL
1 tbsp	turbinado sugar	15 mL

Suggested Accompaniments

Warm or cold plain non-dairy milk (such as soy, almond, rice or hemp)

Liquid honey or pure maple syrup

1. In a medium saucepan, combine quinoa, cinnamon, salt and milk. Bring to a boil over medium-high heat. Reduce heat to low, cover and simmer for 15 minutes.

2. Meanwhile, in a small bowl, whisk together eggs, applesauce, maple syrup and vanilla until blended.

3. Add the egg mixture to the quinoa mixture and stir until just blended. Gently fold in apples and cranberries (if using). Spread evenly in prepared baking dish and sprinkle with sugar.

4. Bake in preheated oven for 20 to 25 minutes or until set at the center and golden. Let cool in pan on a wire rack for 5 minutes. Serve warm with any of the suggested accompaniments, as desired.

Nutrients per serving	
Calories	358
Fat	7 g
Carbohydrate	64 g
Fiber	5 g
Protein	13 g
Calcium	219 mg
Vitamin D	73 IU

Quinoa Coconut Fruit Sushi

This playful breakfast is perfect for breakfast on the run — and for satisfying a morning sweet tooth. Use any fresh or canned fruit you like, or use colorful dried fruits, such as diced dried apricots, dates or cherries.

Tips

For the fruit, try raspberries, blueberries, kiwifruit and/or mandarin oranges.

Let your little ones help decorate the sushi.

- **Large baking sheet, lined with waxed paper or foil**

⅔ cup	sushi rice or other short-grain white rice	150 mL
⅓ cup	black or white quinoa, rinsed	75 mL
1 tbsp	cornstarch or arrowroot starch	15 mL
⅛ tsp	fine sea salt	0.5 mL
1 cup	water	250 mL
¾ cup	light coconut milk, divided	175 mL
¼ cup	agave nectar or liquid honey	60 mL
	Nonstick cooking spray	
	Assorted small-diced fruit or berries	
⅔ cup	vanilla-flavored cultured non-dairy yogurt (such as soy or rice)	150 mL

1. In a medium saucepan, combine rice, quinoa, cornstarch, salt, water, ½ cup (125 mL) of the coconut milk and agave nectar. Bring to a boil over medium-high heat. Reduce heat to low, cover and simmer for 15 minutes. Remove from heat and gently stir in the remaining coconut milk. Cover and let stand for 30 minutes.

2. Lightly coat your hands with cooking spray. Using your hands, press 1½-tbsp (22 mL) portions of rice mixture into an oval shape. Place on prepared baking sheet. Cover and refrigerate for at least 1 hour, until chilled, or for up to 24 hours.

3. Just before serving, top each oval with a few pieces of fruit or berries, gently pressing them into the rice mixture so they adhere. Serve with yogurt for dipping.

Nutrients per piece	
Calories	61
Fat	1 g
Carbohydrate	12 g
Fiber	0 g
Protein	1 g
Calcium	15 mg
Vitamin D	0 IU

Crispy Bacon Strips

Make your meal sizzle. Perfect crispy bacon strips will make you a hero every time you serve them.

Tips

Crumble your crispy bacon strips to add to a lunch salad or egg salad sandwiches.

For some picky eaters, crispy bacon strips might be the motivation your child needs to taste-test that broccoli tree.

| 8 | slices GF bacon | 8 |

1. Place bacon slices side by side in a single layer in a rectangular dish lined with 6 sheets of paper towel. Top with 2 more sheets of paper towel and microwave on High for 7 minutes, or until crispy.

Nutrients per serving			
Calories	87	Protein	6 g
Fat	7 g	Calcium	2 mg
Carbohydrate	0 g	Vitamin D	7 IU
Fiber	0 g		

Tofu Quinoa Scramble

Health food gets fancy, turning tofu, quinoa and vegetables into a truly delectable morning meal.

Tips

Tofu is a good source of protein, calcium and fiber.

Use this delicious and nutritious scramble to introduce tofu to your child.

1 tbsp	extra virgin olive oil	15 mL
1	large red bell pepper, chopped	1
1 cup	chopped mushrooms	250 mL
16 oz	extra-firm or firm tofu, drained and coarsely mashed with a fork	500 g
1 cup	cooked quinoa, cooled	250 mL
1/4 cup	chopped green onions	60 mL
1 tbsp	reduced-sodium GF tamari or soy sauce	15 mL
Pinch	freshly ground black pepper	Pinch

1. In a small skillet, heat oil over medium-high heat. Add red pepper and mushrooms; cook, stirring, for 4 to 5 minutes or until softened. Add tofu, quinoa, green onions and tamari; cook, stirring, for 5 to 6 minutes or until tofu is golden brown. Season with pepper.

Nutrients per serving			
Calories	217	Protein	15 g
Fat	11 g	Calcium	103 mg
Carbohydrate	16 g	Vitamin D	2 IU
Fiber	4 g		

Akoori
(South Asian Scrambled Eggs)

Makes 4 to 6 servings

The dish is of Parsi origin and much loved by Mumbaians and other South Asians.

Tips

Akoori is wonderful as a filling for a wrap or stuffed into pita bread.

The important thing in South Asian cooking is to use a chile pepper with spirit. Fresh cayenne peppers, or any similar ones, would work very well. If using fresh Thai peppers, now readily available in North America, use only half the amount called for in the recipe. In a pinch, jalapeños could also be used.

Turmeric is a healthy addition to any meal, and this dish is perfect for spice lovers.

Nutrients per 1 of 6 servings	
Calories	174
Fat	14 g
Carbohydrate	5 g
Fiber	1 g
Protein	9 g
Calcium	52 mg
Vitamin D	55 IU

8	large eggs	8
1 tsp	salt (or to taste)	5 mL
¼ tsp	freshly ground black pepper	1 mL
3 tbsp	vegetable oil	45 mL
1 tsp	cumin seeds	5 mL
1 cup	chopped onion	250 mL
2 tsp	finely chopped green chile pepper (see tip, at left)	10 mL
1 cup	chopped tomato	250 mL
½ tsp	cayenne pepper	2 mL
¼ tsp	ground turmeric	1 mL
¼ cup	chopped fresh cilantro	60 mL
	Tomato wedges and cilantro sprigs	

1. In a bowl, gently whisk eggs, salt and pepper. Do not beat.

2. In a large skillet, heat oil over medium-high heat and add cumin seeds. Stir in onion and green chile and sauté until golden, 3 to 4 minutes.

3. Add tomato and sauté, stirring continuously, for 1 minute. Stir in cayenne, turmeric and cilantro. Cook for 1 minute longer. Reduce heat to medium-low and slowly add egg mixture. Cook, stirring gently, until eggs are soft and creamy, 3 to 4 minutes. Do not overcook.

4. Serve garnished with tomato wedges and cilantro sprigs.

Aamlete
(South Asian Omelet)

Aamlete is very popular with urban South Asians. Served in every corner tea shop in Mumbai for breakfast or lunch, it is also offered on breakfast menus on trains in India. Aamlete sandwiches served with ketchup (called tomato sauce) are standard lunch fare on the streets of Mumbai when office workers are looking for fast food.

Tips

Aamletes are traditionally flatter and not as fluffy as an omelet, and are often served with hot toast or sandwiched between 2 slices of thin sandwich bread as a quick, tasty and nutritious lunch or snack for all ages.

For a milder version, use a green bell pepper instead of a green chile.

Nutrients per serving	
Calories	105
Fat	7 g
Carbohydrate	5 g
Fiber	1 g
Protein	6 g
Calcium	17 mg
Vitamin D	0 IU

6	large eggs	6
1 tsp	salt	5 mL
¼ tsp	freshly ground black pepper	1 mL
2 to 3 tbsp	vegetable oil, divided	30 to 45 mL
¾ cup	chopped onion, divided	175 mL
¾ cup	chopped tomato, divided	175 mL
2 tsp	chopped green chile pepper (see tip, page 210), divided	10 mL
¼ cup	chopped fresh cilantro, divided	60 mL

1. In a bowl, beat together eggs, salt, pepper and 2 tbsp (30 mL) water until blended.

2. In a large nonstick skillet, heat 1 tbsp (15 mL) of the oil over medium heat. Pour one-quarter of the eggs into skillet. Scatter one-quarter each of the onion, tomato, chile and cilantro evenly on top. Cook, without stirring, until edges can be lifted with spatula, about 2 minutes. Fold over to form semicircle. Cook for 30 seconds longer.

3. Transfer to platter and keep warm. Repeat to make remaining 3 omelets, adding enough oil between batches to prevent sticking.

Individual Salsa Fresca Omelets

Makes 2 servings

This is an easy meal for older children or teens to prepare for themselves or their family. The ingredients can easily be doubled to serve four.

Tips

With all the ingredients on hand, this recipe is quick to prepare and serve for breakfast, lunch or dinner. If you don't have time to make the salsa, use a commercially prepared GFCF salsa instead.

Prepare the salsa the night before; put in an airtight container and store in the fridge. Use about ½ cup (125 mL) salsa per omelet. The extra 1 cup (250 mL) salsa can be used as a dip for Fresh Tortilla Chips (page 371).

Serve with whole-grain GF toast, in a GF pita pocket or wrapped up in a GF flour or corn tortilla.

Nutrients per omelet with ½ cup (125 mL) salsa	
Calories	194
Fat	12 g
Carbohydrate	8 g
Fiber	2 g
Protein	14 g
Calcium	104 mg
Vitamin D	82 IU

Salsa Fresca

1 cup	diced seeded tomatoes	250 mL
1 cup	diced cucumber	250 mL
⅓ cup	chopped red onions	75 mL
¼ cup	chopped fresh cilantro or parsley	60 mL
2 tbsp	freshly squeezed lime juice	30 mL
	Salt and freshly ground black pepper	

Omelets

4	large eggs	4
1 tbsp	water	15 mL
	Salt and freshly ground black pepper	
1 tsp	vegetable oil, divided	5 mL

1. *Salsa:* In a bowl, combine tomatoes, cucumber, red onions, cilantro, lime juice, and salt and pepper to taste. Let stand 10 minutes. Drain well.

2. *Omelet:* In a bowl, beat together eggs, water, and salt and pepper to taste. In a small 8-inch (20 cm) nonstick skillet over medium-high heat, heat ½ tsp (2 mL) oil. Making one omelet at a time, pour half of egg mixture into pan. As eggs begin to set at edges, use a spatula to gently push cooked portions to the center, tilting pan to allow uncooked egg to flow into empty spaces.

3. When egg is almost set on the surface but still looks moist, fill half the omelet with some of the Salsa Fresca. Slip spatula under unfilled side, fold over filling and slide omelet onto plate. Top with additional Salsa Fresca. Repeat with remaining egg mixture.

This recipe courtesy of the Canadian Egg Marketing Agency.

Variation

Dress up your omelet with chopped ham and green onions or diced leftover cooked potatoes.

Banana Pecan Waffles

Makes six 4½-inch (11 cm) waffles		

Kids love these for breakfast. Make ahead and freeze for weekday use, then just pop them in the toaster to reheat and crisp up.

Tips

Recipe can be doubled or tripled.

Store extra waffles between layers of waxed paper in an airtight container in the refrigerator for up to 3 days, or in a plastic freezer bag in the freezer for up to 1 month. Reheat from frozen in the toaster.

Resist the temptation to add extra liquid — the batter should be thick.

Beat the batter until smooth — no need to leave it lumpy.

Nutrients per waffle	
Calories	275
Fat	14 g
Carbohydrate	36 g
Fiber	4 g
Protein	6 g
Calcium	101 mg
Vitamin D	14 IU

- **Waffle maker, lightly greased, then preheated**

¾ cup	sorghum flour	175 mL
¼ cup	quinoa flour	60 mL
¼ cup	tapioca starch	60 mL
2 tbsp	granulated sugar	30 mL
½ tsp	xanthan gum	2 mL
2¼ tsp	GF baking powder	11 mL
¾ tsp	baking soda	3 mL
Pinch	salt	Pinch
½ cup	chopped pecans	125 mL
2	large eggs, separated	2
1 cup	mashed bananas	250 mL
2 tbsp	vegetable oil	30 mL

1. In a large bowl or plastic bag, combine sorghum flour, quinoa flour, tapioca starch, sugar, xanthan gum, baking powder, baking soda, salt and pecans. Mix well and set aside.

2. In a small bowl, using an electric mixer, preferably with wire whisk attachment, beat egg whites until stiff but not dry.

3. In a separate bowl, using an electric mixer, beat egg yolks, bananas and oil until combined. Add dry ingredients and beat until smooth. Fold in beaten egg whites.

4. Pour in enough batter to fill preheated waffle maker two-thirds full. Close lid and cook for 5 to 7 minutes or until no longer steaming. Repeat with remaining batter, greasing waffle maker between waffles as necessary.

Variation

Increase the sugar to ¼ cup (60 mL) to turn these into dessert waffles, and serve with fresh fruit and Tangy Fruit Sauce (page 197).

Tasty Potato Pancakes

Kids will rave about these, so be sure to make extra! Serve warm or cold, as a side dish or a snack. They'll keep in the fridge for up to 2 days.

Tip
Use these pancakes to help replace grains with gluten in your child's diet.

3	potatoes, peeled and shredded	3
2	large eggs, lightly beaten	2
½	onion, finely chopped	½
Pinch	salt	Pinch
2 to 3 tbsp	vegetable oil (approx.), divided	30 to 45 mL

1. In a medium bowl, combine potatoes, eggs, onion and salt. Form into 2-inch (5 cm) diameter patties.

2. In a skillet, heat 2 tbsp (30 mL) of the oil over medium-high heat. Cook patties, in batches, for 2 to 3 minutes per side or until lightly browned on both sides, adding oil to the skillet and adjusting heat between batches as necessary. Transfer to a plate lined with paper towels.

Nutrients per pancake	
Calories	70
Fat	3 g
Carbohydrate	9 g
Fiber	1 g
Protein	2 g
Calcium	10 mg
Vitamin D	7 IU

Maple Breakfast Biscotti

Makes 3 dozen cookies

These crisp biscotti have a plethora of good-for-you ingredients and are great on the go or slowly savored (and dunked) with a morning cup of joe, or non-dairy milk or hot chocolate for your child.

Tips

For the nuts, you can also try walnuts, hazelnuts, pistachios or almonds. For the dried fruit, try raisins, cherries or chopped apricots.

The biscotti will continue to harden as they cool after the second bake.

Store the cooled biscotti in an airtight container at room temperature for up to 5 days.

Kids who like crunchy foods will love these, and kids who like soft foods will love to dip them in their hot chocolate.

Nutrients per cookie	
Calories	71
Fat	2 g
Carbohydrate	12 g
Fiber	1 g
Protein	2 g
Calcium	17 mg
Vitamin D	2 IU

- **Preheat oven to 300°F (150°C)**
- **Food processor**
- **Large rimmed baking sheet, lined with parchment paper**

1½ cups	certified GF large-flake (old-fashioned) rolled oats, divided	375 mL
1 cup	quinoa flour	250 mL
1 tsp	GF baking powder	5 mL
½ tsp	baking soda	2 mL
¼ tsp	fine sea salt	1 mL
⅔ cup	chopped toasted pecans	150 mL
⅔ cup	chopped pitted dates	150 mL
⅓ cup	natural cane sugar or packed light brown sugar	75 mL
2	large eggs	2
⅓ cup	pure maple syrup	75 mL
1 tsp	GF vanilla extract	5 mL

1. In food processor, pulse ¾ cup (175 mL) of the oats until they resemble fine flour.

2. Transfer ground oats to a medium bowl and whisk in the remaining oats, quinoa flour, baking powder, baking soda and salt. Stir in pecans and dates.

3. In a large bowl, whisk together sugar, eggs, maple syrup and vanilla until blended. Gradually add the flour mixture, stirring until just blended. Divide dough in half.

4. Place dough on prepared baking sheet and, using moistened hands, shape into two parallel 12- by 2-inch (30 by 5 cm) rectangles, spaced about 3 inches (7.5 cm) apart.

5. Bake in preheated oven for 30 to 35 minutes or until set at the center and golden. Let cool on pan on a wire rack for 15 minutes.

6. Cut rectangles crosswise into ½-inch (1 cm) slices. Place slices, cut side down, on baking sheet. Bake for 8 to 10 minutes or until edges are golden. Let cool on pan for 1 minute, then transfer to wire racks to cool completely.

Cocoa Quinoa Breakfast Squares

The intense flavor of cocoa powder and natural sweetness of plump dates coalesce with quinoa for a power-packed breakfast.

Tips

This makes a nutritionally rich snack with an energy kick and surprising flavors — an excellent source of omega-3 fatty acids and high in fiber.

Lining a pan with foil is easy. Begin by turning the pan upside down. Tear off a piece of foil longer than the pan, then mold the foil over the pan. Remove the foil and set it aside. Flip the pan over and gently fit the shaped foil into the pan, allowing the foil to hang over the sides (the overhang ends will work as "handles" when the contents of the pan are removed).

Nutrients per square	
Calories	190
Fat	4 g
Carbohydrate	34 g
Fiber	6 g
Protein	7 g
Calcium	95 mg
Vitamin D	23 IU

- **Preheat oven to 350°F (180°C)**
- **Blender or food processor**
- **8-inch (20 cm) square metal baking pan, lined with foil (see tip, at left) and sprayed with nonstick cooking spray**

1 cup	pitted soft dates (such as Medjool)	250 mL
1/3 cup	unsweetened cocoa powder (not Dutch process)	75 mL
1/4 tsp	fine sea salt	1 mL
2 cups	plain non-dairy milk (such as soy, rice, almond or hemp)	500 mL
1 tsp	GF vanilla extract	5 mL
3 cups	hot cooked quinoa	750 mL
1/2 cup	ground flax seeds (flaxseed meal)	125 mL

1. In blender, combine dates, cocoa, salt, milk and vanilla; purée until smooth.

2. Transfer date mixture to a large bowl and stir in quinoa and flax seeds. Spread evenly in prepared pan.

3. Bake in preheated oven for 55 to 60 minutes or until firmly set. Let cool completely in pan on a wire rack. Using foil liner, lift mixture from pan onto a cutting board; peel off foil and cut into 9 squares.

Breads
and Muffins

White Bread 218

Brown Sandwich Bread 220

Egg-Free, Corn-Free, Dairy-Free,
    Soy-Free Brown Bread 222

Crunchy Multigrain Bâtarde 224

Honey Dijon Toastie 226

Date Cashew Loaf 228

Simple Corn Tortillas 229

Biscuit Mix 230

Bacon and Tomato Biscuits 231

Breadsticks 232

Sesame Crispbread 234

Oatmeal Muffin Mix 236

Carrot Oatmeal Muffins 237

Pear Buckwheat Muffins 238

Almond Flour Blackberry Muffins 239

Gingerbread Muffins 240

Pumpkin Almond Flour Muffins 242

White Bread

Makes 15 slices

This is sure to become your whole family's favorite nutritious white sandwich bread. It won't crumble in a packed lunch.

Tips

Be sure not to substitute or omit any ingredients and to measure accurately.

This is a very nutritious bread — tell your children it will turn them into super-kids.

Nutrients per slice	
Calories	129
Fat	5 g
Carbohydrate	20 g
Fiber	2 g
Protein	3 g
Calcium	16 mg
Vitamin D	6 IU

- **Bread machine or 9- by 5-inch (23 by 12.5 cm) loaf pan, lightly greased**

1 cup	brown rice flour	250 mL
½ cup	amaranth flour	125 mL
⅓ cup	almond flour	75 mL
⅓ cup	quinoa flour	75 mL
¼ cup	potato starch	60 mL
2 tbsp	tapioca starch	30 mL
1 tbsp	xanthan gum	15 mL
1 tbsp	bread machine or instant yeast	15 mL
1½ tsp	salt	7 mL
1 cup	water	250 mL
2 tbsp	vegetable oil	30 mL
2 tbsp	liquid honey	30 mL
1 tsp	cider vinegar	5 mL
2	large eggs	2

Bread Machine Method

1. In a large bowl or plastic bag, combine brown rice flour, amaranth flour, almond flour, quinoa flour, potato starch, tapioca starch, xanthan gum, yeast and salt. Mix well and set aside.

2. Pour water, oil, honey and vinegar into the bread machine baking pan. Add eggs.

3. Select the Gluten-Free Cycle. As the bread machine is mixing, gradually add the dry ingredients, scraping bottom and sides of pan with a rubber spatula. Try to incorporate all the dry ingredients within 1 to 2 minutes. When the mixing and kneading are complete, remove the kneading blade, leaving the bread pan in the bread machine. Quickly smooth the top of the loaf. Allow the cycle to finish.

Variation

Raisin Bread: Add ½ cup (125 mL) raisins and 1 tsp (5 mL) ground cinnamon with the dry ingredients.

4. At the end of the cycle, take the temperature of the loaf using an instant-read thermometer. It is baked at 200°F (100°C). If it's between 180°F (85°C) and 200°F (100°C), leave machine on the Keep Warm Cycle until baked. If it's below 180°F (85°C), turn on the Bake Cycle and check the internal temperature every 10 minutes. (Some bread machines are automatically set for 60 minutes; others need to be set by 10-minute intervals.)

5. Once the loaf has reached 200°F (100°C), remove it from the pan immediately and let cool completely on a rack.

Mixer Method

1. In a large bowl or plastic bag, combine brown rice flour, amaranth flour, almond flour, quinoa flour, potato starch, tapioca starch, xanthan gum, yeast and salt. Mix well and set aside.

2. In a separate bowl, using a heavy-duty electric mixer with paddle attachment, combine water, oil, honey, vinegar and eggs until well blended. With the mixer on its lowest speed, slowly add the dry ingredients until combined. Stop the machine and scrape the bottom and sides of the bowl with a rubber spatula. With the mixer on medium speed, beat for 1 minute or until smooth.

3. Spoon dough into prepared pan. Let rise, uncovered, in a warm, draft-free place for 60 to 75 minutes or until dough has risen to the top of the pan. Meanwhile, preheat oven to 350°F (180°C).

4. Bake for 35 to 40 minutes or until internal temperature of loaf registers 200°F (100°C) on an instant-read thermometer. Remove from the pan immediately and let cool completely on a rack.

Brown Sandwich Bread

For those who want a rich, golden, wholesome, nutritious sandwich bread for your family to carry for lunch, this is your loaf.

Tips

Pea flour, like soy flour, has a distinctive odor when wet; it disappears with baking.

This bread is an excellent source of calcium.

If your child likes soft food, try an old-fashioned way to serve it by putting a slice of this bread in a saucer. Pour a little plain non-dairy milk over it and top with fruit topping or a little maple syrup.

Nutrients per slice	
Calories	121
Fat	4 g
Carbohydrate	18 g
Fiber	3 g
Protein	4 g
Calcium	16 mg
Vitamin D	6 IU

- **Bread machine or 9- by 5-inch (23 by 12.5 cm) loaf pan, lightly greased**

1 cup	sorghum flour	250 mL
½ cup	pea flour	125 mL
⅓ cup	tapioca starch	75 mL
⅓ cup	rice bran	75 mL
2 tbsp	packed brown sugar	30 mL
1 tbsp	xanthan gum	15 mL
2 tsp	bread machine or instant yeast	10 mL
1½ tsp	salt	7 mL
1¼ cups	water	300 mL
3 tbsp	vegetable oil	45 mL
2 tbsp	light (fancy) molasses	30 mL
1 tsp	cider vinegar	5 mL
2	large eggs, lightly beaten	2
1	large egg white, lightly beaten	1

Bread Machine Method

1. In a large bowl or plastic bag, combine sorghum flour, pea flour, tapioca starch, rice bran, brown sugar, xanthan gum, yeast and salt. Mix well and set aside.

2. Pour water, oil, molasses and vinegar into the bread machine baking pan. Add eggs and egg white.

3. Select the Gluten-Free Cycle. As the bread machine is mixing, gradually add the dry ingredients, scraping bottom and sides of pan with a rubber spatula. Try to incorporate all the dry ingredients within 1 to 2 minutes. When the mixing and kneading are complete, remove the kneading blade, leaving the bread pan in the bread machine. Quickly smooth the top of the loaf. Allow the cycle to finish.

Variations

Any type of bean flour can be substituted for the pea flour.

Substitute GF oat bran for the rice bran.

4. At the end of the cycle, take the temperature of the loaf using an instant-read thermometer. It is baked at 200°F (100°C). If it's between 180°F (85°C) and 200°F (100°C), leave machine on the Keep Warm Cycle until baked. If it's below 180°F (85°C), turn on the Bake Cycle and check the internal temperature every 10 minutes. (Some bread machines are automatically set for 60 minutes; others need to be set by 10-minute intervals.)

5. Once the loaf has reached 200°F (100°C), remove it from the pan immediately and let cool completely on a rack.

Mixer Method

1. In a large bowl or plastic bag, combine sorghum flour, pea flour, tapioca starch, rice bran, brown sugar, xanthan gum, yeast and salt. Mix well and set aside.

2. In a separate bowl, using a heavy-duty electric mixer with paddle attachment, combine water, oil, molasses, vinegar, eggs and egg white until well blended. With the mixer on its lowest speed, slowly add the dry ingredients until combined. Stop the machine and scrape the bottom and sides of the bowl with a rubber spatula. With the mixer on medium speed, beat for 4 minutes.

3. Spoon dough into prepared pan. Let rise, uncovered, in a warm, draft-free place for 60 to 75 minutes or until dough has risen to the top of the pan. Meanwhile, preheat oven to 350°F (180°C), with rack set in bottom third of oven.

4. Bake for 25 minutes. Tent loosely with foil (dull side out) and bake for 10 to 15 minutes or until internal temperature of loaf registers 200°F (100°C) on an instant-read thermometer. Remove from the pan immediately and let cool completely on a rack.

This recipe courtesy of CanolaInfo.

Egg-Free, Corn-Free, Dairy-Free, Soy-Free Brown Bread

Though shorter than some loaves, this is the perfect brown sandwich bread for those who must eliminate eggs, corn, dairy and/or soy from their diet. It carries well, for a tasty lunch.

Tip

Keep this bread on hand for any GI flare-ups your child may have.

Nutrients per slice	
Calories	131
Fat	4 g
Carbohydrate	24 g
Fiber	3 g
Protein	3 g
Calcium	23 mg
Vitamin D	0 IU

- **Bread machine or 9- by 5-inch (23 by 12.5 cm) loaf pan, lightly greased**

¼ cup	flax flour or ground flax seeds (flaxseed meal)	60 mL
⅓ cup	warm water	75 mL
1¼ cups	brown rice flour	300 mL
¾ cup	sorghum flour	175 mL
⅓ cup	rice bran	75 mL
3 tbsp	tapioca starch	45 mL
1 tbsp	xanthan gum	15 mL
1 tbsp	bread machine or instant yeast	15 mL
1¼ tsp	salt	6 mL
1 cup	water	250 mL
2 tbsp	vegetable oil	30 mL
3 tbsp	liquid honey	45 mL
1 tbsp	light (fancy) molasses	15 mL
1 tsp	cider vinegar	5 mL

Bread Machine Method

1. In a small bowl or measuring cup, combine flax flour and warm water; mix well. Let stand for 5 minutes.

2. In a large bowl or plastic bag, combine brown rice flour, sorghum flour, rice bran, tapioca starch, xanthan gum, yeast and salt. Mix well and set aside.

3. Pour water, oil, honey, molasses and vinegar into the bread machine baking pan.

4. Select the Gluten-Free Cycle. As the bread machine is mixing, add the flax flour mixture. Gradually add the dry ingredients, scraping bottom and sides of pan with a rubber spatula. Try to incorporate all the dry ingredients within 1 to 2 minutes. When the mixing and kneading are complete, remove the kneading blade, leaving the bread pan in the bread machine. Quickly smooth the top of the loaf. Allow the cycle to finish.

Variations

For a milder bread, substitute 1 tbsp (15 mL) packed brown sugar for the molasses.

The rice bran can be replaced by an equal amount of GF oat bran or brown or white rice flour.

5. At the end of the cycle, take the temperature of the loaf using an instant-read thermometer. It is baked at 200°F (100°C). If it's between 180°F (85°C) and 200°F (100°C), leave machine on the Keep Warm Cycle until baked. If it's below 180°F (85°C), turn on the Bake Cycle and check the internal temperature every 10 minutes. (Some bread machines are automatically set for 60 minutes; others need to be set by 10-minute intervals.)

6. Once the loaf has reached 200°F (100°C), remove it from the pan immediately and let cool completely on a rack.

Mixer Method

1. In a small bowl or measuring cup, combine flax flour and warm water; mix well. Let stand for 5 minutes.

2. In a large bowl or plastic bag, combine brown rice flour, sorghum flour, rice bran, tapioca starch, xanthan gum, yeast and salt. Mix well and set aside.

3. In a separate bowl, using a heavy-duty electric mixer with paddle attachment, combine water, oil, honey, molasses, vinegar and flax flour mixture until well blended. With the mixer on its lowest speed, slowly add the dry ingredients until combined. Stop the machine and scrape the bottom and sides of the bowl with a rubber spatula. With the mixer on medium speed, beat for 1 minute or until smooth.

4. Spoon dough into prepared pan. Let rise, uncovered, in a warm, draft-free place for 75 to 90 minutes or until dough has risen almost to the top of the pan. Meanwhile, preheat oven to 350°F (180°C).

5. Bake for 25 minutes. Check to see if loaf is getting too dark and tent with foil if necessary. Bake for 10 to 20 minutes or until internal temperature of loaf registers 200°F (100°C) on an instant-read thermometer. Remove from the pan immediately and let cool completely on a rack.

Crunchy Multigrain Bâtarde

Makes one 12-inch (30 cm) loaf, 12 slices

The attractive grainy slices from this loaf are the perfect accompaniment to your family's favorite soup or salad.

Tips

Store this bread loosely covered in a paper bag to maintain the crisp crust.

Use an electric or serrated knife to thickly slice this loaf on the diagonal.

Nutrients per slice	
Calories	105
Fat	2 g
Carbohydrate	20 g
Fiber	3 g
Protein	3 g
Calcium	13 mg
Vitamin D	0 IU

- **Bread machine or baguette pan or baking sheet, lightly greased and lined with parchment paper**

¾ cup	brown rice flour	175 mL
¼ cup	quinoa flour	60 mL
⅓ cup	potato starch	75 mL
1 tsp	granulated sugar	5 mL
2 tsp	xanthan gum	10 mL
2 tsp	bread machine or instant yeast	10 mL
1 tsp	salt	5 mL
¼ cup	millet seeds	60 mL
¼ cup	cracked flax seeds	60 mL
2 tbsp	certified GF large-flake (old-fashioned) rolled oats	30 mL
¾ cup	water	175 mL
1 tsp	cider vinegar	5 mL
1	large egg white	1

Bread Machine Method

1. In a large bowl or plastic bag, combine brown rice flour, quinoa flour, potato starch, sugar, xanthan gum, yeast, salt, millet seeds, flax seeds and oats. Mix well and set aside.

2. Pour water and vinegar into the bread machine baking pan. Add egg white.

3. Select the Gluten-Free Cycle. As the bread machine is mixing, gradually add the dry ingredients, scraping bottom and sides of pan with a rubber spatula. Try to incorporate all the dry ingredients within 1 to 2 minutes. When the mixing and kneading are complete, remove the kneading blade, leaving the bread pan in the bread machine. Quickly smooth the top of the loaf. Allow the cycle to finish.

4. At the end of the cycle, take the temperature of the loaf using an instant-read thermometer. It is baked at 200°F (100°C). If it's between 180°F (85°C) and 200°F (100°C), leave machine on the Keep Warm Cycle until baked. If it's below 180°F (85°C), turn on the Bake Cycle and check the internal temperature every 10 minutes. (Some bread machines are automatically set for 60 minutes; others need to be set by 10-minute intervals.)

5. Once the loaf has reached 200°F (100°C), remove it from the pan immediately and let cool completely on a rack.

Mixer Method

1. In a bowl or plastic bag, combine brown rice flour, quinoa flour, potato starch, sugar, xanthan gum, yeast, salt, millet seeds, flax seeds and oats. Mix well and set aside.

2. In a separate bowl, using a heavy-duty electric mixer with paddle attachment, combine egg white, water and vinegar until well blended. With the mixer on its lowest speed, slowly add the dry ingredients until combined. Stop the machine and scrape the bottom and sides of the bowl with a rubber spatula. With the mixer on medium speed, beat for 1 minute or until smooth.

3. Spoon dough into one side of prepared pan or onto the baking sheet in the shape of a French loaf. Using a sharp knife, draw 3 or 4 diagonal lines, $1/4$ inch (0.5 cm) deep, across the top of the loaf. Let rise, uncovered, in a warm, draft-free place for 70 minutes. Meanwhile, preheat oven to 425°F (220°C).

4. Bake for 18 to 22 minutes or until internal temperature of loaf registers 200°F (100°C) on an instant-read thermometer. Remove from the pan immediately and let cool completely on a rack.

Honey Dijon Toastie

Makes 4 wedges	

Honey mustard added
to the dough makes this
open-textured bread an
ideal sandwich bread.

Tips

Measure any oil in the
recipe before any sticky
ingredients, such as
molasses or honey. This
greases the measuring
spoon, allowing the sticky
ingredient to slide right out.

You can use a plain Dijon
mustard in place of the
honey Dijon.

- **Bread machine (optional)**
- **6-inch (15 cm) round casserole dish, lightly greased and lined with parchment paper**

¾ cup	whole bean flour	175 mL
¼ cup	quinoa flour	60 mL
¼ cup	tapioca starch	60 mL
2 tsp	xanthan gum	10 mL
2 tbsp	bread machine or instant yeast	30 mL
¼ tsp	salt	1 mL
1 tbsp	dried thyme	15 mL
1	clove garlic, minced	1
¾ cup	water	175 mL
2 tbsp	extra virgin olive oil	30 mL
¼ cup	liquid honey	60 mL
2 tbsp	honey Dijon mustard	30 mL
1 tsp	cider vinegar	5 mL
1	large egg	1

Bread Machine Method

1. In a large bowl or plastic bag, combine whole bean flour, quinoa flour, tapioca starch, xanthan gum, yeast, salt and thyme. Mix well and set aside.

2. Pour garlic, water, oil, honey, mustard and vinegar into the bread machine baking pan. Add egg. Select the Dough Cycle. As the bread machine is mixing, gradually add the dry ingredients, scraping bottom and sides of pan with a rubber spatula. Try to incorporate all the dry ingredients within 1 to 2 minutes. Stop bread machine as soon as the kneading portion of the cycle is complete. Do not let bread machine finish cycle.

Nutrients per wedge	
Calories	371
Fat	14 g
Carbohydrate	52 g
Fiber	6 g
Protein	12 g
Calcium	48 mg
Vitamin D	10 IU

Tips

This is best served hot out of the oven.

If you find this too sweet, decrease the honey to 1 tbsp (15 mL).

Toasties are great for dipping in family-favorite or new dips, sauces and dressings. Give your picky eater some sweet, tart or spicy choices to try something new. For more selective tasters, try making your dips all the same color but different flavors.

Mixer Method

1. In a bowl or plastic bag, combine whole bean flour, quinoa flour, tapioca starch, xanthan gum, yeast, salt and thyme. Mix well and set aside.

2. In a separate bowl, using a heavy-duty electric mixer with paddle attachment, combine garlic, water, oil, honey, mustard, vinegar and egg until well blended. With the mixer on its lowest speed, slowly add the dry ingredients until combined. Stop the machine and scrape the bottom and sides of the bowl with a rubber spatula. With the mixer on medium speed, beat for 1 minute or until smooth.

For Both Methods

3. Gently transfer dough to prepared dish and spread evenly to the edges. With wet fingers, make deep indents all over the dough, pressing all the way down to the bottom. Let rise, uncovered, in a warm, draft-free place for 60 minutes or until dough has doubled in volume. Meanwhile, preheat oven to 375°F (190°C).

4. Bake for 20 minutes. Check to see if loaf is getting too dark and tent with foil if necessary. Bake for 14 to 17 minutes or until top is deep golden. Remove from the dish immediately. Cut into 4 wedges and serve hot, or transfer to a rack and let cool completely.

Date Cashew Loaf

This dark loaf will satisfy your child's need for something slightly sweet and crunchy.

Tips

Instead of chopping with a knife, snip dates with kitchen shears. Dip the blades in hot water when they become sticky.

This is a very dark loaf, and will appear baked before it is, so it is important to take the internal temperature.

This loaf is bound to be a favorite with the crunchy crew! You may need to hide some for later.

This loaf is energy-dense and great for kids who are underweight or need extra calories. It is also a good source of calcium. Set it out of sight, though, for children who tend to overeat.

Nutrients per slice	
Calories	257
Fat	11 g
Carbohydrate	38 g
Fiber	4 g
Protein	5 g
Calcium	92 mg
Vitamin D	6 IU

- **5³⁄₄- by 3¹⁄₄-inch (14 by 8 cm) mini loaf pan, lightly greased**

²⁄₃ cup	coarsely snipped dates	150 mL
¹⁄₂ cup	boiling water	125 mL
¹⁄₂ cup	teff flour	125 mL
¹⁄₄ cup	brown rice flour	60 mL
2 tbsp	tapioca starch	30 mL
2 tbsp	packed brown sugar	30 mL
1¹⁄₂ tsp	GF baking powder	7 mL
¹⁄₂ tsp	baking soda	2 mL
1 tsp	xanthan gum	5 mL
¹⁄₄ tsp	salt	1 mL
1	large egg yolk	1
2 tbsp	vegetable oil	30 mL
¹⁄₂ cup	chopped cashews	125 mL

1. In a large bowl, combine dates and boiling water. Let stand for 5 minutes.

2. In a bowl or plastic bag, combine teff flour, brown rice flour, tapioca starch, brown sugar, baking powder, baking soda, xanthan gum and salt. Mix well and set aside.

3. Add egg yolk and oil to date mixture and, using an electric mixer, beat until combined. Add dry ingredients and mix just until combined. Stir in cashews.

4. Spoon batter into prepared pan. Let stand for 30 minutes. Meanwhile, preheat oven to 350°F (180°C).

5. Bake for 25 minutes. Check to see if loaf is getting too dark and tent with foil if necessary. Bake for 11 to 15 minutes or until internal temperature of loaf registers 200°F (100°C) on an instant-read thermometer. Let cool in pan on a rack for 5 minutes. Remove from pan and let cool completely on rack.

Variation

Substitute macadamia nuts for the cashews.

Simple Corn Tortillas

Makes 16 tortillas

Tortillas with a hint of salt are perfectly balanced with the flavor of the corn. The soda adds an extra-light texture to these tortillas.

Tip

Fresh corn tortillas do not stay fresh. They need to be used within hours of making them.

- **16 sheets waxed paper, cut into 10-inch (25 cm) squares**
- **Tortilla press**

2 cups	masa harina	500 mL
½ tsp	salt	2 mL
¼ tsp	baking soda	1 mL
1½ cups	very warm (almost hot) water	375 mL

1. In a large bowl, mix together masa harina, salt, baking soda and water. Knead with your hands to form the masa, or dough.

2. Pinch off a golf-ball-size piece of masa and roll into a smooth ball. Place balls in an airtight container as you make each one until ready to use, for up to 1 hour. Continue with remaining masa to make 16 balls.

3. To press tortillas, place a piece of waxed paper in tortilla press and place masa ball on top. Place another piece of waxed paper on top of masa ball and press to a 6-inch (15 cm) circle. Continue with remaining masa balls, stacking uncooked tortillas on a platter with a waxed paper sheet in between each one.

4. Heat a dry nonstick or cast-iron skillet over medium heat. Remove waxed paper and transfer tortillas to skillet, one at a time, and cook, turning once, for about 45 seconds per side or until bubbling and lightly browned. Transfer tortillas to a towel-lined platter. Wrap in towel to keep warm.

Nutrients per tortilla	
Calories	50
Fat	1 g
Carbohydrate	11 g
Fiber	1 g
Protein	2 g
Calcium	20 mg
Vitamin D	0 IU

Biscuit Mix

Does your family crave hot, homemade, melt-in-your-mouth biscuits? Have this mix ready to quickly whip up a batch for breakfast, lunch or dinner. They'll disappear right before your eyes.

Tip

Select a shortening that is low in trans fat, if available in your area.

2 cups	brown rice flour	500 mL
2 cups	sorghum flour	500 mL
1 cup	amaranth flour	250 mL
1 cup	tapioca starch	250 mL
½ cup	granulated sugar	125 mL
1 tbsp	xanthan gum	15 mL
¼ cup	GF baking powder	60 mL
1 tbsp	baking soda	15 mL
2 tsp	salt	10 mL
2 cups	vegetable shortening	500 mL

1. In a large bowl, combine brown rice flour, sorghum flour, amaranth flour, tapioca starch, sugar, xanthan gum, baking powder, baking soda and salt. Using a pastry blender or two knives, cut in shortening until mixture resembles coarse crumbs about the size of small peas.

2. Immediately divide into 8 equal portions of approximately 1¼ cups (300 mL) each. Seal tightly in plastic bags, removing as much air as possible. Store at room temperature for up to 3 days or freeze for up to 6 months.

Working with Biscuit Mix

- Stir the mix before spooning very lightly into the dry measures when dividing into portions in step 2 of method. Do not pack.
- Be sure to divide the mix into 8 equal portions before using to make up an individual recipe. Depending on how much air you incorporate into the mix and the texture of the individual gluten-free flours, the total volume of the mix can vary slightly. The important thing is to make 8 equal portions.
- Label and date packages before storing. Add the page number of the recipe to the label as a quick reference.
- Let warm to room temperature and mix well before using.
- Mix can be halved to make 4 batches of 6 biscuits each.
- If you prefer to make a dozen biscuits at a time, divide the mix into 4 equal portions of approximately 2½ cups (625 mL) and double all the ingredients listed in the Bacon and Tomato Biscuits recipe (page 231).

Nutrients per biscuit	
Calories	146
Fat	9 g
Carbohydrate	16 g
Fiber	1 g
Protein	2 g
Calcium	58 mg
Vitamin D	0 IU

Bacon and Tomato Biscuits

Enjoy the salty tang of these quick and easy savory biscuits hot from the oven.

Tips

Use dry, not oil-packed, sun-dried tomatoes. Snip soft sun-dried tomatoes into $\frac{1}{4}$-inch (0.5 cm) pieces for a stronger burst of tomato goodness.

A mouthwatering recipe for a quick after-school snack, perfect for the picky eater who could put on a few pounds.

Soy milk or another non-dairy milk alternative is appropriate for the casein-free diet plan.

* **Preheat oven to 400°F (200°C)**
* **Baking sheet, lightly greased**

$\frac{1}{4}$ cup	fortified soy beverage	60 mL
1 tsp	freshly squeezed lemon juice	5 mL
$1\frac{1}{4}$ cups	Biscuit Mix (page 230)	300 mL
3	slices GF bacon, cooked crisp and crumbled	3
$\frac{1}{4}$ cup	snipped dry-packed sun-dried tomatoes	60 mL
1 tsp	dried basil	5 mL

1. In a measuring cup or bowl, combine soy beverage and lemon juice; set aside for 5 minutes.

2. In a medium bowl, combine biscuit mix, bacon, tomatoes and basil. Add soy beverage mixture all at once, stirring with a fork or rubber spatula to make a soft, slightly sticky dough.

3. Drop by heaping spoonfuls onto prepared baking sheet.

4. Bake in preheated oven for 13 to 15 minutes, or until tops are golden. Serve immediately.

Variations

Substitute sliced kalamata olives for the bacon, and oregano or rosemary for the basil.

Substitute 1 tbsp (15 mL) snipped fresh basil for the dried.

Nutrients per biscuit	
Calories	170
Fat	10 g
Carbohydrate	17 g
Fiber	1 g
Protein	3 g
Calcium	73 mg
Vitamin D	4 IU

Breadsticks

Serve these breadsticks
as Italian restaurants
do — with a dish
of flavored olive oil
for dipping.

Tips

Thoroughly mix the dry
ingredients before adding
them to the liquids — they
are powder-fine and can
clump together.

Don't worry when seeds
move as you spread the
dough to the edges of the
pan — they will still coat
the breadsticks.

For uniform breadsticks,
cut bread in half, then
lengthwise into quarters.
Finally, cut each quarter
lengthwise into 3 strips.

Nutrients per breadstick	
Calories	84
Fat	3 g
Carbohydrate	13 g
Fiber	1 g
Protein	2 g
Calcium	27 mg
Vitamin D	0 IU

- 9-inch (23 cm) square baking pan, lightly greased
- Baking sheet, ungreased

²⁄₃ cup	brown rice flour	150 mL
2 tbsp	almond flour	30 mL
¼ cup	potato starch	60 mL
2 tbsp	tapioca starch	30 mL
1 tbsp	granulated sugar	15 mL
1¼ tsp	xanthan gum	6 mL
2 tsp	bread machine or instant yeast	10 mL
¾ tsp	salt	3 mL
¾ cup	water	175 mL
1 tbsp	vegetable oil	15 mL
1 tsp	cider vinegar	5 mL
3 tbsp	sesame seeds, divided	45 mL

Bread Machine Method

1. In a large bowl or plastic bag, combine brown rice flour, almond flour, potato starch, tapioca starch, sugar, xanthan gum, yeast and salt. Mix well and set aside.

2. Pour water, oil and vinegar into the bread machine baking pan. Select the Dough Cycle. As the bread machine is mixing, gradually add the dry ingredients, scraping bottom and sides of pan with a rubber spatula. Try to incorporate all the dry ingredients within 1 to 2 minutes. Stop bread machine as soon as the kneading portion of the cycle is complete. Do not let bread machine finish the cycle.

Mixer Method

1. In a large bowl or plastic bag, combine brown rice flour, almond flour, potato starch, tapioca starch, sugar, xanthan gum, yeast and salt. Mix well and set aside.

2. In a separate bowl, using a heavy-duty electric mixer with paddle attachment, combine water, oil and vinegar until well blended. With the mixer on its lowest speed, slowly add the dry ingredients until combined. Stop the machine and scrape the bottom and sides of the bowl with a rubber spatula. With the mixer on medium speed, beat for 4 minutes.

Tips

If breadsticks become soft, crisp in a toaster oven or conventional oven at 350°F (180°C) for a few minutes.

Save these breadsticks for special days when your little person needs a calm-me-down. Spread some waxed paper at his favorite quiet eating place, turn the lights down a bit, put on his headphones with his favorite calm music, and let him paint using breadsticks for paintbrushes and red pepper hummus for his edible masterpiece.

Variations

Substitute poppy seeds for the sesame seeds.

For an Italian herb flavor, add 2 to 3 tsp (10 to 15 mL) of your favorite dried herb with the dry ingredients and use extra virgin olive oil instead of vegetable oil.

For Both Methods

3. Sprinkle 2 tbsp (30 mL) of the sesame seeds in bottom of prepared pan. Drop dough by spoonfuls over the sesame seeds. Using a moistened rubber spatula, spread dough evenly to the edges of the pan. Sprinkle with the remaining sesame seeds. Using moistened rubber spatula, press seeds into dough. Let rise, uncovered, in a warm, draft-free place for 30 minutes. Meanwhile, preheat oven to 400°F (200°C).

4. Bake for 10 to 12 minutes or until light brown. Remove from the pan and transfer immediately to a cutting board. Reduce oven temperature to 350°F (180°C). With a pizza wheel or a sharp knife, cut bread into 12 equal strips. Roll strips in loose sesame seeds in pan, pressing seeds into cut sides.

5. Arrange slices, with cut sides exposed, at least $1/2$ inch (1 cm) apart on baking sheet. Bake for 20 to 25 minutes, or until dry, crisp and golden brown. Immediately transfer to a cooling rack and let cool completely.

Sesame Crispbread

Makes about 32 crackers

Quick and easy to make, this crisp flatbread is similar to chapati in texture, appearance and use.

Tips

Use this tasty treat to add new flavor and texture sensations to your child's diet. Try it with different dips, such as hummus, guacamole or salsa. Let her taste new flavors on her finger or with a kiss to the food. Baby steps when it comes to new flavors.

To toast sesame seeds, spread seeds in a single layer in a large skillet and toast over medium heat for 5 to 8 minutes, shaking pan frequently. This is an important step for the flavor of the crispbread.

- **Preheat oven to 400°F (200°C)**
- **Food processor**
- **15- by 10-inch (40 by 25 cm) jelly roll pan, lightly greased**

¾ cup	water	175 mL
1 tbsp	vegetable oil	15 mL
¾ cup	brown rice flour	175 mL
⅓ cup	tapioca starch	75 mL
1 tsp	granulated sugar	5 mL
1½ tsp	xanthan gum	7 mL
½ tsp	GF baking powder	2 mL
½ tsp	salt	2 mL
½ cup	sesame seeds, toasted (see tip, at left)	125 mL
1 to 2 tbsp	sweet rice flour	15 to 30 mL

1. In a small bowl, whisk together water and oil. Set aside.

2. In food processor, pulse brown rice flour, tapioca starch, sugar, xanthan gum, baking powder, salt and sesame seeds until combined. With the motor running, through the feed tube, gradually add water mixture in a steady stream. Process for 15 seconds or until smooth and lump-free.

3. Drop dough by heaping spoonfuls onto prepared pan. Sprinkle with sweet rice flour. With floured fingers, gently and evenly pat out dough right to the edges of the pan, sprinkling with sweet rice flour as required.

Nutrients per 2 crackers	
Calories	71
Fat	3 g
Carbohydrate	10 g
Fiber	1 g
Protein	2 g
Calcium	21 mg
Vitamin D	0 IU

Tips

Spreading the dough is similar to patting out pizza dough; continue all the way to the edge, or it will be too thick.

During baking, the crispbread will crack and curl up.

Store in an airtight container at room temperature for up to 3 months.

4. Bake in preheated oven for 20 to 23 minutes or until lightly browned. Let cool in pan on a wire rack. Break into large pieces.

Variations

Add 1 to 2 tbsp (15 to 30 mL) dried herbs with the sesame seeds.

For a stronger sesame flavor, substitute sesame oil for the vegetable oil.

Oatmeal Muffin Mix

Makes 1½ cups (375 mL), enough for 6 muffins		

This family favorite needs no introduction except to say that it is an upscale GF version loaded with nutrients and bursting with flavor! You'd better make a double batch.

Tips

Loaded with fiber, these muffins will help your child when she is miserable from being constipated. You won't have to ask children twice to finish these off.

Bedtime snacks that are high in carbohydrate (especially starches) and low in protein may help promote sleep in some children as a result of temporary changes in the brain's chemical balance.

⅔ cup	sorghum flour	150 mL
¼ cup	GF oat flour	60 mL
¼ cup	certified GF large-flake (old-fashioned) rolled oats	60 mL
1 tbsp	GF oat bran	15 mL
2 tbsp	tapioca starch	30 mL
2 tsp	GF baking powder	10 mL
½ tsp	baking soda	2 mL
1 tsp	xanthan gum	5 mL
¼ tsp	salt	1 mL

1. In a bowl or plastic bag, combine sorghum flour, oat flour, oats, oat bran, tapioca starch, baking powder, baking soda, xanthan gum and salt. Mix well.

2. Seal tightly in a plastic bag, removing as much air as possible. Store at room temperature for up to 3 days or in the freezer for up to 6 months.

Nutrients per ¼ cup (60 mL)	
Calories	95
Fat	1 g
Carbohydrate	20 g
Fiber	3 g
Protein	3 g
Calcium	76 mg
Vitamin D	0 IU

Carrot Oatmeal Muffins

Makes 6 muffins

These golden muffins are speckled with moist orange strands of carrot. High in nutrients and beautiful to behold, an orange muffin is hard to turn down.

Tips

Don't grate the carrots too far ahead, as they can darken. You can, however, grate extra and freeze in a freezer bag for up to 1 month.

If you prefer a sweeter muffin, increase the honey to 3 tbsp (45 mL).

Variation

Add $\frac{1}{2}$ cup (125 mL) raisins or coarsely chopped pecans with the muffin mix.

- **6-cup muffin pan, lightly greased**

2 tsp	grated orange zest	10 mL
1	large egg	1
$\frac{1}{2}$ cup	freshly squeezed orange juice	125 mL
3 tbsp	vegetable oil	45 mL
2 tbsp	liquid honey	30 mL
1 tbsp	light (fancy) molasses	15 mL
$1\frac{1}{2}$ cups	Oatmeal Muffin Mix (page 236)	375 mL
$\frac{2}{3}$ cup	shredded carrots	150 mL

1. In a bowl, using an electric mixer, beat orange zest, egg, orange juice, oil, honey and molasses until combined. Add muffin mix and carrots; mix just until combined.

2. Spoon batter into prepared muffin cups, dividing evenly. Let stand for 30 minutes. Meanwhile, preheat oven to 350°F (180°C).

3. Bake for 20 to 23 minutes or until firm to the touch. Remove from the pan immediately and let cool completely on a rack.

Nutrients per muffin	
Calories	214
Fat	9 g
Carbohydrate	32 g
Fiber	3 g
Protein	4 g
Calcium	98 mg
Vitamin D	7 IU

Pear Buckwheat Muffins

Here, pears and applesauce are transformed into scrumptious muffins with nutmeg and gems of crystallized ginger stirred into the batter. And the topping? A sparkling sugar-crunch coating made with turbinado sugar and great ease.

Tip

Easy on allergies and high in fiber, these muffins are a dietitian's dream come true.

- **Preheat oven to 375°F (190°C)**
- **12-cup muffin pan, greased**

2½ cups	buckwheat flour	625 mL
½ cup	tapioca flour	125 mL
2 tsp	gluten-free baking powder	10 mL
1 tsp	baking soda	5 mL
1 tsp	ground nutmeg	5 mL
½ tsp	salt	2 mL
½ cup	packed light brown sugar	125 mL
2	large eggs	2
1½ cups	unsweetened applesauce	375 mL
¼ cup	vegetable oil	60 mL
2 tsp	GF vanilla extract	10 mL
1⅓ cups	shredded firm-ripe pears	325 mL
¼ cup	minced crystallized ginger	60 mL
2 tbsp	turbinado sugar	30 mL

1. In a large bowl, whisk together buckwheat flour, tapioca flour, baking powder, baking soda, nutmeg and salt.

2. In a medium bowl, whisk together brown sugar, eggs, applesauce, oil and vanilla until well blended.

3. Add the egg mixture to the flour mixture and stir until just blended. Gently fold in pears and crystallized ginger.

4. Divide batter equally among prepared muffin cups. Sprinkle with turbinado sugar.

5. Bake in preheated oven for 24 to 28 minutes or until a toothpick inserted in the center comes out clean. Let cool in pan on a wire rack for 5 minutes, then transfer to the rack to cool.

Nutrients per muffin	
Calories	232
Fat	6 g
Carbohydrate	42 g
Fiber	4 g
Protein	5 g
Calcium	69 mg
Vitamin D	3 IU

Almond Flour Blackberry Muffins

Here, fail-safe almond flour muffins are pepped up with a combination of honey and fresh blackberries. They'll be jumping out of bed for these.

Tip

Thoroughly rinse all fruits and vegetables under running water to remove any potential contaminants. This includes scrubbing the peel for fruits such as avocados and melons.

- **12-cup muffin pan, lined with paper liners**

2 cups	fresh or frozen (thawed) blackberries	500 mL
2½ cups	almond flour	625 mL
1 tsp	ground cinnamon	5 mL
½ tsp	baking soda	2 mL
½ tsp	salt	2 mL
3	large eggs	3
½ cup	liquid honey	125 mL
1 tsp	GF vanilla extract	5 mL

1. In a small saucepan, bring blackberries and ½ cup (125 mL) water to a boil over medium-high heat. Reduce heat to low and simmer, stirring often, until thickened slightly and blackberries have released their juice. Let cool.

2. Preheat oven to 325°F (160°C).

3. In a medium bowl, whisk together flour, cinnamon, baking soda and salt.

4. In another medium bowl, whisk together eggs, honey and vanilla until well blended.

5. Add the berry mixture and the egg mixture to the flour mixture and stir until just blended.

6. Divide batter equally among prepared muffin cups.

7. Bake for 25 to 30 minutes or until a toothpick inserted in the center comes out clean. Let cool in pan on a wire rack for 5 minutes, then transfer to the rack to cool.

Nutrients per muffin	
Calories	208
Fat	13 g
Carbohydrate	19 g
Fiber	4 g
Protein	7 g
Calcium	66 mg
Vitamin D	10 IU

Gingerbread Muffins

Holiday spices and molasses give these muffins seasonal charm — but why wait for Christmas when they can be served and enjoyed all year round?

Tip

Substitutions are a particular temptation, and challenge, with gluten-free baking, because gluten-free cooks have become accustomed to swapping ingredients. When it comes to baking, though, stick to the recipe as much as possible, as changing too much (especially fats, sugars and leavening) can wreck the underlying chemistry of the baked goods, wreaking havoc on the end results. The best practice is to follow the recipe, period.

- **Preheat oven to 350°F (180°C)**
- **12-cup muffin pan, greased**

1⅔ cups	Brown Rice Flour Blend (see recipe, opposite)	400 mL
2 tsp	ground ginger	10 mL
1¼ tsp	baking soda	6 mL
1 tsp	ground cinnamon	5 mL
¾ tsp	salt	3 mL
¾ tsp	xanthan gum	3 mL
½ tsp	ground nutmeg	2 mL
⅛ tsp	ground cloves	0.5 mL
½ cup	granulated sugar	125 mL
1	large egg	1
½ cup	dark (cooking) molasses	125 mL
½ cup	vegetable oil	125 mL
½ cup	boiling water	125 mL
2 tbsp	confectioners' (icing) sugar	30 mL

1. In a large bowl, whisk together flour blend, ginger, baking soda, cinnamon, salt, xanthan gum, nutmeg and cloves.

2. In a medium bowl, whisk together granulated sugar, egg, molasses and oil until well blended.

3. Using an electric mixer on low speed, beat egg mixture and boiling water into flour mixture until well blended.

4. Divide batter equally among prepared muffin cups.

5. Bake in preheated oven for 20 to 25 minutes or until a toothpick inserted in the center comes out clean. Let cool in pan on a wire rack for 5 minutes, then transfer to the rack to cool.

6. Sprinkle cooled muffin tops with confectioners' sugar.

Nutrients per muffin	
Calories	165
Fat	10 g
Carbohydrate	21 g
Fiber	0 g
Protein	1 g
Calcium	72 mg
Vitamin D	3 IU

Here's an all-purpose gluten-free baking blend that can be used to replace all-purpose flour in most standard recipes.

Tips

You can also make the blend in smaller amounts by using the basic proportions: 2 parts finely ground brown rice flour, $\frac{2}{3}$ part potato starch and $\frac{1}{3}$ part tapioca starch.

You can double, triple or quadruple the recipe to have it on hand. Store the blend in an airtight container in the refrigerator for up to 4 months, or in the freezer for up to 1 year. Let warm to room temperature before using.

Nutrients per $\frac{1}{4}$ cup (60 mL)	
Calories	140
Fat	1 g
Carbohydrate	32 g
Fiber	1 g
Protein	2 g
Calcium	0 mg
Vitamin D	0 IU

Brown Rice Flour Blend

2 cups	finely ground brown rice flour	500 mL
$\frac{2}{3}$ cup	potato starch	150 mL
$\frac{1}{3}$ cup	tapioca starch	75 mL

1. In a bowl, whisk together brown rice flour, potato starch and tapioca starch. Use as directed in recipes.

Pumpkin Almond Flour Muffins

Makes 12 muffins

Watch out, pumpkin pie! These are downright delectable: a rich and flavorful muffin consisting mostly of almonds (in the form of almond flour), a great source of high-quality protein, with just the right amounts of pumpkin, sugar and spice.

Tips

To make this recipe casein-free, replace the butter with melted vegetable shortening or olive oil margarine. Make sure to choose a margarine that is free of trans fat.

For an even higher nutrient kick in this high-fiber recipe, use blackstrap instead of dark molasses. Let your child taste the blackstrap molasses first to be sure the flavor is not too strong.

Nutrients per muffin	
Calories	307
Fat	25 g
Carbohydrate	17 g
Fiber	4 g
Protein	8 g
Calcium	110 mg
Vitamin D	10 IU

- **Preheat oven to 325°F (160°C)**
- **12-cup muffin pan, lined with paper liners**

3 cups	almond flour	750 mL
2½ tsp	pumpkin pie spice	12 mL
¾ tsp	baking soda	3 mL
¼ tsp	salt	1 mL
¼ cup	granulated sugar	60 mL
2	large eggs	2
¾ cup	pumpkin purée (not pie filling)	175 mL
¼ cup	dark (cooking) molasses	60 mL
¼ cup	unsalted butter, melted (see tip, at left)	60 mL
1 tsp	GF vanilla extract	5 mL
1 cup	chopped pecans, toasted	250 mL

1. In a large bowl, whisk together flour, pumpkin pie spice, baking soda and salt.

2. In a medium bowl, whisk together sugar, eggs, pumpkin, molasses, butter and vanilla until well blended.

3. Add the egg mixture to the flour mixture and stir until just blended. Gently fold in pecans.

4. Divide batter equally among prepared muffin cups.

5. Bake in preheated oven for 25 to 30 minutes or until tops are set and a toothpick inserted in the center comes out clean. Let cool in pan on a wire rack for 5 minutes, then transfer to the rack to cool.

Appetizers, Dips and Sauces

Chicken Satays with Peanut Dipping Sauce. 244

Barbecued Beef Satays 245

Oven-Baked Tofu "Fries" 246

Eggplant and Tuna Antipasto Appetizer 247

Grilled Bacon and Zucchini–Wrapped Scallops 248

Mexican Shrimp Cocktail 249

Grilled Cilantro Shrimp Skewers. 250

Crispy Calamari. 251

Creamy Crab Salad Spread. 252

Egg Salad Spread 253

Fiesta Guacamole. 254

Hummus 255

Black Bean Salsa. 255

Tomatillo and Chia Seed Salsa 256

Basic Tomato Sauce 257

Creamy Mayonnaise. 258

Honey Mustard Dipping Sauce. 259

Mock Soy Sauce 259

Fiesta Taco Sauce 260

Chicken Satays with Peanut Dipping Sauce

Makes 24 satays

These flavorful skewers make a great starter for a summer barbecue or light meal for your child. Set them out on a tray with the Peanut Dipping Sauce and watch them disappear.

Tips

Soak wooden skewers in cold water for 15 minutes to prevent them from burning when you're grilling the chicken.

Satays are family favorites in any season, whether you have to grill them while standing in a snowbank on your deck or using your oven's broiler.

Nutrients per 3 satays	
Calories	160
Fat	8 g
Carbohydrate	7 g
Fiber	1 g
Protein	15 g
Calcium	16 mg
Vitamin D	2 IU

- **Twenty-four 6-inch (15 cm) wooden skewers, soaked**

Satays

3	boneless skinless chicken breasts (about 1 lb/500 g)	3
¼ cup	GF soy sauce	60 mL
1 tbsp	vegetable oil	15 mL
1 tbsp	minced gingerroot	15 mL
1 tsp	granulated sugar	5 mL
2	cloves garlic, minced	2

Peanut Dipping Sauce

⅓ cup	GF peanut butter	75 mL
3 tbsp	freshly squeezed lime juice	45 mL
2 tbsp	GF soy sauce	30 mL
1 tbsp	packed brown sugar	15 mL
2 tsp	minced gingerroot	10 mL
1 tsp	Asian chili sauce (or to taste)	5 mL
1	clove garlic, minced	1
2 tbsp	chopped fresh cilantro	30 mL

1. *Satays:* Place chicken on a plate and cover with plastic wrap. Freeze for 1 to 2 hours or until firm to the touch but not solidly frozen. Cut each breast against the grain into 8 long, thin strips, each about ¼ inch (0.5 cm) thick. Thread chicken onto skewers accordion-style. Arrange in a shallow baking dish.

2. In a bowl, combine soy sauce, oil, ginger, sugar and garlic. Pour over chicken. Cover and refrigerate; marinate for 1 hour or overnight, turning chicken occasionally.

3. *Peanut Dipping Sauce:* In a bowl, whisk together peanut butter, lime juice, soy sauce, brown sugar, ginger, chili sauce and garlic until smooth. (Can be covered and refrigerated up to 1 day.) Stir in cilantro.

4. Preheat greased barbecue grill to medium. Remove chicken from marinade, discarding marinade, and place on grill; grill for 3 minutes on each side or until cooked through. Serve warm with dipping sauce.

Barbecued Beef Satays

Serve these satays as a main meal with rice and stir-fried vegetables. They're also great as an appetizer or snack anytime. If the weather isn't suitable for barbecuing, the satays can be broiled instead.

Tips

Remember to use a clean plate to bring cooked satays back in from the barbecue. Raw meat juices can contaminate cooked foods.

Start marinating the beef strips the night before and the satays will take only a few minutes to prepare the next day. Soak wooden skewers for about 30 minutes to prevent them from burning on the barbecue. Be careful with skewers when children are around.

Remove leftovers from their sticks and freeze for a great surprise snack.

Nutrients per 3 satays	
Calories	103
Fat	3 g
Carbohydrate	3 g
Fiber	0 g
Protein	16 g
Calcium	18 mg
Vitamin D	1 IU

- **Twenty-four 6-inch (15 cm) wooden skewers, soaked**

1¼ lbs	sirloin or round steak, cut into 3- by ½-inch (7.5 by 1 cm) strips	625 g
¼ cup	sodium-reduced GF soy sauce	60 mL
1 tbsp	freshly squeezed lemon juice	15 mL
1 tbsp	packed brown sugar	15 mL
½ tsp	minced garlic	2 mL
½ tsp	ground coriander	2 mL
¼ tsp	ground cumin	1 mL
¼ tsp	ground ginger	1 mL
	Prepared peanut sauce	

1. Place beef strips in a large freezer bag. Set aside.

2. In a small bowl, blend together soy sauce, lemon juice, brown sugar, garlic, coriander, cumin and ginger. Pour over beef strips; seal bag. Marinate in refrigerator for at least 4 hours or overnight.

3. Remove meat from marinade; place on wooden skewers. Discard marinade.

4. Barbecue or broil over medium-high heat, turning once, for 4 to 5 minutes or until brown and cooked to desired doneness. Serve with your favorite peanut sauce.

This recipe courtesy of dietitian Lorna Driedger.

Oven-Baked Tofu "Fries"

Makes 6 servings

Fast food, meet your match. Crispy and undeniably dippable, these superfood fries are rich in nutrients, including protein, iron and omega-3 fatty acids. Serve with warmed marinara sauce for the ultimate taste-testing.

Tips

The pressed tofu sticks can be stored in an airtight container in the refrigerator for up to 2 days.

These baked "fries" may be the beginning of a long love affair with tofu for your family.

- **2 rimmed baking sheets**

1 lb	extra-firm tofu, drained and patted dry	500 g
	Nonstick cooking spray	
¼ tsp	fine sea salt	1 mL
¼ tsp	freshly ground black pepper	1 mL

1. Line one of the baking sheets with a kitchen towel or a double layer of paper towels.

2. Cut tofu crosswise into 8 rectangles. Cut each rectangle lengthwise into 3 sticks. Arrange in a single layer on towel-lined baking sheet. Place second baking sheet on top and weigh down with 6 to 8 heavy cans. Let stand for 1 hour to drain liquid from tofu.

3. Preheat oven to 375°F (190°C).

4. Remove weights and lift top baking sheet off tofu. Wipe any dampness from bottom. Spray top of baking sheet with cooking spray. Remove tofu sticks from towel-lined baking sheet and arrange in single layer on sprayed baking sheet. Lightly spray tofu sticks with cooking spray. Sprinkle with salt and pepper.

5. Bake in preheated oven for 8 minutes. Carefully turn tofu sticks over. Bake for 6 to 8 minutes or until tofu is crispy and golden. Serve warm or let cool completely in pan.

Nutrients per serving	
Calories	74
Fat	4 g
Carbohydrate	2 g
Fiber	1 g
Protein	8 g
Calcium	144 mg
Vitamin D	0 IU

Eggplant and Tuna Antipasto Appetizer

Makes 8 to 10 servings

This antipasto is also delicious as a sauce over 8 oz (250 g) of GF pasta.

Tips

Prepare up to 2 days before and keep refrigerated.
Stir before serving cold or reheating to serve with GF crackers or French bread.

Read all labels and lists of ingredients to check for gluten and casein.

- **Food processor**

1 tbsp	olive oil	15 mL
1½ cups	chopped peeled eggplant	375 mL
1 cup	sliced mushrooms	250 mL
¾ cup	chopped red bell peppers	175 mL
½ cup	chopped onions	125 mL
2 tsp	minced garlic	10 mL
1 tsp	dried basil	5 mL
½ tsp	dried oregano	2 mL
½ cup	ready-to-use chicken broth or water	125 mL
½ cup	crushed tomatoes (canned or fresh)	125 mL
⅓ cup	sliced pimiento-stuffed green olives	75 mL
⅓ cup	chili sauce	75 mL
2 tsp	drained capers	10 mL
1	can (6 oz/170 g) water-packed tuna, drained	1

1. Spray a nonstick pan with vegetable spray. Heat oil in pan over medium-high heat; add eggplant, mushrooms, red peppers, onions, garlic, basil and oregano. Cook for 8 minutes, stirring occasionally, or until vegetables are softened.

2. Add broth, tomatoes, olives, chili sauce and capers; simmer, uncovered, for 6 minutes, stirring occasionally until most of the liquid is absorbed.

3. Transfer to food processor and add tuna; process for 20 seconds or until combined but still chunky.

Nutrients per 1 of 10 servings	
Calories	73
Fat	3 g
Carbohydrate	7 g
Fiber	1 g
Protein	5 g
Calcium	9 mg
Vitamin D	0 IU

Grilled Bacon and Zucchini–Wrapped Scallops

<table>
<tr><td colspan="2">**Makes
20 appetizers**</td></tr>
</table>

Smoky bacon and sweet scallops combine with strips of zucchini to make an attractive, impressive starter or light meal for your child.

Tips

Use the best-quality bacon you can find for this recipe, preferably naturally smoked and thinly sliced.

If using wooden skewers for this dish, be sure to soak them in water for 1 hour beforehand.

Skewers may be dangerous around any child.

If your child refuses to eat vegetables, keep the zucchini in this recipe your little secret.

Nutrients per appetizer	
Calories	78
Fat	6 g
Carbohydrate	1 g
Fiber	0 g
Protein	4 g
Calcium	6 mg
Vitamin D	3 IU

- **Preheat lightly greased grill to medium**

20	medium sea scallops	20
2 tbsp	lemon-pepper seasoning	30 mL
1 tbsp	chopped fresh coriander	15 mL
¼ cup	olive oil	60 mL
2 tsp	finely grated lemon zest	10 mL
3	zucchini, sliced lengthwise into 20 equal strips	3
20	slices bacon	20

1. In a bowl, toss scallops with lemon-pepper seasoning, coriander, olive oil and lemon zest. Let marinate for at least 20 minutes but no longer than 1 hour.

2. Meanwhile, in a pot of boiling water, blanch zucchini strips for about 2 minutes. Remove from hot water; plunge into a bowl of ice-cold water for 1 minute. Transfer to paper towels; set aside.

3. In a large skillet over medium heat, cook bacon for about 1 minute per side or until partially cooked. Transfer to paper towels; drain and cool slightly.

4. When bacon is cool enough to handle, lay 4 strips on a work surface. Lay a slice of zucchini onto each bacon slice. Place a scallop, round-side down, 1 inch (2.5 cm) from bottom of bacon/zucchini strip.

5. Keeping scallop centered, roll bacon/zucchini up and over scallop, wrapping it as securely as you can. Secure with a wooden skewer if necessary. Immediately thread 2 to 3 scallops onto each skewer.

6. Grill scallops on preheated grill for 3 to 5 minutes per side or until just browned.

Mexican Shrimp Cocktail

Makes 4 to 6 servings		

Your whole family will enjoy this saucy Mexican-style shrimp cocktail. It's a little thinner than a regular cocktail sauce, with a spicy twist. Fresh avocado accents this tangy, refreshing cocktail.

Tip

Regular vegetable juice cocktail and mild salsa will dampen the fires and add to the appeal of this shrimp cocktail for some.

Variation

For a thicker, richer flavor, add 1 cucumber, peeled, seeded and finely diced, in step 2.

16 to 24	medium shrimp, peeled and deveined	16 to 24
1 cup	finely chopped celery	250 mL
3	green onions, green parts only, chopped	3
2 tbsp	minced fresh cilantro	30 mL
1	tomato, seeded and chopped	1
3 cups	spicy vegetable juice cocktail	750 mL
1/2 cup	picante salsa	125 mL
	Juice of 2 limes	
	Salt and freshly ground black pepper	
2	avocados	2

1. In a large pot of boiling water, boil shrimp until opaque and pink, about 2 minutes. Drain and let cool slightly. Place shrimp in a bowl, cover and refrigerate until chilled, for at least 30 minutes or for up to 2 hours.

2. In a large bowl, combine celery, green onions, cilantro, tomato, vegetable juice and salsa. Add shrimp and lime juice and mix well. Season with salt and pepper to taste. Just before serving, dice avocado and add to mixture. Serve in decorative glassware.

Nutrients per 1 of 6 servings	
Calories	161
Fat	10 g
Carbohydrate	14 g
Fiber	6 g
Protein	6 g
Calcium	43 mg
Vitamin D	0 IU

Grilled Cilantro Shrimp Skewers

Makes 6 servings

Whether for a summertime barbecue or an easy weeknight meal, this simple shrimp recipe comes alive with the sharp flavors of cilantro and lime.

Tips

Barbecue Method: Preheat barbecue to 350°F (180°C) and cook for 2½ minutes per side, or until shrimp are pink and opaque.

Cook extra shrimp and serve over a green salad for a main course another day.

These shrimp are a high-protein, low-calorie, mega-flavor option that's just right if your child is always hungry.

- Six 6-inch (15 cm) wooden skewers
- Baking sheet, greased

2	cloves garlic, minced	2
¼ cup	chopped fresh cilantro	60 mL
2 tbsp	olive oil	30 mL
½ tsp	ground coriander	2 mL
	Grated zest and juice of 2 limes	
	Salt and freshly ground black pepper	
1 lb	extra-large shrimp, peeled and deveined	500 g

1. In a small bowl, combine garlic, cilantro, olive oil, coriander, lime zest, lime juice and salt and pepper to taste.

2. Place shrimp in a shallow dish and pour in marinade. Cover and refrigerate for at least 30 minutes or for up to 2 hours. Meanwhile, soak skewers in hot water for 30 minutes and preheat broiler.

3. Thread shrimp evenly onto skewers and place on prepared baking sheet.

4. Broil, turning once, for 2½ minutes per side or until shrimp are pink and opaque.

This recipe courtesy of chef Eileen Campbell.

Nutrients per serving	
Calories	97
Fat	5 g
Carbohydrate	1 g
Fiber	0 g
Protein	10 g
Calcium	43 mg
Vitamin D	2 IU

Crispy Calamari

Makes 4 servings

If you're looking for a crunchy, crispy outside with a tasty, tender bite in the middle, this is your dish. High in protein and calories, these calamari will fuel your child's energy rockets and desire for crunchy food.

Tips

The cayenne pepper helps the batter to brown, but if cayenne is too spicy for your child's taste, omit it and add another ½ tsp (2 mL) paprika.

You can use cleaned fresh squid rings instead of frozen.

Use this coating to make onion rings as well.

- **Candy/deep-fry thermometer**

¼ cup	sweet rice flour	60 mL
2 tbsp	cornstarch	30 mL
½ tsp	paprika	2 mL
¼ tsp	cayenne pepper	1 mL
1 lb	frozen calamari (squid) rings, thawed and patted dry	500 g
	Vegetable oil	
¼ tsp	salt	1 mL
	Lemon wedges	

1. In a plastic bag, combine sweet rice flour, cornstarch, paprika and cayenne. Add calamari and shake to coat. Transfer to a sieve and shake off excess flour mixture.

2. In a wok or a deep saucepan, heat 1½ to 2 inches (4 to 5 cm) of oil until it registers 375°F (190°C) on the thermometer. Working in batches, fry calamari for 2 to 3 minutes or until golden. Using a slotted spoon, transfer to a plate lined with paper towels. Sprinkle with salt just before serving. Serve with lemon wedges to squeeze over top.

Nutrients per serving	
Calories	148
Fat	2 g
Carbohydrate	13 g
Fiber	0 g
Protein	18 g
Calcium	37 mg
Vitamin D	0 IU

Creamy Crab Salad Spread

Makes 2½ cups
(625 mL)

A quick-to-prepare soft, zesty seafood spread. Use as an appetizer spread on GF crackers or as a spread for a sandwich.

Tips

This smooth-textured, spicy spread will appeal if your child prefers soft foods.

For warm open-face sandwiches or appetizers, spread onto single slices of GF bread or biscuits and pop under the broiler until lightly browned.

- **Food processor**

1	can (10 to 12 oz/300 to 375 g) lump crabmeat, drained	1
8 oz	cooked salad shrimp	250 g
½	red onion, cut into quarters	½
½	red bell pepper, quartered and seeded	½
1 tbsp	fresh dill fronds	15 mL
½ tsp	hot pepper flakes	2 mL
½ tsp	freshly ground white pepper	2 mL
	Salt	

1. In food processor, process crabmeat, shrimp, red onion, bell pepper, dill, hot pepper flakes and white pepper until smooth, about 20 seconds, stopping and scraping down sides of the bowl once or twice. Season with salt to taste.

2. Serve immediately or cover and refrigerate for up to 2 hours or overnight.

Nutrients per ¼ cup (60 mL)	
Calories	69
Fat	4 g
Carbohydrate	2 g
Fiber	1 g
Protein	7 g
Calcium	31 mg
Vitamin D	0 IU

Egg Salad Spread

<table>
<tr><td colspan="2">Makes 2 cups
(500 mL)</td></tr>
</table>

This egg salad is a great spread on crostini for appetizers. And when you have an abundance of colored eggs after Easter, this spread will make them disappear quickly and provide light meals for a few days.

Tips

This is a high-protein spread that will be popular with everyone's kids.

You can hard-cook the eggs a few days before serving.

Spread keeps, covered and refrigerated, for up to 3 days.

Serve with Honey Dijon Toastie (page 226) or Simple Corn Tortillas (page 229).

- **Food processor**

8	large eggs	8
1/3 cup	GF mayonnaise	75 mL
4 oz	cooked ham or salami (optional)	125 g
1 tsp	prepared mustard	5 mL
1 tsp	loosely packed fresh dill fronds	5 mL
1/8 tsp	ground nutmeg	0.5 mL
Pinch	salt	Pinch

1. Place eggs on the bottom of a saucepan in a single layer and add enough cold water to cover by 1 inch (2.5 cm). Bring to a boil over high heat. Remove from heat and, without draining the water, cover and let stand for 10 minutes. With a slotted spoon, carefully place eggs in a large bowl filled with ice water. Let cool completely for 5 minutes. Remove eggshells under cool running water. Let eggs come to room temperature.

2. In food processor, process eggs, mayonnaise, ham (if using), mustard, dill, nutmeg and salt until smooth, about 30 seconds, stopping and scraping down sides of the bowl once or twice. Taste and add more salt, if desired.

Nutrients per 1/4 cup (60 mL)	
Calories	106
Fat	8 g
Carbohydrate	1 g
Fiber	0 g
Protein	6 g
Calcium	29 mg
Vitamin D	41 IU

Fiesta Guacamole

**Makes 3 cups
(750 mL)**

A good guacamole
has to have balance in
flavor. The avocados,
fresh vegetables and
jalapeño chile blend
well with the flavors of
the citrusy juices.

Tip

This is a dip that older
children can easily learn to
make for their lunch, snacks
after school or anytime at
all. Great by itself or with
GF crackers, breadsticks,
tortilla chips or cut-up
vegetables.

6	avocados, mashed	6
1	tomato, seeded and chopped	1
¼ cup	minced onion	60 mL
1	jalapeño pepper, diced	1
2	green onions, green parts only, chopped	2
2 tbsp	freshly squeezed lime juice	30 mL
	Kosher or sea salt	

1. In a large bowl, gently combine avocados, tomato,
   onion, jalapeño and green onions. Add lime juice and
   mix well. Add salt to taste.

2. Serve immediately or transfer to an airtight container
   and refrigerate, stirring occasionally, for 30 minutes or
   for up to 2 hours.

Variations

Add 1 tbsp (15 mL) minced cilantro.

When pressed for time, omit the tomato, onion and
green onions and add ½ cup (125 mL) tomato-based
salsa instead.

Nutrients per ¼ cup (60 mL)	
Calories	167
Fat	15 g
Carbohydrate	10 g
Fiber	7 g
Protein	2 g
Calcium	16 mg
Vitamin D	0 IU

Hummus

Tips

The perfect after-school treat — a good time for your child to try new foods, with no pressure.

Surround this nutritious dip with GF crackers, fresh vegetable sticks or GF pita bread pieces.

Prepare dip up to a day before. Stir just before serving and garnish with parsley.

- **Food processor**

1/4 cup	water	60 mL
1 cup	drained canned chickpeas	250 mL
3/4 tsp	crushed garlic	3 mL
2 tbsp	freshly squeezed lemon juice	30 mL
4 tsp	olive oil	20 mL
1/4 cup	tahini	60 mL
1 tbsp	chopped fresh parsley	15 mL

1. In food processor, combine water, chickpeas, garlic, lemon juice, oil and tahini; process until smooth.

2. Transfer to serving dish; sprinkle with parsley.

Nutrients per 2 tbsp (30 mL)			
Calories	93	Protein	3 g
Fat	7 g	Calcium	17 mg
Carbohydrate	6 g	Vitamin D	0 IU
Fiber	1 g		

Black Bean Salsa

Eating more meals with beans and corn is one way to increase your family's intake of fiber and folate. Serve this zesty salsa with Fresh Tortilla Chips (page 371), or as a condiment for any plain grilled or baked meat, fish or chicken.

Tip

For a fast meal to go, spoon 1/2 cup (125 mL) salsa into half a GF pita pocket with lettuce.

1	can (19 oz/540 mL) black beans, drained and rinsed	1
1 cup	drained canned corn kernels	250 mL
1 cup	diced tomatoes	250 mL
1 tbsp	extra virgin olive oil	15 mL
2 tbsp	freshly squeezed lime juice or cider vinegar	30 mL
2 tbsp	finely chopped fresh cilantro or parsley	30 mL
1/2 tsp	minced garlic	2 mL
1/8 tsp	freshly ground black pepper	0.5 mL

1. Combine all ingredients in a medium bowl and gently toss together.

This recipe courtesy of dietitian Alice Lee.

Nutrients per 1/2 cup (125 mL)			
Calories	133	Protein	5 g
Fat	3 g	Calcium	49 mg
Carbohydrate	19 g	Vitamin D	0 IU
Fiber	4 g		

Tomatillo and Chia Seed Salsa

Makes 2 cups (500 mL)

The chia seeds in this recipe provide omega-3 fatty acids, which have many health benefits. Serve this tangy salsa as a side with dishes that have strong Southwest flavors, or as a quick midday snack.

Tip

Tomatillos resemble small green tomatoes. They come wrapped in a husk, which needs to be removed before using. They are quite tart but very tasty.

1½ cups	diced tomatillos (see tip, at left)	375 mL
¼ cup	chopped fresh cilantro leaves	60 mL
2 tbsp	chia seeds	30 mL
1 tbsp	freshly squeezed lemon juice	15 mL
2 tsp	extra virgin olive oil	10 mL
½ tsp	fine sea salt	2 mL

1. In a bowl, combine tomatillos, cilantro, chia seeds, lemon juice, olive oil and salt. Toss well. Cover and set aside for 10 minutes to allow the chia seeds to swell, which will add texture and body to the salsa.

2. Serve immediately or cover and refrigerate for up to 2 days.

Variation

Substitute an equal quantity of fresh tomatoes for the tomatillos.

Nutrients per ¼ cup (60 mL)	
Calories	32
Fat	1 g
Carbohydrate	3 g
Fiber	1 g
Protein	1 g
Calcium	21 mg
Vitamin D	0 IU

Basic Tomato Sauce

<table>
<tr><td colspan="3">• 3¹⁄₂- to 5-quart slow cooker</td></tr>
</table>

1 tbsp	olive oil	15 mL
2	onions, finely chopped	2
2	carrots, peeled and diced	2
4	cloves garlic, minced	4
1 tsp	dried thyme, crumbled	5 mL
¹⁄₂ tsp	cracked black peppercorns	2 mL
2	cans (each 28 oz/796 mL) tomatoes, with juice, coarsely chopped	2
	Salt (optional)	

Makes about 8 cups (2 L)

Not only is this sauce tasty and easy to make, it is also much lower in sodium than prepared sauces. It keeps, covered, for up to 1 week in the refrigerator and can be frozen for up to 6 months.

Tips

If you are halving this recipe, be sure to use a small (1¹⁄₂ to 3¹⁄₂ quart) slow cooker.

This rich tomato sauce hides carrots from the unsuspecting veggie haters.

Serve with GF pasta, with spaghetti squash for a fun variation, or on baked chicken with a sprinkle of vegan cheese.

1. In slow cooker stoneware, combine olive oil, onions and carrots. Stir well to ensure vegetables are coated with oil. Cover and cook on High for 1 hour, until vegetables are softened. Add garlic, thyme and peppercorns. Stir well. Stir in tomatoes with juice.

2. Place a clean tea towel, folded in half (so you will have two layers), over top of stoneware to absorb moisture. Cover and cook on Low for 6 hours or on High for 3 hours, until sauce is thickened and flavors are melded. Season to taste with salt, if desired.

Nutrients per ¹⁄₂ cup (125 mL)	
Calories	40
Fat	1 g
Carbohydrate	7 g
Fiber	2 g
Protein	1 g
Calcium	40 mg
Vitamin D	0 IU

Creamy Mayonnaise

<table>
<tr><td colspan="2">Makes about
¾ cup (175 mL)</td></tr>
</table>

This creamy and absolutely delicious spread has the consistency and taste of mayonnaise and uses dry mustard powder to give it a little snap. It is excellent on sandwiches. Easily infused with roasted garlic, chopped herbs, curry or a multitude of flavorings, it is equally at home in a macaroni, grain or potato salad. Thin with water or juice for a quick dressing or sauce.

Tip

Read ingredient lists for hidden gluten or casein.

- **Immersion blender or small food processor**

4 oz	firm or extra-firm silken tofu	125 g
2 oz	extra-firm tofu, drained	60 g
4¾ tsp	freshly squeezed lemon juice	23 mL
4 tsp	olive oil	20 mL
¼ tsp	Dijon mustard	1 mL
⅛ tsp	salt (approx.)	0.5 mL
⅛ tsp	dry mustard (approx.)	0.5 mL

1. In a small deep bowl, combine silken and extra-firm tofu, lemon juice, oil, Dijon mustard, salt and dry mustard. Use an immersion blender to thoroughly blend ingredients into a very creamy, smooth mixture with the texture of mayonnaise, 2 to 3 minutes. Taste and adjust seasoning, adding a pinch each of dry mustard and salt, if desired. Store mayonnaise in an airtight container in the refrigerator for up to 1 week.

Nutrients per 1 tbsp (15 mL)	
Calories	33
Fat	3 g
Carbohydrate	1 g
Fiber	0 g
Protein	2 g
Calcium	68 mg
Vitamin D	0 IU

Honey Mustard Dipping Sauce

Makes ½ cup (125 mL)

Kids love this yummy sauce, which is a perfect companion to Crispy Pecan Chicken Fingers (page 312).

Tip
Try pairing this dipping sauce with mixed steamed vegetables to turn your child into a veggie lover.

| ¼ cup | Dijon mustard | 60 mL |
| ¼ cup | liquid honey | 60 mL |

1. In a small bowl, combine Dijon mustard and honey. Serve at room temperature. (If the honey becomes too thick to pour, microwave, uncovered, on Medium for a few seconds until it pours easily.)

Variation
Substitute prepared or grainy mustard for the Dijon.

Nutrients per 1 tbsp (15 mL)			
Calories	42	Protein	0 g
Fat	0 g	Calcium	0 mg
Carbohydrate	10 g	Vitamin D	0 IU
Fiber	0 g		

Mock Soy Sauce

Makes 2 cups (500 mL)

If you are having trouble finding GF soy sauce in your area, try this soy-free version.

3	GF beef bouillon cubes (or 3 tbsp/45 mL GF beef stock powder)	3
1½ cups	boiling water	375 mL
¼ cup	cider vinegar	60 mL
2 tbsp	sesame oil	30 mL
2 tbsp	light (fancy) molasses	30 mL
Pinch	freshly ground black pepper	Pinch

1. Dissolve bouillon cubes in boiling water. Gradually whisk in vinegar, sesame oil, molasses and pepper until blended.

2. Store in a covered jar in the refrigerator for up to 1 month.

Nutrients per 1 tbsp (15 mL)			
Calories	12	Protein	0 g
Fat	1 g	Calcium	4 mg
Carbohydrate	1 g	Vitamin D	0 IU
Fiber	0 g		

Fiesta Taco Sauce

Makes 3½ cups (875 mL)

This spicy tomato sauce has a unique balance of flavors, accented with Mexican oregano. Hot pepper flakes add heat, while the onion adds texture and taste.

Tips

This sauce will be a winner with kids who prefer high-texture, spicy foods.

Mexican oregano is dried, but sometimes it comes with big pieces that need to be crushed or minced.

This taco sauce has a thinner consistency than most. For a thicker sauce, add less water.

- **Blender or food processor**

1¾ cups	tomato sauce	425 mL
1	onion, chopped	1
1 tbsp	crushed Mexican oregano (see tip, at left)	15 mL
1 tbsp	minced garlic	15 mL
1	can (28 oz/796 mL) crushed or diced tomatoes	1
2 tbsp	hot pepper flakes	30 mL
1 tbsp	kosher salt	15 mL

1. In a large bowl, combine tomato sauce, onion, oregano, garlic and tomatoes. Add hot pepper flakes and salt.

2. In blender, in batches, pulse tomato mixture until smooth. Pour into a large bowl and add up to 1½ cups (375 mL) of water, depending on the consistency you desire (see tip, at left). Mix well. Repeat until all tomato mixture has been blended with water.

3. Transfer sauce to a large airtight container. Cover and refrigerate, stirring occasionally, for 1 hour or for up to 4 days.

Nutrients per ¼ cup (60 mL)	
Calories	37
Fat	0 g
Carbohydrate	7 g
Fiber	1 g
Protein	2 g
Calcium	6 mg
Vitamin D	0 IU

Soups and Salads

Cold Mango Soup 262

Sweet Pea Soup 263

Fresh Tomato Dill Soup. 264

Coconut-Spiked Pumpkin Soup with Cumin
    and Ginger 265

Southwestern Turkey Chowder 266

Hungarian Chicken Soup 268

Strawberry Salad. 269

Thai Yellow Curry Mango Salad 270

Festive Mexican Slaw. 271

Kasha and Beet Salad with Celery and Feta. 272

Roasted Sweet Potato Salad 273

Asian-Style Quinoa Salad with Chili-Orange
    Dressing 274

Sticky Rice Salad with Asparagus
    and Mushrooms in Soy Vinaigrette. 275

Shrimp Caesar Salad with Garlic Croutons. 276

Mediterranean Tuna Risotto Salad 278

Warm Chicken Salad with Peanut Dressing. 279

Taco Salad 280

Waldorf Parma Salad 282

Sesame Tofu Vinaigrette. 283

Clear Coleslaw Dressing. 283

Ranch Dressing. 284

Cold Mango Soup

Makes 4 servings

Try to ensure that the mango is ripe. If not, add some sugar to taste. This soup can be frozen for up to 3 weeks.

Tips

This soup will give your child's taste buds — and immune system — a boost.

Rich in vitamins, minerals, and fiber, mango has the ultimate soft and smooth texture to please any highly selective eater.

Prepare and refrigerate up to 2 days before.

• **Food processor**

2 tsp	vegetable oil	10 mL
½ cup	chopped onions	125 mL
2 tsp	minced garlic	10 mL
2 cups	ready-to-use vegetable broth	500 mL
2½ cups	chopped ripe mango (about 2 large)	625 mL
	Fresh cilantro leaves (optional)	

1. In a nonstick saucepan, heat oil over medium heat. Add onions and garlic; cook, stirring, for 4 minutes or until browned.

2. Add broth. Bring to a boil; reduce heat to medium-low and cook for 5 minutes or until onions are soft.

3. Transfer mixture to food processor. Add 2 cups (500 mL) of the mango. Purée until smooth. Stir in remaining chopped mango.

4. Chill 2 hours or until cold. If desired, garnish with cilantro.

Nutrients per serving	
Calories	105
Fat	3 g
Carbohydrate	19 g
Fiber	3 g
Protein	1 g
Calcium	26 mg
Vitamin D	0 IU

Sweet Pea Soup

This fragrant and nutritious soup is delicious with or without tarragon, so prepare it to suit your family's preferences.

Tips

Prepare and refrigerate this soup early in the day and reheat gently before serving.

In place of the dried tarragon, you can use 3 tbsp (45 mL) chopped fresh.

- **Food processor**

1½ tsp	vegetable oil	7 mL
¾ cup	chopped onion	175 mL
1 tsp	crushed garlic	5 mL
1	carrot, chopped	1
4 oz	mushrooms, sliced	125 g
3 cups	ready-to-use chicken broth	750 mL
1	potato, peeled and chopped	1
1	package (10 oz/300 g) frozen sweet peas	1
½ cup	corn kernels	125 mL
2 tsp	dried tarragon (optional)	10 mL

1. In a large nonstick saucepan, heat oil; sauté onion, garlic, carrot and mushrooms until softened, approximately 5 minutes.

2. Add broth, potato and all but ¼ cup (60 mL) of the peas; reduce heat, cover and simmer for 20 to 25 minutes or until potato is tender.

3. Purée soup in food processor until creamy and smooth. Return to pan and add reserved peas and corn. Season with tarragon (if using).

Nutrients per serving	
Calories	175
Fat	4 g
Carbohydrate	29 g
Fiber	7 g
Protein	10 g
Calcium	41 mg
Vitamin D	1 IU

Fresh Tomato Dill Soup

<table>
<tr><td>Makes 6 servings</td></tr>
</table>

Tomato dill soup is a longtime family favorite.

Tips

Prepare and refrigerate this soup early in the day, then serve cold or reheat gently.

Over the centuries, dill has been used to treat digestive upset. Try serving this soup if your child has a GI flare-up.

- **Food processor**

1 tbsp	olive oil	15 mL
1 tsp	crushed garlic	5 mL
1	carrot, chopped	1
1	celery stalk, chopped	1
1 cup	chopped onion	250 mL
2 cups	ready-to-use chicken broth	500 mL
5 cups	chopped ripe tomatoes	1.25 L
3 tbsp	tomato paste	45 mL
2 tsp	granulated sugar	10 mL
3 tbsp	chopped fresh dill	45 mL

1. In a large nonstick saucepan, heat oil; sauté garlic, carrot, celery and onion until softened, approximately 5 minutes.

2. Add broth, tomatoes and tomato paste; reduce heat, cover and simmer for 20 minutes, stirring occasionally.

3. Purée in food processor until smooth. Add sugar and dill; mix well.

Nutrients per serving	
Calories	93
Fat	3 g
Carbohydrate	14 g
Fiber	3 g
Protein	4 g
Calcium	32 mg
Vitamin D	0 IU

Coconut-Spiked Pumpkin Soup with Cumin and Ginger

Makes 6 to 8 servings

Here's a healthy, hearty soup with Asian flavors that makes a nice centerpiece for lunch or a light supper or an elegant starter to a more substantial dinner.

Tips

For the best flavor, toast cumin seeds and grind them yourself. To toast cumin seeds, place in a dry skillet over medium heat and cook, stirring, until fragrant, about 3 minutes. Immediately transfer to a spice grinder or mortar and grind finely.

You may need to adjust the quantity of salt depending upon the saltiness of the broth you're using.

If you like heat, increase the quantity of cayenne to ½ tsp (2 mL).

Nutrients per 1 of 8 servings	
Calories	94
Fat	4 g
Carbohydrate	14 g
Fiber	3 g
Protein	2 g
Calcium	61 mg
Vitamin D	0 IU

- **4- to 6-quart slow cooker**
- **Immersion blender, stand blender or food processor**

1 tbsp	vegetable oil	15 mL
2	onions, finely chopped	2
2	carrots, peeled and diced	2
2	stalks celery, diced	2
4	cloves garlic, minced	4
2 tbsp	minced gingerroot	30 mL
1 tbsp	ground cumin (see tip, at left)	15 mL
½ tsp	salt (see tip, at left)	2 mL
½ tsp	cracked black peppercorns	2 mL
5 cups	ready-to-use vegetable broth, divided	1.25 L
6 cups	cubed peeled pumpkin or butternut squash (½-inch/1 cm cubes)	1.5 L
¼ tsp	cayenne pepper (see tip, at left)	1 mL
2 tbsp	freshly squeezed lime juice	30 mL
1 cup	coconut milk	250 mL

1. In a skillet, heat oil over medium heat. Add onions, carrots and celery and cook, stirring, until softened, about 7 minutes. Add garlic, ginger, cumin, salt and peppercorns and cook, stirring for 1 minute. Add 1 cup (250 mL) of the broth and bring to a boil. Transfer to slow cooker stoneware.

2. Add remaining 4 cups (1 L) of broth and pumpkin. Cover and cook on Low for 6 hours, until pumpkin is tender. Purée using an immersion blender. (If you don't have an immersion blender, do this in a stand blender or food processor, in batches, and return to stoneware.)

3. In a small bowl, combine cayenne and lime juice, stirring until cayenne dissolves. Add to slow cooker along with coconut milk. Stir well. Cover and cook on High for 15 minutes to meld flavors.

Southwestern Turkey Chowder

This soup is the best way to use up leftover turkey and long-cooking whole grains. If you're planning to eat lightly following a holiday, it makes a perfect dinner with the addition of salad and maybe some GF biscuits.

Tips

For the best flavor, toast and grind whole cumin seeds rather than buying ground cumin. Simply stir seeds in a dry skillet over medium heat until fragrant, about 3 minutes. Immediately transfer to a spice grinder or mortar and grind.

Use any combination of long-cooking whole grains in this soup, such as barley, wheat berries or brown, red or wild rice. All will be delicious.

Nutrients per serving	
Calories	335
Fat	7 g
Carbohydrate	47 g
Fiber	8 g
Protein	21 g
Calcium	76 mg
Vitamin D	0 IU

- **Blender**

1 tbsp	olive oil	15 mL
3	onions, diced	3
4	stalks celery, diced	4
1 tbsp	ground cumin (see tip, at left)	15 mL
2 tsp	dried oregano	10 mL
4	cloves garlic, minced	4
1/2 tsp	cracked black peppercorns	2 mL
1 1/2 cups	long-cooking whole grains, rinsed and drained (see tip, at left)	375 mL
1	can (28 oz/796 mL) no-salt-added diced tomatoes, with juice	1
10 cups	turkey stock (see box, opposite)	2.5 L
2 to 3	ancho, guajillo or mild New Mexico dried chiles	2 to 3
1 cup	loosely packed fresh cilantro leaves	250 mL
2 cups	diced cooked turkey	500 mL
2 cups	corn kernels	500 mL

1. In a stockpot, heat oil over medium heat for 30 seconds. Add onions and celery and cook, stirring, until vegetables are softened, about 5 minutes. Add cumin, oregano, garlic and peppercorns and cook, stirring, for 1 minute. Add whole grains and toss until coated. Add tomatoes with juice and stock and bring to a boil.

2. Reduce heat to low. Cover and simmer until grains are tender, about 1 hour.

3. In a heatproof bowl, 30 minutes before grains have finished cooking, combine dried chiles and 2 cups (500 mL) boiling water. Set aside for 30 minutes, weighing chiles down with a cup to ensure they remain submerged. Drain, discarding soaking liquid and stems, and chop coarsely. Transfer to blender. Add cilantro and 1/2 cup (125 mL) of stock from the chowder. Purée. Add to stockpot along with the turkey and corn. Cover and cook until corn is tender and flavors meld, about 20 minutes.

Tips

Slow Cooker Method:
Complete step 1, reducing
the quantity of turkey stock
to 9 cups (2.25 L), and
transfer to slow cooker
stoneware. Cover and cook
on Low for 8 hours or High
for 4 hours, until grains are
tender. Complete step 3.
After adding the chile
mixture, turkey and corn,
cover and cook on High
until corn is tender, about
20 minutes.

Variation

Southwestern Chicken Chowder: Substitute ready-to-
use chicken stock for the turkey stock and diced cooked
chicken for the turkey.

Turkey Stock

To make turkey stock, break a turkey carcass into
manageable pieces and place in a stockpot. Add 2 each
carrots, celery stalks and onions, quartered, plus
8 whole peppercorns. Add water to cover. Bring to a
boil over medium-high heat. Reduce heat to low. Cover
and simmer for 3 hours. Strain, reserving liquid and
discarding solids.

Hungarian Chicken Soup

Makes 8 servings

Here's a good opportunity for you and your kids to try some vegetables that you may not have very often — kohlrabi and parsnips, which add a sweet flavor to this soup.

Tips

Serve this hearty soup over cooked rice or GF noodles.

If you are serving buckwheat noodles with this dish, check the ingredient list to be sure they are 100% buckwheat.

4	skin-on bone-in chicken thighs, rinsed under cold running water	4
5 cups	water	1.25 L
1 tsp	salt	5 mL
1/4 tsp	freshly ground black pepper	1 mL
2	carrots, peeled and sliced	2
2	parsnips, peeled and sliced	2
1	kohlrabi, peeled and chopped	1
3	sprigs fresh parsley, chopped	3

1. In a large saucepan, combine chicken and water. Add salt and pepper. Bring to a boil; reduce heat and simmer, skimming off any froth from the surface, for $1\frac{1}{2}$ hours or until chicken falls off the bone.

2. Remove bones from broth and add vegetables. Simmer for another 45 minutes or until the vegetables are tender. Transfer soup to a serving bowl and garnish with parsley.

Nutrients per serving	
Calories	92
Fat	2 g
Carbohydrate	8 g
Fiber	2 g
Protein	8 g
Calcium	28 mg
Vitamin D	2 IU

Strawberry Salad

Just the name of this salad is appealing to kids. They'll love it even more when they taste it!

Variation

Try replacing the strawberries with mandarin segments and add ¼ cup (60 mL) mushrooms.

Salad

1	bunch fresh spinach (about 6 oz/150 g), washed and torn into bite-size pieces	1
2 cups	lettuce, washed and torn into bite-size pieces	500 mL
2 cups	sliced fresh strawberries	500 mL
2 tbsp	sesame seeds	30 mL

Dressing

2 tbsp	olive oil	30 mL
2 tbsp	white vinegar	30 mL
1 tbsp	granulated sugar	15 mL
Pinch	paprika	Pinch

1. *Salad:* In a salad bowl, toss spinach and lettuce until combined. Add strawberries. Sprinkle with sesame seeds.

2. *Dressing:* In a small bowl, whisk together oil, vinegar, sugar and paprika.

3. Just before serving, pour dressing over salad and toss lightly.

Nutrients per serving	
Calories	71
Fat	5 g
Carbohydrate	7 g
Fiber	2 g
Protein	1 g
Calcium	35 mg
Vitamin D	0 IU

Thai Yellow Curry Mango Salad

Here's a salute to one of Thai cuisine's most famous salads, using the green mangos that are ubiquitous in that tropical country and are easily found in Asian markets on this side of the world.

Tip

Green mangos are firm enough to peel with a sharp vegetable peeler or paring knife. Peel off skin and cut flesh away from the pit in slices. Cut each slice crosswise into thin strips.

2 tbsp	vegetable oil	30 mL
1 tsp	Thai yellow curry paste	5 mL
1	clove garlic, minced	1
2 tbsp	packed brown or palm sugar	30 mL
2 tbsp	freshly squeezed lime juice	30 mL
1 tbsp	fish sauce (nam pla) or soy sauce	15 mL
¼ tsp	Asian chili sauce	1 mL
1	large green mango (or 2 small), peeled and julienned (see tip, at left)	1
½	red bell pepper, finely chopped	½
¼ cup	very thinly sliced red onion	60 mL
1 tbsp	chopped fresh cilantro	15 mL
1 tsp	chopped fresh mint	5 mL
	Salt (optional)	
	Ground or chopped roasted peanuts	

1. In a small saucepan, heat oil over medium-low heat. Add curry paste and cook, stirring, until softened and fragrant, about 2 minutes. Add garlic, brown sugar, lime juice, fish sauce and chili sauce; cook, stirring occasionally, just until sugar is dissolved, about 1 minute. Transfer to a bowl and let cool completely.

2. In a large bowl, combine mango, red pepper, onion, cilantro and mint. Add dressing and toss to coat. Season to taste with salt (if using). Serve immediately, sprinkled with peanuts, or cover and refrigerate for up to 8 hours. Let stand at room temperature for 30 minutes before serving.

Nutrients per serving	
Calories	150
Fat	7 g
Carbohydrate	22 g
Fiber	2 g
Protein	1 g
Calcium	23 mg
Vitamin D	0 IU

Festive Mexican Slaw

<table>
<tr><td>Makes 4 to
6 servings</td></tr>
</table>

Makes 4 to 6 servings

A simple coleslaw marinated with tangy vinegar is perfect for any Mexican meal. Serve as a side dish or as garnish for tacos, tortas or enchiladas.

Tips

For a different flavor, substitute olive oil for the canola oil.

The vitamin C in the cabbage will help your child's digestive system absorb iron from the meal.

Variations

For a simpler version, omit red cabbage and red bell pepper and use 5 cups (1.25 L) green cabbage instead.

For additional flavor, add juice of 1 lime.

½ cup	canola oil	125 mL
⅓ cup	white vinegar	75 mL
½ tsp	salt	2 mL
3 cups	finely shredded green cabbage	750 mL
2 cups	finely shredded red cabbage	500 mL
⅓ cup	diced red bell pepper	75 mL
	Cracked black peppercorns	

1. In a large bowl, whisk together oil, vinegar and salt until well blended. Add green and red cabbage and bell pepper and toss until well coated. Season with pepper to taste.

2. Transfer to an airtight container and refrigerate, stirring occasionally, for up to 1 hour before serving. Coleslaw will keep, covered and refrigerated, for up to 2 days.

Nutrients per 1 of 6 servings	
Calories	180
Fat	19 g
Carbohydrate	5 g
Fiber	2 g
Protein	1 g
Calcium	28 mg
Vitamin D	0 IU

Kasha and Beet Salad with Celery and Feta

Makes 6 to 8 servings

In this hearty salad, beets, parsley and vegan feta are the perfect balance for assertive buckwheat (also known as kasha when it's toasted).

Tips

If you prefer a milder buckwheat flavor, use groats rather than kasha in this dish. Just place them in a dry skillet over medium-high heat and cook, stirring constantly, until they are nicely fragrant, about 4 minutes. In the process, they will darken from a light shade of sand to one with a hint of brown.

Place the celery and green onions in the feed tube together so that the celery provides support for the less rigid onions.

Nutrients per 1 of 8 servings	
Calories	188
Fat	10 g
Carbohydrate	21 g
Fiber	4 g
Protein	6 g
Calcium	72 mg
Vitamin D	0 IU

- **Food processor**

Salad

2 cups	ready-to-use chicken or vegetable broth	500 mL
2	cloves garlic, minced	2
1 cup	kasha or buckwheat groats (see tip, at left)	250 mL
3	beets, cooked, peeled and cut to fit feed tube	3
4	stalks celery, cut to fit feed tube	4
6	green onions, white part only	6
3 oz	crumbled vegan feta cheese alternative	90 g

Dressing

1 cup	fresh flat-leaf (Italian) parsley leaves	250 mL
1/4 cup	red wine vinegar	60 mL
1 tsp	Dijon mustard	5 mL
1/2 tsp	salt	2 mL
1/2 tsp	freshly ground black pepper	2 mL
1/4 cup	extra virgin olive oil	60 mL

1. *Salad:* In a saucepan over medium-high heat, bring broth and garlic to a boil. Gradually add kasha, stirring constantly to prevent clumping. Reduce heat to low. Cover and simmer until all the liquid is absorbed and kasha is tender, about 10 minutes. Remove from heat. Fluff up with a fork, transfer to a serving bowl and let cool slightly.

2. *Dressing:* Meanwhile, in food processor, pulse parsley, vinegar, mustard, salt and pepper until parsley is chopped and mixture is blended, about 5 times, stopping and scraping down sides of the bowl once or twice. With motor running, add olive oil through feed tube, stopping and scraping down sides of the bowl as necessary. Pour over kasha.

3. Replace the food processor's metal blade with the slicing blade and slice beets, celery and green onions (see tip, at left). Add to kasha and toss well. Chill until ready to serve. Just before serving, sprinkle feta over top.

Roasted Sweet Potato Salad

This hearty, alkalizing salad can be served on its own or as a side dish.

Tips

As a side dish, this salad serves 4 people.

Known as a superfood, sweet potatoes deliver quite a punch when it comes to nutrients, with all of the vitamin A and one-third of the vitamin C your child needs in a day. They are high in beta-carotene and fiber as well. And it doesn't hurt that they're super-sweet too. Be careful that your child doesn't eat orange vegetables *too* frequently, though — her skin may turn orange from too much beta-carotene. If this happens, don't fret: it's unlikely to cause illness, and the change in skin tone is reversible.

Nutrients per serving	
Calories	109
Fat	4 g
Carbohydrate	19 g
Fiber	3 g
Protein	2 g
Calcium	20 mg
Vitamin D	0 IU

- **Preheat oven to 350°F (180°C)**

1	large sweet potato, peeled (if desired) and cut into bite-size chunks	1
1 tsp	extra virgin olive oil	5 mL
2 tsp	freshly squeezed lemon juice	10 mL
1 tsp	liquid honey	5 mL
½ tsp	flaxseed oil or extra virgin olive oil	2 mL
Pinch	sea salt	Pinch
	Freshly ground black pepper	
4 oz	mixed salad leaves (about 4 cups/1 L)	125 g

1. Place the sweet potato in a bowl and mix with the olive oil, then place on a baking sheet and bake in preheated oven for 30 minutes or until pieces are soft and browned (not mushy). Remove from the oven and set aside.

2. In a large bowl, combine the lemon juice, honey, flaxseed oil, salt and pepper. Then add the sweet potato and salad leaves and mix gently.

Asian-Style Quinoa Salad with Chili-Orange Dressing

Makes 6 side-dish servings

Perhaps surprisingly, since quinoa is a "New World" grain, it takes very well to Asian ingredients such as water chestnuts. This is a nice light salad that is perfect for summer dining or a buffet. It's an ideal accompaniment to grilled meat or fish.

Tips

The chili sauce adds a pleasant bit of zest, but if your child is heat averse, you can omit it. You can increase the quantity to taste for heat seekers.

The crunchiness of the water chestnuts in this recipe will appeal if your child prefers food that snaps.

Chili-Orange Dressing

1 tsp	finely grated orange zest	5 mL
¼ cup	freshly squeezed orange juice	60 mL
1 tbsp	reduced-sodium GF soy sauce	15 mL
1 tbsp	liquid honey	15 mL
2 tsp	sesame oil	10 mL
½ tsp	Asian chili sauce (such as sambal oelek)	2 mL
	Freshly ground black pepper	

Salad

3 cups	cooked quinoa, cooled	750 mL
1	can (8 oz/227 g) water chestnuts, drained and chopped	1
1	red bell pepper, seeded and chopped	1
1½ cups	chopped snow peas, cooked until tender-crisp and cooled	375 mL
4	green onions, white part with a bit of green, thinly sliced	4

1. *Dressing:* In a small bowl, whisk together orange zest and juice, soy sauce, honey, sesame oil, chili sauce and pepper to taste. Set aside.

2. *Salad:* In a serving bowl, combine quinoa, water chestnuts, bell pepper, snow peas and green onions. Add dressing and toss until combined. Chill thoroughly.

Variation

Asian-Style Millet Salad with Chili-Orange Dressing: Substitute 3 cups (750 mL) cooked toasted millet for the quinoa.

Nutrients per serving	
Calories	176
Fat	4 g
Carbohydrate	31 g
Fiber	5 g
Protein	5 g
Calcium	29 mg
Vitamin D	0 IU

Sticky Rice Salad with Asparagus and Mushrooms in Soy Vinaigrette

---

Makes 4 to 8 servings

"Sticky rice" is the Chinese term for any short-grain or glutinous rice. Italian Arborio or Japanese sushi rice make good substitutes. For this recipe, the rice must be cooked until soft, then drained and set out to dry on a baking sheet. The resulting dense, chewy rice will readily absorb the flavors of the vinaigrette.

Nutrients per 1 of 8 servings	
Calories	263
Fat	6 g
Carbohydrate	45 g
Fiber	3 g
Protein	5 g
Calcium	9 mg
Vitamin D	1 IU

Rice

2 cups	short-grain rice	500 mL
1 tsp	salt	5 mL
4 cups	water	1 L

Dressing

3 tbsp	GF soy sauce or Mock Soy Sauce (page 259)	45 mL
1 tbsp	prepared mustard (yellow, Dijon or grainy)	15 mL
4 tbsp	rice vinegar	60 mL
2 tbsp	vegetable oil	30 mL
1 tsp	sesame oil	5 mL
	Salt and freshly ground black pepper	

Salad

1 tbsp	vegetable oil	15 mL
8 oz	asparagus, trimmed and cut into 1-inch (2.5 cm) pieces	250 g
1 tbsp	minced garlic	15 mL
8 oz	mushrooms, thinly sliced	250 g
1 tbsp	minced fresh cilantro	15 mL

1. *Rice:* In a small pot, combine rice, salt and water. Bring to a boil, stir and reduce heat to low. Cover tightly and cook for 20 minutes. Remove from heat and let sit for at least 5 minutes. Spread rice evenly on a baking sheet and let cool to room temperature.

2. *Dressing:* In a small bowl, combine soy sauce, mustard and rice vinegar. Add the oils in a slow stream, whisking constantly. Season to taste with salt and pepper; set aside.

3. *Salad:* In a nonstick skillet, heat oil over medium-high heat for 30 seconds. Add asparagus, garlic and mushrooms. Sauté until asparagus is tender and mushrooms are soft, about 4 to 5 minutes.

4. In a large salad bowl, combine rice and asparagus mixture. Add dressing and toss to combine. Garnish with cilantro and serve at room temperature.

Shrimp Caesar Salad with Garlic Croutons

Restaurant sales of Caesar salads increase daily. Carry your own Dijon dressing and gluten-free croutons or make them to serve at home.

Tips

Extra salad dressing can be stored in the refrigerator for up to 3 weeks.

For a milder mustard flavor, reduce the Dijon mustard to 1 tbsp (15 mL).

Helping your child develop a taste for a Caesar salad, one bite at a time, would mean she can order one food item in most restaurants.

Dijon Dressing

¾ cup	extra virgin olive oil	175 mL
⅓ cup	freshly squeezed lemon juice	75 mL
2 to 3 tbsp	Dijon mustard	30 to 45 mL

Salad

1	head romaine lettuce, torn into bite-size pieces	1
8 oz	large shrimp, cooked, peeled and deveined	250 g
	Garlic Croutons (see recipe, opposite)	

1. *Dressing:* In a small bowl, whisk together olive oil, lemon juice and Dijon mustard to taste. Set aside for at least 1 hour before serving to allow flavors to develop and blend.

2. *Salad:* In a large bowl, combine lettuce, shrimp and just enough dressing to moisten. Top with gluten-free garlic croutons.

Nutrients per serving	
Calories	484
Fat	44 g
Carbohydrate	9 g
Fiber	3 g
Protein	15 g
Calcium	105 mg
Vitamin D	2 IU

This is a good way to
use up day-old gluten-
free bread!

Variation

Use any GF bread (store-
bought or see recipes,
pages 218–222) to make
these croutons.

Garlic Croutons

- **Preheat oven to 375°F (190°C)**

4	slices day-old White Bread (page 218), cut into 1-inch (2.5 cm) cubes	4
1 tbsp	extra virgin olive oil	15 mL
2	cloves garlic, minced	2

1. In a bowl, toss bread cubes with oil and garlic. Spread in a single layer on a baking sheet.

2. Bake in preheated oven for 10 to 15 minutes or until crisp and golden, turning frequently. Let cool completely, then store in an airtight container.

Nutrients per 10 croutons	
Calories	84
Fat	2 g
Carbohydrate	15 g
Fiber	1 g
Protein	2 g
Calcium	10 mg
Vitamin D	4 IU

Mediterranean Tuna Risotto Salad

Filling and flavorful, this salad makes for a quick and easy side dish or meal.

Tips

Arborio is an Italian rice traditionally used for risotto and great for making a creamy rice pudding. The surface starch should not be washed off before cooking, as it gives the finished dish its creamy texture.

Serve on top of mixed greens and garnish with sliced tomato and parsley.

You can serve this as a main course, if you wish, instead of as a side salad. As a main course, it serves 6.

4 cups	water	1 L
2 cups	Arborio rice	500 mL
2	cans (each 6 oz/170 g) water-packed albacore tuna, drained and flaked	2
1	red bell pepper, finely chopped	1
½	small red onion, diced	½
½ cup	oil-packed sun-dried tomatoes, drained and finely chopped	125 mL
½ cup	chopped pitted kalamata olives	125 mL
½ cup	finely chopped celery or fennel	125 mL
½ cup	chopped fresh Italian (flat-leaf) parsley	125 mL
2 tbsp	olive oil	30 mL
2 tbsp	red wine vinegar	30 mL
	Salt and freshly ground black pepper	
	Sliced tomatoes and fresh parsley sprigs	

1. In a large saucepan, bring water to a boil. Add rice and bring back to a boil. Stir well, then reduce heat, cover and simmer for about 15 minutes or until rice is al dente (tender to the bite). Drain and rinse under cold water to cool rice. Set aside to cool completely.

2. In a large salad bowl, combine cooked rice, tuna, red pepper, red onion, sun-dried tomatoes, olives, celery and parsley. Stir in oil and vinegar. Taste and adjust seasoning with salt and pepper. Garnish with fresh tomatoes and parsley.

This recipe courtesy of chef Eileen Campbell.

Variation

Substitute 10 oz (300 g) cooked diced chicken breast or cooked shrimp or crab for the tuna.

Nutrients per serving	
Calories	216
Fat	5 g
Carbohydrate	32 g
Fiber	2 g
Protein	11 g
Calcium	22 mg
Vitamin D	0 IU

Warm Chicken Salad with Peanut Dressing

Makes 4 servings

Serve this warm dinner salad with grilled flatbread.

Tip

Besides high levels of protein, chicken also provides high levels of niacin (vitamin B_3) and vitamin B_6, which are both important nutrients for supporting the nervous system.

2	boneless skinless chicken breasts	2
Peanut Dressing		
¼ cup	GF peanut butter (smooth or chunky)	60 mL
2 tbsp	freshly squeezed lime or lemon juice	30 mL
1 tbsp	hot water	15 mL
2 tsp	reduced-sodium GF soy sauce	10 mL
1	clove garlic, minced	1
Salad		
1	small apple, chopped	1
1	stalk celery, thinly sliced	1
½ cup	drained canned sliced water chestnuts	125 mL
½ cup	grated carrot	125 mL
½ cup	bean sprouts	125 mL

1. In a large skillet, bring 1 inch (2.5 cm) water to a boil. Add chicken, reduce heat to medium-low, cover and simmer for about 12 minutes or until chicken is no longer pink inside. Transfer to a plate and let cool for 10 minutes.

2. *Peanut Dressing:* In a small bowl, whisk together peanut butter, lime juice, hot water, soy sauce and garlic, adding more hot water, if necessary, to thin.

3. *Salad:* Cut chicken into 1-inch (2.5 cm) pieces. Place in a large bowl and add apple, celery, water chestnuts and carrot. Add peanut dressing and stir to coat. Garnish with bean sprouts.

Nutrients per serving	
Calories	212
Fat	10 g
Carbohydrate	15 g
Fiber	3 g
Protein	18 g
Calcium	33 mg
Vitamin D	3 IU

Taco Salad

Makes 2 servings

Quick, easy, tasty, nutritious — and on top of all that, a meal with hardly any cleanup! What more could you ask?

Tips

If you purchase a sirloin steak, cut it across the grain into thin strips for a tender result.

Read ingredient lists on containers to check for gluten and casein.

If your child prefers a milder-tasting salad, leave out the hot pepper and use a mild chili powder and barbecue sauce.

2	Tortilla Bowls (see recipe, opposite)	2
4 cups	shredded lettuce	1 L
2	tomatoes, diced	2
¼	orange bell pepper, finely chopped	¼
¼	yellow bell pepper, finely chopped	¼
¼ cup	GF barbecue sauce	60 mL
¾ tsp	chili powder	3 mL
Pinch	ground hot pepper	Pinch
1 tsp	extra virgin olive oil	5 mL
6 oz	beef sirloin stir-fry strips	175 g

1. Place tortilla bowls on individual plates. Divide the lettuce evenly between the tortilla bowls. Top each with tomatoes, orange pepper and yellow pepper. Set aside.

2. In a small bowl, combine barbecue sauce, chili powder and hot pepper. Set aside.

3. In a skillet, heat oil over medium-high heat. Brown beef strips, turning occasionally, for 2 to 3 minutes or until just slightly pink in the center. Pour in the barbecue sauce mixture and heat just until steaming.

4. Top each tortilla bowl with half the beef mixture.

Variations

Top the salad with guacamole or salsa.

Marinate the beef strips in the sauce for 30 minutes before cooking them. Drain beef and discard marinade before browning.

Nutrients per serving	
Calories	366
Fat	8 g
Carbohydrate	50 g
Fiber	8 g
Protein	25 g
Calcium	104 mg
Vitamin D	2 IU

Make these neat containers to hold anything from salads to entrées. Children and adults alike will love to eat from them.

Tips

Warm the tortillas in the oven slightly before molding them into the bowl, for easier handling.

Allow your child to use a tortilla bowl as a reward after eating a refused food. Research has shown that children will eat for a reward of a treat or toy they desire (rather than being paid with a bribe before eating the offending food).

Nutrients per serving	
Calories	120
Fat	2 g
Carbohydrate	23 g
Fiber	3 g
Protein	3 g
Calcium	72 mg
Vitamin D	0 IU

Tortilla Bowls

- **Preheat oven to 350°F (180°C)**
- **5$\frac{1}{2}$-inch (14 cm) ovenproof bowl, at least 3$\frac{1}{2}$ inches (9 cm) deep**

2	8-inch (20 cm) GF tortillas	2

1. Gently place a tortilla in the bowl, easing it in to fit the bottom and up the sides. Bake in preheated oven for 15 minutes or until crisp. Let cool in bowl for 5 minutes. Carefully remove from bowl and repeat for remaining tortilla. Let cool completely before filling.

Waldorf Parma Salad

Makes 4 servings

This is a hybrid of New York and Italian flavors. It's a rendition of the salad made popular by the Waldorf Astoria Hotel in New York City, with the addition of Parma ham.

Tips

To toast walnuts: Preheat oven to 350°F (180°C). Spread walnuts on a baking sheet and bake, shaking the pan several times, until fragrant and toasted; 6 to 9 minutes for walnut halves; 4 to 7 minutes for chopped walnuts.

Walnuts are high in omega-3 fatty acids.

- **Food processor**

3	apples (such as Golden Delicious or Jonagold), peeled and quartered	3
8 oz	Parma ham, cut into chunks to fit feed tube	250 g
3	celery stalks, cut into 3-inch (7.5 cm) lengths	3
½	head radicchio, cut to fit feed tube	½
½ cup	toasted walnuts (see tip, at left)	125 mL
2 cups	torn butter lettuce	500 mL
½ cup	GF mayonnaise	125 mL
	Salt and freshly ground black pepper	

1. In food processor fitted with slicing blade, slice apples, ham and celery. Transfer to a salad bowl.

2. Replace slicing blade with shredding blade and shred radicchio. Add to salad bowl.

3. Replace shredding blade with metal blade and pulse walnuts about 10 times. Add to salad bowl. Add butter lettuce and mayonnaise to bowl and toss to coat fully. Season with salt and pepper to taste.

Nutrients per serving	
Calories	364
Fat	24 g
Carbohydrate	23 g
Fiber	6 g
Protein	17 g
Calcium	41 mg
Vitamin D	19 IU

Sesame Tofu Vinaigrette

Makes about 1 cup (250 mL)

Serve with poached vegetable salads, Chinese cabbage coleslaw or fish and seafood salads.

- **Blender or food processor**

1	small clove garlic	1
6 tbsp	canola oil	90 mL
¼ cup	cubed silken tofu	60 mL
3 tbsp	rice vinegar	45 mL
2 tbsp	toasted sesame oil	30 mL
1 tsp	GF soy sauce	5 mL
¼ cup	toasted sesame seeds	60 mL

1. In blender, purée garlic, canola oil, tofu, vinegar, sesame oil and soy sauce, thinning with a few drops of water, if necessary. Stir in sesame seeds.

Nutrients per 1 tbsp (15 mL)			
Calories	76	Protein	1 g
Fat	8 g	Calcium	32 mg
Carbohydrate	1 g	Vitamin D	0 IU
Fiber	0 g		

Clear Coleslaw Dressing

Makes about ¾ cup (175 mL)

Combining energizing cider vinegar with omega-3-rich canola oil makes this clear coleslaw dressing a healthy complement to any salad. Caraway seeds add a touch of savory to the mix.

6 tbsp	canola oil	90 mL
6 tbsp	cider vinegar	90 mL
1 tbsp	granulated sugar	15 mL
2 tsp	caraway seeds	10 mL
1 tsp	kosher salt	5 mL

1. In a bowl, thoroughly whisk together oil, vinegar, sugar, caraway seeds and salt.

Nutrients per 1 tbsp (15 mL)			
Calories	67	Protein	0 g
Fat	7 g	Calcium	3 mg
Carbohydrate	1 g	Vitamin D	0 IU
Fiber	0 g		

Ranch Dressing

<table>
<tr><td colspan="3">• Food processor</td></tr>
<tr><td>8 oz</td><td>firm or extra-firm silken tofu</td><td>250 g</td></tr>
<tr><td>2 tbsp</td><td>freshly squeezed lemon juice</td><td>30 mL</td></tr>
<tr><td>2 tbsp</td><td>white wine vinegar</td><td>30 mL</td></tr>
<tr><td>1 tbsp</td><td>sunflower oil</td><td>15 mL</td></tr>
<tr><td>1½ tsp</td><td>onion powder</td><td>7 mL</td></tr>
<tr><td>1 tsp</td><td>garlic powder</td><td>5 mL</td></tr>
<tr><td>Pinch</td><td>granulated sugar</td><td>Pinch</td></tr>
<tr><td>1 cup</td><td>Creamy Mayonnaise (page 258) or store-bought GF alternative</td><td>250 mL</td></tr>
<tr><td>3 tbsp</td><td>minced fresh chives</td><td>45 mL</td></tr>
<tr><td>½ tsp</td><td>salt</td><td>2 mL</td></tr>
<tr><td>½ tsp</td><td>freshly ground black pepper</td><td>2 mL</td></tr>
</table>

Makes about 2 cups (500 mL)

A family favorite far and wide, homemade ranch dressing is far superior to store-bought. Use it as a dip for crudités or steamed artichokes, toss with chilled potatoes and vegetables, or dollop on baked potatoes.

Tip

The tofu in this recipe puts this ranch dressing on a nutrition pedestal. Enjoy!

1. In food processor, combine tofu, lemon juice, vinegar, oil, onion powder, garlic powder and sugar and process until very smooth.

2. Add mayonnaise, chives, salt and pepper and process until thoroughly combined. Taste and adjust seasoning. If thinner dressing is desired, add a little water, 1 tsp (5 mL) at a time, to thin.

3. Use immediately or refrigerate in an airtight container for up to 10 days.

Variation

Think of this dressing as a base recipe to which you can add fresh herbs, spices and flavors to create your own signature dressing. Try adding 1 tbsp (15 mL) fresh parsley, dill, marjoram, tarragon or cilantro; ¼ or ½ tsp (1 to 2 mL) paprika, cracked peppercorns, cayenne, dry mustard or GF Cajun seasoning; 1 to 2 tsp (5 to 10 mL) hot sauce, tamari, chopped capers, sun-dried tomatoes or minced black olives. You are limited only by your imagination.

Nutrients per 1 tbsp (15 mL)	
Calories	28
Fat	2 g
Carbohydrate	1 g
Fiber	0 g
Protein	2 g
Calcium	51 mg
Vitamin D	0 IU

Meatless Mains

Grilled Portobello on Greens. 286

Vegetarian Chili 287

Mixed Vegetables in Spicy Peanut Sauce 288

Sautéed Mushrooms and Potatoes with
    Garlic, Parsley and Poached Egg. 290

Cold Buckwheat Noodles with Broccoli and
    Sesame Dressing 292

Vegetable Tamale Pie 294

Kale Quinoa Tabbouleh. 295

Rolled Veggie Tacos with Spicy Asian Sauce 296

Rice and Black Bean–Stuffed Peppers. 298

Mushroom and Chickpea Stew with Roasted
    Red Pepper Coulis. 300

Chickpeas in Tomato Sauce 302

Asian Barbecued Tofu Cubes 303

Tofu Patties 304

Grilled Portobello on Greens

This salad combines the smokiness of grilled portobellos with fresh greens in a balsamic vinaigrette with a big taste.

Tips

To make this recipe casein-free, use a vegan Parmesan cheese, such as Parma!, in place of the Parmigiano-Reggiano.

If portobellos are not available, try grilling an assortment of mushrooms tossed with a little olive oil. If they are particularly small, you might want to use a grill basket to keep them from falling through the grate.

- **Preheat grill to medium-high, lightly greased**

2 tbsp	balsamic vinegar	30 mL
1 tbsp	chopped fresh oregano	15 mL
1	clove garlic, minced	1
1/2 tsp	granulated sugar	2 mL
1/3 cup	extra virgin olive oil	75 mL
	Salt and freshly ground black pepper	
2 lbs	portobello mushrooms, stems removed	1 kg
2 to 3 tbsp	extra virgin olive oil	30 to 45 mL
1/2 tsp	coarse salt	2 mL
6 cups	mixed salad greens	1.5 L
2 oz	Parmigiano-Reggiano cheese, shaved (see tip, at left)	60 g

1. In a small bowl, combine balsamic vinegar, oregano, garlic and sugar. Whisk together until well blended. Add olive oil in a steady stream, whisking until well combined. Season to taste with salt and pepper. Set aside.

2. In a bowl, toss portobello caps with olive oil and coarse salt. Place on grill; close lid and grill for 15 minutes, turning frequently, or until edges are a little crispy and mushrooms are tender.

3. Line 4 plates with salad greens. Slice mushrooms fairly thickly; arrange on greens. Drizzle with vinaigrette; top with Parmigiano-Reggiano. Serve immediately.

Nutrients per serving	
Calories	304
Fat	27 g
Carbohydrate	10 g
Fiber	2 g
Protein	7 g
Calcium	180 mg
Vitamin D	0 IU

Vegetarian Chili

Makes 3½ cups (875 mL)		

Children enjoy this good-for-you vegetarian chili for the simple reason that it tastes great — and so will their parents! Serve with cooked brown or white rice or GF toast.

Tips

Use homemade or reduced-sodium broth to lower the sodium content of this recipe.

Use red lentils in this recipe. They cook down to a nice mushy consistency that's ideal for chili.

If your kids don't like chili powder, wait until after you have removed their portion to add it.

Leftover chickpeas can be used to make Hummus (page 255).

1 cup	tomato juice	250 mL
1 cup	ready-to-use vegetable or beef broth	250 mL
1 cup	canned chickpeas, drained and rinsed	250 mL
1	potato, diced	1
¼ cup	red lentils, washed (see tip, at left)	60 mL
1	carrot, chopped	1
½	small onion, chopped	½
½ cup	finely chopped green bell pepper	125 mL
1	clove garlic, minced	1
1 tbsp	chili powder (see tip, at left)	15 mL
¼ tsp	salt	1 mL
¼ tsp	freshly ground black pepper	1 mL

1. In a saucepan, combine tomato juice, broth, chickpeas, potato, lentils, carrot, onion, green pepper and garlic. Cover and bring to a boil. Reduce heat and simmer, covered, for about 20 minutes or until vegetables and lentils are tender. Stir frequently, since the mixture has a tendency to stick as it thickens.

2. Taste and adjust flavor by adding chili powder, salt and pepper; cook for another 5 minutes and serve.

Nutrients per ½ cup (125 mL)	
Calories	85
Fat	1 g
Carbohydrate	17 g
Fiber	4 g
Protein	4 g
Calcium	24 mg
Vitamin D	0 IU

Mixed Vegetables in Spicy Peanut Sauce

<table>
<tr><td colspan="3">Makes 8 servings</td></tr>
</table>

As long as kids don't have peanut allergies, here's one way to get them to eat their vegetables — cook them in a spicy sauce made from peanut butter and add a garnish of chopped roasted peanuts. All you need to add is some steaming rice or brown rice noodles.

- **3½- to 6-quart slow cooker**

1 tbsp	olive oil	15 mL
2	onions, finely chopped	2
6	carrots, peeled and thinly sliced (about 4 cups/1 L)	6
4	stalks celery, diced (about 2 cups/500 mL)	4
2 tbsp	minced gingerroot	30 mL
4	cloves garlic, minced	4
½ tsp	cracked black peppercorns	2 mL
1 cup	ready-to-use vegetable broth	250 mL
3 cups	frozen sliced green beans (see tip, at right)	750 mL
½ cup	smooth natural GF peanut butter	125 mL
2 tbsp	GF soy sauce	30 mL
2 tbsp	freshly squeezed lemon juice	30 mL
1 tbsp	pure maple syrup	15 mL
2 tsp	Thai red curry paste	10 mL
4 cups	shredded napa cabbage	1 L
2 cups	bean sprouts	500 mL
½ cup	finely chopped green onions, white part only	125 mL
½ cup	chopped dry roasted peanuts	125 mL

1. In a large skillet, heat oil over medium heat for 30 seconds. Add onions, carrots and celery and cook, stirring, until softened, about 7 minutes. Add ginger, garlic and peppercorns and cook, stirring, for 1 minute. Transfer to slow cooker stoneware. Add broth and stir well.

2. Add green beans and stir well. Cover and cook on Low for 6 hours or on High for 3 hours, until vegetables are tender.

Nutrients per serving	
Calories	246
Fat	15 g
Carbohydrate	21 g
Fiber	6 g
Protein	10 g
Calcium	98 mg
Vitamin D	0 IU

Tips

If you prefer, substitute fresh green beans for the frozen. Blanch in boiling water for 4 minutes after the water returns to a boil and add to the slow cooker along with the cabbage.

This dish can be partially prepared before it is cooked. Complete step 1. Cover and refrigerate overnight or for up to 2 days. When you're ready to cook, continue with steps 2 and 3.

3. In a bowl, beat together peanut butter, soy sauce, lemon juice, maple syrup and red curry paste until blended. Add to slow cooker stoneware and stir well. Add napa cabbage, in batches, stirring until each batch is submerged in liquid. Cover and cook for 10 minutes, until heated through. Stir in bean sprouts. Garnish each serving with a sprinkle of green onions, then peanuts.

Variation

Add 2 cups (500 mL) cooked broccoli florets along with the cabbage.

Sautéed Mushrooms and Potatoes with Garlic, Parsley and Poached Egg

Makes 4 servings

This makes a lovely light main course. Choose the assortment of mushrooms you wish or even just good old white button mushrooms. Serve over thick-cut GF toast.

Tip

To make this recipe casein-free, replace the butter with olive oil margarine. Make sure to choose a non-hydrogenated margarine that is free of trans fat.

- **Large cast-iron or heavy skillet**

8 oz	waxy potatoes, scrubbed	250 g
1 tsp	salt	5 mL
¼ cup	butter (see tip, at left)	60 mL
3 tbsp	extra virgin olive oil	45 mL
1 lb	assorted mushrooms, trimmed and sliced ¼ inch (0.5 cm) thick	500 g
6	cloves garlic, finely chopped	6
	Salt and freshly ground black pepper	
1 tbsp	freshly squeezed lemon juice	15 mL
1 cup	finely chopped flat-leaf (Italian) parsley leaves	250 mL
1 tsp	white vinegar	5 mL
4	large eggs	4

1. Place potatoes in a large saucepan and add boiling water to barely cover. Add salt, cover loosely and bring to a boil over high heat. Reduce heat and cook for 15 minutes or until potatoes are just tender. Drain well and let cool enough to handle. Cut each potato in half (if large, cut into chunks).

2. In a skillet, heat butter and oil over medium-high heat. Sauté mushrooms and potatoes for about 15 minutes or until golden brown. Toss in garlic, season to taste with salt and freshly ground pepper and sauté for about 1 minute. Remove from heat. Stir in lemon juice and parsley. Reduce heat to very low and cover to keep warm.

Nutrients per serving	
Calories	368
Fat	30 g
Carbohydrate	17 g
Fiber	3 g
Protein	12 g
Calcium	69 mg
Vitamin D	49 IU

Tips

Remove each poached egg from the simmering water with a slotted spoon. Pat the bottom of the spoon on paper towels to absorb any water before transferring to the plate.

If you prefer, you can gently fry the eggs instead of poaching them. Just make sure they are softly fried so you still have some lovely liquid yolk to blend with the mushrooms.

3. Pour enough water into a large, shallow saucepan to come 3 inches (7.5 cm) up the sides. Bring to a boil over high heat. Add vinegar and reduce heat to a simmer. Break each egg into a little dish or cup and gently slip, one at a time (or all together if you are a confident egg poacher), into simmering water. Cook for 5 minutes for a soft yolk and a cooked white, or as desired.

4. Evenly divide mushroom mixture among four warmed individual serving plates and top each with a poached egg. Serve immediately.

Cold Buckwheat Noodles with Broccoli and Sesame Dressing

<table>
<tr><td>

Makes 4 to 6 servings

</td></tr>
</table>

This enticing entrée with flavors of a traditional Japanese buckwheat noodle salad is ideal served on a warm summer day, with chilled sake for the adults and their favorite cold drink for the kids.

Tips

You can also toast sesame seeds in a 350°F (180°C) oven for 10 to 15 minutes.

Recipe can be made in advance and refrigerated in an airtight container for up to 4 hours. Bring to room temperature and add garnishes just before serving.

Nutrients per 1 of 6 servings	
Calories	388
Fat	15 g
Carbohydrate	52 g
Fiber	6 g
Protein	13 g
Calcium	69 mg
Vitamin D	0 IU

- **Blender**
- **Steamer basket**

6 tbsp	sesame seeds, divided (see tip, at left)	90 mL
1 tbsp	grated lemon zest	15 mL
2 tbsp	freshly squeezed lemon juice	30 mL
1 tbsp	grated gingerroot	15 mL
2 tbsp	agave nectar	30 mL
1/4 cup	rice wine vinegar	60 mL
1/3 cup	GF soy sauce	75 mL
2 tbsp	grapeseed oil	30 mL
2 tbsp	toasted sesame oil	30 mL
1/4 tsp	hot pepper flakes	1 mL
8 cups	water	2 L
1	package (12 oz/375 g) dried buckwheat soba noodles	1
5 cups	broccoli florets (about 2 bunches)	1.25 L
3 cups	ice	750 mL
6	green onions, thinly sliced	6
1/2 cup	finely chopped fresh cilantro	125 mL
	Cilantro sprigs or fresh shiso leaves (optional)	

1. In a heavy-bottomed skillet over medium heat, toast sesame seeds, shaking pan frequently, until golden, 4 to 6 minutes. Transfer to plate and let cool.

2. In blender, blend 2 tbsp (30 mL) of the sesame seeds, lemon zest, lemon juice, ginger, agave nectar, vinegar, soy sauce, grapeseed oil, sesame oil and hot pepper flakes until smooth. Set dressing aside.

3. Pour water into stockpot and bring to a boil over high heat. Add noodles and boil, stirring occasionally to deter sticking, until al dente (tender to the bite), about 5 minutes. Drain noodles and transfer to a large serving bowl. Add dressing and toss to coat. Let noodles cool to room temperature, stirring occasionally to recoat with dressing.

Tip

Check the soba noodle label for 100% buckwheat.

Variations

Use asparagus or green beans in place of the broccoli.

For additional protein, add pan-fried tofu cubes.

4. Place a steamer basket into same stockpot. Add water, making sure it is below bottom of steamer basket and bring to a boil. Add broccoli and steam until crisp and just tender, 4 to 5 minutes. Meanwhile, place ice in a large bowl of water. Transfer broccoli to ice bath and when cool, drain in colander. Add broccoli to noodles. Add green onions and chopped cilantro, tossing to combine. Taste and adjust seasoning with additional hot pepper flakes.

5. Serve at room temperature, garnished with remaining $1/4$ cup (60 mL) toasted sesame seeds and sprigs of cilantro or shiso leaves.

Vegetable Tamale Pie

This recipe is a great example of the richness and flavor that can be achieved with vegan and gluten-free recipes!

Tips

For flavor notes that range from savory to sweet, use a combination of green, yellow, red and/or orange bell peppers in this recipe, instead of just one color.

If your child will eat one kind of pepper, this recipe may help widen the variety she will accept. Take baby steps and request tastes of new foods. If rejected, don't give up — it takes 10 to 15 attempts at offering new foods before children will accept them.

Nutrients per 1 of 10 servings	
Calories	110
Fat	2 g
Carbohydrate	19 g
Fiber	3 g
Protein	3 g
Calcium	35 mg
Vitamin D	0 IU

- **8-inch (20 cm) square baking dish**

½ cup	polenta (yellow cornmeal)	125 mL
¼ cup	shredded vegan Cheddar cheese alternative	60 mL
1½ tsp	vegetable oil	7 mL
3	cloves garlic, minced	3
1	onion, finely chopped	1
1	small zucchini, diced	1
½	red, yellow or orange bell pepper, finely chopped	½
1 tbsp	chili powder	15 mL
1 tsp	ground cumin	5 mL
1 tsp	dried oregano	5 mL
1	can (14 to 19 oz/398 to 540 mL) pinto beans, drained and rinsed	1
1	can (14½ oz/411 mL) tomato purée (or 1¾ cups/425 mL crushed tomatoes)	1
½ cup	frozen corn kernels	125 mL
2 tsp	brown rice flour	10 mL
¼ cup	cold water	60 mL
½ tsp	salt	2 mL
½ tsp	freshly ground black pepper	2 mL

1. In a medium saucepan, bring 2 cups (500 mL) water to a boil over high heat. Stir in polenta, reduce heat and simmer, stirring often, for 30 minutes or until thick. Add cheese alternative and stir until melted. Remove from heat and set aside. Preheat oven to 375°F (190°C).

2. In a large skillet, heat oil over medium-high heat. Sauté garlic and onion for 5 to 7 minutes or until tender. Add zucchini, red pepper, chili powder, cumin and oregano; sauté for 5 minutes. Stir in beans, tomato purée and corn.

3. In a small bowl, whisk together rice flour and cold water to form a slurry. Stir into vegetable mixture and cook, stirring, for 3 minutes or until mixture thickens slightly. Season with salt and pepper. Spread in baking dish. Spread polenta mixture over top. Bake for 40 minutes or until bubbling. Let cool for 5 minutes before serving.

Kale Quinoa Tabbouleh

Halfway between a tabbouleh and a fresh vegetable slaw, this dish brightens everything it shares a plate with. Serve it alongside a burger or sandwich, or as a breezy cooldown to a spicy casserole.

Tip

A small serving of this super-salad goes a long way!

Variation

Southwestern Tabbouleh: Add 1 cup (250 mL) cooked black beans, ½ jalapeño pepper, minced, and ¾ tsp (3 mL) ground cumin.

1	bunch kale, stems removed, leaves finely chopped	1
2 cups	cooked quinoa, cooled	500 mL
2	tomatoes, seeded and finely chopped	2
4	green onions, white and light green parts only, chopped	4
2	cloves garlic, finely minced	2
½ cup	finely chopped fresh parsley	125 mL
¼ cup	finely chopped fresh mint	60 mL
½ cup	freshly squeezed lemon juice	125 mL
¼ cup	olive oil	60 mL
1 tsp	salt	5 mL
½ tsp	freshly ground black pepper	2 mL
Pinch	cayenne pepper	Pinch

1. In a large bowl, combine kale, quinoa, tomatoes, green onions, garlic, parsley and mint.

2. In a small bowl, whisk together lemon juice, oil, salt, black pepper and cayenne and pour over vegetables. Gently toss to combine. Let stand for 10 minutes at room temperature before serving.

Nutrients per serving	
Calories	290
Fat	17 g
Carbohydrate	31 g
Fiber	5 g
Protein	7 g
Calcium	146 mg
Vitamin D	0 IU

Rolled Veggie Tacos with Spicy Asian Sauce

Makes 8 tacos

Enjoy this crispy golden corn tortilla stuffed with fresh veggies and dipped in a spicy Asian sauce.

Tip

This is great finger food for all ages. If spicy is not your child's favorite dipping sauce, try Tangy Fruit Sauce (page 197).

Variation

In a large skillet, heat 1 tbsp (15 mL) olive oil over medium-high heat, coating bottom of pan. Add 2 eggs and sauté until set. Let cool. Add to zucchini mixture (step 1) and continue with the recipe.

- **Candy/deep-fry thermometer**

1 cup	shredded zucchini	250 mL
1 cup	shredded cabbage	250 mL
1	carrot, shredded	1
	Salt and freshly ground black pepper	
12	6-inch (15 cm) corn tortillas, micro-warmed (see box, below)	12
	Vegetable oil	
	Spicy Asian Sauce (see recipe, opposite)	

1. In a large bowl, combine zucchini, cabbage and carrot. Season with salt and pepper to taste.

2. To build tacos, place 2 heaping tbsp (30 mL) of zucchini mixture at one end of each tortilla, forming a thin straight line across end of tortilla. Gently roll tortilla and secure with a toothpick. Deep-fry immediately or place rolled tacos in a large sealable plastic bag to keep moist and refrigerate until ready to cook or for up to 24 hours.

3. Fill deep-fryer, deep heavy pot or deep skillet with 3 inches (7.5 cm) of oil and heat to 350°F (180°C). Using tongs, gently place 2 to 3 tacos at a time in the hot oil and deep-fry, turning once, until crispy and golden brown, 2 to 3 minutes. Drain on paper towels. Season lightly with salt. Serve with Spicy Asian Sauce.

Micro-Warmed Tortillas

This method gives you a very pliable and soft tortilla and allows you to roll the tacos tightly, so it's perfect for preparing rolled tacos and taquitos. It is also quick and easy for soft tacos.

Place 4 tortillas at a time in a small microwave-safe plastic bag and close or fold over the opening. Microwave on High for 25 to 45 seconds (depending on the power of your microwave). Remove from plastic bag. The tortillas should be warm and pliable. If you leave them in too long, they will be too hot to handle and will be overdone. Place in a tortilla warmer or wrap in foil to keep warm until ready to use.

Nutrients per taco	
Calories	78
Fat	1 g
Carbohydrate	16 g
Fiber	2 g
Protein	1 g
Calcium	8 mg
Vitamin D	0 IU

Add this sauce to meat, chicken and fish fillings for tacos, or toss it with fresh produce, such as cabbage and lettuce. It is a spicy sauce full of Asian flavors, with a little chile for some kick.

Tip

Use your imagination to include this and some of the other tasty sauces in this cookbook to excite your child's taste buds.

Spicy Asian Sauce

¾ cup	granulated sugar	175 mL
2 tbsp	cornstarch	30 mL
½ cup	GF soy sauce	125 mL
⅓ cup	red wine vinegar	75 mL
1 tbsp	ketchup	15 mL
2 tsp	hot pepper flakes	10 mL

1. In a small bowl, combine sugar and cornstarch.

2. In a saucepan, combine ⅔ cup (150 mL) water, soy sauce, vinegar, ketchup and hot pepper flakes. Add sugar mixture and mix well. Bring to a boil over medium-high heat. Reduce heat and boil gently, stirring, until sauce thickens, 4 to 6 minutes. Let sauce cool.

3. Serve immediately or transfer to an airtight container or squeeze bottle and refrigerate, stirring occasionally, for up to 4 days.

Nutrients per 1 tbsp (15 mL)	
Calories	63
Fat	0 g
Carbohydrate	15 g
Fiber	0 g
Protein	1 g
Calcium	1 mg
Vitamin D	0 IU

Rice and Black Bean–Stuffed Peppers

These peppers are intended to be eaten at room temperature, when their various flavors really blossom. They make a perfect buffet item, especially because they can be (carefully) cut in half to double the number of servings. They also keep well (covered) in the fridge; just let them come back to room temperature before serving.

- **Preheat oven to 375°F (190°C)**
- **Large roasting pan or baking dish**

12	bell peppers (various colors)	12
2 lbs	onions, stemmed and peeled	1 kg
½ tsp	ground cinnamon	2 mL
½ tsp	salt	2 mL
¼ tsp	freshly ground black pepper	1 mL
¼ cup	pine nuts	60 mL
¼ cup	currants	60 mL
¼ cup	olive oil	60 mL
1 cup	short-grain rice	250 mL
1 cup	diced peeled tomatoes, with juices, or canned tomatoes	250 mL
1½ cups	boiling water, divided	375 mL
¼ cup	chopped fresh mint	60 mL
¼ cup	chopped fresh dill	60 mL
2 cups	cooked black beans (or one 19-oz/ 540 mL can), drained and rinsed	500 mL

1. Slice a ½-inch (1 cm) round (including the stem, if any) from the top of each pepper. Set these aside. (They'll serve later as "lids" for the stuffed peppers.) Trim the cavity of the peppers, discarding seed pod and seeds, without puncturing the walls or bottom of the peppers. Set aside.

2. In a bowl, shred the onions through the grater's largest holes (you'll have about 3 cups/750 mL grated onions and juices). Transfer to a large nonstick frying pan. Add cinnamon, salt and pepper; cook, stirring, over high heat for 5 minutes or until most of the juices have evaporated. Add pine nuts, currants and olive oil; cook, stirring, for 3 minutes or until the onions start to catch on bottom of pan.

Nutrients per serving	
Calories	471
Fat	15 g
Carbohydrate	74 g
Fiber	13 g
Protein	12 g
Calcium	113 mg
Vitamin D	0 IU

3. Immediately add rice; cook, stirring, for 2 minutes or until the rice is thoroughly coated with oil. Add tomatoes with juices and $\frac{1}{2}$ cup (125 mL) of the boiling water; cook, stirring, for about 4 minutes or until the tomatoes have broken down and the water is absorbed. Remove from heat. Stir in mint, dill and black beans until well mixed.

4. Stuff a scant $\frac{1}{2}$ cup (125 mL) of the rice-bean stuffing into each pepper. (It should be about two-thirds full to allow for expansion.) Place stuffed peppers into roasting pan, fitting the peppers snugly in a single layer. Place the reserved tops on the peppers to act as lids. Add 1 cup (250 mL) boiling water around the peppers.

5. Cover and bake for 40 minutes, undisturbed. Uncover and bake for 30 to 40 minutes more to char the peppers and reduce the liquid. Remove from oven and cover the peppers. Let them cool down completely (about $1\frac{1}{2}$ hours) before serving.

Mushroom and Chickpea Stew with Roasted Red Pepper Coulis

Makes 6 servings

Topped with luscious red pepper coulis, this delicious stew is divine. Vegetarians and non-vegetarians alike will come back for seconds. Add whole-grain rolls and a green salad or steamed asparagus, in season.

- **3½- to 6-quart slow cooker**
- **Food processor**

1 tbsp	cumin seeds	15 mL
1 tbsp	olive oil	15 mL
2	onions, finely chopped	2
2	carrots, peeled and diced	2
4	stalks celery, thinly sliced (or 1 bulb fennel, trimmed, cored and thinly sliced on the vertical)	4
4	cloves garlic, minced	4
1 tsp	ground turmeric	5 mL
1 tsp	salt	5 mL
½ tsp	cracked black peppercorns	2 mL
8 oz	cremini mushrooms, thinly sliced	250 g
1	can (28 oz/796 mL) tomatoes, with juice, coarsely chopped	1
1	can (14 to 19 oz/398 to 540 mL) chickpeas, drained and rinsed	1

Red Pepper Coulis

2	roasted red bell peppers	2
3	oil-packed sun-dried tomatoes, drained and chopped	3
2 tbsp	extra virgin olive oil	30 mL
1 tbsp	balsamic vinegar	15 mL
10	fresh basil leaves (optional)	10

1. In a large dry skillet over medium heat, toast cumin seeds, stirring, until fragrant and they just begin to brown, about 3 minutes. Immediately transfer to a mortar or a spice grinder and grind. Set aside.

Nutrients per serving	
Calories	210
Fat	9 g
Carbohydrate	28 g
Fiber	8 g
Protein	7 g
Calcium	100 mg
Vitamin D	3 IU

Tips

This dish can be partially prepared before it is cooked. Complete steps 1 and 2. Cover and refrigerate overnight or for up to 2 days. When you're ready to cook, continue with steps 3 and 4.

To meet food guide recommendations, this recipe should be served with another protein-based dish, or try adding cubed tofu to the pot to simmer in the flavors.

2. In same skillet, heat oil over medium heat for 30 seconds. Add onions, carrots and celery and cook, stirring, until vegetables are tender, about 7 minutes. Add garlic, turmeric, salt, peppercorns and reserved cumin and cook, stirring, for 1 minute. Add mushrooms and toss until coated. Add tomatoes with juice and bring to a boil. Transfer to slow cooker stoneware.

3. Add chickpeas and stir well. Cover and cook on Low for 6 hours or on High for 3 hours, until hot and bubbly.

4. *Coulis:* In food processor, combine roasted peppers, sun-dried tomatoes, oil, vinegar, and basil (if using). Process until smooth. Ladle stew into bowls and top with coulis.

Chickpeas in Tomato Sauce

There are many variations on the theme of chickpeas in tomato sauce, most of which can be found in Mediterranean or Indian cooking.

Tips

If you prefer a zippier version of this dish, add 1 tbsp (15 mL) minced gingerroot along with the garlic. If you don't have fresh parsley in the fridge, garnish with finely chopped red or green onion instead.

Chickpeas are a good source of protein, fiber and folate — an excellent dish if your child suffers from constipation.

1	large onion, cut into thin wedges	1
2	cloves garlic, minced	2
1 tbsp	olive oil	15 mL
1	can (28 oz/796 mL) chickpeas, drained and rinsed	1
1½ cups	canned crushed tomatoes	375 mL
½ tsp	salt	2 mL
½ tsp	freshly ground black pepper	2 mL
½ tsp	dried thyme	2 mL
¼ tsp	cayenne pepper	1 mL
1	bay leaf	1
	Chopped fresh parsley	

1. In a large saucepan over medium-high heat, cook onion and garlic in oil for about 5 minutes or until tender. Add chickpeas; cook for 3 to 4 minutes. Add tomatoes, salt, black pepper, thyme, cayenne and bay leaf; cook over low heat for about 25 minutes. Remove bay leaf before serving; garnish with chopped parsley.

This recipe courtesy of Chantal Haddad.

Nutrients per serving	
Calories	242
Fat	6 g
Carbohydrate	38 g
Fiber	8 g
Protein	10 g
Calcium	47 mg
Vitamin D	0 IU

Asian Barbecued Tofu Cubes

Makes 3 servings

In this recipe, tofu cubes adopt the Asian tastes of their marinade — soy, garlic and ginger. While tofu is a mainstay of vegetarian diets, non-vegetarians will learn to appreciate how tasty tofu can be.

Tips

Use more or less garlic, according to taste.

If using wooden skewers, remember to soak them in water for at least 30 minutes before use. This will prevent the wood from burning on the grill.

Skewers are unsafe for children under the age of 4 years, and some older children as well, so remove them before serving.

- **Metal or wooden skewers (see tip, at left)**

8 oz	firm tofu, cubed	250 g
1 to 2 tbsp	reduced-sodium GF soy sauce	15 to 30 mL
½	small garlic clove, crushed (see tip, at left)	½
1 tsp	minced gingerroot	5 mL
1 tsp	freshly squeezed lemon juice	5 mL
1 tsp	olive oil	5 mL

1. Place tofu cubes in a small, sealable plastic bag.

2. In a small bowl, combine soy sauce, garlic, ginger, lemon juice and oil. Pour over tofu, seal bag and refrigerate for several hours.

3. Preheat grill to medium.

4. Remove cubes from marinade and thread onto skewers. Reserve marinade. Grill skewers on preheated barbecue for 10 minutes or until crisp. Baste frequently with reserved marinade.

Variation

Substitute an equal amount of cubed chicken for the tofu. In step 4, boil the marinade for 5 minutes before using it to brush on chicken while it is being grilled. Or discard marinade if not using.

Nutrients per serving	
Calories	129
Fat	8 g
Carbohydrate	4 g
Fiber	2 g
Protein	12 g
Calcium	570 mg
Vitamin D	0 IU

Tofu Patties

This is a fun way for the family to help prepare tofu together. For children, make mini patties and place on whole-grain dinner rolls with their choice of condiments.

Tips

Look for tofu made with calcium. Look for "calcium sulfate" or "calcium chloride" in the ingredients list to make sure the tofu you are buying is a source of calcium.

Place on a GF multigrain bun and top with sliced tomato, leaf lettuce and a dab of your favorite mustard or salsa.

Adding toasted ground pepitas (pumpkin seeds) to the mix will add 7 grams of protein per ounce (30 g) of seeds.

To increase the protein provided by this meal, serve a glass of soy milk alongside it.

Nutrients per serving	
Calories	121
Fat	5 g
Carbohydrate	11 g
Fiber	2 g
Protein	10 g
Calcium	331 mg
Vitamin D	0 IU

- **Preheat oven to 325°F (160°C)**
- **9-inch (23 cm) square baking pan, lightly greased**

10 oz	firm tofu, mashed	300 g
3/4 cup	certified GF quick-cooking rolled oats	175 mL
2 tbsp	GF soy sauce	30 mL
1/2 tsp	dried basil	2 mL
1/2 tsp	dried oregano	2 mL
1/2 tsp	garlic powder	2 mL
1/2 tsp	onion powder	2 mL
	Salt and freshly ground black pepper	

1. In a medium bowl, combine tofu, oats, soy sauce, basil, oregano, garlic powder, onion powder, and salt and pepper to taste. Knead for a few minutes. Shape into 1-inch (2.5 cm) thick patties and place in prepared pan.

2. Bake in preheated oven for 20 to 25 minutes or until lightly browned.

This recipe courtesy of dietitian Sue Minicucci.

Seafood and Meaty Mains

Baked Mediterranean Salmon Fillets 306

Thai-Style Coconut Fish Curry 307

Rice Stick Noodles with Crab in a
    Basil-Tomato Sauce 308

Sweet Potato Coconut Curry with Shrimp 309

Coconut-Battered Shrimp 310

Sticky Honey-Garlic Chicken Wings 311

Crispy Pecan Chicken Fingers 312

Coconut Chicken with Quinoa 313

Turkey Apple Meatloaf 314

Broiled Ham Steak with Pineapple-Mango Salsa . . . 315

Curried Pork Chops with Crispy Sweet Potatoes . . . 316

Pacific Rim Coconut Ribs 318

Italian Sausage Patties 320

Tangy Orange Beef 321

Buckwheat Noodle Bowls with Beef and
    Snap Peas 322

Meatballs for Everyday 323

Lean Lamb and Three Veg 324

Baked Mediterranean Salmon Fillets

Adding Mediterranean flavors to succulent salmon gives a delightful twist to this favorite fish. Baking the salmon in broth ensures that the fish remains moist — which makes it easier (and more enjoyable) for children to eat.

Tips

If you don't have fresh salmon, you can use frozen fillets.

Salmon is rich in omega-3 fatty acids, low in saturated fat, and a good source of protein.

With a soft, smooth texture, salmon is a favorite with children who prefer soft foods.

- **Preheat oven to 400°F (200°C)**
- **8-inch (20 cm) square baking pan, greased**

1 lb	salmon fillets (about 4)	500 g
¼ tsp	dried oregano	1 mL
¼ tsp	dried thyme	1 mL
½	lemon, thinly sliced	½
1	large tomato, sliced	1
½	green bell pepper, diced	½
¼ cup	finely chopped onion	60 mL
½ cup	ready-to-use chicken broth	125 mL
1 tbsp	freshly squeezed lemon juice	15 mL
	Chopped fresh parsley (optional)	

1. Arrange fish fillets in prepared baking pan. Sprinkle with oregano and thyme. Place lemon and tomato slices, green pepper and onion over fish.

2. In a small bowl, combine broth and lemon juice; pour over vegetables and fish. Cover and bake in preheated oven for 20 minutes or until fish flakes easily with a fork at its thickest part. If desired, garnish with parsley before serving.

Nutrients per serving	
Calories	167
Fat	5 g
Carbohydrate	5 g
Fiber	1 g
Protein	25 g
Calcium	22 mg
Vitamin D	493 IU

Thai-Style Coconut Fish Curry

This luscious dish has everything going for it: a centerpiece of succulent fish, a sauce of creamy coconut accented with zesty Asian flavors and an abundance of tasty vegetables to complement the mix. Serve this over brown basmati rice to add fiber and complete the meal.

Tips

This dish can be partially prepared ahead of time. Complete step 1. Cover and refrigerate for up to 2 days. When you're ready to cook, complete step 2.

Sesame seeds are a good source of calcium. Sprinkling each serving of this curry with 1 tbsp (15 mL) toasted sesame seeds adds about 90 mg of calcium.

Nutrients per serving	
Calories	208
Fat	6 g
Carbohydrate	11 g
Fiber	4 g
Protein	27 g
Calcium	62 mg
Vitamin D	463 IU

- **3¹⁄₂- to 6-quart slow cooker**

1 tbsp	olive oil or extra virgin coconut oil	15 mL
2	onions, finely chopped	2
4	cloves garlic, minced	4
1 tbsp	minced gingerroot	15 mL
1 tsp	finely grated lime zest	5 mL
1 cup	ready-to-use vegetable broth	250 mL
¹⁄₂ cup	fish stock or clam juice	125 mL
2 tbsp	freshly squeezed lime juice	30 mL
2 tsp	Thai green curry paste	10 mL
1 cup	coconut milk	250 mL
2 tbsp	fish sauce (nam pla)	30 mL
2 lbs	firm white fish (such as snapper), skin removed, cut into bite-size pieces	1 kg
2 cups	drained rinsed canned bamboo shoot strips	500 mL
2 cups	sweet green peas, thawed if frozen	500 mL
1	red bell pepper, finely chopped	1
¹⁄₂ cup	finely chopped fresh cilantro leaves	125 mL
	Toasted sesame seeds (optional)	

1. In a skillet, heat oil over medium heat for 30 seconds. Add onions and cook, stirring, until softened, about 3 minutes. Add garlic, ginger and lime zest and cook, stirring, for 1 minute. Add broth and fish stock and stir well. Transfer to slow cooker stoneware. Cover and cook on Low for 6 to 8 hours or on High for 3 to 4 hours.

2. In a bowl, combine lime juice and curry paste. Add to slow cooker stoneware and stir well. Stir in coconut milk, fish sauce, fish, bamboo shoots, green peas and red pepper. Cover and cook on High for 20 to 30 minutes, until fish flakes easily when pierced with a fork and mixture is hot. Garnish with cilantro and toasted sesame seeds (if using).

Variation

Substitute 12 oz (375 g) peeled cooked shrimp for half of the fish.

Rice Stick Noodles with Crab in a Basil-Tomato Sauce

In this simple but delicious dish, thin rice stick noodles are combined with a distinctly West Coast combination of crab, tomatoes and basil. Although best with fresh crab, a can of snow crab, lightly rinsed in water to reduce the salt, will do just fine.

Tips

Picky eaters will like this mild, fresh-flavored crab and pasta dish.

Like most seafood, crab is low in saturated fat and an excellent source of protein.

8 oz	thin vermicelli (thin rice stick noodles) or GF spaghettini	250 g
	Extra virgin olive oil	
1	can (19 oz/540 mL) tomatoes, with juice	1
1 tbsp	extra virgin olive oil	15 mL
1	onion, finely chopped	1
1 tsp	minced garlic	5 mL
4 oz	fresh or canned crabmeat	125 g
2 tbsp	finely chopped basil (or $\frac{1}{2}$ tsp/2 mL dried)	30 mL
	Salt and freshly ground black pepper	

1. In a heatproof bowl or pot, cover noodles with boiling water and soak for 3 minutes. (If using GF pasta, prepare according to package instructions.) Drain, toss with a little olive oil and set aside.

2. In a medium-size bowl, crush tomatoes with a fork (or process on and off in a food processor) until they are in bite-size pieces.

3. In a nonstick wok or skillet, heat oil over medium-high heat for 30 seconds. Add onion and garlic and cook, stirring often, until onion has softened and is just beginning to color, about 5 minutes. Add tomatoes and their juice. Increase heat and cook until liquid is reduced and sauce is slightly thickened, about 5 minutes.

4. Reduce heat to a gentle simmer, add crab, stir, and cook for 2 to 3 minutes. Add basil and noodles and mix well to distribute the sauce. Season to taste with salt and pepper. Serve immediately.

Nutrients per serving	
Calories	324
Fat	4 g
Carbohydrate	54 g
Fiber	3 g
Protein	12 g
Calcium	79 mg
Vitamin D	0 IU

Sweet Potato Coconut Curry with Shrimp

This luscious dish features both sweet and spicy flavors. Serve over brown basmati rice and add a platter of steamed spinach sprinkled with toasted sesame seeds to complete the meal.

Tips

If you are adding the almond garnish, try to find slivered almonds with the skin on. They add color and nutrients to the dish.

This dish can be partially prepared before it is cooked. Complete step 1. Cover and refrigerate overnight or for up to 2 days. When you're ready to cook, continue with steps 2 and 3.

- **3½- to 6-quart slow cooker**

1 tbsp	olive oil or extra virgin coconut oil	15 mL
2	onions, finely chopped	2
4	cloves garlic, minced	4
1 tbsp	minced gingerroot	15 mL
1 cup	ready-to-use vegetable broth	250 mL
2	sweet potatoes, peeled and cut into 1-inch (2.5 cm) cubes	2
2 tsp	Thai green curry paste	10 mL
1 tbsp	freshly squeezed lime juice	15 mL
½ cup	coconut milk	125 mL
1 lb	cooked peeled shrimp, thawed if frozen	500 g
¼ cup	toasted slivered almonds (optional)	60 mL
¼ cup	finely chopped fresh cilantro leaves	60 mL

1. In a skillet, heat oil over medium heat for 30 seconds. Add onions and cook, stirring, until softened, about 3 minutes. Add garlic and ginger and cook, stirring, for 1 minute. Add broth. Transfer to slow cooker stoneware.

2. Add sweet potatoes and stir well. Cover and cook on Low for 6 to 8 hours or on High for 3 to 4 hours, until sweet potatoes are tender.

3. In a small bowl, combine curry paste and lime juice. Add to slow cooker stoneware and stir well. Stir in coconut milk and shrimp. Cover and cook on High for 20 minutes, until shrimp are hot. Transfer to a serving dish. Garnish with almonds (if using) and cilantro and serve.

Nutrients per serving	
Calories	305
Fat	12 g
Carbohydrate	18 g
Fiber	3 g
Protein	32 g
Calcium	137 mg
Vitamin D	0 IU

Coconut-Battered Shrimp

Makes 4 servings

Rice flour makes for a crisp batter and the coconut milk adds a hint of sweetness. This tasty batter can be used for fish and chicken strips as well.

Tip

This dish is bound to be a family favorite with everyone around the table, and the crispy batter will appeal to any child who prefers crunchy foods.

- **Deep-fryer or wok**
- **Candy/deep-fry thermometer**

½ cup	rice flour	125 mL
½ cup	coconut milk	125 mL
3 tbsp	unsweetened coconut powder or desiccated coconut	45 mL
1	large egg, beaten	1
1 tsp	nigella seeds (kalaunji)	5 mL
½ tsp	salt	2 mL
1 lb	large shrimp, peeled with tail left on, deveined	500 g
1½ tsp	salt (or to taste)	7 mL
1 tsp	freshly ground black pepper	5 mL
	Vegetable oil	

1. In a bowl, mix together rice flour, coconut milk, coconut powder, egg, nigella and salt.

2. In another bowl, mix together shrimp, salt and pepper.

3. In a wok or deep-fryer, heat oil to 350°F (180°C). Drop shrimp in batches into batter and coat evenly. Deep-fry without crowding, turning once, until golden, 5 to 6 minutes per batch. Remove with large-hole strainer and drain on paper towels. Discard any excess batter.

4. Serve hot with dipping chutney of your choice.

Nutrients per serving	
Calories	206
Fat	7 g
Carbohydrate	19 g
Fiber	1 g
Protein	17 g
Calcium	67 mg
Vitamin D	2 IU

Sticky Honey-Garlic Chicken Wings

Wings are a very kid-friendly meal.

Tips

Save time with pre-separated chicken wings (wing tips removed), available at some grocery stores. Chicken drumettes can also be substituted for all or half of the wings.

Wings can be made ahead and refrigerated for up to 2 days or frozen (thaw before reheating). Reheat in a single layer on baking sheet for 10 to 15 minutes at 350°F (180°C).

Serve with rice and a vegetable. For a snack, serve with raw vegetables and Honey Mustard Dipping Sauce (page 259) and whole-grain rolls.

Provide lots of wipes and hand cleaner if your child doesn't like to get his hands or face messy.

Nutrients per serving	
Calories	250
Fat	4 g
Carbohydrate	26 g
Fiber	0 g
Protein	26 g
Calcium	24 mg
Vitamin D	6 IU

- **Preheat oven to 425°F (220°C)**
- **13- by 9-inch (33 by 23 cm) nonstick baking pan**

3 lbs	chicken wings, tips removed and split into 2 pieces at joint (about 24 pieces)	1.5 kg
⅓ cup	liquid honey	75 mL
¼ cup	packed brown sugar	60 mL
3 tbsp	GF soy sauce	45 mL
2 tbsp	freshly squeezed lemon juice or white vinegar	30 mL
1 tsp	garlic powder	5 mL
½ tsp	ground ginger (optional)	2 mL

1. Place wings in a single layer in baking pan. Bake in preheated oven for 20 minutes; drain fat.

2. Meanwhile, in a bowl, blend together honey, brown sugar, soy sauce, lemon juice, garlic powder and ginger (if using). Set aside.

3. Pour sauce over wings. Reduce oven temperature to 400°F (200°C); bake, turning twice during cooking time, for 40 to 45 minutes or until wings are browned and glazed.

This recipe courtesy of Shelagh Rowney.

Crispy Pecan Chicken Fingers

Makes 4 servings

Slender strips of succulent chicken inside a crunchy pecan coating — what an updated, healthier way to eat "fried" chicken! Serve with Honey Mustard Dipping Sauce (page 259).

Tips

Shake off excess egg and crumbs before baking.

Discard both leftover crumb mixture and the plastic bag — it is not safe to reuse either when raw chicken is involved.

Warning: If your child has meltdowns over great food, you may want to stay away from this recipe.

- **Preheat oven to 425°F (220°C)**
- **Baking sheet, lightly greased**

4	boneless skinless chicken breasts (about 1 lb/500 g)	4
1/3 cup	brown rice flour	75 mL
2	large eggs, beaten	2
1 tbsp	water	15 mL
1 tbsp	Dijon mustard	15 mL
1 cup	fresh GF bread crumbs	250 mL
2/3 cup	pecans, coarsely chopped	150 mL
1/2 cup	cornmeal	125 mL
1/4 tsp	salt	1 mL
1/4 tsp	freshly ground black pepper	1 mL

1. Cut each breast into strips 3/4 inch (2 cm) wide. Pat dry.

2. Place the rice flour in a shallow dish or pie plate. In a second shallow dish or pie plate, whisk together eggs, water and Dijon mustard.

3. In a large plastic bag, combine bread crumbs, pecans, cornmeal, salt and pepper.

4. Coat chicken strips, a few at a time, first in rice flour, then in egg mixture. Shake in pecan–bread crumb mixture. Place in a single layer 1 inch (2.5 cm) apart on prepared baking sheet.

5. Bake in preheated oven for 20 to 25 minutes, or until chicken is no longer pink inside and coating is golden brown and crispy.

Variations

Florentine Chicken Fingers: Top baked chicken fingers with grated soy Asiago-style cheese, 1 leaf of arugula and a strip of roasted red pepper and broil just until cheese melts.

Pizza Chicken Fingers: Top baked chicken fingers with GF pizza sauce, grated soy mozzarella and, if desired, crumbled cooked bacon. Broil just until cheese melts.

Nutrients per serving	
Calories	504
Fat	22 g
Carbohydrate	44 g
Fiber	4 g
Protein	32 g
Calcium	46 mg
Vitamin D	26 IU

Coconut Chicken with Quinoa

Makes 4 servings

This delightfully different chicken is a potpourri of mouthwatering flavors and beneficial nutrients. Add the chile if you like heat and keep the accompaniments simple. Steamed green beans make a nice finish.

Tips

If you prefer, you can substitute already-ground spices for the cumin seeds and allspice and skip the toasting step. Use 1 tsp (5 mL) ground cumin and 1/2 tsp (2 mL) ground allspice.

Though this recipe has intriguing flavors and combinations, this is, in essence, a traditional meal with an updated grain and just a few vegetables to help your child stay calm and in control.

Nutrients per serving	
Calories	355
Fat	11 g
Carbohydrate	31 g
Fiber	4 g
Protein	32 g
Calcium	66 mg
Vitamin D	4 IU

2 tsp	cumin seeds (see tip, at left)	10 mL
1 tsp	whole allspice (see tip, at left)	5 mL
1 tbsp	olive oil	15 mL
1 1/2 lbs	skin-on bone-in chicken breasts, rinsed and patted dry	750 g
1	onion, finely chopped	1
1	red bell pepper, finely chopped	1
1	green bell pepper, finely chopped	1
6	cloves garlic, minced	6
1/2 to 1	chile pepper, seeded and minced (optional)	1/2 to 1
1 tsp	curry powder	5 mL
1/2 tsp	salt	2 mL
1/2 tsp	freshly ground black pepper	2 mL
3/4 cup	quinoa, rinsed	175 mL
1 1/2 cups	ready-to-use reduced-sodium chicken broth	375 mL
1/2 cup	coconut milk	125 mL

1. In a large dry skillet over medium heat, combine cumin seeds and allspice. Toast, stirring constantly, until fragrant, about 4 minutes. Immediately transfer to a mortar or a spice grinder and grind. Set aside.

2. In same skillet, heat oil over medium heat for 30 seconds. Add chicken, in batches, skin side down, and brown well, about 4 minutes. Turn chicken over, cover and cook for 10 minutes. Remove from pan and keep warm. Drain all but 1 tbsp (15 mL) fat from pan.

3. Add onion, bell peppers, garlic and chile pepper (if using) and cook, stirring, until vegetables are softened, about 5 minutes. Add curry powder, salt, black pepper, reserved ground spices and quinoa and cook, stirring, until quinoa is well integrated into mixture, about 1 minute. Add broth and coconut milk and bring to a boil. Lay chicken, skin side up, over mixture. Reduce heat to low. Cover and cook until chicken is no longer pink inside, about 30 minutes.

Turkey Apple Meatloaf

Makes 6 servings

This recipe is a good one for kids to help prepare. They will enjoy adding ingredients to the bowl and patting down the loaf in the pan. (Just make sure they wash their hands before and after!) Ground turkey is lean and pairs well with the tart apple.

Tips

Make extra turkey mixture and form into burger patties. After cooking, freeze in freezer bags for quick healthy lunches. Reheat burgers in the microwave on High for about 1 minute.

An extra meatloaf can be sliced to use in sandwiches or frozen for another day.

The ground flax seeds up the omega-3 ante in this dish.

- **Preheat oven to 350°F (180°C)**
- **9- by 5-inch (23 by 12.5 cm) loaf pan, lightly greased**

2	cloves garlic, minced	2
1	large egg	1
1	tart apple (such as Mutsu or Granny Smith), finely chopped	1
1 lb	lean ground turkey	500 g
½ cup	chopped onion	125 mL
⅓ cup	GF oat bran	75 mL
⅓ cup	ground flax seeds (flaxseed meal)	75 mL
3 tbsp	prepared yellow mustard	45 mL
1 tbsp	ketchup	15 mL
1 tsp	salt	5 mL

1. In a large bowl, combine garlic, egg, apple, turkey, onion, oat bran, flax seeds, mustard, ketchup and salt. Pack into prepared loaf pan.

2. Bake in preheated oven for 45 to 60 minutes or until a meat thermometer inserted in the center registers an internal temperature of 175°F (80°C).

This recipe courtesy of dietitian Gillian Proctor.

Variation

Turkey Apple Burgers: This mixture can also be used to make burgers, which can be cooked on a barbecue or grill or in the oven. They're excellent served on a whole wheat bun with sliced tomato and a spoonful of low-fat cucumber dressing.

Nutrients per serving	
Calories	200
Fat	10 g
Carbohydrate	12 g
Fiber	4 g
Protein	19 g
Calcium	50 mg
Vitamin D	17 IU

Broiled Ham Steak with Pineapple-Mango Salsa

The salsa in this recipe is also great with grilled salmon or swordfish. For lunch, try it stuffed in a pita with chicken salad or rolled up in a tortilla with light vegan cream cheese and some thinly sliced ham or smoked turkey.

Tips

Fresh pineapple tastes best in this recipe, but you can use canned pineapple instead.

Choose a ripe mango that is red or orange-yellow and soft to the touch.

The salsa can be made ahead and kept in the refrigerator for several days.

For children who have trouble digesting sulphur-based foods, leave the onions out of this recipe.

- Preheat broiler
- Shallow baking dish, greased

2	6-oz (175 g) packaged ham steaks	2
2 tsp	Dijon or other mustard	10 mL
2 tsp	packed brown sugar	10 mL
1 tbsp	orange juice or pineapple juice	15 mL

Pineapple-Mango Salsa

1 cup	diced fresh mango	250 mL
1 cup	diced fresh pineapple	250 mL
1/2 cup	chopped red onions	125 mL
1/4 cup	finely chopped cilantro	60 mL
2 tbsp	freshly squeezed lime juice	30 mL

1. Place ham steaks in baking dish and spread with mustard. Sprinkle with brown sugar, then orange juice. Broil for 2 to 3 minutes or until golden and bubbling.

2. *Salsa:* In a bowl, stir together mango, pineapple, red onions, cilantro and lime juice. Chill until ready to use. Warm to room temperature before serving with ham steak.

This recipe courtesy of dietitian Bev Callaghan.

Nutrients per serving	
Calories	172
Fat	4 g
Carbohydrate	17 g
Fiber	2 g
Protein	18 g
Calcium	21 mg
Vitamin D	0 IU

Curried Pork Chops with Crispy Sweet Potatoes

Sweet potato and pork in an aromatic curry sauce team up to nourish like any other plate of pork chop and spuds, but in a way that will add sunshine to the bleakest winter's eve.

Tips

If you don't have parchment paper, you can line the baking sheet with foil and grease the foil — or use nonstick foil.

If lime leaves aren't available, substitute $\frac{1}{2}$ tsp (2 mL) finely grated lime zest and stir into sauce before adding pork chops in step 6.

To get a nice brown crust, be sure the pan and oil are well heated before adding the pork. Don't try to turn the pork too soon, or it will stick and tear.

Read the chicken broth label to check for gluten.

Nutrients per serving	
Calories	540
Fat	24 g
Carbohydrate	20 g
Fiber	3 g
Protein	59 g
Calcium	158 mg
Vitamin D	54 IU

- **Preheat oven to 425°F (220°C)**
- **Rimmed baking sheet, lined with parchment paper**

2	sweet potatoes	2
1½ tsp	curry powder, divided	7 mL
½ tsp	salt, divided	2 mL
4	boneless pork chops, about ¾-inch (2 cm) thick	4
2 tbsp	vegetable oil, divided	30 mL
2	wild lime leaves (see tip, at left)	2
1 cup	Basic Gravy (see recipe, opposite)	250 mL
½ cup	ready-to-use GF chicken broth	125 mL
2 tbsp	chopped fresh Thai or sweet basil	30 mL

1. Peel sweet potatoes, if desired, and cut into $\frac{1}{2}$-inch (1 cm) thick slices. Sprinkle with 1 tsp (5 mL) of the curry powder and about three-quarters of the salt. Set aside. Sprinkle pork chops with remaining curry powder and salt. Set aside separately.

2. In a large skillet, heat half the oil over medium heat. Add sweet potatoes, in batches as necessary, and cook, turning once, until well browned on both sides, about 5 minutes per batch. Transfer to prepared baking sheet. Add more of the oil between batches as necessary.

3. Bake potatoes in preheated oven until tender, about 10 minutes.

4. Meanwhile, increase heat to medium-high, add remaining oil to pan and heat for 15 seconds. Add pork chops and cook, turning once, until well browned, 1 to 2 minutes per side. Transfer to a plate and set aside.

5. Add lime leaves and gravy to pan and cook, stirring, for 2 minutes. Stir in broth and bring to a boil, scraping up bits stuck to pan. Boil for 3 minutes or until thickened.

6. Return pork chops and any accumulated juices to pan, turning to coat in sauce. Reduce heat and simmer, turning pork once, until just a hint of pink remains in pork, about 5 minutes. Serve pork and sauce over sweet potatoes and sprinkle with basil.

This aromatic sauce enhancer speeds up curry recipes.

Tips

Older children will appreciate the more subtle curry flavors in this recipe.

If you don't have a food processor, you can use a blender. Just add enough of the tomato purée to the onion mixture to help the blender purée more easily.

Let extra gravy cool completely, then transfer to an airtight container, cover and refrigerate for up to 1 week. Or divide into $\frac{1}{2}$-cup (125 mL) and/ or 1-cup (250 mL) portions in airtight containers and freeze for up to 2 months. Thaw overnight in the refrigerator or defrost in the microwave.

Nutrients per $\frac{1}{4}$ cup (60 mL)	
Calories	163
Fat	8 g
Carbohydrate	23 g
Fiber	4 g
Protein	4 g
Calcium	129 mg
Vitamin D	0 IU

Basic Gravy

- **Food processor**

1	can (28 oz/796 mL) tomatoes, with juice	1
2 cups	coarsely chopped onions	500 mL
$\frac{1}{3}$ cup	whole garlic cloves (about 12)	75 mL
$\frac{1}{3}$ cup	thinly sliced gingerroot	75 mL
2 tbsp	vegetable oil	30 mL
$\frac{1}{4}$ cup	ground coriander	60 mL
1 tbsp	ground turmeric	15 mL
1 tbsp	garam masala	15 mL
2 tsp	salt	10 mL
1 tsp	cayenne pepper	5 mL

1. In food processor, purée tomatoes with juice until smooth. Pour back into the can or into a bowl and set aside.

2. Add onions, garlic and ginger to food processor and pulse until very finely chopped but not juicy.

3. In a skillet, heat oil over medium heat. Add onion mixture and cook, stirring, until onions start to release their liquid, about 3 minutes. Stir in coriander, turmeric, garam masala, salt and cayenne. Cook, stirring, until well blended and mixture is starting to dry and get thick and paste-like, about 3 minutes.

4. Stir in puréed tomatoes and bring to a simmer, scraping up bits stuck to pan. Reduce heat and boil gently, stirring often, until slightly thickened and flavors are blended, about 5 minutes. Use as directed in recipes.

This recipe courtesy of Chef Prasannan of the Lonely Planet restaurant in Kovalam Beach, Kerala.

Pacific Rim Coconut Ribs

	Makes 4 to 6 servings	

Lemongrass and coconut milk give these terrific ribs contemporary appeal.

Tips

Cut the racks into individual portions and then, using a sharp knife, diamond-score them before marinating.

When using canned coconut milk, be sure to shake the can before opening; stir milk before using.

Check the soy sauce ingredients list for gluten or casein.

- **Preheat oven to 350°F (180°C)**
- **Large baking dish (glass, ceramic or other nonreactive material) with rack**
- **Food processor or blender**

½ tsp	Chinese five-spice powder	2 mL
½ tsp	ground ginger	2 mL
1 tsp	paprika	5 mL
½ tsp	lemon-pepper seasoning	2 mL
½ tsp	cayenne pepper	2 mL
½ tsp	salt	2 mL
1 tsp	freshly ground black pepper	5 mL
2	baby back pork ribs (1½ to 2 lbs/750 g to 1 kg)	2
1¼ cups	canned unsweetened low-fat coconut milk	300 mL
½ cup	unsweetened pineapple juice	125 mL
¾ cup	chopped fresh cilantro	175 mL
½ cup	packed light brown sugar	125 mL
3	shallots, finely chopped	3
⅓ cup	reduced-sodium GF soy sauce	75 mL
	Juice of 2 lemons	
	Juice of 2 limes	
3	cloves garlic, minced	3
2 tbsp	chopped gingerroot	30 mL
2	lemongrass stalks, chopped (see tip, opposite)	2
1 tsp	salt	5 mL
2	lemons, thinly sliced	2

1. In a small bowl, combine five-spice powder, ground ginger, paprika, lemon-pepper, cayenne, salt and black pepper. Rub thoroughly over ribs.

2. In a bowl, combine coconut milk, pineapple juice, cilantro, brown sugar, shallots, soy sauce, lemon juice, lime juice, garlic, gingerroot, lemongrass and salt.

Nutrients per 1 of 6 servings	
Calories	420
Fat	24 g
Carbohydrate	27 g
Fiber	1 g
Protein	25 g
Calcium	74 mg
Vitamin D	53 IU

Tips

When buying lemongrass, look for firm stalks with a nice-size bulb. When fresh, it should be firm with a pale to light green hue and a bulb of palest pink. Pass over any that are dry and yellowed. Before chopping, peel away the tough outer layer of the stalk and trim the root end. To make the stalks easier to chop finely, slice them (as you would a green onion) into thin rounds, removing any long fibrous bits as you work. This process may be done in a food processor if you plan on chopping a great deal of lemongrass.

Get out the bibs and washcloths to keep up with the messy hands and smiling faces.

3. Place ribs on rack in baking dish. Cover with coconut milk mixture and lemon slices. Cover with foil. Cook in preheated oven for 1½ hours or until tender when pierced with a knife. Remove ribs and cool slightly.

4. Transfer the coconut milk mixture to the food processor, along with 3 or 4 lemon slices; process until relatively smooth.

5. Preheat grill to medium-high heat. Grill ribs for 5 minutes or until brown on all sides, brushing with coconut milk mixture. Transfer to a serving platter. Use any remaining marinade to pour over ribs or serve alongside.

Italian Sausage Patties

Makes 12 patties

Serve these spicy meat patties over pasta, in a pesto sauce or with a mild tomato sauce. Make ahead and freeze for up to 3 months for a last-minute supper or snack.

Tips

If you use an indoor contact grill, there is no need to turn the patties. Cooking time will be much shorter; check the manufacturer's instructions.

For a stronger flavor, substitute caraway or anise seed for the fennel.

Meatballs are a fabulous snack anytime for all ages. They also make a great reward for staying seated at the table during mealtimes.

- **Barbecue, grill or broiler, preheated**

1 lb	lean ground beef	500 g
3	cloves garlic, minced	3
2 tsp	fennel seeds	10 mL
1 tsp	hot pepper flakes	5 mL
¾ tsp	salt	3 mL
½ tsp	freshly ground black pepper	2 mL
¼ tsp	cayenne pepper (optional)	1 mL

1. In a medium bowl, using a fork, gently combine beef, garlic, fennel seeds, hot pepper flakes, salt, black pepper and cayenne (if using). Form into 12 patties, 2 inches (5 cm) in diameter.

2. On preheated barbecue, grill patties for 2 to 3 minutes, turning only once, until meat thermometer registers 160°F (71°C) and patties are no longer pink inside.

Variations

Substitute ground veal, pork, chicken or turkey for the ground beef.

Make into meatballs. Bake on a baking sheet at 400°F (200°C) for 15 to 20 minutes, or until no longer pink in the center.

Nutrients per patty	
Calories	55
Fat	2 g
Carbohydrate	1 g
Fiber	0 g
Protein	8 g
Calcium	9 mg
Vitamin D	1 IU

Tangy Orange Beef

Makes 4 servings

This hearty dish has a light, bright flavor, thanks to the inclusion of orange juice and orange zest. You can omit the zest if you don't have an orange handy, and still have a tasty dish. A green salad and rice make it a meal.

Tip

Check the soy sauce label for gluten and casein.

1 tbsp	GF soy sauce	15 mL
2 tsp	white or cider vinegar	10 mL
2 tsp	cornstarch	10 mL
1 tsp	salt (or to taste)	5 mL
12 oz	lean boneless beef, thinly sliced	375 g
1 tsp	grated orange zest (optional)	5 mL
3 tbsp	orange juice	45 mL
1 tbsp	granulated sugar	15 mL
2 tbsp	vegetable oil	30 mL
1 tbsp	chopped gingerroot	15 mL
½ cup	shredded carrot	125 mL
¼ cup	chopped green onions	60 mL

1. In a bowl, combine soy sauce, vinegar, cornstarch and salt and mix well into a smooth sauce. Add beef and stir to coat well. Set aside.

2. In a small bowl, combine orange zest (if using), orange juice and sugar and stir well. Set aside.

3. Heat a wok or a large deep skillet over high heat. Add oil and swirl to coat pan. Add ginger and carrot and toss well, until ginger is fragrant and carrots are beginning to soften, about 30 seconds.

4. Push carrots to the side and add beef mixture. Spread into a single layer and cook, undisturbed, until edges change color, about 1 minute. Toss well. Cook, tossing occasionally, until beef is cooked through, 1 to 2 minutes more.

5. Add orange juice mixture, pouring in around sides of pan. When it begins to sizzle, toss well to season beef evenly. Add green onions and toss well. Transfer to a serving plate. Serve hot or warm.

Nutrients per serving	
Calories	168
Fat	9 g
Carbohydrate	8 g
Fiber	1 g
Protein	13 g
Calcium	24 mg
Vitamin D	1 IU

Buckwheat Noodle Bowls with Beef and Snap Peas

8 oz	soba (buckwheat) noodles	250 g
2 tsp	vegetable oil	10 mL
12 oz	sugar snap peas, strings removed	375 g
1 cup	thinly sliced green onions, white and green parts separated	250 mL
1 tbsp	minced gingerroot	15 mL
1/4 tsp	hot pepper flakes	1 mL
2 tsp	cornstarch	10 mL
3 tbsp	reduced-sodium GF tamari or soy sauce	45 mL
1 tbsp	brown rice syrup or liquid honey	15 mL
2 tsp	unseasoned rice vinegar	10 mL
8 oz	thinly sliced lean deli roast beef, cut crosswise into 1/2-inch (1 cm) strips	250 g

Makes 4 servings

Roast beef from the deli counter, coupled with hearty buckwheat noodles, makes these Japanese-inspired noodle bowls hearty and satisfying, in spite of their turbo assembly.

Tip

Check that your soba noodles are 100% buckwheat.

1. In a large pot of boiling salted water (see tip, at left), cook noodles according to package directions until al dente (tender to the bite). Drain, reserving 1/3 cup (75 mL) noodle water.

2. In a large skillet, heat oil over medium-high heat. Add peas, white parts of green onions, ginger and hot pepper flakes; cook, stirring, for 1 minute. Add the reserved noodle water and cook, stirring, for 1 to 2 minutes or until peas turn bright green.

3. In a small bowl, whisk together cornstarch, tamari, brown rice syrup and vinegar.

4. Reduce heat to medium and add cornstarch mixture to skillet. Bring to a simmer, stirring constantly. Add noodles and beef, gently tossing to combine. Simmer for 1 minute or until heated through. Serve sprinkled with green parts of green onions.

Nutrients per serving	
Calories	399
Fat	8 g
Carbohydrate	57 g
Fiber	6 g
Protein	24 g
Calcium	80 mg
Vitamin D	0 IU

Meatballs for Everyday

Whether you serve these meatballs with spaghetti or sweet-and-sour sauce or as hot hors d'oeuvres, they are sure to be a hit.

Tips

To freeze: Let cool slightly, then freeze baked meatballs on the jelly roll pan. Once frozen, remove meatballs from pan and place in a heavy-duty freezer bag. Remove only the number you need — they won't stick together. Reheat meatballs from frozen directly in sauce, or microwave just until thawed and then add to the sauce.

Vitamin-packed fresh herbs top the anti-inflammatory scale. Add fresh herbs whenever possible at the end of the cooking process (dried herbs go into the pot at the beginning). Reducing inflammation for your child may reduce GI symptoms.

Nutrients per meatball	
Calories	40
Fat	2 g
Carbohydrate	2 g
Fiber	0 g
Protein	4 g
Calcium	5 mg
Vitamin D	1 IU

- **Preheat oven to 400°F (200°C)**
- **15-by 10-inch (40 by 25 cm) jelly roll pan, lightly greased**

1 lb	extra-lean ground beef	500 g
8 oz	ground pork	250 g
½ cup	finely chopped onion	125 mL
1	large egg, lightly beaten	1
1 cup	soft GF bread crumbs	250 mL
2 tbsp	snipped fresh parsley	30 mL
2 tbsp	snipped fresh basil	30 mL
2 tbsp	snipped fresh oregano	30 mL
¼ tsp	freshly ground black pepper	1 mL

1. In a large bowl, gently mix together beef, pork, onion, egg, bread crumbs, parsley, basil, oregano and pepper. Shape into 1-inch (2.5 cm) balls. Place in a single layer on prepared pan.

2. Bake in a preheated oven for 20 minutes or until no longer pink in the center.

Variations

Use commercial gluten-free rice crackers to make crumbs and substitute for gluten-free bread crumbs. If using flavored crackers, such as barbecue or teriyaki, omit the basil and oregano.

Substitute ground turkey or chicken for all or part of the ground beef and pork.

Lean Lamb and Three Veg

Makes 4 servings

This tasty lamb dish is balanced with specially selected vegetables.

Tips

Mashed sweet potatoes will be the hit of the meal with a soft-food-loving child. Make the first helping a small one, and offer a second helping after the beans have disappeared.

Either cut the beans up in small pieces and suggest your child build a fire with the beans and put the fire out by eating them. Or leave the beans in one place and tell her to think of all the possible things that the beans could be and tell you one of these things with every bite. Have fun!

- **Preheat barbecue grill to high**
- **Steamer**

2	sweet potatoes (about 1 lb/500 g total), peeled and diced	2
1/3 cup	organic malt-free soy milk	75 mL
	Freshly ground black pepper	
1 lb	lean lamb loin chops or leg cutlets, fat trimmed	500 g
1 tsp	dried rosemary	5 mL
10 oz	yellow wax beans or frenched green beans	300 g
3 cups	chopped broccoli	750 mL

1. In a saucepan, bring some water to a boil and cook the sweet potato for 10 minutes or until very soft, then drain and return the sweet potato to the saucepan. Mash the sweet potato until lump-free, then stir in soy milk and pepper. Keep the mixture in the saucepan.

2. Place the lamb on the preheated grill and sprinkle with rosemary. Grill for about 5 minutes per side or until cooked to your liking.

3. In a steamer, cook the beans and broccoli for 2 to 3 minutes (maximum). Set the timer so you don't overcook the vegetables; they must be slightly crisp.

4. Reheat the mash if necessary and serve immediately with lamb and vegetables.

Nutrients per serving	
Calories	397
Fat	12 g
Carbohydrate	33 g
Fiber	7 g
Protein	39 g
Calcium	142 mg
Vitamin D	11 IU

Side Dishes

Orange Broccoli 326

Glazed Carrots. 327

Corn with Tomatoes and Basil 328

Green Beans with Mustard Seeds 329

Sautéed Spinach with Pine Nuts 330

Sweet Baked Tomatoes 331

Tomato and Zucchini Sauté. 332

Hot-Bag Vegetables 333

Squash with Quinoa and Apricots 334

Ratatouille 336

Batter-Dipped Vegetable Fritters 338

Sweet Potato "Fries" 339

Mashed Sweet Potatoes with Rosemary 340

Yukon Gold Bay Leaf Mash 341

Florentine Potato Cakes 342

Basic Beans 343

Caramelized Peppers and Onions with Pasta 344

Steamed Rice Noodle Cakes 345

Egg and Mushroom Fried Rice. 346

Orange Broccoli

Makes 6 servings

Citrus juice, mustard, herbs and spices give broccoli a taste makeover.

Tips

Blanching enhances the color of vegetables while maintaining their crispy raw texture. Even undercooking broccoli just slightly will help keep its crisp texture and bright color for the duration of the meal.

If you don't have sunflower seeds on hand, substitute toasted nuts, such as pine nuts, walnuts or almonds.

1	bunch broccoli florets	1
2 tbsp	orange juice	30 mL
2 tsp	freshly squeezed lemon juice	10 mL
1 tbsp	vegetable oil	15 mL
1½ tsp	granulated sugar	7 mL
½ tsp	crushed dried basil	2 mL
¼ tsp	coarsely ground black pepper	1 mL
¼ tsp	Dijon mustard	1 mL
2 tbsp	unsalted sunflower seeds, toasted	30 mL

1. In a large saucepan of boiling water, blanch broccoli for 2 minutes. Drain and plunge into ice water. Return to saucepan.

2. In a bowl, whisk together orange juice, lemon juice, oil, sugar, basil, pepper and mustard until blended.

3. Drizzle mixture over broccoli. Cover and heat until warm. Sprinkle with sunflower seeds.

This recipe courtesy of chef Murray Henderson and dietitian Carole Doucet Love.

Nutrients per serving	
Calories	80
Fat	4 g
Carbohydrate	9 g
Fiber	3 g
Protein	3 g
Calcium	52 mg
Vitamin D	0 IU

Glazed Carrots

Can't get your kids to eat their carrots? It's amazing what adding a light glaze can do. Your entire family will love it!

Tips

Make sure to choose a margarine that is free of trans fat.

Try other fresh herbs for a change of pace.

3 tbsp	olive oil margarine, divided	45 mL
1/4 cup	water	60 mL
Pinch	salt	Pinch
1 lb	carrots, thinly sliced	500 g
1 tsp	granulated sugar	5 mL
2 tbsp	minced fresh basil	30 mL

1. In a large skillet, melt 1 tbsp (15 mL) of the margarine over medium-low heat, along with water and salt. Stir in carrots. Cook, covered, for 8 to 10 minutes or until tender. Drain carrots and set aside.

2. Using the same skillet, melt remaining margarine. When margarine begins to sizzle, add sugar. Shake pan a few times, then add carrots and basil; cook, tossing carrots gently, for 3 to 5 minutes or until glazed.

Nutrients per serving	
Calories	126
Fat	9 g
Carbohydrate	12 g
Fiber	3 g
Protein	1 g
Calcium	41 mg
Vitamin D	45 IU

Corn with Tomatoes and Basil

Makes 4 to 6 servings

Fresh corn is a real summer treat. Serve this tasty summer side dish with grilled meats.

Tips

Fresh corn works best, but frozen kernels can be substituted. To cut corn kernels from cobs, stand ears on end and cut straight down using a small, sharp knife.

If your child shouts for more corn, you'll have to sympathize — but hand it over when they use an appropriate mealtime voice.

2 tsp	vegetable or olive oil	10 mL
3	green onions, sliced	3
1	small green bell pepper, diced	1
3 cups	corn kernels (about 5 ears)	750 mL
2	tomatoes, seeded and diced	2
2 tbsp	chopped fresh basil (or 1 tsp/5 mL dried)	30 mL
Pinch	granulated sugar	Pinch
	Salt and freshly ground black pepper	

1. In a large nonstick skillet, heat oil over medium-high heat. Cook green onions, green pepper, corn, tomatoes and basil (if using dried), stirring often, for 5 to 7 minutes (8 to 10 minutes, if using frozen corn) or until corn is tender.

2. Add sugar; season with salt and pepper to taste. Sprinkle with chopped basil (if using fresh).

Nutrients per 1 of 6 servings	
Calories	81
Fat	3 g
Carbohydrate	15 g
Fiber	2 g
Protein	3 g
Calcium	7 mg
Vitamin D	0 IU

Green Beans with Mustard Seeds

This recipe is excellent as a side dish to chicken, fish and pork entrées.

Tip

Make sure that there is an audible sizzle at all times to indicate that vegetables are cooking.

2 tbsp	vegetable oil	30 mL
1½ tsp	mustard seeds	7 mL
1½ lbs	green beans, fresh or frozen, cut into ½-inch (1 cm) pieces	750 g
3	potatoes, cut into ½-inch (1 cm) cubes (unpeeled if thin-skinned)	3
1½ tsp	ground coriander	7 mL
¾ tsp	ground turmeric	3 mL
½ tsp	cayenne pepper	2 mL
1½ tsp	salt (or to taste)	7 mL

1. In a large skillet with a tight-fitting lid, heat oil over high heat until a couple of mustard seeds thrown in start to sputter. Add remaining mustard seeds and cover quickly.

2. When seeds stop popping in a few seconds, uncover and reduce heat to medium. Add green beans and potatoes.

3. Sprinkle mixture with coriander, turmeric, cayenne and salt. Mix well. Sprinkle with 1 tbsp (15 mL) water. Reduce heat to low (see tip, at left). Cover and cook, stirring once to prevent sticking, until vegetables are tender, about 10 minutes.

Nutrients per 1 of 8 servings	
Calories	116
Fat	4 g
Carbohydrate	19 g
Fiber	4 g
Protein	3 g
Calcium	41 mg
Vitamin D	0 IU

Sautéed Spinach with Pine Nuts

This is a great way to jazz up plain spinach. You can easily substitute Swiss chard, kale, rapini, or mustard greens for the spinach.

Tip

Stir-frying vegetables is a great way to preserve nutrients. When boiled, vegetables can lose up to 45% of vitamin C compared to losing only 5% when stir-fried.

2 tsp	olive oil	10 mL
¼ cup	pine nuts	60 mL
1	package (10 oz/300 g) fresh spinach, trimmed of tough stalks	1
1 tsp	minced garlic	5 mL
1 tsp	freshly squeezed lemon juice	5 mL
⅛ tsp	ground nutmeg	0.5 mL
	Freshly ground black pepper	

1. In a large nonstick skillet, heat 1 tsp (5 mL) of the oil over medium heat. Add pine nuts and cook, stirring constantly, for 2 to 3 minutes or until golden. Remove pine nuts from pan and set aside.

2. Add remaining oil to pan. Add spinach in several bunches (it will cook down quickly), stirring constantly. Add garlic and cook for 1 to 2 minutes. Stir in lemon juice and nutmeg. Season to taste with pepper. Add reserved pine nuts. Cook until heated through.

This recipe courtesy of dietitian Bev Callaghan.

Nutrients per serving	
Calories	97
Fat	9 g
Carbohydrate	4 g
Fiber	2 g
Protein	3 g
Calcium	72 mg
Vitamin D	0 IU

Sweet Baked Tomatoes

Makes 4 servings

In this tasty recipe, tomatoes serve as the container for an unusual fruit and nut filling. Serve at room temperature, or chilled if desired.

Tips

Toasting nuts and seeds helps to bring out their flavor. To toast, preheat oven (350°F/180°C) and spread nuts or seeds on a baking sheet. Place in oven and roast, shaking pan occasionally, for 5 to 6 minutes. Or toast in a nonstick skillet over medium heat, shaking pan often. Watch carefully.

Sultanas are usually larger and paler than most raisins and have a slightly higher acid content. If you can't find sultanas, use any other variety of raisin instead.

- **Preheat oven to 325°F (160°C)**
- **Baking dish**

4	tomatoes	4
1/4 cup	sultana raisins	60 mL
1/4 cup	currants	60 mL
2 tbsp	liquid honey	30 mL
1 tbsp	freshly squeezed lemon juice	15 mL
1/4 tsp	ground cinnamon	1 mL
1/4 tsp	ground ginger	1 mL
1/4 cup	chopped walnuts or pecans, lightly toasted (see tip, at left)	60 mL
	Salt	
1/2 cup	apple cider or juice	125 mL
	Grated orange zest or 4 mint leaves	

1. Slice tops off tomatoes; seed, scoop out pulp and reserve. Invert tomato shells on paper towels to drain for at least 15 minutes.

2. In a bowl, coarsely mash tomato pulp; stir in raisins, currants, honey, lemon juice, cinnamon and ginger. Refrigerate for 1 hour to allow flavors to blend. Stir in nuts.

3. Sprinkle inside of each tomato shell lightly with salt; evenly spoon in raisin mixture. Place in small baking dish or pie plate; drizzle cider over and around tomatoes. Bake in preheated oven for 15 to 20 minutes or just until soft.

4. With slotted spoon, transfer tomatoes to serving dish or small individual dishes, reserving juice. Cover tomatoes and juice; refrigerate for at least 2 hours or until thoroughly chilled. At serving time, drizzle some juice over each tomato and garnish with orange zest or mint.

This recipe courtesy of chef Ralph Graham and dietitian Rosanne E. Maluk.

Nutrients per serving	
Calories	152
Fat	5 g
Carbohydrate	28 g
Fiber	2 g
Protein	2 g
Calcium	27 mg
Vitamin D	0 IU

Tomato and Zucchini Sauté

This colorful vegetable medley is a classic summer side dish.

Tips

To toast pine nuts: Place nuts in dry skillet over medium heat, stirring, for 3 to 4 minutes.

Mint is a vitamin- and mineral-packed fresh herb.

1 tbsp	olive oil	15 mL
3	small zucchini, halved lengthwise and thinly sliced	3
2 cups	cherry tomatoes, halved	500 mL
½ tsp	ground cumin (optional)	2 mL
2	green onions, sliced	2
2 tsp	balsamic vinegar	10 mL
	Salt and freshly ground black pepper	
2 tbsp	chopped fresh basil or mint	30 mL
2 tbsp	lightly toasted pine nuts (optional)	30 mL

1. In a large nonstick skillet, heat oil over medium-high heat. Add zucchini and cook, stirring, for 1 minute. Add cherry tomatoes, cumin (if using), green onions and balsamic vinegar. Cook, stirring, for 1 to 2 minutes or until zucchini is tender-crisp and tomatoes are heated through. Season with salt and pepper to taste.

2. Sprinkle with basil and pine nuts (if using) and serve immediately.

Nutrients per serving	
Calories	62
Fat	4 g
Carbohydrate	6 g
Fiber	2 g
Protein	2 g
Calcium	27 mg
Vitamin D	0 IU

Hot-Bag Vegetables

This is an easy-peasy barbecue recipe, but on rainy days you can also cook it in the oven (see variation) and save on cleanup.

Tips

Roasting bags are heat-resistant clear plastic bags with plastic closures. Look for them in the meat department of your grocery store.

This recipe will work with any of your favorite fresh vegetables — just chop them into bite-size pieces.

For the seasonings, try any combination of dried basil, dried rosemary, dried thyme, dried parsley, salt, pepper and garlic powder.

If your child is overwhelmed by a lot of different foods on her plate, try moving a small amount of one type of vegetable at a time, cut into small pieces, from your plate to hers.

Nutrients per serving	
Calories	67
Fat	2 g
Carbohydrate	12 g
Fiber	3 g
Protein	1 g
Calcium	33 mg
Vitamin D	0 IU

- **Preheat barbecue to medium**
- **Roasting bag, lightly greased**
- **Vegetable basket for barbecue**

1 cup	chopped carrots	250 mL
1 cup	chopped peeled parsnips	250 mL
1 cup	chopped peeled potato	250 mL
1 cup	chopped red bell pepper	250 mL
1 cup	cauliflower florets	250 mL
1 cup	chopped onion	250 mL
1 tbsp	vegetable oil	15 mL
2 tbsp	seasonings (see tip, at left)	30 mL

1. In a large bowl, toss carrots, parsnips, potato, red pepper, cauliflower, onion, oil and seasonings. Pour into prepared roasting bag. Fold opening of bag twice to ensure it stays closed.

2. Place roasting bag in a vegetable basket on preheated barbecue and cook, turning occasionally, for 17 to 20 minutes or until vegetables are tender.

This recipe courtesy of Susanna Herczeg.

Variation

Oven Method: Place roasting bag in preheated 350°F (180°C) oven and roast for 30 to 40 minutes or until vegetables are tender.

Squash with Quinoa and Apricots

Banish the blahs with this robust combination of fruits, vegetables and a nutritious whole grain seasoned with ginger, orange and a hint of cinnamon. In season, accompany with a serving of watercress tossed in a simple vinaigrette.

Tip

If you prefer, use frozen chopped butternut squash in this recipe. Reduce the quantity to 2 cups (500 mL).

- **$3\frac{1}{2}$- to 6-quart slow cooker**

1 tbsp	cumin seeds	15 mL
1 tbsp	olive oil	15 mL
2	onions, finely chopped	2
2	cloves garlic, minced	2
1 tbsp	minced gingerroot	15 mL
2 tsp	finely grated orange zest	10 mL
1	2-inch (5 cm) cinnamon stick	1
1 tsp	ground turmeric	5 mL
1 tsp	salt	5 mL
$\frac{1}{2}$ tsp	cracked black peppercorns	2 mL
1 cup	ready-to-use vegetable broth	250 mL
$\frac{1}{2}$ cup	orange juice	125 mL
4 cups	cubed peeled squash (1 inch/2.5 cm cubes)	1 L
2	apples, peeled, cored and sliced	2
$\frac{1}{2}$ cup	chopped dried apricots	125 mL
$1\frac{1}{2}$ cups	quinoa, rinsed	375 mL

1. In a large dry skillet over medium heat, toast cumin seeds, stirring, until fragrant and they just begin to brown, about 3 minutes. Immediately transfer to a mortar or spice grinder and grind. Set aside.

2. In same skillet, heat oil over medium heat for 30 seconds. Add onions and cook, stirring, until softened, about 3 minutes. Add garlic, ginger, orange zest, cinnamon stick, turmeric, salt and peppercorns and cook, stirring, for 1 minute. Add broth and orange juice and bring to a boil. Transfer to slow cooker stoneware.

Nutrients per serving	
Calories	226
Fat	4 g
Carbohydrate	44 g
Fiber	6 g
Protein	6 g
Calcium	65 mg
Vitamin D	0 IU

Tips

Be sure to rinse the quinoa thoroughly before using because some quinoa has a resinous coating called saponin, which needs to be rinsed off. To ensure your quinoa is saponin-free, before cooking fill a bowl with warm water and swish the kernels around, then transfer to a sieve and rinse thoroughly under cold running water.

This dish can be partially prepared before it is cooked. Complete steps 1 and 2. Cover and refrigerate overnight or for up to 2 days. When you're ready to cook, continue with steps 3 and 4.

Candied ginger or ginger tea can settle an upset tummy or GI issues. But some children may find the flavor of ginger very sharp, so be sensitive to their ability to handle strong flavors.

3. Add squash, apples and apricots to stoneware and stir well. Cover and cook on Low for 6 hours or on High for 3 hours, until vegetables are tender.

4. In a pot, bring 3 cups (750 mL) of water to a boil. Add quinoa in a steady stream, stirring to prevent lumps from forming, and return to a boil. Cover, reduce heat to low and simmer for 15 minutes, until tender and liquid is absorbed. Add to slow cooker and stir well. Serve immediately.

Ratatouille

Ratatouille makes a great accompaniment to roast meat or, if you're a vegetarian, served over baked tofu. It's also delicious on its own with some warm whole-grain bread.

Tip

Try using Italian San Marzano tomatoes in this recipe. They are richer and thicker and have more tomato flavor than domestic varieties. If you are using a domestic variety, add 1 tbsp (15 mL) tomato paste along with the tomatoes.

- **Preheat oven to 400°F (200°C)**
- **Rimmed baking sheet, ungreased**
- **Minimum 5-quart slow cooker**

2	eggplants (each about 12 oz/375 g), peeled and cut into 1-inch (2.5 cm) cubes	2
2 tbsp	kosher or coarse sea salt	30 mL
3 tbsp	olive oil, divided	45 mL
4	zucchini (about 1½ lbs/750 g total), peeled and thinly sliced	4
2	cloves garlic, minced	2
2	onions, thinly sliced	2
1 tsp	dried herbes de Provence	5 mL
½ tsp	salt	2 mL
½ tsp	cracked black peppercorns	2 mL
8 oz	mushrooms, sliced	250 g
1	can (28 oz/796 mL) tomatoes, with juice, coarsely chopped	1
2	green bell peppers, cut into ½-inch (1 cm) pieces	2
½ cup	chopped fresh parsley or basil	125 mL

1. In a colander over a sink, combine eggplant and salt. Toss to ensure eggplant is well coated and let stand for 30 minutes to 1 hour.

2. Rinse eggplant thoroughly under cold running water. Lay a clean tea towel on a work surface. Working in batches over the sink and using your hands, squeeze liquid out of eggplant. Transfer to the tea towel. When batches are complete, roll the towel up and press down to remove remaining liquid.

Nutrients per serving	
Calories	127
Fat	6 g
Carbohydrate	18 g
Fiber	6 g
Protein	5 g
Calcium	65 mg
Vitamin D	1 IU

Tips

Be sure to rinse the salted eggplant thoroughly after sweating. Otherwise it may retain salt and your ratatouille will be too salty.

Ratatouille is a soft and smooth-textured multi-vegetable recipe that would likely be selected as number 1 by soft food lovers everywhere.

This dish can be partially prepared before it is cooked. Complete steps 1 through 3. Cover and refrigerate stoneware and zucchini mixture separately overnight. The next day, continue with step 4.

3. Transfer eggplant to baking sheet and toss with 1 tbsp (15 mL) of the olive oil. Spread evenly on baking sheet. Cover with foil and bake in preheated oven until soft and fragrant, about 15 minutes. Remove from oven and transfer to slow cooker stoneware.

4. Meanwhile, in a skillet, heat 1 tbsp (15 mL) of the oil over medium-high heat. Add zucchini and cook, stirring, for 6 minutes. Add garlic and cook, stirring, until zucchini is soft and browned, about 1 minute. Transfer to a bowl. Cover and refrigerate.

5. Reduce heat to medium. Add remaining 1 tbsp (15 mL) oil. Add onions and cook, stirring, until softened, about 3 minutes. Add herbes de Provence, salt and peppercorns and cook, stirring, about 1 minute. Add mushrooms and toss until coated. Stir in tomatoes and bring to a boil. Transfer to stoneware.

6. Cover and cook on Low for 6 to 8 hours or on High for 3 to 4 hours, until vegetables are tender. Add green peppers, reserved zucchini mixture and parsley and stir well. Cover and cook on High for 25 minutes, until peppers are tender and zucchini is heated through.

Batter-Dipped Vegetable Fritters

These fritters are very easy to make and have wide appeal. You can use a variety of vegetables, including cauliflower, sweet potato and even fresh spinach. Pass your favorite chutney alongside and urge people to put a small dollop on top before inhaling.

Tips

These fritters are best eaten as soon as they are cooked; they lose their crispness as they sit.

Fritters are a favorite for kids who like crispy. Use this crunchy packaging to add new vegetables to your child's diet. Give your child the same variety a few times before you add a new vegetable flavor or texture.

Nutrients per serving	
Calories	120
Fat	2 g
Carbohydrate	20 g
Fiber	5 g
Protein	6 g
Calcium	18 mg
Vitamin D	0 IU

- **Deep-fryer or wok**
- **Candy/deep-fry thermometer**

2 cups	chickpea flour (besan)	500 mL
1 tsp	salt	5 mL
½ tsp	cayenne pepper	2 mL
½ tsp	baking soda	2 mL
8	eggplant slices (unpeeled), cut ¼ inch (0.5 cm) thick	8
8	red or green bell pepper slices, cut ¼ inch (0.5 cm) thick	8
8	zucchini slices (unpeeled), cut ¼ inch (0.5 cm) thick	8
8	peeled potato slices, cut ⅛ inch (0.25 cm) thick	8
	Vegetable oil	

1. In a bowl, mix together chickpea flour, salt, cayenne pepper and baking soda. Slowly pour in 1 cup (250 mL) water, stirring to a smooth consistency and adding up to ¼ cup (60 mL) more water, a little at a time, until batter is slightly thinner than pancake batter. Set aside for 15 minutes.

2. Heat oil in deep-fryer to 375°F (190°C). One at a time, dip slices of eggplant, pepper, zucchini and potato into batter. Add to hot oil in batches of 5 or 6 and deep-fry until golden, 3 to 4 minutes. Remove with slotted spoon and drain on paper towels. Serve immediately with chutney of your choice.

Sweet Potato "Fries"

Makes 4 servings

Here's a delicious alternative to french fries — with more nutrients and less fat.

Tips

Sweet potatoes are cooked when you can easily insert a fork into the flesh.

Turning on the broiler once the potatoes are cooked will help the skins become crispy. Don't leave the oven for an instant, however.

- **Preheat oven to 375°F (190°C)**
- **Nonstick baking sheet**

1 lb	sweet potatoes, each cut lengthwise into 6 wedges	500 g
2 tsp	vegetable oil	10 mL
¼ tsp	paprika	1 mL
⅛ tsp	garlic powder	0.5 mL
	Freshly ground black pepper	

1. Place potatoes in a bowl. Add oil, paprika and garlic powder. Season with pepper to taste. Toss to coat. Transfer to baking sheet.

2. Bake in preheated oven for 25 minutes or until tender and golden, turning once.

This recipe courtesy of dietitian Bev Callaghan.

Nutrients per serving	
Calories	119
Fat	2 g
Carbohydrate	23 g
Fiber	4 g
Protein	2 g
Calcium	34 mg
Vitamin D	0 IU

Mashed Sweet Potatoes with Rosemary

Sweetness, fruity olive oil and the aroma of rosemary, all coming together for a truly special dish.

Tip

Rosemary has quite a strong flavor, so reduce the amount in this recipe if you aren't sure whether young taste buds will approve.

2 lbs	sweet potatoes, peeled and diced	1 kg
2½ tsp	minced fresh rosemary	12 mL
¼ tsp	fine sea salt	1 mL
¼ tsp	freshly ground black pepper	1 mL
2 tsp	extra virgin olive oil	10 mL

1. Place sweet potatoes in a medium saucepan and cover with water. Bring to a boil over high heat. Boil for 8 minutes or until tender. Drain, reserving ⅓ cup (75 mL) of the cooking water.

2. In a large bowl, using an electric mixer on medium speed, beat sweet potatoes and reserved cooking liquid until smooth. Beat in rosemary, salt and pepper. Spoon into a bowl and drizzle with oil.

Nutrients per serving	
Calories	120
Fat	2 g
Carbohydrate	25 g
Fiber	4 g
Protein	2 g
Calcium	46 mg
Vitamin D	0 IU

Yukon Gold Bay Leaf Mash

These potatoes are as good as gold. The recipe was developed by chef Stephen Treadwell when he was at the Tiara Dining Room of the Queen's Landing Inn in Niagara-on-the-Lake, Ontario. The chef paired this simple yet sumptuous side dish with maple roasted salmon and a reduction of Cabernet Sauvignon and mustard seed.

Tips

Use the very best extra virgin olive oil for this recipe.

If you're not using the skins to hold the mash, top them with olive oil margarine or vegan butter substitute and gobble them up.

3 to 4	bay leaves, crushed	3 to 4
1 cup	extra virgin olive oil	250 mL
5	large Yukon gold potatoes, baked and cooled enough to handle	5
1/4 cup	chopped fresh flat-leaf (Italian) parsley	60 mL
	Salt and freshly ground black pepper	

1. Place bay leaves in a small bowl. In a small sauté pan, warm oil over medium heat. Pour over bay leaves and set aside to infuse for 1 hour.

2. Halve each potato lengthwise and scoop flesh into a bowl. Cover with a clean tea towel to keep warm and set aside.

3. Strain oil through a fine-mesh sieve into a small jug or bowl, discarding bay leaves. Stir in parsley until just blended.

4. Using a fork, gradually stir oil into potato flesh, roughly incorporating it and slightly mashing the flesh. Transfer to a serving dish or divide evenly among the skins. Season to taste with salt and pepper and serve immediately.

Nutrients per 1 of 4 servings	
Calories	663
Fat	54 g
Carbohydrate	42 g
Fiber	7 g
Protein	5 g
Calcium	31 mg
Vitamin D	0 IU

Florentine Potato Cakes

Makes 4 servings

A comfort food for sure, these potatoes take the cake for being irresistible, with a little smoky bite from the pancetta and a breath of fresh air from the parsley. Your fans will keep you busy at the skillet until they're all gone.

Tips

You can make the cakes a little smaller and serve them as an appetizer.

Pancetta is unsmoked Italian-style bacon and is widely available.

This recipe uses potatoes that are parboiled, not cooked completely through, making them easier to shred.

Sea salt has a much cleaner, crisper taste than refined table salt, and an enhanced mineral content.

Fresh parsley is packed with nutrients.

Nutrients per serving	
Calories	219
Fat	14 g
Carbohydrate	20 g
Fiber	3 g
Protein	5 g
Calcium	20 mg
Vitamin D	3 IU

- **Preheat oven to 140°F (60°C)**

1 lb	floury potatoes, scrubbed	500 g
1 tsp	salt	5 mL
4	slices pancetta, diced	4
1	small red onion, diced	1
3 tbsp	finely chopped flat-leaf (Italian) parsley leaves	45 mL
	Salt and freshly ground black pepper	
3 tbsp	olive oil	45 mL

1. Place potatoes in a large saucepan and add cold water to barely cover. Add salt, cover loosely and bring to a boil over high heat. Reduce heat, cover and cook until potatoes are tender around the edges but relatively firm in the center, about 10 minutes. Drain well and set aside until cool enough to handle. Using a sharp paring knife, peel the skins. Using the coarse side of a box grater, shred potatoes into a large bowl. Set aside.

2. In a skillet over medium heat, cook pancetta and onion, stirring, until softened, about 6 minutes. Add to potato mixture, making sure to scrape up any brown bits from bottom of pan and the accumulated pan drippings. Add parsley, and salt and pepper to taste. Mix well.

3. Shape mixture into 3-inch (7.5 cm) round cakes. (Cakes may be made ahead to this point, covered with plastic wrap and refrigerated for up to 2 days.)

4. In same skillet, heat oil over medium-high heat. Add potato cakes in batches (unless skillet is very large) and cook until golden brown on both sides, about 10 minutes a batch. Transfer to a platter and keep warm in preheated oven as completed. Serve hot.

Basic Beans

**Makes about
2 cups (500 mL)**

Loaded with nutrition
and high in fiber, beans
are one of our most
healthful edibles.

Tips

This recipe may be doubled
or tripled to suit the quantity
of beans required for a
recipe. Remember to
increase the size of your
slow cooker accordingly.

Generally, the older the
beans are, the longer they
will take to cook. If beans
are still tough after a long
cooking, they are probably
past their prime.

Cooked legumes can
be covered and stored
in the refrigerator for 4
to 5 days or frozen in an
airtight container for up to
6 months.

If your child is not used to
having much fiber, try small
servings to start, then build
up to a regular serving.

Nutrients per ½ cup (125 mL)	
Calories	139
Fat	1 g
Carbohydrate	25 g
Fiber	7 g
Protein	10 g
Calcium	44 mg
Vitamin D	0 IU

- **2-quart slow cooker**

1 cup	dried beans or chickpeas	250 mL
3 cups	water	750 mL

1. *Long soak:* In a bowl, combine beans and water. Soak for at least 6 hours or overnight. Drain and rinse thoroughly with cold water. Beans are now ready for cooking.

2. *Quick soak:* In a pot, combine beans and water. Cover and bring to a boil. Boil for 3 minutes. Turn off heat and soak for 1 hour. Drain and rinse thoroughly under cold water. Beans are now ready to cook.

3. *Cooking:* In slow cooker, combine 1 cup (250 mL) presoaked beans and 3 cups (750 mL) fresh cold water. Season with garlic, bay leaves or a bouquet garni made from your favorite herbs tied together in a piece of cheesecloth, if desired. Add salt to taste. Cover and cook on Low for 10 to 12 hours or overnight or on High for 5 to 6 hours, until beans are tender. Drain and rinse. If not using immediately, cover and refrigerate. The beans are now ready for use in your favorite recipe.

Variation

Basic Lentils: These instructions also work for lentils, with the following changes: Do not presoak them and reduce the cooking time to about 6 hours on Low, 3 hours on High.

Caramelized Peppers and Onions with Pasta

Enjoy this colorful, tasty, upscale spin on traditional Italian peppers and onions. Just add cooked meat or seafood to complete the meal.

Tips

Don't rush this dish — the more the vegetables caramelize, the deeper the flavor.

Try wild rice fusilli for the pasta, or use any kind you like.

The fresh herbs in this recipe will reduce inflammation and support the immune system.

- 9- to 10-inch (23 to 25 cm) skillet, 2 inches (5 cm) deep

2 tsp	extra virgin olive oil	10 mL
3	red bell peppers, cut into 1/4-inch (0.5 cm) slices	3
3	cloves garlic, minced	3
2	Vidalia or other sweet onions, thinly sliced	2
1 tsp	liquid honey	5 mL
1/4 cup	snipped fresh parsley	60 mL
2 tbsp	snipped fresh oregano	30 mL
1/4 cup	balsamic vinegar	60 mL
	Salt and freshly ground black pepper	
2 cups	GF pasta	500 mL

1. In a large nonstick skillet, heat olive oil over low heat. Add red peppers, garlic, onions and honey; cover and cook, stirring occasionally, for 15 to 20 minutes or until tender and deep golden brown. Remove from heat and stir in parsley, oregano and vinegar. Season to taste with salt and pepper.

2. Meanwhile, cook pasta according to package directions or just until tender. Drain well. Toss with caramelized peppers and onions.

Variation

To turn this recipe into a complete entrée, add a protein (such as two 6-oz/170 g cans of tuna, drained, or 12 oz/375 g cooked sliced GF Italian sausage) when tossing vegetables with pasta.

Nutrients per serving	
Calories	237
Fat	4 g
Carbohydrate	47 g
Fiber	3 g
Protein	5 g
Calcium	67 mg
Vitamin D	0 IU

Steamed Rice Noodle Cakes

This easy-to-make recipe can be used as a base for many different toppings — try serving it under a green salad tossed in your favorite dressing.

Tips

If you don't have a steamer, pan-fry cakes in a little oil over medium heat until just golden and lightly crisp, about 1 minute per side.

Cakes can be prepared up to 2 hours ahead. Follow recipe to the end of step 3; allow cakes to cool, and steam briefly to reheat, or pan-fry until golden and crisp, or reheat in a microwave oven.

Steamed rice noodles are very low in salt, cholesterol and saturated fat.

- **Steamer, preferably bamboo**

7 oz	thin rice vermicelli (thin rice stick noodles)	210 g
1/4 cup	cornstarch	60 mL
1/2 tsp	salt	2 mL
1/2 tsp	ground pepper	2 mL
2 tbsp	finely chopped fresh cilantro or green onions	30 mL
1 tbsp	sesame oil	15 mL

1. In a heatproof bowl or pot, cover noodles with boiling water and soak for 3 minutes. Drain. Using chopsticks (or two forks), toss noodles lightly to dry. Divide noodles into 4 equal portions.

2. In a small bowl, combine cornstarch, salt and pepper; mix well. Sprinkle a noodle portion with one-quarter of the cornstarch mixture and one-quarter of the cilantro. Toss until well distributed. Form noodle mixture into a 6-inch (15 cm) round cake, using a spatula to flatten.

3. Brush steamer rack lightly with sesame oil and place over rapidly boiling water. Place one noodle cake on steamer rack and press down to firm. Cover and steam for 2 minutes. Remove cake and cover with plastic wrap to keep warm. Repeat procedure for remaining cakes.

Nutrients per serving	
Calories	248
Fat	4 g
Carbohydrate	46 g
Fiber	1 g
Protein	4 g
Calcium	4 mg
Vitamin D	0 IU

Egg and Mushroom Fried Rice

Here's a great way to use up leftover rice. You can easily divide the ingredients in half to share between two.

Tip

Serve rice for supper and pack up leftovers for lunch the next day. Keep in a cold container until ready to reheat in a microwave.

4	large eggs	4
2 tsp	vegetable oil	10 mL
1 cup	sliced mushrooms	250 mL
1 tsp	minced garlic	5 mL
1 tsp	minced gingerroot (or $\frac{1}{2}$ tsp/2 mL ground ginger)	5 mL
3 cups	cooked rice	750 mL
$\frac{1}{2}$ cup	frozen peas	125 mL
$\frac{1}{2}$ cup	chopped green onions	125 mL
$\frac{1}{3}$ cup	sodium-reduced GF soy sauce	75 mL
$\frac{1}{2}$ to 1 tsp	sesame oil	2 to 5 mL
$\frac{1}{8}$ tsp	freshly ground black pepper	0.5 mL

1. In a small bowl, whisk eggs until well blended. Pour into a large nonstick skillet; cook undisturbed over low heat for 4 to 5 minutes or until bottom is lightly browned and mixture is almost set. Flip eggs over and cook for 1 to 2 minutes. Remove from pan; cool slightly. Cut into $\frac{1}{4}$-inch (0.5 cm) strips. Set aside.

2. In the same skillet, heat oil over medium-high heat. Add mushrooms; cook for 4 to 5 minutes or until lightly browned. Add garlic and ginger; cook for 1 minute. Stir in rice, peas and onions until combined. Stir in soy sauce, sesame oil and pepper; add cooked egg strips. Cook for 2 minutes or until piping hot.

This recipe courtesy of dietitian Bev Callaghan.

Nutrients per serving	
Calories	290
Fat	8 g
Carbohydrate	40 g
Fiber	2 g
Protein	12 g
Calcium	57 mg
Vitamin D	42 IU

Desserts

Crunchy Flaxseed Cookies 348

Chocolate Chip Cookies 349

Black Bean Brownies 350

Apple Ginger Pudding Cake 351

Harvest Cupcakes. 352

The Ultimate Baked Apples 353

Trendy Pastry 354

Strawberry Rhubarb Pie 356

Medley of Fruit Crisp 357

Fresco de Fruit Taco Cupitas 358

Easy Homemade Applesauce 360

Fruit Salad with Ginger and Honey. 361

Fruit Salad with Flax Seeds. 362

Berry Pops 362

Peaches and Cream Frozen Pops. 363

Pumpkin Pudding 364

Coconut Butter Vanilla Icing 365

Chocolate Hazelnut Spread 366

Almond Crème Fraîche. 368

Crunchy Flaxseed Cookies

Makes 3½ dozen cookies

These perfect back-to-school lunch box treats will remind you of oatmeal cookies. Try to eat just one!

Tips

Try this cookie with sprouted flax powder, flaxmeal, ground flax seeds or flax flour. All are delicious, so you can substitute one for another.

Whole flax seeds can be stored at room temperature for up to 1 year. Ground flaxseed can be stored in the refrigerator for up to 90 days, but for optimum freshness it is best to grind as you need it.

This dough doesn't hold in the refrigerator or freezer, so don't attempt to make these into refrigerator slice-and-bake cookies.

Substitute raw hemp powder for ground flaxseed, and hemp hearts for half the cracked flaxseed.

Nutrients per cookie	
Calories	70
Fat	4 g
Carbohydrate	9 g
Fiber	1 g
Protein	1 g
Calcium	9 mg
Vitamin D	1 IU

- **Preheat oven to 350°F (180°C)**
- **Baking sheets, lightly greased**

⅓ cup	sorghum flour	75 mL
¼ cup	whole bean flour	60 mL
¼ cup	tapioca starch	60 mL
¼ cup	ground flax seeds (flaxseed meal)	60 mL
⅔ cup	cracked flax seeds	150 mL
1 tsp	baking soda	5 mL
1 tsp	xanthan gum	5 mL
¼ tsp	salt	1 mL
½ cup	vegetable shortening, softened	125 mL
½ cup	packed brown sugar	125 mL
⅓ cup	granulated sugar	75 mL
1	large egg	1
½ tsp	GF vanilla extract	2 mL
⅔ cup	buckwheat flakes	150 mL

1. In a medium bowl or plastic bag, combine sorghum flour, whole bean flour, tapioca starch, ground flaxseed, cracked flaxseed, baking soda, xanthan gum and salt. Mix well and set aside.

2. In a large bowl, using an electric mixer, cream the shortening, brown sugar and granulated sugar until combined. Add egg and vanilla and cream until light and fluffy. Slowly beat in the dry ingredients until combined. Stir in buckwheat flakes. Roll into 1-inch (2.5 cm) balls. Place 2 inches (5 cm) apart on prepared baking sheets and flatten with a fork or the bottom of a drinking glass.

3. Bake in preheated oven for 10 to 15 minutes or until set. Remove from baking sheets to cooling rack immediately.

Variation

Make date- or jam-filled sandwich cookies or add 1 cup (250 mL) GFCF semisweet chocolate chips or raisins to the batter and bake as drop cookies.

Chocolate Chip Cookies

No point trying to freeze these — the minute anyone knows they are in the house, these cookies disappear.

Tips

Read chocolate ingredient labels carefully for gluten-, milk- and casein-related food products. Choose GFCF or vegan chocolate.

For crisper cookies, replace the shortening with vegan butter substitute and replace half the brown sugar with granulated sugar.

- **Preheat oven to 350°F (180°C)**
- **Baking sheets, lightly greased**

1 cup	sorghum flour	250 mL
⅔ cup	whole bean flour	150 mL
½ cup	tapioca starch	125 mL
1 tsp	baking soda	5 mL
1 tsp	xanthan gum	5 mL
½ tsp	salt	2 mL
1 cup	vegetable shortening, softened	250 mL
1⅓ cups	packed brown sugar	325 mL
2	large eggs	2
1 tsp	GF vanilla extract	5 mL
2 cups	mini GFCF semisweet chocolate chips (see tip, at left)	500 mL
1 cup	chopped walnuts	250 mL

1. In a bowl or plastic bag, combine sorghum flour, whole bean flour, tapioca starch, baking soda, xanthan gum and salt. Mix well and set aside.

2. In a separate bowl, using an electric mixer, cream shortening and brown sugar. Add eggs and vanilla extract and beat until light and fluffy. Slowly beat in the dry ingredients until combined. Stir in chocolate chips and walnuts. Drop dough by level teaspoonfuls (5 mL), 1½ inches (4 cm) apart on prepared baking sheets. Let stand for 30 minutes. Bake in preheated oven for 8 to 10 minutes or until set. Remove from baking sheets to a cooling rack immediately.

Variations

Substitute white chocolate chips and macadamia nuts for the mini chocolate chips and walnuts.

To bake a dozen cookies at a time or to turn these into slice-and-bake cookies, form the dough into 1-inch (2.5 cm) logs, 6 inches (15 cm) in length, and freeze for up to 1 month. To bake, thaw slightly and cut into ½-inch (1 cm) slices. Bake for 10 to 12 minutes.

Nutrients per cookie	
Calories	83
Fat	5 g
Carbohydrate	9 g
Fiber	1 g
Protein	1 g
Calcium	8 mg
Vitamin D	1 IU

Black Bean Brownies

Black bean brownies are all the rage, but not all versions are worthy of the "brownie" moniker. This very fudgy option is.

Tips

Lining a pan with foil is easy. Begin by turning the pan upside down. Tear off a piece of foil longer than the pan, then mold the foil over the pan. Remove the foil and set it aside. Flip the pan over and gently fit the shaped foil into the pan, allowing the foil to hang over the sides (the overhang ends will work as "handles" when the contents of the pan are removed).

Read chocolate ingredient labels carefully for gluten-, milk- and casein-related food products. Choose GFCF or vegan chocolate.

Store the cooled brownies in an airtight container in the refrigerator for up to 3 days.

Nutrients per square	
Calories	149
Fat	7 g
Carbohydrate	18 g
Fiber	4 g
Protein	5 g
Calcium	23 mg
Vitamin D	5 IU

- **Preheat oven to 350°F (180°C)**
- **Food processor**
- **8-inch (20 cm) square metal baking pan, lined with foil (see tip, at left) and sprayed with nonstick cooking spray**

3 cups	rinsed drained canned black beans	750 mL
1/3 cup	unsweetened cocoa powder (not Dutch process)	75 mL
1/8 tsp	fine sea salt	0.5 mL
2	large eggs, at room temperature	2
2	large egg whites, at room temperature	2
1/3 cup	warmed virgin coconut oil	75 mL
1/3 cup	brown rice syrup or liquid honey	75 mL
2 tsp	GF vanilla extract	10 mL
1/2 cup	GFCF bittersweet (dark) or semisweet chocolate chips, roughly chopped (see tip, at left)	125 mL
1/3 cup	finely chopped toasted pecans or walnuts (optional)	75 mL

1. In food processor, combine beans, cocoa powder, salt, eggs, egg whites, coconut oil, brown rice syrup and vanilla; purée until smooth.

2. Spread bean mixture in prepared pan. Sprinkle with chocolate chips and pecans (if using).

3. Bake in preheated oven for 30 to 35 minutes or until just set at the center. Let cool completely in pan on a wire rack. Using foil liner, lift mixture from pan and invert onto a cutting board; peel off foil and cut into 16 squares.

Apple Ginger Pudding Cake

Makes 3 servings

This comforting autumnal dessert has a sweet fruit bottom and a cake top!

Tips

Choose apples that hold their shape when cooked, such as Northern Spy, Spartan or Golden Delicious.

Make sure to place the bowls on a baking sheet, as they are quite full and may boil over in the oven.

Apples contain fiber, which helps support a healthy digestive system. Include them in your child's diet as often as possible.

Nutrients per serving

Calories	267
Fat	3 g
Carbohydrate	60 g
Fiber	6 g
Protein	5 g
Calcium	286 mg
Vitamin D	14 IU

- **Preheat oven to 350°F (180°C)**
- **Three 10-oz (300 mL) ovenproof bowls or ramekins, lightly greased**

Base

2	small apples, sliced	2
1 tbsp	packed brown sugar	15 mL
2 tsp	freshly squeezed lemon juice	10 mL

Cake

1/3 cup	teff flour	75 mL
2 tbsp	amaranth flour	30 mL
1 tbsp	tapioca starch	15 mL
1/4 cup	packed brown sugar	60 mL
1 tbsp	GF baking powder	15 mL
1 tsp	baking soda	5 mL
1/2 tsp	xanthan gum	2 mL
1/8 tsp	salt	0.5 mL
1/2 tsp	ground ginger	2 mL
1/4 tsp	ground cinnamon	1 mL
1	large egg	1
1/2 cup	unsweetened apple cider or apple juice	125 mL

1. *Base:* In a small bowl, combine apples, brown sugar and lemon juice, tossing to coat apples. Evenly distribute among prepared ovenproof bowls.

2. *Cake:* In a bowl or plastic bag, combine teff flour, amaranth flour, tapioca starch, brown sugar, baking powder, baking soda, xanthan gum, salt, ginger and cinnamon. Mix well and set aside.

3. In a separate bowl, using a handheld electric mixer, combine egg and apple cider. Gradually add dry ingredients and mix just until combined. Spoon over apple mixture, dividing evenly. Place bowls on a small baking sheet.

4. Bake in preheated oven for 20 to 25 minutes or until cake is firm when gently touched. Serve warm.

Variation

Add 2 tbsp (30 mL) fresh or thawed frozen cranberries or blueberries with the apples.

Harvest Cupcakes

Makes 24 cupcakes	

These moist cupcakes make an excellent snack to carry in a lunch bag for a midmorning break.

Tips

Be sure to buy pumpkin purée, not pumpkin pie filling, which is too sweet and contains too much moisture for these cupcakes.

Letting the batter stand for 30 minutes before baking results in lighter-textured, more tender cupcakes. But if you're short on time, you can bake the cupcakes immediately.

• **Two 12-cup muffin pans, lined with paper liners**

1 cup	sorghum flour	250 mL
¾ cup	whole bean flour	175 mL
¼ cup	potato starch	60 mL
¼ cup	tapioca starch	60 mL
1½ tsp	GF baking powder	7 mL
¾ tsp	baking soda	3 mL
2 tsp	xanthan gum	10 mL
½ tsp	salt	2 mL
1 tsp	ground cinnamon	5 mL
½ tsp	ground allspice	2 mL
½ tsp	ground ginger	2 mL
½ tsp	ground nutmeg	2 mL
½ cup	vegetable shortening	125 mL
1 cup	packed brown sugar	250 mL
2	large eggs	2
1 cup	canned pumpkin purée (not pie filling)	250 mL
¼ cup	frozen orange juice concentrate, thawed	60 mL
1 tsp	GF vanilla extract	5 mL

1. In a large bowl or plastic bag, combine sorghum flour, whole bean flour, potato starch, tapioca starch, baking powder, baking soda, xanthan gum, salt, cinnamon, allspice, ginger and nutmeg. Mix well and set aside.

2. In a separate bowl, using a handheld electric mixer, cream shortenng until fluffy. Gradually beat in brown sugar. Continue beating until light and fluffy. Add eggs, one at a time, beating well after each. Stir in pumpkin purée, orange juice and vanilla until light and fluffy. Gradually beat in dry ingredients. Continue beating just until smooth, about 2 minutes.

3. Spoon batter into prepared muffin cups, dividing evenly. Let stand for 30 minutes. Meanwhile, preheat oven to 350°F (180°C).

4. Bake for 20 to 23 minutes or until a tester inserted in the center of a cupcake comes out clean. Let cool in pans on a rack for 5 minutes. Remove from pans and let cool completely on rack.

Nutrients per cupcake	
Calories	133
Fat	5 g
Carbohydrate	21 g
Fiber	2 g
Protein	2 g
Calcium	34 mg
Vitamin D	3 IU

The Ultimate Baked Apples

These luscious apples, simple to make yet delicious, are the definitive autumn dessert.

Tips

When buying nuts, be sure to source them from a purveyor with high turnover. Because nuts are high in fat (but healthy fat), they tend to become rancid very quickly. This is especially true of walnuts. The vast majority of walnuts sold in supermarkets have already passed their peak. Taste before you buy, if possible. If they are not sweet, substitute an equal quantity of pecans.

For the casein-free diet plan, vegan non-dairy whipped topping is a good option in place of the yogurt.

- **Minimum 5-quart oval slow cooker**

½ cup	chopped toasted walnuts (see tip, at left)	125 mL
½ cup	dried cranberries	125 mL
2 tbsp	packed muscovado or other evaporated cane juice sugar	30 mL
1 tsp	grated orange zest	5 mL
8	apples, cored	8
1 cup	cranberry juice	250 mL
	Vanilla-flavored cultured non-dairy yogurt (optional)	

1. In a bowl, combine walnuts, cranberries, sugar and orange zest. To stuff the apples, hold your hand over the bottom of the apple and, using your fingers, tightly pack core space with filling. One at a time, place filled apples in slow cooker stoneware. Drizzle cranberry juice evenly over tops.

2. Cover and cook on Low for 8 hours or on High for 4 hours, until apples are tender.

3. Transfer apples to a serving dish and spoon cooking juices over them. Serve hot with a dollop of yogurt, if desired.

Nutrients per serving	
Calories	183
Fat	5 g
Carbohydrate	36 g
Fiber	5 g
Protein	3 g
Calcium	20 mg
Vitamin D	0 IU

Trendy Pastry

People today are
concerned about what
type of fat they're
eating. This recipe is
made with vegetable
oil. Though not quite
as tender as pastry
made with shortening
or butter, this is just
as easy to work with.

Tips

If the pastry cracks while
you're handling it, don't
worry: just use the excess
to patch.

This pastry can also be
made into tart shells to fill
with custard and fresh fruit
or to make mini quiches or
hors d'oeuvre tartlets.

1½ cups	sorghum flour	375 mL
1 cup	cornstarch	250 mL
½ cup	tapioca starch	125 mL
1 tbsp	granulated sugar	15 mL
2 tsp	GF baking powder	10 mL
1 tsp	salt	5 mL
1	large egg	1
½ cup	ice water	125 mL
⅓ cup	vegetable oil	75 mL
2 tbsp	cider vinegar	30 mL

Food Processor Method

1. In a food processor, pulse sorghum flour, cornstarch, tapioca starch, sugar, baking powder and salt until mixed. Set aside.

2. In a small bowl, whisk together egg, ice water, oil and vinegar.

3. With food processor running, add egg mixture through feed tube in a slow, steady stream. Process until dough just holds together. Do not let it form a ball.

Traditional Method

1. In a large bowl, sift sorghum flour, cornstarch, tapioca starch, sugar, baking powder and salt. Set aside.

2. In a small bowl, whisk together egg, ice water, oil and vinegar.

3. Stirring with a fork, sprinkle egg mixture, a little at a time, over the flour mixture to make a soft dough.

Nutrients per 1 of 8 servings	
Calories	272
Fat	11 g
Carbohydrate	42 g
Fiber	2 g
Protein	4 g
Calcium	58 mg
Vitamin D	5 IU

You can freeze the pastry for up to 3 months. Thaw in refrigerator. Bring to room temperature before rolling out.

While rolling out the first half of the dough, cover remaining half to prevent it from drying out.

For Both Methods

4. Divide dough in half. Gently gather each piece into a ball and flatten into a disc. Place the pastry disc between two sheets of parchment paper. Using quick, firm strokes of the rolling pin, roll out the dough into a circle about 1 inch (2.5 cm) larger than the diameter of the inverted pie plate. Carefully remove the top sheet of parchment paper and invert the pastry over the pie plate, easing it in. Carefully peel off the remaining sheet of parchment paper.

5. To prepare another single-crust pie, repeat step 4 with the remaining dough. To prepare the top crust for a double-crust pie, roll out the remaining dough as directed above, then set aside.

For a Single-Crust Pie

Trim excess pastry to edge of pie plate, patch any cracks with trimmings, and press edges with a fork. Or, for a more attractive finish, using a sharp knife, trim the pastry evenly, leaving a 1-inch (2.5 cm) overhang. Tuck pastry under to form a raised double rim. Flute or crimp the edges.

To Bake an Unfilled Pastry Shell

To prevent pastry from shrinking or puffing up, prick bottom and sides with a fork. Bake in oven preheated to 425°F (220°C) for 18 to 20 minutes, or until golden. Let cool completely before filling.

To Bake a Filled Pastry Shell

Do not prick the pastry. Spoon filling into unbaked pastry shell and bake according to individual recipe directions.

For a Double-Crust Pie

For instructions on finishing and baking, see recipe for Strawberry Rhubarb Pie, page 356.

Strawberry Rhubarb Pie

Makes 6 to 8 servings

This pie is a sure-fire winner when fresh local rhubarb and strawberries are at their prime.

Tip

For the best flavor and color, purchase fresh local berries while they're in season. Choose firm stalks of rhubarb that are fresh and crisp; slender stalks are more tender than thick ones.

- **9-inch (23 cm) deep-dish pie plate**

4 cups	chopped fresh rhubarb (or frozen rhubarb, thawed)	1 L
2 cups	quartered fresh strawberries	500 mL
1 cup	granulated sugar	250 mL
$\frac{1}{3}$ cup	tapioca starch	75 mL
2 tsp	freshly squeezed lemon juice	10 mL
	Trendy Pastry (see recipe, page 354)	

1. In a large bowl, toss together rhubarb, strawberries, sugar and tapioca starch. Add the lemon juice. Let stand for 15 minutes. Meanwhile, preheat oven to 425°F (220°C).

2. Roll out pastry for a double-crust pie and press the bottom pastry into pie plate as directed on page 355. Spoon filling into the unbaked pie shell and moisten the edge. Carefully remove the top sheet of parchment paper from the top pastry, invert and cover the filling. Carefully peel off the remaining sheet of parchment paper. Trim pastry, leaving a $\frac{3}{4}$-inch (2 cm) overhang. Fold overhang under bottom pastry rim, seal and flute edge.

3. Make numerous $\frac{1}{2}$-inch (1 cm) slits near the center of the pie through the crust to the filling or cut out a 1-inch (2.5 cm) circle in the center of the crust.

4. Position the oven racks to divide the oven into thirds. Place a baking sheet on the bottom rack to catch the drips if pie boils over. Bake in preheated oven on the top rack for 20 minutes. Reduce heat to 350°F (180°C) and bake for 40 to 50 minutes or until crust is golden and filling is bubbly. Shield edges with foil if they are browning too quickly. Let cool completely on a rack.

Variation

To make a rhubarb pie, substitute rhubarb for the strawberries and increase the granulated sugar to $1\frac{1}{4}$ cups (300 mL).

Nutrients per 1 of 8 servings	
Calories	411
Fat	11 g
Carbohydrate	77 g
Fiber	4 g
Protein	5 g
Calcium	117 mg
Vitamin D	5 IU

Medley of Fruit Crisp

	Makes 4 servings

Old-fashioned, but never out of fashion, this dessert is truly a comfort food!

Tips

If you are not familiar with cardamom, it has a strong, warmly spiced flavor that your child may enjoy. It's often used in Scandinavian and Indian cuisines. Cinnamon, ginger or nutmeg can be used as a substitute.

If you use a smaller or deeper casserole dish, the baking time may be up to twice as long.

If your child cannot tolerate cornstarch, substitute an equal amount of arrowroot starch.

If your child refuses to eat fruit, this dish might appeal, since it has a crumbly top and alluring spice notes.

Nutrients per serving	
Calories	364
Fat	8 g
Carbohydrate	69 g
Fiber	8 g
Protein	9 g
Calcium	129 mg
Vitamin D	0 IU

- **Preheat oven to 375°F (190°C)**
- **8-cup (2 L) shallow casserole dish, lightly greased**

Base

4 cups	frozen unsweetened mixed peaches, blackberries and strawberries	1 L
2 tbsp	cornstarch	30 mL
2 tbsp	granulated sugar	30 mL

Topping

1½ cups	certified GF large-flake (old-fashioned) rolled oats	375 mL
⅓ cup	GF oat flour	75 mL
3 tbsp	packed brown sugar	45 mL
1 tsp	ground cardamom	5 mL
⅓ cup	vegan butter substitute, melted	75 mL

1. *Base:* In prepared casserole dish, combine fruit, cornstarch and sugar. Bake in preheated oven for 30 minutes, or until fruit begins to thicken and steam.

2. *Topping:* Meanwhile, in a medium bowl, combine oats, oat flour, brown sugar and cardamom. Drizzle with butter substitute and mix until crumbly. Sprinkle topping over hot fruit. Do not pack.

3. Bake for 25 to 30 minutes, or until fruit is bubbly around the edges, juices are thickened and clear, a tester inserted in the center is hot to the touch and topping is browned. Serve warm.

Variations

You can use other mixed fruit combinations; the baking time will vary according to the type of fruit selected. If using larger fruit pieces, increase the baking time.

Instead of baking, microwave the base, uncovered, on High for 5 minutes. Stir and microwave on High for 5 minutes, or until fruit is steaming. Sprinkle topping over hot fruit. Microwave on High for 7 minutes. Let stand for 5 minutes.

Fresco de Fruit Taco Cupitas

Mexico is famous for adding a hint of chile to unsuspecting dishes. Enjoy this fresh fruit bowl laced with lime and hot pepper flakes.

Tip

If your child would prefer a less spicy version, set aside the hot pepper flakes.

2 cups	sliced strawberries	500 mL
1 cup	diced pineapple	250 mL
½ cup	chopped jicama	125 mL
2	kiwifruit, peeled and cut into chunks	2
	Grated zest and juice of 1 lime	
½ tsp	hot pepper flakes	2 mL
4	corn cupitas (see recipe, opposite)	4
¼ cup	sweetened shredded coconut	60 mL

1. In a large bowl, combine strawberries, pineapple, jicama, kiwis, lime zest, lime juice and hot pepper flakes. Let stand for 10 minutes to let hot pepper flakes soften and bloom.

2. Divide fruit equally among cupitas. Top with coconut.

Nutrients per cupita	
Calories	162
Fat	3 g
Carbohydrate	33 g
Fiber	6 g
Protein	3 g
Calcium	79 mg
Vitamin D	0 IU

Small tortillas make the perfect shell for fruit and creamy fillings. These little cups are quick to make and delicious.

Tip

It can be very difficult to find 6-inch (15 cm) GF flour tortillas unless you make them yourself. When pressed for time, buy a high-quality 8-inch (20 cm) GF flour tortilla and trim it to 6 inches (15 cm). An 8-inch (20 cm) GF tortilla is too large for the dessert tacos.

Cupitas

- **Preheat oven to 400°F (200°C)**
- **4 deep ovenproof cereal bowls**

| 4 | 6-inch (15 cm) GF flour or corn tortillas (see tip, at left) | 4 |
| | Vegetable cooking spray | |

1. Lightly coat tortillas with cooking spray on both sides. Place tortillas, 2 at a time, in a small plastic bag and microwave on High for 15 seconds. Tortillas should be moist and pliable, but not too hot to handle. Remove from plastic bag. Fit each tortilla in deep bowl, carefully using your fingers to fold and mold the edges into a curvy shape. Place bowls in preheated oven immediately.

2. Bake in preheated oven until tortillas are crispy and golden brown, 10 to 12 minutes. Let cool in bowls. Transfer to platter.

Nutrients per cupita	
Calories	58
Fat	1 g
Carbohydrate	12 g
Fiber	1 g
Protein	2 g
Calcium	46 mg
Vitamin D	0 IU

Easy Homemade Applesauce

	Makes about 3 cups (750 mL)	

The ultimate comfort food, and a fast and delicious recipe.

8	McIntosh apples, peeled and cut in 1-inch (2.5 cm) chunks	8
1/3 cup	granulated sugar (approx.)	75 mL
1 tbsp	freshly squeezed lemon juice	15 mL
1/2 tsp	ground cinnamon	2 mL

1. In an 8-cup (2 L) bowl, combine apple chunks, sugar, lemon juice and cinnamon. Cover tightly with microwave-safe plastic wrap and microwave on High for 6 to 8 minutes, or until apples are steaming and starting to soften.

2. Remove wrap, stir and microwave on High for 6 to 8 minutes, or until apples are completely soft.

3. Remove wrap, mash with a fork and stir in additional sugar, if desired, depending on your family's taste and the sweetness of the apples.

Nutrients per 1/2 cup (125 mL)

Calories	171
Fat	0 g
Carbohydrate	45 g
Fiber	6 g
Protein	1 g
Calcium	17 mg
Vitamin D	0 IU

Fruit Salad with Ginger and Honey

Makes 6 to 8 servings

In Asia, a dessert called icy bowls (which resembles this fruit salad) is served over shaved ice, sometimes topped with coconut milk.

Tips

Feel free to add or substitute any fruits of your choice. Canned Asian fruits such as lychee and jackfruit will work very well in this recipe. And, of course, you can enrich it with coconut milk, if desired.

Take your time in introducing new fruits, such as lychee or jackfruit. And don't feel bad if your child rejects the fruit, but offer it again tomorrow.

Sauce

¼ cup	liquid honey	60 mL
2 tsp	minced gingerroot	10 mL
1 tsp	grated lime zest	5 mL
1 tsp	grated orange zest	5 mL

Salad

1 cup	cubed apples (1-inch/2.5 cm cubes)	250 mL
1 cup	cubed cantaloupe (1-inch/2.5 cm cubes)	250 mL
2 cups	cubed honeydew melon (1-inch/2.5 cm cubes)	500 mL
1 cup	cubed pineapple (1-inch/2.5 cm cubes)	250 mL
1 cup	seedless red grapes	250 mL

1. *Sauce:* In a small bowl or pot, combine honey, ginger, lime zest and orange zest. Heat 30 seconds in microwave or until warmed through on top of stove. Set aside to cool.

2. *Salad:* In a mixing bowl, combine fruits; add sauce and mix well.

Nutrients per 1 of 8 servings	
Calories	86
Fat	0 g
Carbohydrate	23 g
Fiber	1 g
Protein	1 g
Calcium	11 mg
Vitamin D	0 IU

Fruit Salad with Flax Seeds

Makes 2 servings

Combining fruit salad with freshly ground flax seeds is simple and sweet, with a summertime feel to it. This salad takes 10 minutes to prepare.

1	pear, peeled and diced	1
1	ripe banana, chopped	1
1½ cups	diced papaya	375 mL
2 tsp	ground flax seeds (flaxseed meal)	10 mL
4 tsp	certified GF rolled oats or rice bran	20 mL

1. Combine pear, banana, papaya, flax seeds and oats. Serve immediately.

Nutrients per serving			
Calories	179	Protein	3 g
Fat	2 g	Calcium	40 mg
Carbohydrate	42 g	Vitamin D	0 IU
Fiber	7 g		

Berry Pops

Makes 12 ice pops

The kids will want to help make these as well as to eat them!

Tip

Ice pops help soothe the sore throats often experienced by children with autism.

- **12 waxed paper cups and 12 wooden sticks**

2 cups	raspberry, strawberry or cherry juice	500 mL
½ cup	freshly squeezed orange juice	125 mL
½ cup	beet juice	125 mL
2 tbsp	liquid honey (optional)	30 mL

1. In a medium bowl, combine raspberry juice, orange juice, beet juice and honey (if using).

2. Pour ¼ cup (60 mL) juice into each waxed paper cup. Freeze for 1 hour or until firm enough to hold a stick. Insert wooden stick in middle and return to freezer for 1 hour or until hard.

Nutrients per ice pop			
Calories	30	Protein	0 g
Fat	0 g	Calcium	8 mg
Carbohydrate	7 g	Vitamin D	0 IU
Fiber	0 g		

Peaches and Cream Frozen Pops

Makes 6 ice pops

Just the thing for the long dog days of summer.

- **Blender**
- **Six ¼-cup (60 mL) frozen pop molds**

1 cup	frozen sliced peaches	250 mL
¾ cup	vanilla-flavored almond milk, divided	175 mL
3 tbsp	packed brown sugar	45 mL

1. In blender, combine peaches, ½ cup (125 mL) of the almond milk and brown sugar and purée until smooth. Add remaining almond milk and process to blend. Divide among molds. Seal molds and freeze until solid, for at least 8 hours or for up to 2 weeks.

2. To serve, run mold under warm water for a few seconds, then unmold pops. Serve immediately.

Nutrients per ice pop	
Calories	45
Fat	0 g
Carbohydrate	11 g
Fiber	0 g
Protein	0 g
Calcium	8 mg
Vitamin D	13 IU

Pumpkin Pudding

This warm comfort food is cake-like in texture.

Tip

This pudding can also be baked in a 4-cup (1 L) casserole dish for 25 to 30 minutes.

- **Preheat oven to 350°F (180°C)**
- **3-cup (750 mL) round casserole dish, lightly greased and bottom lined with parchment paper**

¼ cup	sorghum flour	60 mL
¼ cup	whole bean flour	60 mL
1 tbsp	tapioca starch	15 mL
2 tsp	GF baking powder	10 mL
¼ tsp	baking soda	1 mL
½ tsp	xanthan gum	2 mL
Pinch	salt	Pinch
⅛ tsp	ground ginger	0.5 mL
⅛ tsp	ground nutmeg	0.5 mL
Pinch	ground cloves	Pinch
¼ cup	packed brown sugar	60 mL
1	large egg	1
⅔ cup	pumpkin purée (not pie filling)	150 mL
2 tbsp	vegetable oil	30 mL
½ tsp	GF vanilla extract	2 mL

1. In a bowl or plastic bag, combine sorghum flour, whole bean flour, tapioca starch, baking powder, baking soda, xanthan gum, salt, ginger, nutmeg and cloves. Mix well and set aside.

2. In a separate bowl, using an electric mixer, combine brown sugar, egg, pumpkin purée, oil and vanilla. Gradually add dry ingredients and mix just until combined. Spoon into prepared casserole dish.

3. Bake in preheated oven for 28 to 32 minutes or until internal temperature of pudding registers 200°F (100°C) on an instant-read thermometer. Carefully remove casserole dish to a rack and let cool for 10 minutes. Serve warm.

Nutrients per 1 of 4 servings	
Calories	215
Fat	9 g
Carbohydrate	31 g
Fiber	4 g
Protein	5 g
Calcium	148 mg
Vitamin D	10 IU

Coconut Butter Vanilla Icing

Makes 2 cups (500 mL)

Here's a rich and creamy vanilla frosting that is actually healthier for you. Make a large batch and keep it in the fridge for when your family is craving something sweet. It makes a perfect frosting for brownies, or spread it on a sliced banana and enjoy it just like that.

Tips

Coconut butter is a blend of coconut oil and coconut meat. You can usually find it in natural foods stores next to the coconut oil.

Some coconut oils are softer than others, so it is often necessary to add liquid to adjust the consistency of recipes containing coconut oil or coconut butter.

Nutrients per 1 tbsp (15 mL)	
Calories	86
Fat	7 g
Carbohydrate	7 g
Fiber	2 g
Protein	1 g
Calcium	5 mg
Vitamin D	0 IU

- **Blender**

1½ cups	coconut butter (see tips, at left)	375 mL
½ cup	agave nectar	125 mL
2 tsp	vanilla seeds (about 1 whole pod) or GF vanilla extract	10 mL

1. In blender, combine coconut butter, agave nectar and vanilla seeds. Blend at high speed until smooth and creamy. If necessary, add water 1 tbsp (15 mL) at a time, pulsing after each addition, until desired consistency is achieved.

Variation

Chocolate Coconut Butter Frosting: Add ½ cup (125 mL) unsweetened cocoa powder and an additional 3 tbsp (45 mL) agave nectar.

Chocolate Hazelnut Spread

Makes about 1¾ cups (425 mL)

This is a sublime spread for sandwiches, morning toast or crêpes, or a delectable dip for fruits. It is also terrific thinned slightly and drizzled on cakes, frozen desserts and waffles. The possibilities are endless.

Tips

To toast and skin hazelnuts: Spread nuts in a single layer on a baking sheet. Toast in a 350°F (180°C) oven, stirring occasionally, until toasted, 8 to 10 minutes. Check constantly because nuts can burn quickly. Transfer to a lightly dampened clean kitchen towel, gather up the sides and rub briskly to dislodge majority of skins.

Hazelnuts are high in calories, with a healthy fat profile, known to lower blood cholesterol.

Nutrients per 2 tbsp (30 mL)

Calories	188
Fat	11 g
Carbohydrate	20 g
Fiber	2 g
Protein	3 g
Calcium	54 mg
Vitamin D	13 IU

- **Food processor**

2 tbsp	powdered soy milk	30 mL
6 tbsp	plain soy milk (approx.)	90 mL
4 oz	vegan dark chocolate, chopped	125 g
1 cup	toasted hazelnuts, skins rubbed off (see tip, at left)	250 mL
¾ cup	Sweetened Condensed Milk (see recipe, opposite) or store-bought vegan alternative	175 mL

1. In a small bowl, whisk powdered milk into soy milk. Set aside.

2. In a small microwave-safe bowl, microwave chopped chocolate on Medium (50%) power in 30-second increments until melted, stirring each time, about 2½ minutes.

3. In food processor, process hazelnuts into a smooth butter, 3 to 5 minutes. Add chocolate and condensed milk and process until combined into a thick paste. With machine running, add soy milk mixture through the feed tube, processing into a thick, smooth but spreadable paste. If mixture is too thick, add soy milk, 1 tsp (5 mL) at a time.

4. Use immediately or transfer to an airtight glass container and refrigerate for up to 1 week. Mixture thickens when chilled, so remove 10 minutes before using to soften.

Thick and sweet, just like the original. Use this luscious sauce as a dip for fruit, in dessert recipes, as a sweetener for breakfast cereals, or add a spoonful to a beverage for a rich spot of decadence.

Tip

This recipe may be doubled if more is needed.

Sweetened Condensed Milk

¾ cup	granulated sugar	175 mL
½ cup	boiling water	125 mL
3 tbsp	vegan hard margarine, melted	45 mL
¾ cup	powdered non-dairy milk (such as soy, hemp or nut)	175 mL

1. In a small heavy-bottomed saucepan, combine sugar, water and margarine. Bring to a low boil over medium heat and cook, swirling pan gently, until sugar is melted. Remove from heat and gradually whisk in powdered milk.

2. Return mixture to medium heat and bring to a gentle boil. Adjust heat as necessary to keep mixture gently boiling with small bubbles breaking the surface consistently, whisking frequently, until slightly thickened and blended, 2 to 3 minutes. Remove from heat and let cool (the mixture will thicken as it cools). Use immediately or refrigerate in an airtight container for up to 2 days.

Nutrients per ¼ cup (60 mL)	
Calories	371
Fat	12 g
Carbohydrate	62 g
Fiber	0 g
Protein	3 g
Calcium	122 mg
Vitamin D	45 IU

Almond Crème Fraîche

| | **Makes about 2¾ cups (675 mL)** | |

Spoon this fabulous thick and perfectly sweetened topping over fresh fruit, pound cake, granola, or baked goods that benefit from a little dab of cream, and stand back for the rave reviews.

Tip

If your child is underweight, this delightful topping with any of the ideas in the headnote should put her back on track!

- **Blender**

1	package (12.3 oz/350 g) firm or extra-firm silken tofu	1
1 cup	Almond Milk (page 377) or store-bought plain almond milk	250 mL
2½ tbsp	coconut oil, liquefied	37 mL
2½ tbsp	agave nectar	37 mL
½ tsp	GF vanilla extract	2 mL
¼ tsp	GF almond extract	1 mL
⅛ tsp	salt	0.5 mL

1. In blender, pulse tofu and almond milk until smooth and well combined. Add coconut oil, agave nectar, vanilla and almond extracts and salt and blend until very smooth and creamy. Mixture will be frothy and is ready to use, or let settle and thicken overnight in refrigerator.

2. Refrigerate crème fraîche in an airtight container for up to 5 days. Stir well before using.

Variation

For an autumn topping, substitute maple syrup for agave nectar and add ¼ tsp (1 mL) maple extract, ¼ tsp (1 mL) ground cinnamon and a sprinkle of nutmeg.

Nutrients per ¼ cup (60 mL)	
Calories	106
Fat	8 g
Carbohydrate	6 g
Fiber	1 g
Protein	6 g
Calcium	226 mg
Vitamin D	0 IU

Snacks and Beverages

Sage Potato Crisps 370

Fresh Tortilla Chips 371

Baked Candied Pecans 372

Spicy, Crispy Roasted Chickpeas 373

Chocolate Date Protein Bars 374

Pumpkin Date Bars 375

Toasted Sesame Quinoa Bars 376

Almond Milk 377

Banana Frappé 378

Berry Frappé 379

Prune Smoothie 379

Green Quinoa Smoothie 380

Hot Carob 380

Electrifying Electrolyte Drink 381

Daterade 382

Nog Me Up 383

Sage Potato Crisps

Makes 4 servings

This is a lovely, simple method of preparing fingerling potatoes — they look so pretty with fresh sage leaves pressed into them. Besides being a nice side dish to accompany roast chicken or other poultry, these make a wonderful accompaniment to glasses of bubbly or an anytime snack.

Tip

These potatoes seem like the perfect food — healthy, attractive, and tasty — to include in a celebration of any sort.

- **Preheat oven to 375°F (190°C)**
- **Baking dish, large enough to accommodate 12 fingerling potato halves**

12	fingerling potatoes (about 1 lb/500 g), scrubbed	12
1 tsp	salt	5 mL
24	fresh sage leaves	24
1/3 cup	olive or canola oil	75 mL
	Salt and freshly ground black pepper	

1. Place potatoes in a large saucepan and add boiling water to barely cover. Add salt, cover loosely and bring to a boil over high heat. Reduce heat and cook for 8 to 10 minutes or until potatoes still offer some resistance when pierced with a small knife. Drain well. Set aside until cool enough to handle. Slice in half lengthwise, then press a sage leaf onto cut side of each half.

2. In baking dish, arrange potatoes cut side up and drizzle with oil. Bake in preheated oven for 15 minutes or until cooked through and golden brown. Using tongs, transfer to a plate lined with paper towels. Season to taste with salt and freshly ground pepper. Serve immediately.

Nutrients per serving	
Calories	241
Fat	18 g
Carbohydrate	18 g
Fiber	3 g
Protein	2 g
Calcium	29 mg
Vitamin D	0 IU

Fresh Tortilla Chips

Makes 72 chips

Freshly made tortilla chips and a big bowl of salsa are the essence of Mexican cuisine. These crispy fried chips, made with either corn or flour tortillas, elevate the flavor of any Mexican salsa or appetizer.

Tips

Peanut oil is a good choice for deep-frying because it has a high smoke point. Canola oil and vegetable oil are good options too.

You can make these chips ahead and store in an airtight container for up to 2 days.

- **Candy/deep-fry thermometer**

	Oil (see tip, at left)	
6	6-inch (15 cm) corn or 8-inch (20 cm) flour tortillas, each cut into 6 wedges	6
	Salt (optional)	

1. Fill a deep-fryer, deep heavy pot or deep skillet with 3 inches (7.5 cm) of oil and heat to 350°F (180°C).

2. Using tongs, gently place 4 to 6 tortilla wedges at a time in the hot oil and deep-fry, turning once, until crisp, 1 to 2 minutes. Drain on paper towels. Salt to taste. Serve chips warm or at room temperature.

Nutrients per 12 chips	
Calories	144
Fat	4 g
Carbohydrate	24 g
Fiber	1 g
Protein	4 g
Calcium	59 mg
Vitamin D	0 IU

Baked Candied Pecans

Makes about 2 cups (500 mL)	

In Chinese cuisine, these popular New Year candied snacks were traditionally made with walnuts because they signify togetherness and are supposedly good for the brain. Pecans are easier to handle, but you can use walnuts if you wish.

Tips

If using walnuts, bring 4 cups (1 L) water to a boil. Add walnuts and blanch for 2 minutes. Remove from heat; drain well, pat dry and proceed with recipe.

These nuts can be served alone as a snack or as a garnish in other dishes.

Young children often throw food as a way of learning about it. Some dropcloths from your local paint store might come in handy!

- **Preheat oven to 275°F (140°C)**
- **Baking sheet sprayed with vegetable spray**

1 lb	shelled raw pecan or walnut halves (see tip, at left)	500 g
1 cup	water	250 mL
1 cup	granulated sugar	250 mL
1/2 cup	liquid honey	125 mL
1/4 tsp	salt	1 mL
2 tbsp	toasted sesame seeds (optional)	30 mL

1. In a large skillet, combine water, sugar, honey and salt. Bring to a boil; cook until liquid coats the back of a spoon with the consistency of corn syrup. Reduce heat to medium. Add nuts; stir and boil for about 1 minute, making sure that nuts are well coated.

2. With a slotted spoon, transfer nuts to prepared baking sheet. (Be sure to separate and spread them out evenly.) Bake in preheated oven for 20 to 25 minutes or until golden brown, turning once.

3. Remove from oven and cool slightly. If you want to eat the nuts as a snack, while they're still warm and sticky, toss them in a mixing bowl with sesame seeds. Spread out coated nuts again on baking sheet; let cool and harden thoroughly. Store in a glass jar with a tight-fitting lid.

Nutrients per 1/4 cup (60 mL)	
Calories	553
Fat	41 g
Carbohydrate	50 g
Fiber	6 g
Protein	5 g
Calcium	42 mg
Vitamin D	0 IU

Spicy, Crispy Roasted Chickpeas

Makes 8 servings	

Chickpeas sprinkled with cayenne and lemon, then roasted until crispy, are a habit-forming snack. They're also great tossed into salads.

Variations

You can use any ground spice or dried herb in place of, or in addition to, the cayenne.

This is a recipe that will appeal if your child prefers crunchy foods.

- **Preheat oven to 425°F (220°C)**
- **Large rimmed baking sheet, lined with parchment paper**

1	can (14 to 19 oz/398 to 540 mL) chickpeas, drained, rinsed and patted dry	1
¾ tsp	fine sea salt	3 mL
⅛ tsp	cayenne pepper	0.5 mL
2 tsp	extra virgin olive oil	10 mL
1 tsp	freshly squeezed lemon juice	5 mL

1. In a large bowl, combine chickpeas, salt, cayenne, oil and lemon juice. Spread in a single layer on prepared baking sheet.

2. Bake in preheated oven for 32 to 38 minutes or until crisp and dry. Let cool completely in pan. Store in an airtight container at room temperature for up to 2 weeks.

Nutrients per serving	
Calories	69
Fat	2 g
Carbohydrate	11 g
Fiber	2 g
Protein	3 g
Calcium	16 mg
Vitamin D	0 IU

Chocolate Date Protein Bars

Makes 8 to 10 bars

These dense treats
are perfect for midday
hunger and take very
little time to prepare.
Try making a double
batch and freezing
some of the mixture
for future use.

Tips

To soak the dates for this
recipe, place them in a bowl
and cover with 4 cups (1 L)
water. Cover and set aside
to soak for 30 minutes.
Drain, discarding any
remaining water.

Dates provide iron, fiber
and potassium and are a
good source of antioxidants.
When you find your child
craving sugar, give him
one or two dates and the
craving will go away.

If caffeine is a concern,
substitute raw carob
powder in place of the
cacao.

- **Food processor**
- **Baking sheet**

2 cups	pitted dates, soaked (see tips, at left)	500 mL
1/4 cup	freshly squeezed orange juice	60 mL
1/4 cup	raw agave nectar	60 mL
1/2 cup	raw cacao powder	125 mL
1 cup	raw shelled hemp seeds	250 mL

1. In food processor, process soaked dates, orange juice, agave nectar and cacao powder until smooth, stopping the motor once and scraping down the sides of the work bowl. Add hemp seeds and pulse several times until well integrated.

2. Transfer onto baking sheet and, using your hands, press out until approximately 8 inches (20 cm) square and 1 inch (2.5 cm) thick. Refrigerate for 1 hour to firm up. Remove and cut into bars. Transfer to an airtight container and store, refrigerated, for up to 7 days.

Nutrients per 1 of 10 bars	
Calories	252
Fat	9 g
Carbohydrate	37 g
Fiber	6 g
Protein	9 g
Calcium	23 mg
Vitamin D	0 IU

Pumpkin Date Bars

Makes 2 dozen bars

These quick and easy, casein-free, moist bars are dotted with dates, nuts and a refreshing touch of orange. No need to frost; simply dust with GF confectioners' (icing) sugar, if desired.

Tips

Check for gluten-free confectioners' (icing) sugar. Some brands may contain up to 5% starch, which could be from wheat.

Store in an airtight container at room temperature for up to 5 days or freeze for up to 2 months.

Substitute an equal amount of dried cranberries for the walnuts.

For a stronger orange flavor, add ½ tsp (2 mL) orange extract.

- **9-inch (23 cm) square baking pan, lined with foil, lightly greased**

¾ cup	soy flour	175 mL
½ cup	packed brown sugar	125 mL
1½ tsp	xanthan gum	7 mL
2 tsp	GF baking powder	10 mL
½ tsp	salt	2 mL
2 tbsp	grated orange zest	30 mL
½ tsp	ground cinnamon	2 mL
½ tsp	ground nutmeg	2 mL
2	large eggs	2
½ cup	canned pumpkin purée (not pie filling)	125 mL
2 tbsp	vegetable oil	30 mL
¾ cup	chopped pitted dates	175 mL
½ cup	chopped walnuts	125 mL

1. In a large bowl or plastic bag, mix together soy flour, brown sugar, xanthan gum, baking powder, salt, orange zest, cinnamon and nutmeg. Set aside.

2. In another large bowl, using an electric mixer, beat eggs, pumpkin purée and oil until combined. Slowly beat in the dry ingredients and mix just until combined. Stir in dates and walnuts. Spoon into prepared pan. Using a moistened rubber spatula, spread to edges and smooth top. Let stand for 30 minutes. Meanwhile, preheat oven to 325°F (160°C).

3. Bake in preheated oven for 25 to 30 minutes, or until a tester inserted in the center comes out clean. Let cool completely in the pan on a rack. Cut into 24 bars.

Nutrients per bar	
Calories	80
Fat	3 g
Carbohydrate	11 g
Fiber	2 g
Protein	3 g
Calcium	38 mg
Vitamin D	3 IU

Toasted Sesame Quinoa Bars

Makes 16 bars

Weary of store-bought power bars and breakfast bars? Then give this no-bake bar a try. The tahini and honey base is amped up with toasted quinoa, sesame seeds and dried fruit, all to delicious, nutritious effect.

Tips

Lining a pan with foil is easy. Begin by turning the pan upside down. Tear off a piece of foil longer than the pan, then mold the foil over the pan. Remove the foil and set it aside. Flip the pan over and gently fit the shaped foil into the pan, allowing the foil to hang over the sides (the overhang ends will work as "handles" when the contents of the pan are removed).

This is a nutrient-rich recipe.

Wrap bars individually and refrigerate for up to 2 weeks.

Nutrients per bar	
Calories	294
Fat	11 g
Carbohydrate	43 g
Fiber	5 g
Protein	8 g
Calcium	64 mg
Vitamin D	0 IU

- **9-inch (23 cm) square metal baking pan, lined with foil (see tip, at left)**

$3/4$ cup	quinoa, rinsed	175 mL
$1/4$ cup	sesame seeds	60 mL
4 cups	certified GF large-flake (old-fashioned) rolled oats	1 L
$3/4$ cup	pitted dates, chopped	175 mL
$3/4$ cup	chopped dried apricots	175 mL
$1/4$ tsp	fine sea salt	1 mL
1 cup	tahini	250 mL
$1/2$ cup	liquid honey or brown rice syrup	125 mL
2 tsp	GF vanilla extract	10 mL

1. In a large skillet over medium heat, toast quinoa and sesame seeds, stirring, for 4 to 5 minutes or until seeds are golden and beginning to pop. Transfer to a large bowl and let cool completely.

2. To the quinoa mixture, add oats, dates, apricots and salt. Stir in tahini, honey and vanilla until blended.

3. Press mixture into prepared pan and refrigerate for at least 30 minutes, until firm. Using foil liner, lift mixture from pan and invert onto a cutting board; peel off foil and cut into 16 bars.

Almond Milk

Makes 4 cups (1 L)

This recipe is very simple to make and, after soaking the almonds, takes no time at all. Use it in smoothies and soups or as a refreshing pick-me-up any time of the day. If you or your child is feeling a bit peckish or having a slight slump, a glass of cold almond milk will provide instant energy.

Tip

To soak the almonds for this recipe, place in a bowl and add 2 cups (500 mL) filtered water. Cover and set aside for at least 30 minutes or up to 12 hours. If you are soaking the nuts at room temperature, change the water every 3 hours (if they are refrigerated, this step isn't necessary). When the soaking time has been completed, drain, discard the soaking water and rinse under cold running water until the water runs clear.

Nutrients per 1 cup (250 mL)	
Calories	206
Fat	18 g
Carbohydrate	8 g
Fiber	4 g
Protein	8 g
Calcium	103 mg
Vitamin D	0 IU

- **Blender**
- **Nut milk bag or cheesecloth (see box, below)**

| 1 cup | whole raw almonds, soaked (see tip, at left) | 250 mL |
| 4 cups | filtered water | 1 L |

1. In blender, combine almonds and water. Blend at high speed for 30 to 60 seconds or until the liquid becomes milky white and no visible pieces of almond remain.

2. Pour into a nut milk bag placed over a pitcher, large enough to accommodate the liquid, and strain. Starting at the top of the bag and using your hands, squeeze in a downward direction to extract the remaining milk. Cover and refrigerate the milk for up to 3 days. Discard the pulp.

Nut Milk Bags

A nut milk bag, which is used to squeeze the liquid from the pulp when making nut or seed milks, is fairly specific to raw food. Typically they are made from nylon mesh. They are available from specialty raw food dealers and most health food stores. If you do not have a nut milk bag, line a sieve with two layers of cheesecloth and place it over a bowl or pitcher. Add the puréed nut and water mixture and strain. Use a wooden spoon to press out the liquid, extracting as much of it as possible. Collect the corners of the cheesecloth and twist them to form a tight ball. Using your hands, squeeze out the remaining liquid. Discard the solids or save for another use.

Variation

Sweetened Almond Milk: After straining, return milk to the blender and add a chopped pitted date, a dash of raw GF vanilla extract and a pinch of sea salt. Blend until smooth.

Banana Frappé

Makes 1 serving

A rich combination of nuts, seeds, dates, banana and cocoa that is a nutritional powerhouse in a glass, this rich frappé goes down well any time of the day.

Tip

Having your child help make the Banana Frappé gives you a chance to talk together about how fresh, delicious food is full of nutrition and energy that makes our bodies and brains run better.

- **Blender**

1 cup	boiling water, divided	250 mL
½ cup	finely chopped almonds	125 mL
1½ tsp	chopped pitted dates	7 mL
1½ tsp	ground flax seeds (flaxseed meal)	7 mL
1½ tsp	chopped vanilla bean	7 mL
½ cup	silken tofu	125 mL
4	frozen banana chunks	4
1 tbsp	carob powder or unsweetened cocoa powder	15 mL
⅛ tsp	almond extract (optional)	0.5 mL

1. In blender, combine ½ cup (125 mL) boiling water, almonds, dates, flax seeds and vanilla bean. Secure lid and blend (from low to high if using a variable speed bender) until smooth.

2. With blender still running, add remaining boiling water through opening in center of lid. Blend until smooth. Let cool.

3. Add tofu, banana, carob powder, and almond extract (if using) to the blender. Secure lid and blend (from low to high if using a variable speed blender) until smooth.

Nutrients per serving	
Calories	483
Fat	33 g
Carbohydrate	38 g
Fiber	10 g
Protein	21 g
Calcium	301 mg
Vitamin D	0 IU

Berry Frappé

Berry Frappé has it all — froth, great color, a nutty taste underlying the sweetness of the berries and the protein from the tofu, and soy or nut milk to carry you through the morning with all the energy you'll need.

Tip

This is a great way to add some fruit if your child either does not eat fruit or has a very limited diet selection.

- **Blender**

1 cup	soy or nut milk	250 mL
1/2 cup	soft tofu	125 mL
1/2 cup	berries, fresh or frozen	125 mL
	Juice of 1/2 lemon	

1. In blender, process soy milk, tofu, berries and lemon juice until smooth. Pour into 1 large or 2 smaller glasses.

Nutrients per serving

Calories	216	Protein	14 g
Fat	8 g	Calcium	448 mg
Carbohydrate	24 g	Vitamin D	105 IU
Fiber	4 g		

Prune Smoothie

Makes 1 serving

A good morning starter, prunes bring their sweet flavor and somewhat chewy texture to make a silky-smooth beverage.

Tip

For children who are suffering from constipation, this smoothie is a gentle solution.

- **Blender**

1 cup	soy milk	250 mL
1/4 cup	pitted prunes	60 mL
1	banana	1

1. In blender, process soy milk, prunes and banana until smooth. Pour into a glass.

Nutrients per serving

Calories	304	Protein	8 g
Fat	4 g	Calcium	304 mg
Carbohydrate	61 g	Vitamin D	105 IU
Fiber	5 g		

Green Quinoa Smoothie

Makes 2 servings

Eschew the drive-through once and for all: this is what real fast food is all about. Ready in minutes, this refreshing, nutrient-dense elixir will satisfy and energize you and your child all morning long.

- **Blender**

2 cups	loosely packed spinach leaves or trimmed kale leaves	500 mL
1 cup	green grapes	250 mL
¾ cup	sliced frozen ripe banana	175 mL
½ cup	chopped kiwifruit	125 mL
3 tbsp	quinoa flakes or flour	45 mL
1 cup	orange juice	250 mL

1. In blender, purée spinach, grapes, banana, kiwi, quinoa flakes and orange juice until smooth. Pour into 2 glasses and serve immediately.

Nutrients per serving

Calories	251	Protein	6 g
Fat	2 g	Calcium	77 mg
Carbohydrate	57 g	Vitamin D	0 IU
Fiber	6 g		

Hot Carob

Makes 1 serving

This makes a great nightcap.

2 cups	date or fig milk or soy milk	500 mL
3 tbsp	powdered carob	45 mL
½ tsp	ground cinnamon	2 mL

1. In a saucepan over medium-low heat, scald milk (heat until little bubbles form around the edge of the pan). Whisk in carob and cinnamon and simmer gently until blended. Serve immediately in warmed mug.

Nutrients per serving

Calories	272	Protein	13 g
Fat	7 g	Calcium	611 mg
Carbohydrate	40 g	Vitamin D	209 IU
Fiber	3 g		

Electrifying Electrolyte Drink

Makes 1½ cups (375 mL)

Tips

If you are using fresh coconut water in this recipe, purchase a white coconut, also known as a young Thai coconut. A brown coconut is mature and will contain no water, although the meat — unlike the meat from a young coconut, which resembles jelly — is ideal for shredding.

Choose decaffeinated green tea if caffeine is a concern.

For children with autism who also have intellectual disabilities (ID) and are nonverbal, it may be more difficult to stay hydrated. Research has shown that people with ID have less self-awareness and are thus at higher risk of self-injury, some forms of illness and even death. This drink helps guard against dehydration.

- **Blender**

1 cup	coconut water (see tip, at left)	250 mL
2 tbsp	cool green tea	30 mL
1	banana	1
8	blueberries	8

1. In blender, combine coconut water, green tea, banana and blueberries. Blend at high speed until smooth. Serve immediately.

Nutrients per 1½ cups (375 mL)

Calories	142
Fat	1 g
Carbohydrate	34 g
Fiber	6 g
Protein	3 g
Calcium	63 mg
Vitamin D	0 IU

Daterade

<table>
<tr><td>

**Makes 2 cups
(500 mL)**

</td></tr>
</table>

Made with coconut water, this simple drink is a great electrolyte replacer. It enables you to avoid those sugar-loaded athletic drinks.

Tips

To soak the dates for this recipe, place in a bowl and add 2 cups (500 mL) water. Cover and set aside for 1 hour. Drain, discarding liquid.

When purchasing coconut water, look for high-quality products that don't contain additives or preservatives (many prepared coconut waters have added sugar and other ingredients).

- **Blender**

10 to 12	pitted Medjool dates, soaked and chopped (see tip, at left)	10 to 12
2 cups	coconut water	500 mL

1. In blender, combine coconut water and soaked dates. Blend at high speed until smooth. Serve immediately.

Nutrients per 1 cup (250 mL)	
Calories	143
Fat	1 g
Carbohydrate	35 g
Fiber	5 g
Protein	2 g
Calcium	80 mg
Vitamin D	0 IU

Nog Me Up

This take on holiday eggnog is rich and perfectly spiced. It *is* sure to be a crowd-pleaser. Although raw, it has all the creaminess and flavor of the traditional version.

Tip

To soak the almonds for this recipe, place in a bowl and add ½ cup (125 mL) water. Cover and set aside for 30 minutes. Drain, discarding soaking water. Rinse under cold running water until the water runs clear.

- **Blender**

¼ cup	whole raw almonds, soaked (see tip, at left)	60 mL
1½ cups	Almond Milk (see recipe, page 377)	375 mL
¼ cup	Date Paste (see recipe, below)	60 mL
1 tbsp	raw agave nectar	15 mL
1 tsp	raw GF vanilla extract or ¼ tsp (1 mL) vanilla seeds	5 mL
1 tsp	ground cinnamon	5 mL
Pinch	ground nutmeg	Pinch
Pinch	ground cloves	Pinch
	Raw agave nectar (optional)	

1. In blender, combine soaked almonds, almond milk, date paste, agave nectar, vanilla, cinnamon, nutmeg and cloves. Blend at high speed until smooth. Taste. If drink is not sweet enough, add 1 to 2 tsp (5 to 10 mL) agave nectar and blend again. Serve immediately.

Nutrients per ½ cup (125 mL)			
Calories	160	Protein	5 g
Fat	11 g	Calcium	70 mg
Carbohydrate	13 g	Vitamin D	0 IU
Fiber	3 g		

Use this paste as a sweetener in place of refined sugar.

Tip

To soak the dates for this recipe, place in a bowl and add 2 cups (500 mL) water. Cover and set aside for 20 minutes. Drain, discarding soaking water.

Date Paste

- **Food processor**

10	chopped pitted dates, soaked (see tip, at left)	10
1 cup	filtered water	250 mL

1. In food processor, process soaked dates and water until smooth. Use immediately or transfer to an airtight container and refrigerate for up to 1 week.

Nutrients per 1 tbsp (15 mL)			
Calories	12	Protein	0 g
Fat	0 g	Calcium	2 mg
Carbohydrate	3 g	Vitamin D	0 IU
Fiber	0 g		

Contributing Authors

Byron Ayanoglu and Jennifer MacKenzie
Complete Curry Cookbook
Recipes from this book are found on pages 270 and 316.

Johanna Burkhard
500 Best Comfort Food Recipes
Recipes from this book are found on pages 244, 328 and 332.

Kelley Cleary Coffeen
200 Easy Mexican Recipes
Recipes from this book are found on pages 249, 254, 271 and 371.

Kelley Cleary Coffeen
300 Best Taco Recipes
Recipes from this book are found on pages 229, 260, 296 and 358.

Pat Crocker
The Juicing Bible, Second Edition
Recipes from this book are found on pages 362 (bottom), 378, 379 (top and bottom) and 380 (bottom).

Dietitians of Canada
Cook Great Food
Recipes from this book are found on pages 255 (bottom), 302, 326, 331 and 339.

Dietitians of Canada
Great Food Fast
Recipes from this book are found on pages 212, 245, 311, 315, 330 and 346.

Dietitians of Canada
Simply Great Food
Recipes from this book are found on pages 250, 278, 304, 314 and 333.

Judith Finlayson
The Complete Gluten-Free Whole Grains Cookbook
A recipe from this book is found on page 266.

Judith Finlayson
The Complete Whole Grains Cookbook
Recipes from this book are found on pages 206, 274 and 313.

Judith Finlayson
The Healthy Slow Cooker, Second Edition
Recipes from this book are found on pages 288, 300, 307, 309, 334 and 336.

Judith Finlayson
The Vegetarian Slow Cooker
Recipes from this book are found on pages 204 (bottom), 257, 265, 343 and 353.

Karen Fischer
The 8-Week Healthy Skin Diet
Recipes from this book are found on pages 203, 205, 273, 324 and 362 (top).

George Geary and Judith Finlayson
650 Best Food Processor Recipes
Recipes from this book are found on pages 195, 252, 253, 272 and 282.

Bill Jones and Stephen Wong
100 Best Asian Noodle Recipes
Recipes from this book are found on pages 308 and 345.

Bill Jones and Stephen Wong
125 Best Chinese Recipes
Recipes from this book are found on pages 275, 361 and 372.

Daina Kalnins and Joanne Saab
Better Baby Food, Second Edition
Recipes from this book are found on pages 186, 188, 189 (top), 191, 194 (top and bottom), 196 (top and bottom), 199, 200, 287, 303 and 306.

Nancie McDermott
300 Best Stir-Fry Recipes
A recipe from this book is found on page 321.

Douglas McNish
Eat Raw, Eat Well
Recipes from this book are found on pages 256, 365, 374, 377, 381, 382 and 383.

Robert Rose Inc.
250 Best Beans, Lentils & Tofu Recipes
Recipes from this book are found on pages 294 and 298.

Lynn Roblin, Nutrition Editor
500 Best Healthy Recipes
Recipes from this book are found on pages 247, 255 (top), 262, 263 and 264.

Deb Roussou
350 Best Vegan Recipes
Recipes from this book are found on pages 202, 258, 284, 292, 295, 363, 366 and 368.

Joanne Saab and Daina Kalnins
Better Food for Kids, Second Edition
Recipes from this book are found on pages 189 (bottom), 190, 192, 193, 197 (top), 197 (bottom), 198, 214, 268, 269, 279 and 327.

Camilla V. Saulsbury
5 Easy Steps to Healthy Cooking
Recipes from this book are found on pages 246, 322, 340, 350 and 373.

Camilla V. Saulsbury
150 Best Gluten-Free Muffin Recipes
A recipe from this book is found on page 240.

Camilla V. Saulsbury
500 Best Quinoa Recipes
Recipes from this book are found on pages 204 (top), 207, 208, 209 (bottom), 215, 216, 376 and 380 (top).

Camilla V. Saulsbury
750 Best Muffin Recipes
Recipes from this book are found on pages 238, 239 and 242.

Andrew Schloss with Ken Bookman
2500 Recipes
Recipes from this book are found on pages 209 (top), 283 (top and bottom) and 360.

Kathleen Sloan-McIntosh
100 Best Grilling Recipes
Recipes from this book are found on pages 248, 286 and 318.

Kathleen Sloan-McIntosh
300 Best Potato Recipes
Recipes from this book are found on pages 290, 341, 342 and 370.

Suneeta Vaswani
Easy Indian Cooking, Second Edition
Recipes from this book are found on pages 210, 211, 310, 329 and 338.

Donna Washburn and Heather Butt
125 Best Gluten-Free Recipes
Recipes from this book are found on pages 276, 323 and 349.

Donna Washburn and Heather Butt
250 Gluten-Free Favorites
Recipes from this book are found on pages 213, 220, 234, 251 and 280.

Donna Washburn and Heather Butt
The Best Gluten-Free Family Cookbook
Recipes from this book are found on pages 259 (top), 312, 320, 348, 354, 356 and 375.

Donna Washburn and Heather Butt
Complete Gluten-Free Cookbook
Recipes from this book are found on pages 230, 231, 232, 259 (bottom), 344 and 357.

Donna Washburn and Heather Butt
The Gluten-Free Baking Book
Recipes from this book are found on pages 187, 218, 222, 224, 226, 228, 236, 237, 351, 352 and 364.

Library and Archives Canada Cataloguing in Publication

Smith, R. Garth, author
    ASD, the complete autism spectrum disorder health & diet guide : includes 175 gluten-free and casein-free recipes / R. Garth Smith, MBBS, FRCPC, Susan Hannah, BA, BScH, and Elke Sengmueller, BASc, RD.

Includes index.
ISBN 978-0-7788-0473-4 (pbk.)

    1. Autism—Nutritional aspects—Popular works. 2. Autism—Diet therapy—Recipes. 3. Gluten-free diet. 4. Casein-free diet. 5. Cookbooks. I. Hannah, Susan, 1956–, author II. Sengmueller, Elke, 1972–, author III. Title. IV. Title: Complete autism spectrum disorder health & diet guide.

RC553.A88S65 2014   616.85'882   C2013-908544-0

Acknowledgments

From Garth Smith

Thanks to all the children who, over 25 years, have taught me to recognize their uniqueness, optimize their strengths, and help mitigate the effects of those who don't acknowledge their "specialness."

From Elke Sengmueller

I would like to express heartfelt appreciation to the families and patients who have invited me into their lives for nearly two decades. It has been a privilege to learn from you, and an honor to have participated in your care.

From Susan Hanna

Special thanks to the folks at ASD-CARC (Autism Spectrum Disorders Canadian-American Research Consortium), in particular Xudong Liu and Melissa Hudson for your support of this book. I'd like to offer recognition in memory of Jeanette Holden, Ph.D., FCCMG, for her efforts to improve the lives of people with ASD. Thank you also to all of the clinicians, therapists, helpers, families, and friends who support families of children with ASD. Much appreciation to the families who shared their stories; your generosity never fails to amaze. Heidi, Olivia, and Hayden, thank you for continuing to motivate others to strive for more. Finally, sincere thanks and appreciation to the team at Robert Rose Inc. for your expertise, patience, and support.

Resources

Internet

Finding what you are seeking on the Internet can be like discovering a needle in a haystack. Experienced marketers design their sites so they pop up to the top of your search list. Although many autism societies have local chapters, we have included national sites here, where you will be able to track down a chapter close to your home. Beware of sites that are offering services that may not be evidence-based. Discuss any therapies you are interested in with your health-care provider.

Autism-Specific Websites

American Psychiatric Association (www.dsm5.org). This site is devoted to the *Diagnostic and Statistical Manual of Mental Disorders* 5 (*DSM-5*) reference book, which was released May 2013.

Autism Canada Foundation (www.autismcanada.org). Offers in-depth information based on recent research; videos on various topics about autism; a physicians' handbook for autism; dietary, nutritional, and medical treatments for autism; and much more.

Autism Research Institute (http://autism.com). This site provides basic information, a signup for an email newsletter, advocacy, resources, information for professionals, news and events, research information, surveys, a support course, and more.

Autism Society of America (www.autism-society.org). A website that offers information on every aspect of living with autism to families, to people with autism, to professionals, and to supporters.

Autism Spectrum Disorders Canadian-American Research Consortium (www.asdcarc.com). An excellent website created by a group of researchers from institutions and laboratories across Canada and the United States, who work with other researchers globally to learn more about the causes and development of ASD and to improve the lives of those affected. Families are welcome to join the registry on this site, to take part in research that examines genes and environmental factors.

Autism World (www.autism-world.com). Autism World exists to raise awareness of autism, to improve the community of autism, to provide information about recent research, and to help the parents of autistic individuals with their daily living. The games for autistic children are especially good.

Centers for Disease Control and Prevention (CDC); Autism Spectrum Disorders (ASDs) (www.cdc.gov/ncbddd/autism/index.html). Topics of information include basics, treatments, research and tracking, screening and diagnosis, data and statistics, and scientific articles.

Children's Hospital Boston; Autism Screening Tool Kit for Primary Care Providers (2010), Compare Screening Tools — Validity Properties Chart (http://autismscreening.org/screening_tools).

Children's Hospital of Eastern Ontario (www.cheo.on.ca/en/ibi). The CHEO's website offers information on treatment programs and the autism program, parent perspectives, events, training, resources, and tips about autism.

Global Autism Collaboration (www.autism.org). This site offers research information, public education, autism awareness, and global collaboration.

Health Canada; About Autism Spectrum Disorders (www.hc-sc.gc.ca/hc-ps/dc-ma/autism-eng.php). Offers basic information about autism and lists government resources, such as links to many Canadian and international autism organizations across Canada.

Mayo Clinic; Autism (www.mayoclinic.org/diseases-conditions/autism/basics/definition/CON-20021148). This not-for-profit organization offers information in easily understood language about all aspects of autism, including warnings about possibly dangerous treatments.

National Autistic Society (www.autism.org.uk). This United Kingdom charity site provides information, support, and pioneering services, and it campaigns for a better world for people with autism.

Society for Treatment of Autism (www.autism.ca). This site offers treatment and educational services for people with autism and related disorders.

U.S. National Library of Medicine; NIH National Institutes of Health; Medline Plus (www.nlm.nih.gov/medlineplus/ency/article/001526.htm). Offers basic information, links to related conditions, and information about drugs and supplements.

Nutrition-Specific Websites

Academy of Nutrition and Dietetics (http://healthycanadians.gc.ca/eating-nutrition/index-eng.php). A trustworthy source of information for general good health, disease conditions, different stages of life, nutrition, cooking tips, book reviews, and lots more.

American Diabetes Association: What Foods Have Gluten? (www.diabetes.org/food-and-fitness/food/planning-meals/gluten-free-diets/what-foods-have-gluten.html).

British Dietetic Association (http://bda.uk.com/index.html). This site offers food facts, tips for nutrition in the workplace, publications and resources, and more.

British Nutrition Foundation-Official Site (www.nutrition.org.uk). Promotes the nutritional well-being of society by interpreting scientifically based nutritional knowledge and advice.

Canadian Pediatric Society (www.caringforkids.cps.ca/handouts/feeding_your_baby_in_the_first_year).

College of Dietitians of Ontario (www.cdo.on.ca).

Dietitians of Canada (www.dietitians.ca). A people-friendly site that offers practice-based evidence answers to your questions, online learning, and recipes.

EatRight Ontario (www.eatrightontario.ca/en/default.aspx). Three easy ways to find nutrition and healthy eating information: 1. Browse by topic. 2. Email a dietitian. 3. Call a dietitian.

Food and Nutrition (http://healthycanadians. gc.ca/eating-nutrition/index-eng.php). Access to Canada's Food Guide, and information about food labeling, food poisoning, food safety, and healthy eating.

Health Canada; Food and Nutrition. (www.hc-sc.gc.ca/fn-an/food-guide-aliment/index-eng. php). Canada's Food Guide website provides information for the public; for educators and communicators; and for First Nations, Inuit, and Metis.

HealthLinkBC (www.healthlinkbc.ca/ healthyeating). An easy-reading site that offers nutrition information for every situation; a phone number to talk to a dietitian is also listed.

Mayo Clinic Healthy Lifestyle Nutrition and Healthy Eating (www.mayoclinic.org/healthy-living/nutrition-and-healthy-eating/basics/ nutrition-basics/HLV-20049477). Provides evidence-based information about diets, cooking, menus and shopping strategies, and nutritional supplements.

National Institutes of Health (http://health.nih. gov/search_results.aspx?terms=Nutrition). Information to help your kids develop healthy eating habits and physical activity habits that last throughout their lives.

Nutrition.gov (www.nutrition.gov). The United States Food and Drug Administration (FDA) offers sound nutrition information, including shopping, cooking and meal planning, and weight management.

Nutrition Source (www.hsph.harvard.edu/ nutritionsource). The Harvard School of Public Health website about nutrition is a knowledge-packed source for all ages and all conditions.

Self Nutrition Data (http://nutritiondata.self.com). A great site that will help you understand the nutrient analysis of what you are eating.

Talk about Curing Autism; GFCF Food Shopping List (www.tacanow.org/family-resources/gfcf-food-shopping-list). A list of gluten-free, casein-free food items.

United States Department of Agriculture; National Agricultural Library; Child Nutrition and Health (http://fnic.nal.usda. gov/lifecycle-nutrition/child-nutrition-and-health). This site offers nutrition information, with credible, accurate, and practical resources for nutrition and health professionals, educators, government personnel, and consumers.

World Health Organization; Nutrition (www. who.int/nutrition/en). Provides information about vitamin and mineral nutrition; child growth standards; nutrition landscape information; information on maternal, infant, and young child nutrition; and information to promote healthy growth and prevent childhood stunting.

Books

There are many books available that are focused on autism. Walk through your local bookstore and create a list of books you are interested in (or take photos with your smartphone). Search the Internet for book reviews. Bring your book list to the next appointment with your health-care provider to discuss which books might be most helpful for you. Your local autism organization may also have recommended books to lend or a suggested book list.

References

Journal Articles

Adams JB, Audhya T, McDonough-Means S, et al. Nutritional and metabolic status of children with autism vs. neurotypical children, and the association with autism severity. *Nutr Metab (Lond)*. 2011; 8 (1): 34.

Afzal N, Murch S, Thirrupathy K, et al. Constipation with acquired megarectum in children with autism. *Pediatrics*, 2003; 112 (4): 939–42.

Ahearn WH, Castine T, Nault K, et al. An assessment of food acceptance in children with autism or pervasive developmental disorder-not otherwise specified. *J Autism Dev Disord*, 2001; 31 (5): 505–11.

Al-Qabandi M, Gorter JW, Rosenbaum P. Early autism detection: Are we ready for routine screening? *Pediatrics*, 2011; 128 (1): e211–17.

Alcantara, J, Alcantara, JD, Alcantara, J. A systematic review of the literature on the chiropractic care of patients with autism spectrum disorder. *Explore (NY)*, 2010; 7 (6): 384–90.

Allison C, Baron-Cohen S, Wheelwright S, et al. The Q-CHAT (Quantitative Checklist for Autism in Toddlers): A normally distributed quantitative measure of autistic traits at 18–24 months of age: Preliminary report. *J Autism Dev Disord*, 2008; 38 (8): 1414–25.

Angelidou A, Alysandratos KD, Asadi S, et al. Brief report: "Allergic symptoms" in children with autism spectrum disorders. More than meets the eye? *J Autism Dev Disord*, 2011; 41 (11): 1579–85.

Arnold GL, Hyman SL, Mooney RA, et al. Plasma amino acids profiles in children with autism: Potential risk of nutritional deficiencies. *J Autism Dev Disord*, 2003; 33 (4): 449–54.

Atladóttir HÓ, Thorsen P, Østergaard L, et al. Maternal infection requiring hospitalization during pregnancy and autism spectrum disorders. *J Autism Dev Disord*, 2010; 40 (12): 1423–30.

Auyeung B, Baron-Cohen S, Wheelwright S, et al. The Autism-Spectrum Quotient: Children's Version (AQ-Child). *J Autism Dev Disord*, 2007; 38 (7): 1230–40.

Badcock C. The imprinted brain: How genes set the balance between autism and psychosis. *Epigenomics*, 2011; 3 (3): 345–59.

Barcia G, Posar A, Santucci M, et al. Autism and coeliac disease. *J Autism Dev Disord*, 2008; 38 (2): 407–8.

Barnevik Olsson M, Carlsson LH, Westerlund J, et al. Autism before diagnosis: Crying, feeding and sleeping problems in the first two years of life. *Acta Paediatr*, 2013; 102 (6): 635–39.

Baron-Cohen S, Hoekstra RA, Knickmeyer R, et al. The Autism-Spectrum Quotient (AQ): Adolescent Version. *J Autism Dev Disord*, 2006; 36 (3): 343–50.

Baron-Cohen S, Knickmeyer RC, Belmonte MK. Sex differences in the brain: Implications for explaining autism. *Science*, 2005; 310 (5749): 819–22.

Baron-Cohen S, Wheelwright S, Skinner R, et al. The Autism-Spectrum Quotient (AQ): Evidence from Asperger syndrome/high-functioning autism, males and females, scientists and mathematicians. *J Autism Dev Disord*, 2001; 31 (1): 5–17.

Barttfeld P, Amoruso L, Ais J, et al. Organization of brain networks governed by long-range connections index autistic traits in general population. *J Neurodev Dis*, 2013; 5 (1): 16.

Battaglia A, Novelli A, Bernardini L, et al. Further characterization of the new microdeletion syndrome of 16p11.2-p12.2. *Am J Med Genet A*, 2009; 149A (6):1200–204.

Berry A, Borgi M, Francia N, et al. Use of assistance and therapy dogs for children with autism spectrum disorders: A critical review of the current evidence. *J Altern Complement Med*, 2013; 19 (2), 73–80.

Berry RJ, Crider KS, Yeargin-Allsopp M. Periconceptional folic acid and risk of autism spectrum disorders. *JAMA*, 2013; 309 (6): 611–13.

Boersma M, Kemner C, de Reus MA, et al. Disrupted functional brain networks in autistic toddlers. *Brain Connect*, 2013; 3 (1): 41–49.

Boles RE, Roberts MC. Supervising children during parental distractions. *J Pediatr Psychol*, 2008; 33 (8): 833–41.

Braunschweig D, Van de Water J. Maternal autoantibodies in autism. *Arch Neurol*, 2012; 69 (6): 693–99.

Brill H. Approach to milk protein allergy in infants. *Can Fam Physician*, 2008; 54 (9):1258–64.

Casanova MF, Buxhoeveden DP, Switala AE, et al. Minicolumnar pathology in autism. *Neurology*, 2002; 58 (3): 428–32.

Chan ES, Cummings C, Canadian Paediatric Society, Community Paediatrics Committee and Allergy Section. Dietary exposures and allergy prevention in high-risk infants: A joint statement with the Canadian Society of Allergy and Clinical Immunology. *Paediatr Child Health*, 2013; 18 (10): 545–54.

Chandler S, Charman T, Baird G, et al. Validation of the social communication questionnaire in a population cohort of children with autism spectrum disorders. *J Am Acad Child Adolesc Psychiatry*, 2007; 46 (10): 1324–32.

Collins SM, Surette M, Bercik P. The interplay between the intestinal microbiota and the brain. *Nat Rev Microbiol*, 2012; 10 (11): 735–42.

Curtin J. Tips on implementing a gluten/casein free diet (without driving yourself crazy). *Pure Facts*, 1998; 22 (4).

Davis TN, O'Reilly M, Kang S, et al. Chelation treatment for autism spectrum disorders: A systematic review. *Res Autism Spect Dis*, 2013; 7 (1): 49–55.

de Magistris L, Familiari V, Pascotto A, et al. Alterations of the intestinal barrier in patients with autism spectrum disorders and in their first-degree relatives. *J Pediatr Gastroenterol Nutr*, 2010; 51 (4): 418–24.

de Theije CG, Bavelaar BM, Lopes da Silva S, et al. Food allergy and food-based therapies in neurodevelopmental disorders. *Pediatr Allergy Immunol*, 2013. doi: 10.1111/pal.12149.

DeMattei R, Cuvo A, Maurizio S. Oral assessment of children with an autism spectrum disorder. *J Dent Hyg*, 2007; 81 (3): 1–11.

Dickie VA, Baranek GT, Schultz B, et al. Parent reports of sensory experiences of preschool children with and without autism: A qualitative study. *Am J Occup Ther*, 2009; 63 (2): 172–81.

Dillenburger K, Keenan M. None of the As in ABA stand for autism: Dispelling the myths. *J Intellect Dev Disabil*, 2009; 34 (2): 193–95.

Dosman C, Adams D, Wudel B, et al. Complementary, holistic, and integrative medicine: Autism spectrum disorder and gluten- and casein-free diet, *Pediatr Rev*, 2013; 34 (10): e36–41.

Ehlers S, Gillberg C, Wing L. A screening questionnaire for Asperger syndrome and other high-functioning autism spectrum disorders in school age children. *J Autism Dev Disord*, 1999; 29 (2): 129–41.

Eichler EE. Copy number variation and human disease. *Nature Education*, 2008; 1 (3): 1.

Elbe D, Lalani Z. Review of the pharmacotherapy of irritability of autism. *J Can Acad Child Adolesc Psychiatry*, 2012; 21 (2): 130–46.

Elsabbagh M, Divan G, Koh Y-J, et al. Global prevalence of autism and other pervasive developmental disorders. *Autism Res*, 2012; 5 (3): 160–79.

Elsabbagh M, Johnson MH. Getting answers from babies about autism. *Trends Cogn Sci*, 2010; 14 (2): 81–87.

Emond A, Emmett P, Steer C, et al. Feeding symptoms, dietary patterns, and growth in young children with autism spectrum disorders. *Pediatrics*, 2010; 126 (2): e337–42.

Eskenazi B, Marks AR, Bradman A, et al. Organophosphate pesticide exposure and neurodevelopment in young Mexican-American children. *Environ Health Perspect*, 2007; 115 (5): 792–98.

Fatemi SH, Aldinger KA, Ashwood P, et al. Consensus paper: Pathological role of the cerebellum in autism. *Cerebellum*, 2012; 11 (3): 777–807.

Fein D, Barton M, Eigsti IM, et al. Optimal outcome in individuals with a history of autism. *J Child Psychol Psychiatry*, 2013; 54 (2): 195–205.

Fernell E, Eriksson MA, Gillberg C. Early diagnosis of autism and impact on prognosis: A narrative review. *Clin Epidemiol*, 2013; 5: 33–43.

Fischer E, Silverman A. Behavioral conceptualization, assessment, and treatment of pediatric feeding disorders. *Semin Speech Lang*, 2007; 28 (3): 223–31.

Gardener H, Spiegelman D, Buka SL. Perinatal and neonatal risk factors for autism: A comprehensive meta-analysis. *Pediatrics*, 2011; 128 (2): 344–55.

Gardener H, Spiegelman D, Buka SL. Prenatal risk factors for autism: Comprehensive meta-analysis. *Br J Psychiatry*, 2009; 195 (1): 7–14.

Gee ME, Bienek A, Campbell NR, et al. Prevalence of, and barriers to, preventive lifestyle behaviors in hypertension (from a national survey of Canadians with hypertension). *Am J Cardiol*, 2012; 109 (4): 570–75.

Geler DA, Kern JK, Geier MR. A comparison of the Autism Treatment Evaluation Checklist (ATEC) and the Childhood Autism Rating Scale (CARS) for the quantitative evaluation of autism. *J Ment Health Res Intellect Disabil*, 2013; 6 (4): 255–67.

Geschwind DH, Levitt P. Autism spectrum disorders: Developmental disconnection syndromes. *Curr Opin Neurobiol*, 2007; 17 (1): 103–11.

Ghanizadeh A. Hyperbaric oxygen therapy for treatment of children with autism: A systematic review of randomized trials. *Med Gas Res*, 2012; 2 (13).

Goodwyn CM, Cruz RF. Communication and symbolic behavior scales. *Assessment for Effective Intervention*, 1997; 23 (1): 233–40.

Gourine AV, Kasymov V, Marina N, et al. Astrocytes control breathing through pH-dependent release of ATP. *Science*, 2010; 329 (5991): 571–75.

Grønborg TK, Schendel DE, Parner ET. Recurrence of autism spectrum disorders in full- and half-siblings and trends over time: A population-based cohort study. *JAMA Pediatr*, 2013; 167 (10): 947–53.

Guthrie W, Swineford LB, Wetherby AM, et al. Comparison of DSM-IV and DSM-5 factor structure models for toddlers with autism spectrum disorder. *J Am Acad Child Adolesc*, 2013; 52 (8): 797–805.e2.

Hadjivassiliou M, Sanders DS, Grünewald RA, et al. Gluten sensitivity: From gut to brain. *Lancet Neurol*, 2010; 9 (3): 318–30.

Hallmayer J, Cleveland S, Torres A, et al. Genetic heritability and shared environmental factors among twin pairs with autism. *Arch Gen Psychiatry*, 2011; 68 (11): 1095–102.

Herbstman JB, Sjödin A, Kurzon M, et al. Prenatal exposure to PBDEs and neurodevelopment. *Environ Health Perspect*, 2010; 118 (5): 712–19.

Herbert MR, Buckeley JA. Autism and dietary therapy: Case report and review of the literature. *J Child Neurol*, 2013; 28: 975.

Herndon AC, DiGuiseppi C, Johnson SL, et al. Does nutritional intake differ between children with autism spectrum disorders and children with typical development? *J Autism Dev Disord*, 2009; 39 (2): 212–22.

Huxham L. Feeding problems and current dietary practices in children with autism spectrum disorder in England (doctoral dissertation, Stellenbosch: Stellenbosch University), 2012.

Hyman SL. New DSM-5 includes changes to autism criteria. *American Academy of Pediatrics*, 2013. APP News.

Ireton H, Glascoe FP. Assessing children's development using parents' reports. The Child Development Inventory. *Clin Pediatr (Phila)*, 1995; 34 (5): 248–55.

Janney DM, Umbreit J, Ferro JB, et al. The effect of the extinction procedure in function-based intervention. *J Posit Behav Interv*, 2013; 15 (2): 113–23.

Johnson CR, Handen BL, Zimmer M, et al. Effects of a gluten free/casein free diet in young children with autism: A pilot study. *J Dev Phys Disabil*, 2011; 23 (3): 213–25.

Jones W, Carr K, Klin A. Absence of preferential looking to the eyes of approaching adults predicts level of social disability in 2-year-old toddlers with autism spectrum disorder. *Arch Gen Psychiatry*, 2008; 65 (8): 946–54.

Jusko TA, Henderson CR, Lanphear BP, et al. Blood lead concentrations < 10 microg/dL and child intelligence at 6 years of age. *Environ Health Perspect*, 2008; 116 (2): 243–48.

Kadar M, McDonald R, Lentin, R. Evidence-based practice in occupational therapy services for children with autism spectrum disorders in Victoria, Australia. *Aust Occup Ther J*, 2012; 59 (4): 284–93.

Kanner L. The birth of infantile autism. *J Autism Child Schizophr*, 1973; 3 (2): 93–95.

Kapur K, Kapur A, Ramachandran S, et al. Barriers to changing dietary behavior. *J Assoc Physicians India*, 2008; 56: 29–32.

Kefeni KK, Okonkwo JO, Olukunie OI, et al. Polybromobiphenyls and polybromodiphenyl ethers in indoor dust. *South Africa Organohalogen Compd*, 2011; 73: 761–63.

Kefeni KK, Okonkwo JO, Olukunie OI. Brominated flame retardants: Sources, distribution, exposure pathways, and toxicity. *Environ Rev*, 2011; 19: 238–53.

Kendall T, Megnin-Viggars O, Gould N, et al. Management of autism in children and young people: Summary of NICE and SCIE guidance. *BMJ*, 2013; 347: f4865: doi: 10.1136/bmj.f4865.

King BH, Bostic JQ. An update on pharmacologic treatments for autism spectrum disorders. *Child Adolesc Psychiatr Clin N Am*, 2006; 15 (1): 161–75.

Klaveness J, Bigam J, Reichelt KL. The varied rate of response to dietary intervention in autistic children. *Open J of Psychiatr*, 2013; 3 (2): 56–60.

Kleinman JM, Robins DL, Ventola PE, et al. The modified checklist for autism in toddlers: A follow-up study investigating the early detection of autism spectrum disorders. *J Autism Dev Disord*, 2008; 38 (5): 827–39.

Knivsberg AM, Reichelt KL, Høien T, et al. A randomised, controlled study of dietary intervention in autistic syndromes. *Nutr Neurosci*, 2002; 5 (4): 251–61.

Knivsberg AM, Reichelt KL, Nødland M, et al. Autistic syndromes and diet: A follow-up study. *Scan J Educ Res*, 1995; 39 (3): 223–36.

Knivsberg AM, Wiig K, Lind G, et al. Dietary intervention in autistic syndromes. *Brain Dysfunction*, 1990; 3: 315–27.

Kral TV, Eriksen WT, Souders MC, et al. Eating behaviors, diet quality, and gastrointestinal symptoms in children with autism spectrum disorders: A brief review. *J Pediatr Nurs*, 2013; 28 (6): 548–56.

Kristjánsson G, Venge P, Hällgren R. Mucosal reactivity to cow's milk protein in coeliac disease. *Clin Exp Immunol*, 2007; 147 (3): 449–55.

Kumar RA, KaraMohamed S, Sudi J, et al. Recurrent 16p11.2 microdeletions in autism. *Hum Mol Genet*, 2008; 17 (4): 628–38.

Kunz C, Lönnerdal B. Human-milk proteins: Analysis of casein and casein subunits by anion-exchange chromatography, gel electrophoresis, and specific staining methods. *Am J Clin Nutr*, 1990; 51 (1): 37–46.

Kurth F, Narr KL, Woods RP, et al. Diminished gray matter within the hypothalamus in autism disorder: A potential link to hormonal effects? *Biol Psychiatry*, 2011; 70 (3): 278–82.

Lai M-C, Lombardo MV, Baron-Cohen S. Autism. *Lancet*, 2014; 383 (9920): 896–910.

Lai M-C, Lombardo MV, Suckling J, et al. Biological sex affects the neurobiology of autism. *Brain*, 2013; 136 (9): 2799–815.

Landrigan PJ, Lambertini L, Birnbaum LS. A research strategy to discover the environmental causes of autism and neurodevelopmental disabilities. *Environ Health Perspect*, 2012; 120 (7): a258–60.

Landrigan, PJ. What causes autism? Exploring the environmental contribution. *Curr Opin Pediatr*, 2010; 22 (2): 219–25.

Lang R, O'Reilly M, Healy O, et al. Sensory integration therapy for autism spectrum disorders: A systematic review. *Res Autism Spect Dis*, 2012; 6 (3): 1004–18.

Ledford JR, Gast DL. Feeding problems in children with autism spectrum disorders: A review. *Focus Autism Other Dev Disabl*, 2006; 21 (3): 153–66.

Lefton-Greif MA, Arvedson JC. Pediatric feeding and swallowing disorders: State of health, population trends, and application of the international classification of functioning, disability, and health. *Semin Speech Lang*, 2007; 28 (3): 161–65.

Li P, Feng X, Qiu G. Methylmercury exposure and health effects from rice and fish consumption: A review. *Int J Res Public Health*, 2010; 7 (6): 2666–91.

Linscheid TR. Behavioral treatments for pediatric feeding disorders. *Behav Modif*, 2006; 3 (1): 6–23.

Liu X, Malenfant P, Reesor C, et al. 2p15-p16.1 microdeletion syndrome: Molecular characterization and association of the OTX1 and XPO1 genes with autism spectrum disorders. *Eur J Hum Genet*, 2011; 19 (12): 1264–70.

London L, Beseler C, Bouchard MF, et al. Neurobehavioral and neurodevelopmental effects of pesticide exposures. *Neurotoxicology*, 2012; 33 (4): 887–96.

Lord C, Risi S, DiLavore PS, et al. Autism from 2 to 9 years of age. *Arch Gen Psychiatry*, 2006; 63 (6): 694–701.

Lucarelli S, Frediani T, Zingoni AM, et al. Food allergy and infantile autism. *Panminerva Med*, 1995; 37 (3): 137–41.

Luyster R, Gotham K, Guthrie W, et al. The Autism Diagnostic Observation Schedule — Toddler Module: A new module of a standardized diagnostic measure for autism spectrum disorders. *J Autism Dev Disord*, 2009; 39 (9): 1305–20.

Mandell DS, Ittenbach RF, Levy SE, et al. Disparities in diagnoses received prior to a diagnosis of autism spectrum disorder. *J Autism Dev Disord*, 2007; 37 (9): 1795–802.

Manning-Courtney P, Murray D, Currans K, et al. Autism spectrum disorders. *Curr Probl Pediatr Adolesc Health Care*, 2013; 43 (1): 2–11.

Martina CA, Weiss B, Swan SH. Lifestyle behaviors associated with exposures to endocrine disruptors. *Neurotoxicology*, 2012; 33 (6): 1427–33.

Matson JL, Tureck K. Early diagnosis of autism: Current status of the Baby and Infant Screen for Children with aUtIsm Traits (BISCUIT), Parts 1, 2, and 3. *Res Autism Spect Dis*, 2012; 6: 1135–41.

Mazefsky CA, Oswald DP. The discriminative ability and diagnostic utility of the ADOS-G, ADI-R and GARS for children in a clinical setting. *Autism*, 2006; 10 (6): 533–49.

Meek SE, Lemery-Chalfant K, Jahromi LB, et al. A review of gene-environment correlations and their implications for autism: A conceptual model. *Psychol Rev*, 2013; 120 (3): 497–521.

Mefford HC, Batshaw ML, Hoffman EP. Genomics, intellectual disability, and autism, *N Engl J Med*, 2012; 366 (8): 733–43.

Mills R, Marchant S. Intervention in autism: A brief review of the literature. *Tizard Learning Disability Review*, 2011; 16 (4): 20–35.

Milton D, Mills R, Pellicano E. Ethics and autism: Where is the autistic voice? Commentary on Post et al. *J Autism Dev Disord*, 2012: 1–2.

Miodovnik A, Engel SM, Zhu C, et al. Endocrine disruptors and childhood social impairment. *Neurotoxicology*, 2011; 32 (2): 261–67.

Mulloy A, Lang R, O'Reilly M, et al. Gluten-free and casein-free diets in the treatment of autism spectrum disorders: A systematic review. *Res Autism Spect Dis*, 2010; 4(3): 328–39.

Nair A, Treiber JM, Shukla DK, et al. Impaired thalamocortical connectivity in autism spectrum disorder: A study of functional and anatomical connectivity. *Brain*, 2013; 136 (6): 1942–55.

Neihart M. Gifted children with Asperger's syndrome. *Gifted Child Quarterly*, 2000; 44 (4): 222–30.

Nielsen JA, Zielinski BA, Ferguson MA, et al. An evaluation of the left-brain vs. right-brain hypothesis with resting state functional connectivity magnetic resonance imaging. *PLoS One*, 2013; 8 (8): e71275.

Oken E, Bellinger DC. Fish consumption, methylmercury and child neurodevelopment. *Curr Opin Pediatr*, 2008; 20 (2); 178–83.

Oosterhof NN, Tipper SP, Downing PE. Crossmodal and action-specific: Neuroimaging the human mirror neuron system. *Trends Cogn Sci*, 2013; 17 (7): 311–18.

Ozonoff S, Young GS, Carter A, et al. Recurrence risk for autism spectrum disorders: A baby siblings research consortium study. *Pediatrics*, 2011; 128 (3): e488–95.

Ozonoff S, Young GS, Steinfeld MB, et al. How early do parent concerns predict later autism diagnosis? *J Dev Behav Pediatr*, 2009; 30 (5): 367–75.

Perera FP, Li Z, Whyatt R, et al. Prenatal airborne polycyclic aromatic hydrocarbon exposure and child IQ at age 5 years. *Pediatrics*, 2009; 124 (2): e195–202.

Radhakrishna S. Application of integrated yoga therapy to increase imitation skills in children with autism spectrum disorder. *Int J Yoga*, 2010; 3 (1): 26–30.

Ratajczak HV. Theoretical aspects of autism: Biomarkers–A review. *J Immunotoxicol*, 2011; 8 (1): 80–94.

Ratajczak HV. Theoretical aspects of autism: Causes–A review. *J Immunotoxicol*, 2011; 8 (1): 68–79.

Reichelt KL, Tveiten D, Knivsbert AM, et al. Peptides' role in autism with emphasis on exorphins. *Microb Ecol Health Dis*, 2012; 23.

Ritvo RA, Ritvo ER, Guthrie D, et al. The Ritvo Autism Asperger Diagnostic Scale-Revised (RAADS-R): A scale to assist the diagnosis of autism spectrum disorder in adults: An international validation Study. *J Autism Dev Disord*, 2011; 41 (8): 1076–89.

Rodier PM. The early origins of autism. *Sci Am*, 2000; 282 (2): 56–63.

Rojahn J, Schroeder SR, Mayo-Ortega L, et al. Validity and reliability of the Behavior Problems Inventory, the Aberrant Behavior Checklist, and the Repetitive Behavior Scale — Revised among infants and toddlers at risk for intellectual or developmental disabilities: A multi-method assessment approach. *Res Dev Disabil*, 2013; 34 (5): 1804–14.

Rue HC, Knox M. Capacity building: Evidence-based practice and adolescents on the autism spectrum. *Psychol Schools*, 2013; 50 (9): 947–56.

Rutishauser U, Tudusciuc O, Wang S, et al. Single-neuron correlates of atypical face processing in autism. *Neuron*, 2013; 80 (4): 887–99.

Saitoh O, Karns CM, Courchesne E. Development of the hippocampal formation from 2 to 42 years: MRI evidence of smaller area dentata in autism. *Brain*, 2001; 124 (7): 1317–24.

Sasson NJ, Lam KS, Parlier M. Autism and the broad autism phenotype: Familial patterns and intergenerational transmission. *J Neurodev Disord*, 2013; 5 (1): 11.

Schmunk G, Gargus JJ. Channelopathy pathogenesis in autism spectrum disorders. *Front Genet*, 2013; 4: 222.

Schreck KA, Williams K, Smith AF. A comparison of eating behaviors between children with and without autism. *J Autism Dev Disord*, 2004; 34 (4): 433–38.

Seneff S, Davidson RM, Liu J. Empirical data confirm autism symptoms related to aluminum and acetaminophen exposure. *Entropy*, 2012; 14 (11): 2227–53.

Sheffield F. Homeopathy and the treatment of autism spectrum disorders (Part 1). *Similia Journal of the Australian Homeopathic Association*, 2007; 19 (2): 9–41.

Silva LM, Schalock M, Gabrielsen, K. Early intervention for autism with a parent-delivered qigong massage program: A randomized controlled trial. *Amer J Occu Thera*, 2011; 65 (5): 550–59.

Silva LM, Schalock M. Autism Parenting Stress Index: Initial psychometric evidence. *J Autism Dev Disord*, 2012; 42 (4): 566–74.

Silva LM, Schalock M. Sense and self-regulation checklist, a measure of comorbid autism symptoms: Initial psychometric evidence. *Am J Occup Ther*, 2012; 66 (2): 177–86.

Smith SL, Smith IT, Branco T, et al. Dendritic spikes enhance stimulus selectivity in cortical neurons in vivo. *Nature*, 2013; 503 (7474): 115–20.

Stahl T, Mattern D, Brunn H. Toxicology of perfluorinated compounds. *Environ Sci Europe*, 2011; 23: 38.

Stein CR, Savitz DA. Serum perfluorinated compound concentration and attention deficit/hyperactivity disorder in children 5–18 years of age. *Environ Health Perspect*, 2011; 119 (10): 1466–71.

Stock R, Mirenda P, Smith IM. Comparison of community-based verbal behavior and pivotal response treatment programs for young children with autism spectrum disorder. *Res Autism Spect Dis*, 2013; 7 (9): 1168–81.

Storch EA, Rasmussen SA, Price LH, et al. Development and psychometric evaluation of the Yale-Brown Obsessive-Compulsive Scale, 2nd ed. *Psychol Assess*, 2010; 22 (2): 223–32.

Theoharides TC, Asadi S, Patel AB. Focal brain inflammation and autism. *J Neuroinflammation*, 2013; 10: 46.

Tomchek SD, Dunn W. Sensory processing in children with and without autism: A comparative study using the short sensory profile. *Am J Occup Ther*, 2007; 61 (2): 190–200.

Trasande L, Liu Y. Reducing the staggering costs of environmental disease in children, estimated at $76.6 billion in 2008. *Health Aff (Millwood)*, 2011; 30 (5): 863–70.

Twachtman-Reilly J, Amaral SC, Zebrowski PP. Addressing feeding disorders in children on the autism spectrum in school-based settings: Physiological and behavioral issues. *Lang Speech Hear Serv Sch*, 2008: 39 (2): 261–72.

Verschuur R, Didden R, Lang R, et al. Pivotal response treatment for children with autism spectrum disorders: A systematic review. *J Autism Dev Disord*, 2003; 1–28.

Volk HE, Hertz-Picciotto I, Delwiche L, et al. Residential proximity to freeways and autism in the CHARGE Study. *Environ Health Perspect*, 2011; 119 (6): 873–77.

Walters RG, Jacquemont S, Valsesia A, et al. A new highly penetrant form of obesity due to deletions on chromosome 16p11.2. *Nature*, 2010; 463 (7281): 671–75.

Weiss LA, Shen Y, Korn JM, et al. Association between microdeletion and microduplication at 16p11.2 and autism. *N Engl J Med*, 2008; 358 (7): 667–75.

Whiteley P, Haracopos D, Knivsberg AM, et al. The ScanBrit randomised, controlled, single-blind study of a gluten-and casein-free dietary intervention for children with autism spectrum disorders. *Nutr Neurosci*, 2010; 13 (2): 87–100.

Whiteley P, Rodgers J, Savery D, et al. A gluten-free diet as an intervention for autism and associated spectrum disorders: Preliminary findings. *Autism*, 1999; 3 (1): 45–65.

Whiteley P, Shattock P, Knivsberg AM, et al. Gluten- and casein-free dietary intervention for autism spectrum conditions. *Front Hum Neurosci*, 2012; 6 (344).

Whyatt CP, Craig CM. Motor skills in children aged 7-10 years, diagnosed with autism spectrum disorder. *J Autism Dev Disord*, 2012; 42 (9): 1799–809.

Williams BL, Hornig M, Buie T, et al. Impaired carbohydrate digestion and transport and mucosal dysbiosis in the intestines of children with autism and gastrointestinal disturbances. *PLoS One*, 2011; 6 (9): e24585.

Williams J, Scott F, Stott C, et al. The CAST (Childhood Asperger Syndrome Test): Test accuracy. *Autism*, 2005; 9 (1): 45–68.

Williams KE, Seiverling L. Eating problems in children with autism spectrum disorders. *Top Clin Nutr*, 2010; 25 (1): 27–37.

Williams PG, Dalrymple N, Neal J. Eating habits of children with autism. *Pediatr Nurs*, 2000; 26 (3): 259–64.

Winburn E, Charlton J, McConachie H, et al. Parents' and child health professionals' attitudes towards dietary interventions for children with autism spectrum disorders. *J Autism Dev Disord*, 2014 Apr; 44 (4): 747–57.

Winneke G. Developmental aspects of environmental neurotoxicology: Lessons from lead and polychlorinated biphenyls. *J Neurol Sci*, 2011; 308 (1–2): 9–15.

Wong VN, Chen WX. Randomized controlled trial of electro-acupuncture for autism spectrum disorder. *Altern Med Rev*, 2010; 15 (2): 136–46.

Zerbo O, Iosif A, Walker C, et al. Is maternal influenza or fever during pregnancy associated with autism or developmental delays? Results from the CHARGE (Childhood Autism Risks from Genetics and Environment) study. *J Autism Dev Disord*, 2013; 43 (1): 25–33.

Zuddas A. Autism assessment tools in the transition from DSM-IV to DSM-5. *Eur Child Adolesc Psychiatry*, 2013; 22 (6): 325–27.

Internet Articles

"A Parent's Guide to Autism Spectrum Disorder; What Is Autism Spectrum Disorder (ASD)?" National Institute of Mental Health, accessed September 2013, www.nimh.nih.gov/health/publications/a-parents-guide-to-autism-spectrum-disorder/index.shtml.

"About Pesticides," U.S. Environmental Protection Agency, last modified December 30, 2013, accessed September 2013, www.epa.gov/pesticides/about.

"About SDP," Sensory Processing Disorder Foundation, last modified March 13, 2014, accessed September 4, 2013, www.spdfoundation.net/about-sensory-processing-disorder.html.

"About TMS; What Is Transcranial Magnetic Stimulation?" Centre for Addiction and Mental Health, accessed October 13, 2013, www.camh.ca/en/research/research_areas/clinical_translational_labs/Pages/About-TMS.aspx.

"Australian Scale for Asperger's Syndrome," Garnett MS, Attwood AJ, Online Asperger Syndrome Information and Support, last modified April 25, 2009, accessed September 4, 2013, www.smccd.edu/accounts/skyecesped/Autism%20spectrum%20Disorder/The%20Australian%20scale%20for%20Asperger's%20syndrome.pdf.

"Autism A.L.A.R.M. Referral Process," American Academy of Pediatricians, accessed December 2013, www.autismgateway.com/cme_20.html.

"Autism Fact Sheet; How Is Autism Diagnosed?" National Institute of Neurological Disorders and Stroke, last modified December 30, 2013, accessed September 12, 2013, www.ninds.nih.gov/disorders/autism/detail_autism.htm.

"Autism Spectrum Disorders (ASDs), Screening and Diagnosis for Healthcare Providers," Centers for Disease Control and Prevention, last modified December 26, 2013, accessed September 10, 2013, www.cdc.gov/ncbddd/autism/hcp-screening.html.

"Autism Spectrum Disorders (ASDs); Research," Centers for Disease Control and Prevention, last modified December 20, 2013, accessed September 12, 2013, www.cdc.gov/ncbddd/autism/research.html.

"Autism Spectrum Disorders — Canadian American Research Consortium, About Us," ASD-CARC, accessed April 29, 2013, www.asdcarc.com/index.php/publisher/articleview/frmArticleID/390/staticId/1234.

"Autism Spectrum Disorders; Data & Statistics," Centers for Disease Control and Prevention, last modified December 20, 2013, accessed September 14, 2013, www.cdc.gov/ncbddd/autism/data.html.

"Autism Spectrum Disorders; Research," Centers for Disease Control and Prevention, last modified December 20, 2013, accessed September 12, 2013, www.cdc.gov/ncbddd/autism/research.html.

"Beat the Bloat," National Health Service, last modified June 21, 2012, accessed September 4, 2013, www.nhs.uk/Livewell/digestive-health/Pages/beat-the-bloat.aspx.

"Blood Testing for Celiac Disease," Canadian Celiac Association, accessed September 10, 2013, www.celiacguide.org/articles/blood_test.pdf.

"BRIEF — Behaviour Rating Inventory of Executive Function," Ann Arbor Publishers, accessed September 14, 2013, www.annarbor.co.uk/index.php?main_page=index&cPath=416_249_123.

"By the Way, Doctor, Children and Soy Milk," Willett WC, Harvard Health Publications, Harvard Medical School, last modified May 2009, accessed September 10, 2013, www.health.harvard.edu/newsletters/Harvard_Health_Letter/2009/May/By-the-way-doctor-Children-and-soy-milk.

"Childhood Lead Poisoning," World Health Organization, Children's Environmental Health (2010), accessed September 2013, www.who.int/ceh/publications/childhoodpoisoning/en.

"Colic — Treatment," National Health Service, last modified January 16, 2014, accessed September 4, 2013, www.nhs.uk/Conditions/Colic/Pages/Treatment.aspx.

"Current Evidence for Diet Therapies in the Treatment and Management of Autism Spectrum Disorder," Presentation by Gutschall M, 2012, accessed September 2013, http://ebookbrowsee.net/gutschall-presentation-current-evidence-for-diet-therapies-in-the-treatment-and-management-of-autism-spectrum-disorder-pdf-d475710134.

"Developmental Checklist — Children's Speech & Language," Kids First's Children's Speech Pathology Team, Kids First Children's Services, accessed March 2014, www.kids-first.com.au/developmental-checklist-childrens-speech-language.

"Diagnostic Instruments for Autism Spectrum Disorder: A Brief Review," McClintock JM and Fraser J, New Zealand Guidelines Group, last modified April 2011, accessed September 17, 2013, www.health.govt.nz/system/files/documents/publications/asd_instruments_report.pdf.

"DSM-5 Implementation and Support," American Psychiatric Association, DSM-5 Development, accessed September 11, 2013, www.dsm5.org/pages/default.aspx.

"Effects of Human Exposure to Hormone-Disrupting Chemicals Examined in Landmark UN Report," World Health Organization, February 19, 2013, accessed September 2013, www.who.int/mediacentre/news/releases/2013/hormone_disrupting_20130219/en.

"Endocrine Disruptors," National Institute of Environmental Health Sciences, last modified February 14, 2014, accessed September 2013, www.niehs.nih.gov/health/topics/agents/endocrine.

"Environment Canada Study Finds Vehicle Exhaust a Significant Source of Isocynaic Acid, Suggests Consideration of New Emission Standard," Green Car Congress, last modified July 12, 2013, accessed September 2013, www.greencarcongress.com/2013/07/ec-20130712.html.

"Facts for Families: The Child with Autism," American Academy of Child & Adolescent Psychiatry, last modified October 2013, accessed September 10, 2013, www.aacap.org/cs/root/facts_for_families/the_child_with_autism.

"Feeding Your Child in the First Year," Canadian Paediatric Centre, Caring for Kids, last modified December 2013, accessed September 14, 2013, www.caringforkids.cps.ca/handouts/feeding_your_baby_in_the_first_year.

"Gastroesophageal Reflux in Infants and Children," Jung AD, American Family Physician, American Academy of Family Physicians, accessed September 2013, www.aafp.org/afp/2001/1201/p1853.html.

"Gilliam Autism Rating Scale, 2nd ed. (GARS-2)," Pearson, accessed September 4, 2013, www.pearson clinical.co.uk/Psychology/ChildMentalHealth/ChildAutisticSpectrumDisorders/GilliamAutism RatingScale-SecondEdition(GARS-2)/Gilliam AutismRatingScale-SecondEdition(GARS-2).aspx.

"Gluten Free Whole Grains," Whole Grain Council, accessed September 9, 2013, http://wholegrainscouncil.org/whole-grains-101/gluten-free-whole-grains.

"Gluten Sensitivity," Canadian Celiac Association, accessed August 29, 2013, www.celiac.ca/?page_id=883.

"International Statistical Classification of Diseases and Related Health Problems 10th Revision," World Health Organization, accessed September 13, 2013, http://apps.who.int/classifications/icd10/browse/2010/en.

"Introducing Solid Foods," Hayes D, Kids Eat Right, Academy of Nutrition and Dietetics Foundation, accessed September 8, 2013, www.eatright.org/kids/article.aspx?id=6442459352&terms=introducing%20food%20textures.

"Lead Poisoning Preventions: Frequently Asked Questions," Minnesota Department of Health, accessed September 2013, www.health.state.mn.us/divs/eh/lead/faqs.html.

"Monitoring Child Development," Royal Children's Hospital Melbourne, Centre for Community Child Health, accessed September 2, 2013, www.rch.org.au/ccch/resources_and_publications/Monitoring_Child_Development.

"Network News: Gene Discoveries for Autism," Collins F, National Institutes of Health, last modified December 2013, accessed December 2013, http://directorsblog.nih.gov/2013/12/03/network-news-gene-discoveries-for-autism.

"Nutrition for Healthy Term Infants: Recommendations from Birth to Six Months (A Joint Statement of Health Canada, the Canadian Paediatric Society, the Dietitians of Canada, and the Breastfeeding Committee for Canada)," Health Canada; Food and Nutrition, last modified October 31, 2012, accessed August 15, 2013, www.hc-sc.gc.ca/fn-an/nutrition/infant-nourisson/recom/index-eng.php.

"Nutrition for Young Children (1 Year and Over)," Ministry of Health 2013, accessed September 4, 2013, www.health.govt.nz/your-health/healthy-living/babies-and-toddlers/nutrition-young-children-1-year-and-over.

"Parent-Child Interaction Therapy," UCDavis Children's Hospital, last modified March 30, 2013, http://pcit.ucdavis.edu.

"Perfluorinated Chemicals (PFCs)," National Institute of Environmental Health Sciences, last modified September 2012, www.niehs.nih.gov/health/materials/perflourinated_chemicals_508.pdf.

"Pervasive Developmental Disorders Screening Test-II," Siegel B, Pearson, accessed September 13, 2013, http://pearsonassess.ca/haiweb/Cultures/en-CA/Products/Product+Detail.htm?CS_ProductID=PDDST-II&CS_Category=ot-asd&CS_Catalog=TPC-CACatalog.

"Picky Eating: 10 Fun Tips to Get Kids to Try New Foods," EatRight Ontario, accessed September 3, 2013, www.eatrightontario.ca/en/Articles/Child-Toddler-Nutrition/Picky-eating—10-fun-tips-to-get-kids-to-try-new-foods.aspx#.UqsQOShnWmA.

"Polychlorinated Biphenyls (PCBs)," Environment Canada, last modified August 26, 2013, accessed September 2013, www.ec.gc.ca/bpc-pcb/Default.asp?lang=En&n=52C1E9EF-1.

"Polycyclic Aromatic Hydrocarbons (PAHs)," Illinois Department of Public Health, last modified February 2009, accessed September 2013, www.idph.state.il.us/envhealth/factsheets/polycyclicaromatichydrocarbons.htm.

"Polycyclic Aromatic Hydrocarbons (PAHs): Health Effects," Government of South Australia, last modified February 2009, accessed September 2013, www.health.sa.gov.au/pehs/PDF-files/ph-factsheet-PAHs-health.pdf.

"Polycyclic Aromatic Hydrocarbons," Environment Canada, last modified July 23, 2013, accessed September 2013, www.ec.gc.ca/toxiques-toxics/default.asp?lang=En&n=9C252383-1.

"Preventing Disease Through Healthy Environments. Exposure to Mercury: A Major Public Health Concern," World Health Organization, 2007, accessed September 2013, www.who.int/phe/news/Mercury-flyer.pdf.

"Reclassification of Rett Syndrome Diagnosis Stirs Concerns," DeWeerdt S, Simons Foundation Autism Research Initiative, July 4, 2011, accessed September 2013, http://sfari.org/news-and-opinion/news/2011/reclassification-of-rett-syndrome-diagnosis-stirs-concerns.

"Reducing Risk of Food Allergy in Your Baby: A Resource for Parents of Babies at Increased Risk of Food Allergy," HealthLink BC, last modified July 26, 2013, accessed August 15, 2013, www.healthlinkbc.ca/healthyeating/pdf/reducing-risk-of-food-allergy-in-your-baby.pdf.

"Resource Handbook for Parents (and Professionals) of Young Children with Autism (or Autistic-Like Tendencies) Who Struggle at Mealtimes," Vittner D and Klein MD (Master's thesis, 2009), The

University of Arizona, Autism Society of America, Pima County Chapter, accessed September 3, 2013, www.mealtimeconnections.com/documents/handbook_compiled.pdf.

"Screening Tools for Autism Spectrum Disorders," Autism Canada Foundation, accessed September 10, 2013, www.autismcanada.org/aboutautism/screeningtools.html.

"Sensitive Gag Reflex: Transition to Textured Foods," About Kids Health, The Hospital for Sick Children, last modified October 11, 2009, accessed September 2013, www.aboutkidshealth.ca/En/HealthAZ/TestsAndTreatments/SpecialDiets/Pages/Sensitive-Gag-Reflex-Transition-to-Textured-Foods.aspx.

"Signed Speech or Simultaneous Communication," Edelson SM, Autism Research Institute, accessed September 14, 2013, www.autism.com/index.php/advocacy_signing.

"Social Stories," by Lara Pullen, Autism Canada Foundation, accessed September 10, 2013, www.autismcanada.org/treatments/comm/socialstories.html.

"Soy Milk, Almond Milk, Hemp Milk, Oat Milk…Oh My!" Withee A, Eat Simply, Real Food Nutrition, last modified November 1, 2011, accessed September 13, 2013, http://eatsimply.org/soy-milk-almond-milk-hemp-milk-oat-milk-oh-my.

"Test Review: Social Responsiveness Scale, Second Edition (SRS-2)," Best Practice Autism, January 13, 2013, accessed September 11, 2013, http://bestpracticeautism.blogspot.ca/2013/01/test-review-social-responsiveness-scale.html.

"Texture Progression: The Effects of Oral Sensory Defensiveness on Oral Motor Function in ASD," Greis SM and Hunt SM, Pediatric Feeding & Swallowing Center, The Children's Hospital of Philadelphia, accessed September 10, 2013, www.chop.edu/export/download/pdfs/articles/pediatric-feeding-and-swallowing/texture-progression.pdf.

"The Sensory World of Autism," National Autistic Society, last modified April 2013, accessed August 2013, www.autism.org.uk/sensory.

"The Shape Autism Takes," Kleiner K, Johns Hopkins Engineering, accessed September 2013, http://eng.jhu.edu/wse/magazine-fall-10/item/the-shape-autism-takes.

"Tips for Milk and Alternatives," Health Canada, Food and Nutrition, last modified September 30, 2009, accessed September 10, 2013, http://hc-sc.gc.ca/fn-an/food-guide-aliment/choose-choix/milk-lait/tips-trucs-eng.php.

"Vision Therapy for ASD, an interview with Melvin Kaplan, OD," Autism Research Institute, accessed September 14, 2013, www.autism.com/index.php/treating_vision.

"What Is a Food Guide Serving?" Health Canada, Food and Nutrition, last modified February 5, 2007, accessed September 12, 2013, www.hc-sc.gc.ca/fn-an/food-guide-aliment/basics-base/serving-portion-eng.php.

"What Is IBI and Is it the Same as ABA"? Geneva Centre for Autism, accessed September 15, 2013, www.autism.net/faqs/595-what-is-ibi-and-is-it-the-same-as-aba.html.

"What Nutritionalists Do," Association for Nutrition, accessed September 11, 2013, www.associationfornutrition.org/Default.aspx?tabid=143.

"When Baby Does Not Latch," Canadian Breastfeeding Association, 2009, accessed September 10, 2013, http://canadianbreastfeedingfoundation.org/basics/does_not_latch.shtml.

"WTC Polychlorinated Biphenyls Fact Sheet," Mount Sinai Pediatric Environmental Health Specialty Unit, accessed September 2013, http://icahn.mssm.edu/static_files/MSSM/Files/Research/Programs/Pediatric%20Environmental%20Health%20Specialty%20Unit/pcbs-faq2.pdf.

Books

American Academy of Pediatrics. *Autism: Caring for Children with Autism Spectrum Disorders: A Resource Toolkit for Clinicians*, 2nd ed. Elk Grove Village, IL: American Academy of Pediatrics, 2012.

Betts DE, Betts SW. *Yoga for Children with Autism Spectrum Disorders: A Step-by-Step Guide*. London, UK: Jessica Kingsley Publishers, 2006.

Bryson SE, Zwaigenbaum L. "The Autism Observation Scale for Infants." In *A Comprehensive Guide to Autism*. Patel VB, Preedy V, Martin CR (eds.). New York: Springer, 2014.

Ernsberger L, Stegen-Hanson T. *Just Take a Bite*. Arlington, Texas: Future Horizons, 2004.

Friedman J, Saunders N. *Canada's Baby Care Book: A Complete Guide from Birth to 12 Months Old*. Toronto: The Hospital for Sick Children and Robert Rose Inc., 2007.

Gardener H, Lyall K. "Perinatal and Neonatal Complications in Autism Etiology." In *A Comprehensive Guide to Autism*. Patel VB, Preedy V, Martin CR (eds.). New York: Springer, 2014: 3–25.

Hilsen L. *A Step-by-Step ABA Curriculum for Young Learners with Autism Spectrum Disorders (Ages 3–10)*. London, UK: Jessica Kingsley Publishers, 2013.

Isles AR. "Genomic Imprinting and Brain Function." In *Neuroscience in the 21st Century*. Pfaff DW (ed.). New York: Springer, 2013: 1917–37.

Karp, H. *The Happiest Toddler on the Block*. New York: Random House Inc., 2014.

Klintwall L, Eikeseth S. "Early and Intensive Behavioral Intervention (EIBI) in Autism." In *A Comprehensive Guide to Autism*. Patel VB, Preedy V, Martin CR (eds.). New York: Springer, 2014: 117–37.

Matson JL, Sturmey P. *International Handbook of Autism and Pervasive Developmental Disorders, Autism and Child Psychopathology Series*. New York: Springer, 2011.

Parmeggiani A. "Gastrointestinal Disorders and Autism." In *A Comprehensive Guide to Autism*. Patel VB, Preedy V, Martin CR (eds.). New York: Springer, 2014: 2035–46.

Prousky J. *Textbook of Integrative Clinical Nutrition*. Toronto: Canadian College of Naturopathic Medicine Press, 2012.

Purves D, Augustine GJ, Fitzpatrick D, Katz LC, LaMantia AS, McNamara JO, Williams SM (eds.), *Neuroscience*, 2nd ed. Sunderland, MA: Sinauer Associates, 2001.

Rogers SJ, Ozonoff S, Hansen RL. "Autism Spectrum Disorders." In *Clinical Manual of Neurodevelopmental Disorders*. Rogers SJ, Hansen RL (eds.) New York: American Psychiatric Publishing Inc., 2014.

Sternberg RJ, Sternberg K. *Cognitive Psychology*, 6th ed. Belmont, CA: Wadsworth, Cengage Learning/ Nelson Education, 2009.

Svedova J, Eigsti IM, Masino SA. "Adenosine and Autism: Physiological Symptoms and Metabolic Opportunities." In *Adenosine: A Key Link Between Metabolism and Brain Activity*. Masino S, Boison D (eds.). New York: Springer, 2013: 513–34.

Zisser A, Eyberg SM. "Parent-Child Interaction Therapy and the Treatment of Disruptive Behavior Disorders." In *Evidence-Based Psychotherapies for Children and Adolescents*, 2nd ed. Weisz JR, Kadkin AE (eds.). New York: Guildford Press, 2001: 179–93.

Index

A

Aamlete (South Asian Omelet), 211
ABA (applied behavior analysis), 101, 102–3, 113
ABC approach, 159
acupuncture, 114–15
ADI-R (Autism Diagnostic Interview — Revised), 43, 48
ADOS (Autism Diagnostic Observation Schedule), 43, 48
Ages and Stages Questionnaires (ASQs), 42
aggression, 95, 105–6, 147, 160
Akoori (South Asian Scrambled Eggs), 210
A.L.A.R.M. guidelines, 97
allergies, 63, 84, 86, 87. See also sensitivities
almond flour
    Almond Flour Blackberry Muffins, 239
    Breadsticks, 232
    Pumpkin Almond Flour Muffins, 242
    White Bread, 218
almond milk
    Almond Crème Fraîche, 368
    Nog Me Up, 383
    Peaches and Cream Frozen Pops, 363
almonds. See also almond flour; almond milk
    Almond Milk, 377
    Banana Frappé, 378
    Easy Homemade Granola, 202
    Gluten-Free Muesli, 203
    Nog Me Up, 383
American Academy of Neurology, 97, 98–99
American Academy of Pediatrics, 97
anaphylaxis, 87
antibodies, 149, 150
antioxidants, 69–70, 118
Apgar score, 64
appetizers, 244–51
apple juice/cider
    Fresh Vegetable Purée, 195
    Sweet Baked Tomatoes, 331
apples, 144. See also apple juice/cider
    Apple Ginger Pudding Cake, 351
    Baked Apple Quinoa, 207
    Baked Apples, The Ultimate, 353
    Breakfast Rice (variation), 204
    Easy Homemade Applesauce, 360
    Fruit Salad with Ginger and Honey, 361
    Mashed Banana and Avocado (variation), 199
    Pear Buckwheat Muffins, 238
    Squash with Quinoa and Apricots, 334
    Turkey Apple Meatloaf, 314
    Waldorf Parma Salad, 282
    Warm Chicken Salad with Peanut Dressing, 279
Asian Barbecued Tofu Cubes, 303
Asian-Style Quinoa Salad with Chili-Orange Dressing, 274
asparagus
    Cold Buckwheat Noodles with Broccoli and Sesame Dressing (variation), 292
    Sticky Rice Salad with Asparagus and Mushrooms in Soy Vinaigrette, 275
Asperger, Hans, 149
attention, 159
attitude, 162, 168
auditory integration, 110–11
autism spectrum disorder (ASD), 15–21. See also behavior; diagnosis; treatment
    biologic risks, 64
    and brain, 74, 89
    causes, 55–89
    disability in, 16
    environmental factors, 56, 63–68, 73
    gender and, 71–72
    genetic factors, 55–56, 60–61
    incidence, 16–17
    information sources, 100
    prognosis, 168
    range, 11, 16, 19
    recognizing, 10, 21–31
    related disorders, 49–53, 83
    sensory symptoms, 18, 54, 123, 131–39
    sibling risk, 55, 57, 73, 98
    social symptoms, 18, 35, 36, 53
    stigmatization of, 11, 38, 168
    symptoms, 17–19, 33–35, 94
    theories about, 56, 59–61
automobile emissions, 67
avocado
    Fiesta Guacamole, 254
    Mashed Banana and Avocado, 199
    Mexican Shrimp Cocktail, 249
axons, 77, 80–82

B

babies. See infants
bacon and pancetta
    Bacon and Tomato Biscuits, 231
    Crispy Bacon Strips, 209
    Florentine Potato Cakes, 342
    Grilled Bacon and Zucchini–Wrapped Scallops, 248
bacteria (gut), 83–84
balance (physical), 50
bananas
    Banana Frappé, 378
    Banana Pecan Waffles, 213
    Electrifying Electrolyte Drink, 381
    Fruit Salad with Flax Seeds, 362
    Gluten-Free Muesli, 203
    Green Quinoa Smoothie, 380
    Mashed Banana and Avocado, 199
    Prune Smoothie, 379
    Special Muffins for Kids, 187
    Spiced Bananas, 198
    Sweet Banana Porridge, 205
Basic Beans, 343
Basic Beef Mixture, 192
Basic Gravy, 317
Basic Tomato Sauce, 257
Batter-Dipped Vegetable Fritters, 338
bean/pea flour
    Brown Sandwich Bread (variation), 220
    Chocolate Chip Cookies, 349
    Crunchy Flaxseed Cookies, 348
    Harvest Cupcakes, 352
    Honey Dijon Toastie, 226
    Pumpkin Pudding, 364
beans. See also bean/pea flour; beans, green/yellow; bean sprouts
    Basic Beans, 343
    Basic Beef Mixture (variation), 192
    Black Bean Brownies, 350
    Black Bean Salsa, 255
    Kale Quinoa Tabbouleh (variation), 295
    Lettuce Wraps (variation), 190
    Rice and Black Bean–Stuffed Peppers, 298
    Vegetable Tamale Pie, 294
beans, green/yellow
    Cold Buckwheat Noodles with Broccoli and Sesame Dressing (variation), 292

beans, green/yellow (*continued*)
  Green Beans with Mustard Seeds, 329
  Lean Lamb and Three Veg, 324
  Mixed Vegetables in Spicy Peanut Sauce, 288
bean sprouts
  Egg Foo Yong, 189
  Mixed Vegetables in Spicy Peanut Sauce, 288
  Warm Chicken Salad with Peanut Dressing, 279
beef
  Barbecued Beef Satays, 245
  Basic Beef Mixture, 192
  Buckwheat Noodle Bowls with Beef and Snap Peas, 322
  Egg Foo Yong, 189
  Italian Sausage Patties, 320
  Meatballs for Everyday, 323
  Puréed Meat, 191
  Taco Salad, 280
  Tangy Orange Beef, 321
behavior, 9. *See also* language
  aggressive, 95, 105–6, 147, 160
  assessing, 32–35, 105
  cusps, 104
  with eating, 121, 122, 131, 133
  fastidious, 19
  GFCF diet and, 159
  repetitive/stereotyped, 32
  symptomatic, 33, 34, 53
  therapies based on, 101–5
  wandering, 95–96
berries. *See also specific types of berries*
  Almond Flour Blackberry Muffins, 239
  Apple Ginger Pudding Cake (variation), 351
  Berry Frappé, 379
  Medley of Fruit Crisp, 357
  Quinoa Coconut Fruit Sushi, 208
  Tangy Fruit Sauce, 197
Berry Pops, 362
beverages, 165, 166, 377–84
BFRs (brominated flame retardants), 68
biopsy, 152
birth complications, 64, 82
Biscuit Mix, 230
Biscuits, Bacon and Tomato, 231
biting, 147
Black Bean Brownies, 350
Black Bean Salsa, 255
blueberries
  Apple Ginger Pudding Cake (variation), 351
  Easy Homemade Granola, 202
  Electrifying Electrolyte Drink, 381
bone health, 157

bottle-feeding, 125, 128–30
brain. *See also* nervous system
  anatomy of, 74–75, 78–79
  and ASD, 74, 89
  dysfunctions of, 73–79
  extreme male brain theory, 71–72
  genetic imprinting of, 79–82
  and mind, 77
breads, 218–34
Breadsticks, 232
Breakfast Rice, 204
breakfasts, 163, 186, 202–16
breastfeeding, 128–30
Bristol Stool Chart, 156
broccoli
  Cold Buckwheat Noodles with Broccoli and Sesame Dressing, 292
  Lean Lamb and Three Veg, 324
  Mixed Vegetables in Spicy Peanut Sauce (variation), 288
  Orange Broccoli, 326
  Vegetable Broth and Puréed Veggies, 188
Brown Bread, Egg-Free, Corn-Free, Dairy-Free, Soy-Free, 222
Brown Rice Flour Blend, 241
Brown Sandwich Bread, 220
buckwheat
  Buckwheat Noodle Bowls with Beef and Snap Peas, 322
  Crunchy Flaxseed Cookies, 348
  Kasha and Beet Salad with Celery and Feta, 272
  Pear Buckwheat Muffins, 238

C

cabbage
  Festive Mexican Slaw, 271
  Mixed Vegetables in Spicy Peanut Sauce, 288
  Rolled Veggie Tacos with Spicy Asian Sauce, 296
Calamari, Crispy, 251
calcium, 119, 156
candida, 84
carob powder. *See also* cocoa/cacao powder
  Banana Frappé, 378
  Hot Carob, 380
carrots. *See also* vegetables
  Carrot Oatmeal Muffins, 237
  Coconut-Spiked Pumpkin Soup with Cumin and Ginger, 265
  Fresh Tomato Dill Soup, 264
  Glazed Carrots, 327
  Lettuce Wraps, 190
  Mushroom and Chickpea Stew with Roasted Red Pepper Coulis, 300

Rolled Veggie Tacos with Spicy Asian Sauce, 296
  Sweet Pea Soup, 263
casein sensitivity, 87, 152–53
case studies
  Adela, 55, 147, 161
  GFCF diet (Elia), 170–71
  picky eaters, 121
  Stephen, 15, 37, 91
celery. *See also* vegetables
  Coconut-Spiked Pumpkin Soup with Cumin and Ginger, 265
  Fresh Tomato Dill Soup, 264
  Kasha and Beet Salad with Celery and Feta, 272
  Mediterranean Tuna Risotto Salad, 278
  Mexican Shrimp Cocktail, 249
  Mushroom and Chickpea Stew with Roasted Red Pepper Coulis, 300
  Southwestern Turkey Chowder, 266
  Waldorf Parma Salad, 282
celiac disease, 87, 149, 150, 151. *See also* gluten sensitivity
Centers for Disease Control and Prevention (CDC), 97
cereals, 127, 163, 202–7
cheese and alternatives
  Crispy Pecan Chicken Fingers (variation), 312
  Grilled Portobello on Greens, 286
  Kasha and Beet Salad with Celery and Feta, 272
  Spiced Bananas, 198
  Vegetable Tamale Pie, 294
chelation, 110
chemicals (environmental), 63, 65–68
chewing, 135, 136
chicken. *See also* turkey
  Asian Barbecued Tofu Cubes (tip), 303
  Chicken Satays with Peanut Dipping Sauce, 244
  Coconut Chicken with Quinoa, 313
  Crispy Pecan Chicken Fingers, 312
  Egg Foo Yong, 189
  Fruity Chicken, 193
  Hungarian Chicken Soup, 268
  Italian Sausage Patties (variation), 320
  Lettuce Wraps, 190
  Mediterranean Tuna Risotto Salad (variation), 278
  Puréed Meat, 191
  Sticky Honey-Garlic Chicken Wings, 311
  Warm Chicken Salad with Peanut Dressing, 279

chickpeas
  Basic Beans, 343
  Chickpeas in Tomato Sauce, 302
  Hummus, 255
  Mushroom and Chickpea Stew
    with Roasted Red Pepper
    Coulis, 300
  Spicy, Crispy Roasted Chickpeas,
    373
  Vegetarian Chili, 287
Child Neurology Society, 97, 98–99
chiropractic therapy, 111
chocolate. See also cocoa/cacao
  powder
  Black Bean Brownies, 350
  Chocolate Chip Cookies, 349
  Chocolate Hazelnut Spread, 366
  Crunchy Flaxseed Cookies
    (variation), 348
  Special Muffins for Kids, 187
chromosomes, 58, 61
cilantro
  Broiled Ham Steak with
    Pineapple-Mango Salsa, 315
  Cold Buckwheat Noodles with
    Broccoli and Sesame Dressing,
    292
  Grilled Cilantro Shrimp Skewers,
    250
  Individual Salsa Fresca Omelets,
    212
  Pacific Rim Coconut Ribs, 318
  Southwestern Turkey Chowder,
    266
  Thai-Style Coconut Fish Curry, 307
  Tomatillo and Chia Seed Salsa,
    256
clustering, 80–82
CNVs (copy number variations), 62
cocoa/cacao powder. See also carob
  powder; chocolate
  Banana Frappé, 378
  Black Bean Brownies, 350
  Chocolate Date Protein Bars, 374
  Cocoa Quinoa Breakfast Squares,
    216
  Coconut Butter Vanilla Icing
    (variation), 365
coconut and coconut milk
  Coconut-Battered Shrimp, 310
  Coconut Chicken with Quinoa,
    313
  Coconut-Spiked Pumpkin Soup
    with Cumin and Ginger, 265
  Fresco de Fruit Taco Cupitas, 358
  Pacific Rim Coconut Ribs, 318
  Quinoa Coconut Fruit Sushi, 208
  Sweet Potato Coconut Curry with
    Shrimp, 309
  Thai-Style Coconut Fish Curry, 307

coconut oil and butter
  Almond Crème Fraîche, 368
  Coconut Butter Vanilla Icing, 365
coconut water
  Daterade, 382
  Electrifying Electrolyte Drink, 381
Cold Buckwheat Noodles with
    Broccoli and Sesame Dressing,
    292
Cold Mango Soup, 262
Coleslaw Dressing, Clear, 283
communication, 112–14. See also
  language
  improving, 106, 159, 161
complementary/alternative medicine,
  109, 114–15
concentration, 159
consciousness (sense of self), 77
cookies and squares, 215–16, 348–50
corn. See also cornmeal/masa harina
  Black Bean Salsa, 255
  Corn with Tomatoes and Basil, 328
  Southwestern Turkey Chowder,
    266
  Sweet Pea Soup, 263
  Vegetable Tamale Pie, 294
cornmeal/masa harina
  Crispy Pecan Chicken Fingers,
    312
  Simple Corn Tortillas, 229
  Vegetable Tamale Pie, 294
crabmeat
  Creamy Crab Salad Spread, 252
  Mediterranean Tuna Risotto Salad
    (variation), 278
  Rice Stick Noodles with Crab in a
    Basil-Tomato Sauce, 308
cranberries
  Apple Ginger Pudding Cake
    (variation), 351
  Baked Apples, The Ultimate, 353
  Cranberry Quinoa Porridge, 206
  Pumpkin Date Bars (tip), 375
Creamy Crab Salad Spread, 252
Creamy Mayonnaise, 258
Crispy Bacon Strips, 209
Crispy Calamari, 251
Crispy Pecan Chicken Fingers, 312
Croutons, Garlic, 277
Crunchy Flaxseed Cookies, 348
Crunchy Multigrain Bâtarde, 224
cucumber
  Individual Salsa Fresca Omelets,
    212
  Lettuce Wraps, 190
  Mexican Shrimp Cocktail
    (variation), 249
Curried Pork Chops with Crispy
    Sweet Potatoes, 316
cysteine, 85–86

D

dairy alternatives, 181, 182. See also
  almond milk; soy milk
  Baked Apple Quinoa, 207
  Breakfast Rice, 204
  Chocolate Hazelnut Spread, 366
  Cocoa Quinoa Breakfast Squares,
    216
  Quinoa Coconut Fruit Sushi,
    208
  Sweetened Condensed Milk, 367
  Vegetable Broth and Puréed
    Veggies (tip), 188
dates
  Almond Milk (variation), 377
  Banana Frappé, 378
  Chocolate Date Protein Bars, 374
  Cocoa Quinoa Breakfast Squares,
    216
  Crunchy Flaxseed Cookies
    (variation), 348
  Date Cashew Loaf, 228
  Date Paste, 383
  Daterade, 382
  Maple Breakfast Biscotti, 215
  Nog Me Up, 383
  Pumpkin Date Bars, 375
  Toasted Sesame Quinoa Bars, 376
DDT, 66
dendrites, 78
desserts, 197–200, 348–68
development, 20, 21–31, 53. See also
  language
  screening tools for, 44–47, 98–99
diabetes (gestational), 64
diagnosis, 37–54
  assessment in, 39–40, 80, 94,
    113
  early, 21, 38, 168
  process of, 37–40, 52
  screening in, 38–39, 41–48, 92,
    98–99
  standards for, 40, 97–99
dietitians, 145
diets. See also GFCF diet; therapies,
  dietary
  antioxidant, 118
  changing, 161–62
  exclusionary, 117, 147–48, 151,
    152, 158
  ketogenic, 118
  specific carbohydrate (SCD),
    118
  supplement needs, 109, 148, 157,
    163
dips and spreads, 143, 252–56
DNA, 58, 60–61
Down syndrome, 61
drooling, 133

DSM-5 (*Diagnostic and Statistical Manual of Mental Disorders*), 39, 40, 97–99
DTT (discrete trial teaching), 104
dyspraxia, 50

E

Easy Homemade Applesauce, 360
Easy Homemade Granola, 202
eating problems, 122–24
  associated behaviors, 121, 122, 131, 133
  developmental, 124–31
  environmental issues, 139–41
  of infants, 128–29
  overeating, 164–65, 181
  physiological causes, 135
  pickiness, 119, 121, 126, 130, 132, 145
  selectivity, 123, 130, 134, 145
  sensory issues, 123, 131–39
  solutions, 123–24, 128–30, 138, 140
  undereating, 130, 164, 182
echolalia, 131
EEG (electroencephalogram), 99
Egg-Free, Corn-Free, Dairy-Free, Soy-Free Brown Bread, 222
eggplant
  Batter-Dipped Vegetable Fritters, 338
  Eggplant and Tuna Antipasto Appetizer, 247
  Ratatouille, 336
eggs, 143
  Aamlete (South Asian Omelet), 211
  Akoori (South Asian Scrambled Eggs), 210
  Banana Pecan Waffles, 213
  Egg and Mushroom Fried Rice, 346
  Egg Foo Yong, 189
  Egg Salad Spread, 253
  Individual Salsa Fresca Omelets, 212
  Sautéed Mushrooms and Potatoes with Garlic, Parsley and Poached Egg, 290
EIBI (early intensive behavior interventions), 103–5
Electrifying Electrolyte Drink, 381
endocrine disruptors, 66
environment, 56, 63–68, 73
enzyme deficiencies, 85–86
epilepsy, 16, 53. *See also* seizures
essential fatty acids, 109, 125
event-related potentials, 99
exercise, 164
extreme male brain theory, 71–72

F

face processing, 82
family, 93, 95, 96. *See also* parents
  and GFCF diet, 119, 162, 164
fast foods, 165
FBA (functional behavioral assessment), 105
fennel
  Mediterranean Tuna Risotto Salad, 278
  Mushroom and Chickpea Stew with Roasted Red Pepper Coulis, 300
Festive Mexican Slaw, 271
Fiesta Guacamole, 254
Fiesta Taco Sauce, 260
finger foods, 126, 127, 128
fish and seafood. *See also* shrimp
  Baked Mediterranean Salmon Fillets, 306
  Caramelized Peppers and Onions with Pasta (variation), 344
  Creamy Crab Salad Spread, 252
  Crispy Calamari, 251
  Eggplant and Tuna Antipasto Appetizer, 247
  Grilled Bacon and Zucchini–Wrapped Scallops, 248
  Mediterranean Tuna Risotto Salad, 278
  Rice Stick Noodles with Crab in a Basil-Tomato Sauce, 308
  Thai-Style Coconut Fish Curry, 307
flame retardants, 68
flax seeds
  Banana Frappé, 378
  Cocoa Quinoa Breakfast Squares, 216
  Crunchy Flaxseed Cookies, 348
  Crunchy Multigrain Bâtarde, 224
  Egg-Free, Corn-Free, Dairy-Free, Soy-Free Brown Bread, 222
  Fruit Salad with Flax Seeds, 362
  Sweet Banana Porridge, 205
  Turkey Apple Meatloaf, 314
Floortime therapy, 110, 112
Florentine Chicken Fingers, 312
Florentine Potato Cakes, 342
fluids, 164. *See also* beverages
fMRI (functional magnetic resonance imaging), 80
folic acid deficiency, 85
food journal, 151, 152, 156
foods. *See also* diets; eating problems; meals
  to avoid, 154–55
  casein-free, 154–55, 165–66
  finger, 126, 127, 128
  fun with, 136, 137, 142–44

gluten-free, 154, 165–66
  groups, 126–27
  health issues, 131
  for infants, 125–28
  introducing, 125, 126, 127, 135–37, 158, 166
  preparation tips, 141–44
  rotating, 152, 166
  shopping for, 163
  texture of, 125
food therapy. *See* therapies, dietary
fragile X syndrome, 51
free radicals, 69–70, 118
Fresco de Fruit Taco Cupitas, 358
fruit, 126–27, 142, 181, 182. *See also* fruit, dried; fruit juices; *specific fruits*
  Fresco de Fruit Taco Cupitas, 358
  Fruit Salad with Flax Seeds, 362
  Fruit Salad with Ginger and Honey, 361
  Quinoa Coconut Fruit Sushi, 208
  Strawberry Rhubarb Pie, 356
  Tangy Fruit Sauce, 197
fruit, dried. *See also* dates; raisins
  Baked Apples, The Ultimate, 353
  Breakfast Rice, 204
  Cooked Oat Bran (variation), 186
  Cranberry Quinoa Porridge, 206
  Easy Homemade Granola, 202
  Fruity Chicken, 193
  Maple Breakfast Biscotti, 215
  Rice and Black Bean–Stuffed Peppers, 298
  Squash with Quinoa and Apricots, 334
  Sweet Baked Tomatoes, 331
  Toasted Sesame Quinoa Bars, 376
fruit juices, 166
  Baked Apples, The Ultimate, 353
  Berry Pops, 362
functional disconnection syndrome, 88
functioning
  academic, 94
  adaptive, 36, 94
  assessments of, 94, 105
  cognitive, 35, 94

G

gagging, 129, 133, 135
gait, 50
gardens, 136
garlic
  Basic Gravy, 317
  Coconut Chicken with Quinoa, 313
  Garlic Croutons, 277
  Sautéed Mushrooms and Potatoes with Garlic, Parsley and Poached Egg, 290

Sweet Potato Coconut Curry with Shrimp, 309
gastrointestinal (GI) system, 83–85
and ASD, 35, 53, 125
diet and, 118–19, 132, 148, 159
leaky gut syndrome, 84, 119, 153
genes, 58–59. *See also* genetics
environment and, 56, 63, 73
mutations in, 58, 60–61, 73
genetics, 55–56, 59. *See also* genes
and brain, 79–82
testing, 98
GFCF (gluten-free, casein-free) diet, 12, 117, 119–20, 147–49, 158. *See also* meal plans
attitude to, 162
behavior and, 159
benefits, 120, 159
costs, 158, 164
goals, 162
implementation steps, 161–67
principles, 148–49
research on, 159
risks, 156–57
shopping for, 163
support for, 164, 166
ginger
Asian Barbecued Tofu Cubes, 303
Basic Gravy, 317
Buckwheat Noodle Bowls with Beef and Snap Peas, 322
Chicken Satays with Peanut Dipping Sauce, 244
Chickpeas in Tomato Sauce (tip), 302
Coconut-Spiked Pumpkin Soup with Cumin and Ginger, 265
Cold Buckwheat Noodles with Broccoli and Sesame Dressing, 292
Fruit Salad with Ginger and Honey, 361
Gingerbread Muffins, 240
Mixed Vegetables in Spicy Peanut Sauce, 288
Pacific Rim Coconut Ribs, 318
Pear Buckwheat Muffins, 238
Squash with Quinoa and Apricots, 334
Sweet Potato Coconut Curry with Shrimp, 309
Tangy Orange Beef, 321
Thai-Style Coconut Fish Curry, 307
glucose metabolism, 118
gluten-free flours. *See also* bean/pea flour; rice flour; sorghum flour
Apple Ginger Pudding Cake, 351
Batter-Dipped Vegetable Fritters, 338

Biscuit Mix, 230
Date Cashew Loaf, 228
Egg-Free, Corn-Free, Dairy-Free, Soy-Free Brown Bread, 222
Pumpkin Date Bars, 375
White Bread, 218
Gluten-Free Muesli, 203
gluten sensitivity, 87–88, 151–52
grains, 127, 181, 182. *See also* specific grains
Breakfast Rice (variation), 204
Crunchy Multigrain Bâtarde, 224
Southwestern Turkey Chowder, 266
grapes
Fruit Salad with Ginger and Honey, 361
Grape and Melon Fruit Cups, 197
Green Quinoa Smoothie, 380
gray matter, 78
Green Beans with Mustard Seeds, 329
Green Quinoa Smoothie, 380
greens. *See also* lettuce; spinach
Crispy Pecan Chicken Fingers (variation), 312
Green Quinoa Smoothie, 380
Grilled Portobello on Greens, 286
Kale Quinoa Tabbouleh, 295
Roasted Sweet Potato Salad, 273
Greenspan, Stanley, 111
grocery shopping, 163
guacamole, 143, 254
gut. *See* gastrointestinal system

H
ham
Broiled Ham Steak with Pineapple-Mango Salsa, 315
Individual Salsa Fresca Omelets (variation), 212
Waldorf Parma Salad, 282
Harvest Cupcakes, 352
head size, 16, 82, 99
health journal, 92, 156, 163
hearing, 94, 110–11
herbs. *See also* cilantro; parsley
Caramelized Peppers and Onions with Pasta, 344
Corn with Tomatoes and Basil, 328
Fresh Tomato Dill Soup, 264
Glazed Carrots, 327
Kale Quinoa Tabbouleh, 295
Mashed Sweet Potatoes with Rosemary, 340
Meatballs for Everyday, 323
Ranch Dressing, 284
Rice and Black Bean–Stuffed Peppers, 298

Sage Potato Crisps, 370
Thai Yellow Curry Mango Salad, 270
Yukon Gold Bay Leaf Mash, 341
HMNS (human mirror neural systems), 82
homeopathy, 114
homocysteine, 85
honey
Almond Flour Blackberry Muffins, 239
Baked Candied Pecans, 372
Fruit Salad with Ginger and Honey, 361
Honey Dijon Toastie, 226
Honey Mustard Dipping Sauce, 259
Sticky Honey-Garlic Chicken Wings, 311
Toasted Sesame Quinoa Bars, 376
hormones, 66, 71–73
Hot-and-Sour Soup, Junior, 189
Hot-Bag Vegetables, 333
Hot Carob, 380
Hummus, 143, 255
Hungarian Chicken Soup, 268
hyperactivity, 159
hypersensitivity, 133, 134, 139. *See also* allergies; sensitivities
hyposensitivity, 133, 134, 140
hypotonia, 50, 135

I
IBI (intensive behavior intervention), 103–5, 107
ice cream, 163
Ig antibodies, 150
immune system, 35, 84, 149
Individual Salsa Fresca Omelets, 212
infants. *See also* birth complications
autism signs in, 17–18, 22–31
eating guides for, 126–27
food issues, 124–30
inflammation, 118, 149
integration therapies, 110–11
intellectual disabilities, 16
interventions. *See* therapies
intestinal permeability (IPT), 153
intolerances (to food), 87. *See also* sensitivities
Italian Sausage Patties, 320

J
Junior Hot-and-Sour Soup, 189

K
Kale Quinoa Tabbouleh, 295
Kanner, Leo, 89, 149

Kasha and Beet Salad with Celery and Feta, 272
kitchen organization, 164
kiwifruit
    Fresco de Fruit Taco Cupitas, 358
    Green Quinoa Smoothie, 380

L

lactose intolerance, 87
lactulose, 153
lamb
    Lean Lamb and Three Veg, 324
    Puréed Meat, 191
language, 19, 20–21
    assessment of, 20–21, 94, 113
    development of, 20–21, 49
    GFCF diet and, 159
    regression in, 32
    therapy for, 106, 110, 113
    use of, 18, 34, 35
Last-Minute Chili, 192
lead exposure, 65
leaky gut syndrome, 84, 119, 153
Lean Lamb and Three Veg, 324
LEAP (Learning Experiences and Alternate Program for Preschoolers and their Parents), 107
leftovers, 144
lemon
    Berry Frappé, 379
    Cold Buckwheat Noodles with Broccoli and Sesame Dressing, 292
    Pacific Rim Coconut Ribs, 318
    Tangy Fruit Sauce, 197
lentils
    Basic Beans (variation), 343
    Vegetarian Chili, 287
lettuce
    Lettuce Wraps, 190
    Shrimp Caesar Salad with Garlic Croutons, 276
    Strawberry Salad, 269
    Taco Salad, 280
    Waldorf Parma Salad, 282
leukocytes, 149
lime
    Chicken Satays with Peanut Dipping Sauce, 244
    Festive Mexican Slaw (variation), 271
    Fresco de Fruit Taco Cupitas, 358
    Grilled Cilantro Shrimp Skewers, 250
    Mexican Shrimp Cocktail, 249
    Pacific Rim Coconut Ribs, 318
    Thai-Style Coconut Fish Curry, 307

M

magnetoencephalography, 99
mango
    Broiled Ham Steak with Pineapple-Mango Salsa, 315
    Cold Mango Soup, 262
    Thai Yellow Curry Mango Salad, 270
mannitol, 153
Maple Breakfast Biscotti, 215
Mashed Banana and Avocado, 199
Mashed Sweet Potatoes with Rosemary, 340
massage, 115
mayonnaise
    Creamy Mayonnaise, 258
    Egg Salad Spread, 253
    Ranch Dressing, 284
    Waldorf Parma Salad, 282
meal plans, 135, 167, 170–80. See also meals
    ages 2–3, 172, 176, 179
    ages 4–8, 172, 176, 179
    ages 9–13, 173, 177, 180
    ages 14–18, 173, 177, 180
    crunchy, high-texture, 176–78
    regular, varied-texture, 179–80
    soft, low-texture, 172–75
meals, 12, 121–22. See also eating problems; meal plans
    involving child in, 123–24, 136–37, 138–39
    location of, 141
    scheduling, 165
    serving sizes, 165, 171
    utensils, 137–38
meat, 127, 181, 182. See also specific meats
    alternatives, 181, 182
    puréed, 191
Meatballs for Everyday, 323
medications, 64, 105, 108
Mediterranean Tuna Risotto Salad, 278
Medley of Fruit Crisp, 357
megalencephaly (large head), 16, 82, 99
melon
    Fruit Salad with Ginger and Honey, 361
    Grape and Melon Fruit Cups, 197
memory, 49
mercury (methylmercury), 65
metabolism, 99
Mexican Shrimp Cocktail, 249
Mexican Slaw, Festive, 271
microbiome, 83–84
microvilli, 84
milk alternatives. See dairy alternatives

millet
    Asian-Style Quinoa Salad with Chili-Orange Dressing (variation), 274
    Crunchy Multigrain Bâtarde, 224
mind, 77
mirror neurons, 82
Mock Soy Sauce, 259
mosaicism, 61
motor skills, 35, 36, 49, 50, 94, 159
mouth and teeth, 133, 135, 136
muffins, 187, 236–42
mushrooms
    Basic Beef Mixture (variation), 192
    Egg and Mushroom Fried Rice, 346
    Eggplant and Tuna Antipasto Appetizer, 247
    Grilled Portobello on Greens, 286
    Mushroom and Chickpea Stew with Roasted Red Pepper Coulis, 300
    Ratatouille, 336
    Sautéed Mushrooms and Potatoes with Garlic, Parsley and Poached Egg, 290
    Sticky Rice Salad with Asparagus and Mushrooms in Soy Vinaigrette, 275
    Strawberry Salad (variation), 269
    Sweet Pea Soup, 263
    Tofu Quinoa Scramble, 209
music therapy, 110, 111
mustard
    Honey Dijon Toastie, 226
    Honey Mustard Dipping Sauce, 259
    Shrimp Caesar Salad with Garlic Croutons, 276
myelin sheath, 77, 78, 81

N

National Institute for Health and Care Excellence (UK), 99
nervous system, 76–78. See also brain
    neural networks, 80–82, 104
    neurons, 76–78, 82
    neurotransmitters, 76–77
neuroimaging, 80, 99
Nog Me Up, 383
noodles and pasta, 163
    Buckwheat Noodle Bowls with Beef and Snap Peas, 322
    Caramelized Peppers and Onions with Pasta, 344
    Cold Buckwheat Noodles with Broccoli and Sesame Dressing, 292
    Rice Stick Noodles with Crab in a Basil-Tomato Sauce, 308
    Steamed Rice Noodle Cakes, 345

nut milk bags, 377
nutritional deficiencies, 85–86, 116, 119, 148, 156
nutritionists, 145
nuts. *See also* almonds; pecans; walnuts
  Chocolate Chip Cookies (variation), 349
  Chocolate Hazelnut Spread, 366
  Date Cashew Loaf, 228
  Easy Homemade Granola, 202
  Maple Breakfast Biscotti, 215
  Orange Broccoli (tip), 326
  Rice and Black Bean–Stuffed Peppers, 298
  Sautéed Spinach with Pine Nuts, 330
  Sweet Baked Tomatoes, 331

O

oat bran. *See also* oats and oat flour
  Brown Sandwich Bread (variation), 220
  Cooked Oat Bran, 186
  Egg-Free, Corn-Free, Dairy-Free, Soy-Free Brown Bread (variation), 222
  Oatmeal Muffin Mix, 236
  Turkey Apple Meatloaf, 314
oats and oat flour. *See also* oat bran
  Carrot Oatmeal Muffins, 237
  Crunchy Multigrain Bâtarde, 224
  Easy Homemade Granola, 202
  Fruit Salad with Flax Seeds, 362
  Maple Breakfast Biscotti, 215
  Medley of Fruit Crisp, 357
  Oatmeal Muffin Mix, 236
  Sweet Banana Porridge, 205
  Toasted Sesame Quinoa Bars, 376
  Tofu Patties, 304
occupational therapy, 110
oligodendrocytes, 77
olives
  Bacon and Tomato Biscuits (variation), 231
  Mediterranean Tuna Risotto Salad, 278
omega-3 fatty acids, 109
onions. *See also* vegetables
  Basic Gravy, 317
  Basic Tomato Sauce, 257
  Buckwheat Noodle Bowls with Beef and Snap Peas, 322
  Caramelized Peppers and Onions with Pasta, 344
  Coconut-Spiked Pumpkin Soup with Cumin and Ginger, 265
  Cold Buckwheat Noodles with Broccoli and Sesame Dressing, 292

Fiesta Taco Sauce, 260
Kasha and Beet Salad with Celery and Feta, 272
Mushroom and Chickpea Stew with Roasted Red Pepper Coulis, 300
Rice and Black Bean–Stuffed Peppers, 298
Southwestern Turkey Chowder, 266
opioid excess theory, 84–85, 119
oral motor tools, 136
orange juice. *See also* oranges
  Berry Pops, 362
  Chocolate Date Protein Bars, 374
  Date Paste (variation), 383
  Easy Homemade Granola, 202
  Fruity Chicken, 193
  Green Quinoa Smoothie, 380
  Harvest Cupcakes, 352
  Orange Broccoli, 326
  Tangy Fruit Sauce, 197
oranges. *See also* orange juice
  Asian-Style Quinoa Salad with Chili-Orange Dressing, 274
  Carrot Oatmeal Muffins, 237
  Spiced Bananas, 198
  Squash with Quinoa and Apricots, 334
  Strawberry Salad (variation), 269
  Tangy Orange Beef, 321
organophosphates, 66
Oven-Baked Tofu "Fries," 246
Oven-Roasted Potato Wedges, 196
oxidative stress, 69–70, 118

P

Pacific Rim Coconut Ribs, 318
PAHs (polycyclic aromatic hydrocarbons), 67
pakoras, 338
pancakes and waffles, 144, 213–14
parents, 64. *See also* family; health journal
  and ASD stigma, 11, 168
  and ASD symptoms, 10, 38, 42
  challenges facing, 11, 96
  principles for, 89, 160
  safety tips, 95, 128
  support for, 93
  and treatment decisions, 102, 109, 110
parsley
  Kasha and Beet Salad with Celery and Feta, 272
  Mediterranean Tuna Risotto Salad, 278
  Sautéed Mushrooms and Potatoes with Garlic, Parsley and Poached Egg, 290

parsnips
  Hot-Bag Vegetables, 333
  Hungarian Chicken Soup, 268
  Vegetable Broth and Puréed Veggies, 188
pasta. *See* noodles and pasta
PCBs (polychlorinated biphenyls), 66
PCIT (parent–child interactive therapy), 106
peaches
  Mashed Banana and Avocado (variation), 199
  Medley of Fruit Crisp, 357
  Peaches and Cream Frozen Pops, 363
pea flour. *See* bean/pea flour
peanuts and peanut butter
  Chicken Satays with Peanut Dipping Sauce, 244
  Mixed Vegetables in Spicy Peanut Sauce, 288
  Special Muffins for Kids, 187
  Warm Chicken Salad with Peanut Dressing, 279
pears
  Breakfast Rice (variation), 204
  Fruit Salad with Flax Seeds, 362
  Pear Buckwheat Muffins, 238
peas (green)
  Asian-Style Quinoa Salad with Chili-Orange Dressing, 274
  Buckwheat Noodle Bowls with Beef and Snap Peas, 322
  Egg and Mushroom Fried Rice, 346
  Rice Salad, 196
  Sweet Pea Soup, 263
  Thai-Style Coconut Fish Curry, 307
pecans. *See also* nuts
  Baked Candied Pecans, 372
  Banana Pecan Waffles, 213
  Carrot Oatmeal Muffins (variation), 237
  Crispy Pecan Chicken Fingers, 312
  Pumpkin Almond Flour Muffins, 242
PEC (picture exchange communication), 112–13
peppers, bell. *See also* vegetables
  Asian-Style Quinoa Salad with Chili-Orange Dressing, 274
  Baked Mediterranean Salmon Fillets, 306
  Caramelized Peppers and Onions with Pasta, 344
  Coconut Chicken with Quinoa, 313
  Corn with Tomatoes and Basil, 328
  Creamy Crab Salad Spread, 252

peppers, bell (*continued*)
Crispy Pecan Chicken Fingers (variation), 312
Eggplant and Tuna Antipasto Appetizer, 247
Festive Mexican Slaw, 271
Mediterranean Tuna Risotto Salad, 278
Mushroom and Chickpea Stew with Roasted Red Pepper Coulis, 300
Rice and Black Bean–Stuffed Peppers, 298
Taco Salad, 280
Thai-Style Coconut Fish Curry, 307
Thai Yellow Curry Mango Salad, 270
Tofu Quinoa Scramble, 209
peppers, chile
Fiesta Guacamole, 254
Kale Quinoa Tabbouleh (variation), 295
Southwestern Turkey Chowder, 266
peptides, 84–85, 119
pesticides, 66
PFCs (perfluorinated compounds), 68
phenylketonuria, 149
phytotoxins, 85
picky eaters, 119, 121, 126, 130, 132, 145
pies, 355–56
pineapple and pineapple juice
Broiled Ham Steak with Pineapple-Mango Salsa, 315
Fresco de Fruit Taco Cupitas, 358
Fruit Salad with Ginger and Honey, 361
Pacific Rim Coconut Ribs, 318
pizza (instant), 143
Pizza Chicken Fingers, 312
pollution, 64–68, 69, 84
popcorn, 144
POPs (persistent organic pollutants), 66
pork. *See also* bacon and pancetta; ham
Curried Pork Chops with Crispy Sweet Potatoes, 316
Egg Foo Yong, 189
Italian Sausage Patties (variation), 320
Meatballs for Everyday, 323
Pacific Rim Coconut Ribs, 318
portion control, 165, 171
potatoes. *See also* vegetables
Florentine Potato Cakes, 342
Green Beans with Mustard Seeds, 329

Individual Salsa Fresca Omelets (variation), 212
Oven-Roasted Potato Wedges, 196
Sage Potato Crisps, 370
Sautéed Mushrooms and Potatoes with Garlic, Parsley and Poached Egg, 290
Sweet Pea Soup, 263
Tasty Potato Pancakes, 214
Yukon Gold Bay Leaf Mash, 341
pregnancy
chemical exposure during, 64–68, 73
and folic acid intake, 85
infections during, 63
medications during, 64
probiotics, 83, 170
prompts, 104–5
proprioception, 137
proteins, 58–59. *See also* peptides in foods, 127
PRT (pivotal response training), 105
Prune Smoothie, 379
pruning, 81–82
psychiatric symptoms, 33, 34, 53, 94, 149, 151
pumpkin. *See also* squash
Coconut-Spiked Pumpkin Soup with Cumin and Ginger, 265
Harvest Cupcakes, 352
Pumpkin Almond Flour Muffins, 242
Pumpkin Date Bars, 375
Pumpkin Pudding, 364
Puréed Meat, 191
Puréed Sweet Potatoes, 194
Puréed Vegetables, 194

Q
quinoa. *See also* quinoa flour/flakes
Asian-Style Quinoa Salad with Chili-Orange Dressing, 274
Baked Apple Quinoa, 207
Cocoa Quinoa Breakfast Squares, 216
Coconut Chicken with Quinoa, 313
Cranberry Quinoa Porridge, 206
Kale Quinoa Tabbouleh, 295
Quinoa Coconut Fruit Sushi, 208
Quinoa Crunch, 204
Squash with Quinoa and Apricots, 334
Toasted Sesame Quinoa Bars, 376
Tofu Quinoa Scramble, 209
quinoa flour/flakes
Banana Pecan Waffles, 213
Crunchy Multigrain Bâtarde, 224
Green Quinoa Smoothie, 380

Honey Dijon Toastie, 226
Maple Breakfast Biscotti, 215
Special Muffins for Kids, 187
White Bread, 218

R
radiation, 69
raisins
Carrot Oatmeal Muffins (variation), 237
Crunchy Flaxseed Cookies (variation), 348
White Bread (variation), 218
Ranch Dressing, 284
Ratatouille, 336
regression, 15, 32, 63
reinforcers (rewards), 104
research studies, 100, 101, 144, 159
restaurants, 166
Rett syndrome, 51
rice. *See also* rice bran; rice flour
Breakfast Rice, 204
Egg and Mushroom Fried Rice, 346
Mediterranean Tuna Risotto Salad, 278
Quinoa Coconut Fruit Sushi, 208
Rice and Black Bean–Stuffed Peppers, 298
Rice Salad, 196
Sticky Rice Salad with Asparagus and Mushrooms in Soy Vinaigrette, 275
Vanilla Soy Milk Pudding, 200
rice bran
Brown Sandwich Bread, 220
Egg-Free, Corn-Free, Dairy-Free, Soy-Free Brown Bread, 222
Fruit Salad with Flax Seeds, 362
Gluten-Free Muesli, 203
rice flour. *See also* gluten-free flours
Breadsticks, 232
Brown Rice Flour Blend, 241
Coconut-Battered Shrimp, 310
Crispy Pecan Chicken Fingers, 312
Crunchy Multigrain Bâtarde, 224
Date Cashew Loaf, 228
Sesame Crispbread, 234
Rice Stick Noodles with Crab in a Basil-Tomato Sauce, 308
Rolled Veggie Tacos with Spicy Asian Sauce, 296

S
safety issues, 95, 128
Sage Potato Crisps, 370
salads, 143, 196, 269–82
dressings, 283–84

Salmon Fillets, Baked Mediterranean, 306
salsas, 255–56, 315
Satays, Barbecued Beef, 245
sauces, 257–60
Sausage Patties, Italian, 320
SCD (specific carbohydrate diet), 118
schedules (visual), 106–7
school, 97, 104, 106, 107, 167
Schwann cells, 77
screening
  for development, 44–47, 98–99
  for diagnosis, 38–39, 41–48, 92, 98–99
  tools for, 38–39, 41–48
scripting, 116
seeds. See also flax seeds; sesame seeds
  Chocolate Date Protein Bars, 374
  Easy Homemade Granola, 202
  Gluten-Free Muesli, 203
  Orange Broccoli, 326
  Tofu Patties (tip), 304
  Tomatillo and Chia Seed Salsa, 256
seizures, 16, 53, 117, 159
self-injury, 159
sensitivities
  as ASD trigger, 63, 84, 116
  to casein, 87, 152–53
  to foods, 86, 150
  to gluten, 87–88,151–52
  sensory, 123
  tests for, 150, 152, 153
sensory integration, 110
service dogs, 115
sesame oil
  Egg and Mushroom Fried Rice, 346
  Junior Hot-and-Sour Soup, 189
  Mock Soy Sauce, 259
  Steamed Rice Noodle Cakes, 345
  Sticky Rice Salad with Asparagus and Mushrooms in Soy Vinaigrette, 275
sesame seeds. See also sesame oil; tahini
  Breadsticks, 232
  Cold Buckwheat Noodles with Broccoli and Sesame Dressing, 292
  Sesame Crispbread, 234
  Sesame Tofu Vinaigrette, 283
  Strawberry Salad, 269
  Thai-Style Coconut Fish Curry (tip), 307
  Toasted Sesame Quinoa Bars, 376
Shepherd's Pie, 192

shrimp
  Coconut-Battered Shrimp, 310
  Creamy Crab Salad Spread, 252
  Grilled Cilantro Shrimp Skewers, 250
  Lettuce Wraps, 190
  Mediterranean Tuna Risotto Salad (variation), 278
  Mexican Shrimp Cocktail, 249
  Shrimp Caesar Salad with Garlic Croutons, 276
  Sweet Potato Coconut Curry with Shrimp, 309
  Thai-Style Coconut Fish Curry (variation), 307
siblings, 96
  ASD risk, 55, 57, 73, 98
signing, 113, 161
Simple Corn Tortillas, 229
Sloppy Joes, 192
smoothies, 142, 379–80
snacks, 163, 164, 370–76
SNPs (single nucleotide polymorphisms), 59–60
social skills, 10, 18, 35, 36, 53, 159
social workers, 108
sorghum flour. See also gluten-free flours
  Banana Pecan Waffles, 213
  Brown Sandwich Bread, 220
  Chocolate Chip Cookies, 349
  Crunchy Flaxseed Cookies, 348
  Harvest Cupcakes, 352
  Oatmeal Muffin Mix, 236
  Pumpkin Pudding, 364
  Special Muffins for Kids, 187
  Trendy Pastry, 354
soups, 188–89, 262–68
South Asian Omelet (Aamlete), 211
South Asian Scrambled Eggs (Akoori), 210
Southwestern Turkey Chowder, 266
soy milk. See also dairy alternatives
  Bacon and Tomato Biscuits, 231
  Berry Frappé, 379
  Hot Carob, 380
  Lean Lamb and Three Veg, 324
  Prune Smoothie, 379
  Sweet Banana Porridge, 205
  Vanilla Soy Milk Pudding, 200
Soy Sauce, Mock, 259
Special Muffins for Kids, 187
specific carbohydrate diet (SCD), 118
speech impairments, 16. See also language
Spiced Bananas, 198
Spicy, Crispy Roasted Chickpeas, 373
Spicy Asian Sauce, 297

spinach
  Green Quinoa Smoothie, 380
  Sautéed Spinach with Pine Nuts, 330
  Strawberry Salad, 269
squash. See also pumpkin; zucchini
  Fresh Vegetable Purée, 195
  Squash with Quinoa and Apricots, 334
Sticky Honey-Garlic Chicken Wings, 311
Sticky Rice Salad with Asparagus and Mushrooms in Soy Vinaigrette, 275
strawberries
  Fresco de Fruit Taco Cupitas, 358
  Strawberry Rhubarb Pie, 356
  Strawberry Salad, 269
stress, 69, 96. See also oxidative stress
supplements (nutritional), 109, 148, 157, 163
Sweet Baked Tomatoes, 331
Sweet Banana Porridge, 205
Sweetened Condensed Milk, 367
Sweet Pea Soup, 263
sweet potatoes
  Curried Pork Chops with Crispy Sweet Potatoes, 316
  Lean Lamb and Three Veg, 324
  Mashed Sweet Potatoes with Rosemary, 340
  Puréed Sweet Potatoes, 194
  Roasted Sweet Potato Salad, 273
  Sweet Potato Coconut Curry with Shrimp, 309
  Sweet Potato "Fries," 339
swimming, 111
synthetic products, 63

T
Taco Salad, 280
tahini
  Hummus, 255
  Toasted Sesame Quinoa Bars, 376
Tangy Fruit Sauce, 197
Tangy Orange Beef, 321
task breakdown, 104
teaching systems, 104, 107
teenagers, 181, 182
  meal plans for, 173, 177, 180
teeth, 133, 135
Thai-Style Coconut Fish Curry, 307
Thai traditional massage (TTM), 115
Thai Yellow Curry Mango Salad, 270
therapies, 100–108, 170. See also treatment; specific therapies
  behavioral, 101–5
  dietary, 116–20
  parents and, 102, 109, 110
  sensory, 110–12

Thomas the Tank Engine, 72
toddlers, 130
meal plans for, 172, 176, 179
tofu
Almond Crème Fraîche, 368
Asian Barbecued Tofu Cubes, 303
Banana Frappé, 378
Berry Frappé, 379
Cold Buckwheat Noodles with Broccoli and Sesame Dressing (variation), 292
Creamy Mayonnaise, 258
Junior Hot-and-Sour Soup, 189
Lettuce Wraps (variation), 190
Oven-Baked Tofu "Fries", 246
Ranch Dressing, 284
Sesame Tofu Vinaigrette, 283
Tofu Patties, 304
Tofu Quinoa Scramble, 209
toiletry items, 163
Tomatillo and Chia Seed Salsa, 256
tomatoes and tomato sauce. *See also* vegetables
Aamlete (South Asian Omelet), 211
Akoori (South Asian Scrambled Eggs), 210
Baked Mediterranean Salmon Fillets, 306
Basic Gravy, 317
Basic Tomato Sauce, 257
Black Bean Salsa, 255
Chickpeas in Tomato Sauce, 302
Corn with Tomatoes and Basil, 328
Eggplant and Tuna Antipasto Appetizer, 247
Fiesta Guacamole, 254
Fiesta Taco Sauce, 260
Fresh Tomato Dill Soup, 264
Individual Salsa Fresca Omelets, 212
Kale Quinoa Tabbouleh, 295
Lettuce Wraps, 190
Mediterranean Tuna Risotto Salad, 278
Mexican Shrimp Cocktail, 249
Mushroom and Chickpea Stew with Roasted Red Pepper Coulis, 300
Rice and Black Bean–Stuffed Peppers, 298
Rice Stick Noodles with Crab in a Basil-Tomato Sauce, 308
Southwestern Turkey Chowder, 266
Sweet Baked Tomatoes, 331
Taco Salad, 280
Tomatillo and Chia Seed Salsa (variation), 256
Tomato and Zucchini Sauté, 332

tortillas
Cupitas, 359
Fresco de Fruit Taco Cupitas, 358
Fresh Tortilla Chips, 371
Rolled Veggie Tacos with Spicy Asian Sauce, 296
Simple Corn Tortillas, 229
Taco Salad, 280
Tortilla Bowls, 281
trail mix, 143
transulfuration, 85–86
treatment. *See also* therapies
assessments for, 94
complementary/alternative, 109, 114–15
health-care team and, 92, 93
interventions, 93, 94–95, 99, 100, 116–20, 168
planning, 91, 93
Trendy Pastry, 354
tuna
Caramelized Peppers and Onions with Pasta (variation), 344
Eggplant and Tuna Antipasto Appetizer, 247
Mediterranean Tuna Risotto Salad, 278
turkey. *See also* chicken
Meatballs for Everyday (variation), 323
Southwestern Turkey Chowder, 266
Turkey Apple Meatloaf, 314
Turkey Stock, 267
Turner syndrome, 61

U

The Ultimate Baked Apples, 353

V

Vanilla Soy Milk Pudding, 200
vegetable juices
Berry Pops, 362
Mexican Shrimp Cocktail, 249
Vegetarian Chili, 287
vegetables, 126–27, 142, 181, 182. *See also* greens; vegetable juices; *specific vegetables*
Basic Beef Mixture, 192
Basic Tomato Sauce, 257
Batter-Dipped Vegetable Fritters, 338
Fresco de Fruit Taco Cupitas, 358
Fresh Vegetable Purée, 195
Hot-Bag Vegetables, 333
Hungarian Chicken Soup, 268
Kasha and Beet Salad with Celery and Feta, 272

Mixed Vegetables in Spicy Peanut Sauce, 288
Puréed Vegetables, 194
Ratatouille, 336
Rice Salad, 196
Vegetable Broth and Puréed Veggies, 188
Vegetable Tamale Pie, 294
Vegetarian Chili, 287
Warm Chicken Salad with Peanut Dressing, 279
verbal behavior (VB) therapy, 113
visual schedules, 106–7
vitamin B, 85
vitamin D, 119
vocal play, 131
vomiting, 129

W

Waldorf Parma Salad, 282
walking, 50
walnuts
Baked Apples, The Ultimate, 353
Baked Candied Pecans, 372
Chocolate Chip Cookies, 349
Pumpkin Date Bars, 375
Waldorf Parma Salad, 282
wandering, 95–96
Warm Chicken Salad with Peanut Dressing, 279
water chestnuts
Asian-Style Quinoa Salad with Chili-Orange Dressing, 274
Warm Chicken Salad with Peanut Dressing, 279
weight management, 164–65, 181–82
White Bread, 218
white matter, 78
World Health Organization, 39

Y

yoga, 115
Yukon Gold Bay Leaf Mash, 341

Z

zucchini
Batter-Dipped Vegetable Fritters, 338
Grilled Bacon and Zucchini–Wrapped Scallops, 248
Ratatouille, 336
Rolled Veggie Tacos with Spicy Asian Sauce, 296
Tomato and Zucchini Sauté, 332
Vegetable Tamale Pie, 294